HEAVY!

Richard B. McKenzie

HEAVY!

The Surprising Reasons America Is the Land of the Free—And the Home of the Fat

 Springer

An Imprint of Springer Science + Business Media

Prof. Richard B. McKenzie
University of California, Irvine
Paul Merage School of Business
IRVINE California
USA
mckenzie@uci.edu

ISBN 978-3-642-20134-9   e-ISBN 978-3-642-20135-6
DOI 10.1007/978-3-642-20135-6
Springer Heidelberg Dordrecht London New York

Library of Congress Control Number: 2011936526

© Springer-Verlag Berlin Heidelberg 2012
An imprint of Springer Science+Business Media.

Copernicus Books
Springer Science+Business Media
233 Spring Street
New York, NY 10013
www.springer.com

Printed on acid-free paper

Springer is part of Springer Science+Business Media (www.springer.com)

Preface

A mericans' growing obesity is self-evident on any street corner in any city in the country. The extra poundage Americans are packing is apparent in the growing percentage of people with overhanging guts and ballooning buttocks, as well as in the number who are turning to three-wheeled electric scooters for mobility around their homes and in stores for a sad reason: they can no longer carry their own weight for more than a few yards. In no small way—no, in very *BIG* and surprising ways—America has become the home of heavies!

Americans' expanding waists are increasing the amounts of fuel required to travel both by car and plane, decreasing fuel efficiency, and increasing the emissions of CO^2 and potentially speeding up the natural long-term global warming trend (if human activity does in fact consequentially affect climate change). A mountain of scholarly studies have documented without doubt that the fattening of America is undercutting worker productivity, lowering wages, and impairing the country's international competitiveness. Excess weight and obesity are increasing both medical and health insurance costs, expanding the number of Americans who can no longer afford private health insurance, truncating many Americans' life expectancy, and offsetting the benefits of tremendous advancements in medical technologies and treatments. Paramedic firms are reinforcing their ambulances and gurneys, enabling their "bariatric rescue squads" to handle a decidedly modern peak-load problem, patients who weight more than half a ton. And this is just a partial list of the effects of overweight.

The many "fatoids" (or facts about fat) and economic arguments presented in this book—with added insights from evolutionary biology, neurobiology, psychology, nutrition, and medicine—lead inextricably to a coming "fat war" to be fought over the regulation and taxation of the food industry and the control of what and how much people are permitted to eat and where. The arsenal for this emerging fat policy war springs from arguments used successfully to control smoking beginning in the 1960s, which can be applied with equal force to eating (or, rather, overeating):

- Fat parents can beget fat children, who can spawn a new generation of fat adults.
- Fat is a "contagious disease" (which suggests a form of "second-hand fat") since fat people tend to congregate in groups and encourage those around them to gain weight.
- Fat can kill and is killing Americans at an increasing rate even as death from smoking has been on the decline.
- And people's excess pounds increase the costs imposed on trim people through lower wages, less room on planes, and increased taxes imposed to cover the health-care costs of heavy people (often through government medical-care subsidies).

The fat war will inevitably spawn policy and legal debates over whether the country's laws against discrimination should be extended to cover heavy people. Studies have piled up on the extent to which workers' excess weight can undercut their job opportunities and their wages. Some retail firms and paramedic services have added surcharges for obese customers where their weight affects the costs of delivering their products and services. Associations set up to defend heavy people have already begun campaigns to declare obesity to be a disease and to require businesses and government agencies alike to accommodate the needs of heavy Americans under the nation's Americans with Disabilities Act, or face the prospects of court-ordered damages. And the legal threats to businesses and public agencies are real. Weight discrimination and disability lawsuits are on the rise.

The recently passed national health insurance program will likely intensify the fat war primarily because national health insurance can encourage weight gain as Americans' pass their costs of overeating on to others through higher premiums on health insurance policies and through higher taxes. And because weight gain has real effects on fuel consumption, controls on people's weight will be pressed for many of the same reasons environmentalists advocate suppression of greenhouse gases.

Packing on the Pounds

HEAVY! The Surprising Reasons America Is the Land of the Free—And the Home of the Fat documents the fattening of the country through the past century (with emphasis on the last fifty years) with both conventional measures (expanding obesity rates) and unconventional measures (increasing sizes of dinner plates and coffins and added cremation times). Beyond the well-reported "fat facts" on the health problems related to weight gain, this book examines the unusual and unheralded causes and consequences of America's weight problems—including some unexpected and counterintuitive, even weird, economic arguments.

The country's weight problems stem from the triumph of modern economic forces, which now move at the speed of the Internet, over ancient evolutionary forces, which always have moved at a tectonic pace. Modern humans' genes and proclivities to eat were shaped long ago when food was scarce and hard to obtain, but people now have an abundance of opportunities to consume cheap calories through sugared and fatty foods. During the past century, Americans' income and wealth have dramatically increased with concomitant declines in the price of calories, especially calories from fatty foods, which are everywhere available in a growing array of foods. The prices of fat-laden foods (French fries) have fallen *relative* to calorie-free foods (carrots), but this book also focuses on a hidden force behind the decline in the *full* price of calorie-laden foods—the decline in the labor cost of meals. For many Americans, the time they spend eating meals is often greater than the time they spend preparing them.

The growth in people's girths also can be traced to an expansion in world trade brought on by a long-term downward trend in trade protectionism and the growth in capital and labor mobility across national borders, which has been aggravated by the computer and telecommunications revolutions and the downfall of communism and expansion of market economies. In an important but unheralded regard, America has become the home of so many heavy people because the country has always been the "land of the free." Now, free markets have broken out all over the world with ever more intense competition in markets that are now global in scope, causing Americans to pack on pounds with escalating efficiency. In other words, the country's weight problems are at least partially a result of the triumph of free-market economics, which the late Milton Friedman and the late Ronald Reagan fervently advocated during the last quarter of the twentieth century, over all the other "isms" that stressed government control of markets.

Given economic forces, Americans should now be expected to be heavier on average than they were decades ago, even if their goal were solely to maximize their life expectancy. Fat can kill, but so can stress—brought on by efforts to curb excess pounds. Americans must balance the life-saving benefits of fewer pounds on their backsides against the life-threatening stress that can come with efforts to achieve idealized weight goals set decades ago when the economic temptations to eat were not as pressing. Because of lower prices of calories, weight loss simply takes more fortitude than it did a generation or more ago. Obviously, many Americans today have settled for new and higher optimum weight levels, while others have simply lost control of their weights.

Moreover, **HEAVY!** explains how the growth in obesity among the young and old can beget growth in kind: When more and more people are gaining weight, the social and economic costs of extra pounds decline relatively, which under-cut people's incentives to avoid packing on more pounds. As friends, clothing designers, restaurants, and employers accommodate people's growing girths, they aggravate the country's weight problems. In no small way, the country's obesity problem is a true "tragedy of the commons" and shares many economic building blocks with global warming. Greater weight translates into greater emissions of greenhouse gases and broader and sooner melting of the Arctic and Antarctic ice shelves. The fate of polar bears *could* be tied to people's growing girths (although the effects of human activities on global warming remains hotly contested by a minority of atmospheric scientists). The real, or just perceived, ties among people's weights, greenhouse gases, and global warming effects will fuel the coming fat policy war, no matter how consequential the effects of human activity are on climate change.

The country's coming fat war and policy debates also have undertones in class inequalities. In the not-too-distant past, excess poundage rose with income and wealth. After all, wealthy people could afford to pay for more calories. Indeed, at one time, extra pounds were a not-so-subtle form of "conspicuous consumption" (with the pun intended). Now, the correlation between income and wealth, on the one hand, and extra poundage, on the other, has been reversed. The battle of the bulge is clearly being lost with more conspicuous effects among lower-income and minority groups who have been sucked into buying low-price, high-calorie food and who are not able to afford what higher-income groups can buy: memberships in fancy gymnasiums (often aided by trainers) and trips to lifestyle-altering "fat farms."

Clearly, food is for many people an addictive good that the "rich" can afford to try knowing that they have the wherewithal to buy their way out of their addictions (through a host of not-always-cheap weight-reduction strategies). The "poor" have no such luxury, which is one unheralded reason the poor can see their economic lot spiral downward in a "cycle of fat"—with their extra weight undercutting their incomes and their lower incomes undercutting their best weight-reduction intentions by inducing them to buy cheaper and fattier foods for themselves and their children.

Paying by the Pound

In a significant way, Americans are paying by the pound, both privately and publicly. But the American battle of the bulge raises the ominous prospect of a new social and economic divide in the country between thin and fat Americans. Many of the economic arguments used to control smoking are arguments that have been, and will continue to be used, to control people's eating in various ways, which means there will likely be growing political tensions between thin and fat Americans; however, the outcomes of these political battles are less certain than in the case of smoking because the number of fat Americans continues to grow.

HEAVY! identifies public policies (especially farm and educational food subsidies) that have aggravated the country's obesity problems, and suggests reforms. But readers should be forewarned that a key solution to slowing down the growth in the country's excess tonnage, if not reversing the growth, is an old-fashioned one: ensure that overweight and obese Americans shoulder the full economic burden of their excess poundage. Our biological propensities to eat, and overeat, make it all the more necessary for individuals to pay the full costs of their overeating. Such "tough love" has a clear goal—weight reduction for the good of overweight and obese Americans as well as for the national economy.

Most overweight people know the underworked rule for losing weight: expend more calories daily than are consumed. This book offers suggestions for effective dieting based on economic arguments for weight gain developed in the book and also critically examines incentive systems that some companies have instituted to effectively pay workers to control their weight, with the aim of controlling health insurance costs.

As I finalize this book, I am also drawing to a close my forty-five-year career as an economics and management professor and am plotting a second career in non-academic writing and business ventures. I feel fortunate to have spent the last twenty years teaching only MBA students in the Merage School of Business at the University of California, Irvine. As all professors know, teaching is the best means of learning. I have been inspired by my students, especially the fully employed and executive MBA students who have juggled their coursework with their careers and family obligations, who have been dedicated to learning, and who have challenged me to make microeconomics relevant to them as they seek to rise to substantial management positions within their organizations or create and build companies of their own. I have also been able to test out my economic arguments captured in my many books, including this one, in my classes and have used my students' reactions to refine and improve my arguments. My MBA students at the Merage Business School have been a joy to teach, which is why I get great pleasure in dedicating this book to them.

Richard B. McKenzie

Acknowledgements

My work on *HEAVY!* has taken several years, which means I am necessarily indebted to a number of research assistants, including Ashish Agarwal, Sarah Hajizadeh, Niraj Jha, and Sriram Narayan, all of whom deserve my considerable gratitude for going way beyond the call of their duties. I am also indebted to three economist colleagues from across the country who read the entire manuscript and recommended numerous improvements in the arguments presented: Daniel Hammond (history of economic thought and economic history, Wake Forest University), Dwight Lee (applied microeconomic theory, Southern Methodist University), and Lorens Helmchen (health care economics, George Mason University), I have also benefited greatly from colleagues from other disciplines who have given me their expert advice on key topics covered in sections of the book: Steve Frank (evolutionary biology, University of California, Irvine), James Fallon (neuroscience, University of California, Irvine), and Paul Zak (neuroeconomics, Claremont Graduate School). Most prominently, I am extraordinarily indebted to journalist and writer Laura Long, who in editing several drafts of the manuscript and adding flow to my words for a general audience, became a true partner in the development of the book.

Richard B. McKenzie

Contents

Chapter 1
Crowding Out

"Continental [now United] flight 1598 for Houston is now ready for boarding," the gate attendant at the Orange County, California airport announced exactly twenty minutes before the plane was scheduled to depart. The people milling about at the gate represented America in microcosm—various ages, various ethnic groups, with some considerable diversity in dress (from business people in dapper suits, male and female, to college students whose stylishly faded and tattered jeans obscured their high prices). Then there was the spread of body types, ranging from petite to way past plus sizes. Even kids in plus and double- and triple-plus sizes stirred about in the gate area, often with parents who were equally oversized. America was there in plain view, well represented, in all its sophistication and debilities, with many wearing their excesses around their waists.

The gate attendee continued the usual routine, "Passengers in rows 30 and higher may board now… 15 and higher." "Ah, that's me." I weaseled my way into the developing queue, avoiding eye contact when I thought I was pressing forward too aggressively, which, of course, everyone else was doing, at least a little. Even with assigned seats, many air travelers often worry that someone will get on board ahead of them and fill the overhead bins above their rows with overstuffed carry-on bags, requiring late boarders to hand off their bags to the flight attendant. These "orphan bags" (as ground crew members call them) end up either in the cargo hold or worse yet, crammed into an overhead bin well behind where their owners are seated. Anxiety-provoking thoughts follow: "How the hell am I going to get my bag until everyone else has left the plane? And I have a tight gate connection!"

As frequent travelers know all too well, running out of overhead bin space has always been a possibility, but one that has jumped as a potential problem since 2007 when American Airlines initiated the airline industry's spreading practice of charging for checked bags.[1] United quickly followed suit with a $15 fee for the first checked bag and $25 for a second.[2] Delta upped the ante by announcing in mid-2008 a $50 fee for the second bag, with total fee for two bags reaching $120 for at least one airline (if you can believe a widely replayed 2010 Southwest Airline television ad pressing its resistance to the trend to charge for bags).

R.B. McKenzie, *HEAVY!*, DOI 10.1007/978-3-642-20135-6_1,
© Springer-Verlag Berlin Heidelberg 2012

Travelers responded as economists would predict: They began taking more (overstuffed) bags on board. Surprise, surprise! The problem of scarce overhead bin space became all the worse. Checked baggage fees have since sensibly, and predictably, morphed into an added charge for excess poundage of unchecked bags as passengers have sought to avoid the bag charges by overstuffing both their checked and carry-on bags. Airlines have since found that passengers' checked bags have, predictably, again, grown in weight, which has caused a movement in the industry toward substantial surcharges for each "overweight" bag (50–70 pounds) of as much as $90 and for each "supersized" bag (over 70 pounds) of as much as $175.[3]

But the shortage of overhead bin space will no doubt grow because airlines are likely to continue to raise baggage fees for a good old-fashioned reason: Luggage is now a substantial profit center, netting more than $1 billion in 2008 and a projected $3.5 billion for 2009 (partially because the fees allow airlines to price discriminate between passengers who pack heavy and light).[4] The baggage revenues help airlines cover their losses from a decrease in fares (inflation-adjusted) driven down through competition and from the increase in the real cost of jet fuel during the past decade.[5]

Bag fees have been roundly criticized as "unfair," but then why shouldn't there be a charge for luggage, or, better yet, a charge *per pound* of luggage? After all, passengers' luggage takes up cargo space that could be used for … well, cargo that is often shipped with per-pound charges. In addition, every added pound on board whatever its source takes extra jet fuel to fly them across country. The tens of millions of passenger bags, whether in the cargo hold or overhead bins, flown across country cost airlines each year hundreds of millions of dollars in jet fuel, which is a cost not subtracted from airline profits (which most airlines haven't seen for years) but a cost that is often added to airlines' perennial losses.

Per-bag or per-pound charges also can do away with the cross-subsidy from passengers who pack light to those who have to use a cart to move their bags up to the check-in counters. But then, I couldn't help but wonder as I sized up the travelers at the gate why it is that all passengers have to pay applicable baggage fees, but the significant number of overweight passengers that day didn't have to pay for the hundreds of extra pounds they were carrying on board not-so-hidden under their clothes? Indeed, a number of the waiting passengers looked as though they had the equivalent of three bags around their waists and on their backsides, several of whom may have paid less for their tickets than the more petite travelers (and I) paid. The issue here is not just economic efficiency but also fairness, and could be at the core of political policy battles over weight (and appearance) in our not-too-distant future. In no small way (no, in a big way), policy and legal battle lines are now being formed in the coming weight war.

A Full Flight, in More Ways than the Obvious

The Continental desk attendee, of course, warned everyone that over-sized carry-on bags would not be allowed and would require checking at the end of the jetway. And of greater concern to me, she cautioned, "The plane will be full," which I translated into a scarcity of space in the overhead bins for carry-on and more cramped quarters during the flight. "Just my luck." I needed to revise a book chapter during the flight and I was hoping against vacant wishes that the middle seat in my row would be empty. That way, I could work on my light-weight laptop without worrying about elbowing anyone, and I could use the tray for the middle seat to extend my "desktop" for the journal articles I had brought with me.

The flight attendant on board was all smiles as I turned the corner to amble down the aisle to 17A, a window seat about halfway into the coach section. As few of my frequent traveling colleagues do, I routinely ask for a window seat and grumble (silently) when none is left. I've never lost the feeling of enchantment from seeing the white topsides of clouds.

The petite and classy older woman, who had taken the aisle seat on my side of row 17 and who could not have weighed more than 110 pounds, even if she had just come out a rain storm, got up with ease to let me slide into my seat. "Maybe we'll get lucky with the middle seat remaining empty," I told the woman in the aisle seat. The two of us looked up occasionally to watch the few stragglers coming down the aisle for any sign that they wanted our middle seat. As each approached our aisle, hesitated to check the row number, and then moved on, I breathed a sigh of relief. When one trim Asian lady looked toward the seat next me, only to pass my row by, I thought, "Whew! A close call."

As the stragglers stopped altogether, I knew it was about time for the flight attendants to close the cabin doors. "Almost there. Lady Luck just could make our day, and flight," I told the woman on the aisle.

But then, my heart skipped more than a beat when a very BIG man in his mid-forties appeared at the head of the aisle. Correction, he wasn't just BIG, he was humongous, maybe my height, five-feet-ten, but possibly 350 pounds, double my weight and more than double the maximum weight nutritionists recommend for someone of his height! But there was some hope left. A couple of middle seats in front and behind my row were still open. "Maybe his number is on one of those seats." He kept coming down the aisle, squeezing his way between every set of aisle seats on every row. I could now see the sweat on his brow and the telltale sweat stains in the armpits of his short-sleeved Hawaiian shirt that gaped to reveal his overhanging gut.

The man looked toward our row; then he looked past our row. But his eyes returned to fix on our row, again. "Damn!" He did what I dreaded. He stopped at our row—17—pointed to the middle seat beside me and then to his chest with the obvious message, "That's mine."

"Damn! Double damn!" My distress probably showed. Only moments earlier I thought the woman on the aisle and I had been saved by the bell, so to speak. Regrets surfaced, "Why couldn't the slim Asian woman have taken the seat?"

The big man pressed his bag into the bin behind us, and the woman on the aisle got up to let him in. And did he ever need all the room he could get, and then some, to get seated. He could only squeeze into his seat with the armrests raised. The people in row 16 were seriously bumped as he pushed their seats forward to press himself into his seat. Once seated, he could not possibly have lowered his tray. The flight attendant saved him the embarrassment of having to ask for a seatbelt extender. Even with the extender, he had trouble snapping the buckle together.

Me? My work plans were terminated, and indeed, any other plans I might have had for the three-hour flight were abruptly shut down. Even though the big man made a valiant effort to minimize the impact of his size on the woman on the aisle and me, he still took over half of our seats. I was jammed against the window, even after crossing my arms to reduce the press at all points of contact between the big man in the middle and myself. The woman on the aisle was also pressed to the far side of her seat, but then she had two advantages. She was less than two-thirds my size, which means she had more room to give up for the big man's encroachment. And she could lean into the aisle, which she had to do, at least a little.

I fretted to myself, "I paid for a *seat*, a full seat, for the trip—not a half seat, but a *full seat*," and here someone had effectively mugged me for half of my space simply because he was large—no, humongous! The big man was not only making work on the plane impossible for me, he was effectively forcing me, as well as the woman in the aisle seat, to subsidize his trip (via his taking over a portion of *our* seats for which he paid nothing), with the prospective similar subsidies on all of his plane trips likely encouraging his overeating (maybe marginally), as well as that of many other Americans of his size. If heavy people had to pay by the pound (or pay for the parts of other people's seats they cover or just pay for wider seats on all their trips by plane, train, bus, and subway), might they not have greater incentive to watch what and how much they eat? If, instead, trim people were given a discount, would not heavy people also have much the same incentive to watch what they eat?

If people in general can be expected to pack lighter when they have to pay for checked luggage by the pound, might not some heavy people be expected to "pack" lighter around their waists when charged by the pound (in some rough and ready way, maybe by paying for extra-wide seats or by buying two seats)? I agree, an added charge for weight on plane trips might have a very small effect, but if the principle were extended to all similar travel situations in which heavy people impose on people around them, the effect on people's weight could be quite significant (or so all economists are bound to think, a line of argument that is backed by a mountain of scholarly studies, as will be explained later).

A number of other thoughts raced through my mind: "If there is a runway accident or if the plane strikes birds on takeoff and has to ditch in the inlet at the end of the runway at the John Wayne/Orange County Airport [as US Airways flight 1549 had to do in the Hudson River in early 2009], there is no way in hell I'm going to get out of my seat, much less the aircraft. I'm a goner."

Plus, he will make it more difficult for everyone else in the plane to exit in the event of an emergency, if he even tries to get out of his seat. If he doesn't try to get out, I'm a total goner. If by some almost nonexistent chance he makes it to the exit, he would surely get stuck in the exit doorway and block the egress of everyone else."

Inevitably, I realized that I should have gone to the bathroom before boarding. There's no way I would have been able to squeeze out of my row during the flight. Of course, the last thing you want to do on an airplane is to think about going to the bathroom because such thoughts can spur the urge to go, which the thought did with force.

My experience on the flight to Houston is important only because it is a widely shared one. More important, it affords me an opportunity to dramatize and preview in this first chapter the varied themes that are developed in some detail throughout this book. The most important theme is the likely growing conflict between heavy and trim people, all very silent for now. Scratch any frequent flier, and most can relate to my story, most often without good feelings. Even heavy travelers can have trouble with other heavy travelers because they are then doubly squeezed.

But my trip saga had a final turn of events after the door was closed, one that was a bit surprising but very instructive. The pilot came over the intercom, "I'm sorry, but we will have a delay. We are too heavy. We need six passengers to disembark." The flight attendant then took over and went through the familiar process offering free tickets at escalating values for those six passengers who voluntarily gave up their seats. The big man beside me muttered, "I'd take them up on their offer if they would count me as two, which they should." Oh well, so much depends on perspective, I guess.[6]

> One pound of body fat is the equivalent to approximately 3,500 calories. This means that in order to lose that pound over the course of a week, you must eat 500 fewer calories a day than the calories required to maintain your body weight. If you can maintain your weight with 2,100 calories consumed a day, then to lose a pound of weight in a week, you must drop your calorie intake to 1,600. To estimate the maximum calories you must consume to maintain your current body weight—given your sex, weight, height, and physical activity— go to a John Hopkins Health Alert provided at http://copdnewsofthe day.com/?p=4111.

The Population Bomb, Redux

As I sat there on the plane, I couldn't help lamenting my bad draw in seatmates (not just row-mates). Then, the economist in me kicked in and I began seeing my predicament on that flight representing, albeit in microcosm and in exaggerated form, a plight of much of modern America, if not Western Civilization. I began to think of the potential for a coming "fat war," pitting trim people against fat people over who pays for all the costs associated with people's excess weight and how the growth in people's weight will be abated with taxes on all tasty but fatty and sugared foods and drinks with the revenues targeted for subsidies on healthy foods, and laws that will try to abate efforts by firms, airlines included, to collect on (weight penalties) the added costs of people's weights on business and their trim customers. Surely, the added costs of people's excess weight is also bound to lead to lawsuits against employers who impose a "wage penalty" on heavy workers for their added workplace costs and against service providers (from airlines to nail shops) who impose price surcharges on heavy customers for accommodating their weight-related service costs.

The planet is getting smaller not only because of increasing population and the ever increasing speed and availability of cheap air travel, but also because so many people in the world—especially Americans—are getting larger, leading to a growing sense of crowdedness and to ever more opportunities for others to invade our individual spaces. And we, as a species, must produce and consume ever more calories just to keep alive and haul around all the fat cells on our backsides filled to the brim from so many people overeating.

Demographers have made much about the effects of the "population bomb" going off in slow motion as the count of human beings has more than doubled during the lifetimes of the middle-aged and older people on that Continental flight. But few have mentioned how the close to seven billion people now on the planet take up substantially more volume today than they would have a mere generation ago. Well, if there had been seven billion people in, say, 1960 or at the time of the Revolution, you can imagine that they would have taken up substantially less volume than the seven billion contemporary people take up today. And the growth in the mass of Americans has outstripped the growing mass of people in most other parts of the world (although people in some countries, most notably England and Mexico, seem to have decided to give Americans a race for added excess pounds).

When I began to think in terms of the volume of people in existence, the gate attendant's announcement that "the flight would be full" took on more meaning than she realized. She meant no seats would be empty. I thought of just how *full* those seats and the plane would be, and how much fuller it would be than a full flight of the Boeing 757 on its maiden flight three or so decades ago.[7]

Americans' growth in weight in the past thirty years alone has literally meant that there would be less empty space—as in volume—in the plane's cabin than there would have been had the passengers' weight been what it was back in, say, 1960. If the 216 passengers on my flight represented America today, each boarded the plane with the average weight of Americans in 1960, *plus* the equivalent of the largest ready-to-cook turkey that can be bought during the Thanksgiving season, with all "turkeys" held on the passengers' laps. And those turkeys took up a lot of the cabin volume. Think about the mass of 216 twenty-eight-pound plucked turkeys spread out in the aisle of the plane, and consider the amount of jet fuel needed to haul those turkeys to Houston and points beyond. The more than two-and-a-half tons of added weight of the passengers (over what a similar count of 1960 passengers would have weighed) required Continental to use close to 500 additional gallons of jet fuel, costing over $1,220 in total (at 2010 prices for jet fuel) or between $5 and $6 for each passenger, for the 1,350 miles of the Orange County-to-Houston leg of the flight alone.[8]

The added weight that year was adding millions of dollars directly to Continental's net loss, which totaled $146 million in the first quarter of 2010.[9] The losses of all world airlines ran into the billions of dollars that year, with some tens of millions of dollars of those losses attributable to the excess weight of a majority of passengers and the outright morbid obesity of some passengers, such as the big guy next to me.

In 2003, a small commuter plane crashed on takeoff in Charlotte, North Carolina, with excess passenger weight found to be a contributing factor to the crash.[10]

Understandably, the Federal Aviation Administration (FAA) began requiring airlines in 2003 to increase their estimated takeoff weights by ten pounds per passenger and five pounds per bag, just to make sure the planes met safety standards.[11] Of course, more jet fuel consumed by airlines to carry the extra human fat converts into tons of additional carbon dioxide that planes dump directly into the upper atmosphere, speeding up and exacerbating global warming, however serious that environmental problem is. Exactly how much passengers' added weight contributes to the CO_2 dumping is not easy to compute, simply because with added passenger weight, airlines have had to curb the cargo they take on board, just to meet maximum takeoff weight limits. No one should be surprised, however, that the *net* effect of people's growing girths in this country and around the world has undermined the efficiency improvements in airplane engines and could, at least beyond some point, give rise to a nontrivial increase in greenhouse gases (the details of which will be covered later in the book). At the core of the problem for economists is that heavy people might not be carrying the full costs of their environmental effects, which can add to heavy people's incentive to add to their girths (or reduce heavy people's incentives to make the required effort to reduce their girths).

In case you think that that there could be no net global warming effects because airlines reduce cargo to compensate for passenger weight, just

If you weigh 160 pounds, you will burn in an hour 584 calories playing in a basketball game, 329 calories golfing, 511 calories running (at eight miles per hour), 292 calories biking (at 10 miles per hour), and 183 calories walking (at 3.5 miles per hour). If you weigh 240 pounds, the calories burned in an hour are 545 for basketball, 491 golfing, 763 running, 436 biking, 273 walking. For the calories burned in a number of other physical activities, see the link in the endnote. As reported by the Mayo Clinic Staff (2010), citing Ainsworth et al. (2000). The link to the complete table is http://www.mayoclinic.com/health/exercise/SM00109.

remember that much of the cargo that is taken off passenger planes will be shifted to other planes or trucks to be hauled to their destinations, likely at added cost and with some inevitable CO_2 emissions. Taken together, heavy people, in no small way, could represent a real threat to polar bears and the ice shelves around both poles of the globe (if, in fact, human activity consequentially elevates the undisputed global warming trend that has been underway for centuries, an active scientific controversy I will shy from even trying to settle in this book[12]).

Okay, not everyone on board was carrying the equivalent of a large Thanksgiving turkey in added weight on that Continental flight. The older woman in the aisle seat of my row, for example, may have been underweight by the equivalent of a ready-to-bake chicken. I was at the time close to my high-school-graduation weight, and within a few pounds of my target weight recommended by nutritionists (I say with some pride, which may have eased my writing of this book, although as I wrote this book I gained weight). However, such observations only mean that others were carrying our turkeys, plus their own. A few passengers were obviously carrying the equivalent of three turkeys. The big man next to me was at least a four-turkey passenger just in gut size. Accommodating for very overweight people on airplanes is a familiar scene for many, but even more distressing is that Americans were, on average, overweight even in the early 1960s.[13]

The Growing Weight Conflict

As the nation's population spreads out in weight (and the weights of already overweight Americans are rising more rapidly than those of thinner Americans), tension and conflict are bound to emerge not just in airplane seating, but in political and business arenas, as well as other social spheres. This book will cover from beginning to end an array of the likely points of conflict. Let me offer a sample.

From Baggage Fees to Fat Fees

The practice of charging for checked bags will likely cause airline executives to ask the question mentioned earlier, "Why should a customer have to pay for her bag plus cover a portion of the air travel costs of overweight travelers?" Might the airline business not see people's excess weight as the same sort of profit center that checked luggage has become? Might we not expect airlines, at some point, to charge passengers by the excess pounds as a means to lower fuel costs and the ticket prices of trimmer passengers who can be hauled around the country even with their bags in the cargo hold for less cost than much heavier passengers with no bags? Might airlines charge more for overweight passengers just so they can reduce their numbers and increase the paying cargo, including checked bags, they can carry? You ask, "How might they proceed?" Ever noticed the rack off to the side of the counter at the gate with a sign with message something to the effect, "If your bag can't fit below, you must check your bag"? Can you not imagine a far less obtrusive human scanning machine through which all passengers must pass before boarding that determines a fare penalty or credit determined by body mass, which is applied to the credit card that is used to buy the tickets? If not that method, might not airlines provide different size seats in the different cabins and sell them off at different prices?

Spreading Fat Fees

These questions are not simply rhetorical. Initial skirmishes in the coming fat wars have already been engaged. After receiving more than seven hundred complaints over the previous twelve months, United Airlines announced in spring 2009 that it will bump severely overweight passengers from sold-out flights and require passengers who cannot comfortably fit into standard coach seats to buy a second adjoining seat on the next flight or to upgrade to business class where the seats are larger. Delta Airlines has established much the same policy.[14] Southwest Airlines soon followed United, requiring its "customers of size" to buy two adjoining seats, with the provision that the charge for the second seat will be refunded if the plane is not full, a new policy it sees as more lenient and considerate (and competitive) than other airlines' policies.[15] At least one nail salon has added (but then retracted) a "surcharge" for severely overweight customers (mostly women) because of the damage the shop has suffered to their pedicure lounge chairs;[16] paramedic squads have begun to add "bariatric" surcharges for the added costs of rescuing seriously overweight patients that require added manpower and reinforced rescue equipment—all topics to which we will return in this book.[17]

Talking heads on television news programs immediately cried "foul" and raised the banner of "discrimination" against the obese on grounds that translate to "fat people should not be held responsible for their weight; their genes made them fat."[18] A medical doctor specializing in the care of the obese blogged, "The rule [for added fares for large people] reinforces the stigma that obese people face every day. Bias against obesity is one of the last socially acceptable forms of discrimination in our society, and forcing an obese person to purchase a second airplane seat would serve only to increase it."[19]

But is the doctor right? Might a heavy person who pays for the space he or she takes up not be less offensive to other passengers since their space will not be invaded? If the doctor's assessment governs, who then is going to pay for the partial seats heavy passengers take up? Trim people? Should heavy passengers be immune to socials and economic slights when they are imposing real costs on others? Granted, there might be a stigma associated with charging fat people for the space they take up, but is there not a problem with charging others around them or asking the airline companies to take the added costs associated with people's excess weight? If others cover the costs of people adding pounds, will heavy people not be less attentive to their weights and gain even more pounds? How in the world are we going to discriminate, legally and practically, between heavy people who have genetic disorders and those who just don't want to work at controlling their weights as so many other people do? And don't forget that many heavy passengers can be just as disturbed about their space being invaded by other heavy passengers and can harbor stigmas and prejudice toward others who have personal characteristics they don't like.

No matter, the added charge for large passengers is spreading internationally, partially at the urging of many trimmer passengers. Ryanair, an Irish airline, is considering a "fat tax" for obese passengers for two reasons. First, it polled a hundred thousand visitors to its Web site on whether they favor an added charge for heavy people. Remarkably, thirty thousand (one in three) of the respondents favored the added charge. But then, *The Daily Telegraph* of London polled its readers and found that 83 percent favored United's added charge for obese passengers, which makes me think that I am a member of a silent majority bothered by the encroachment of large people into space of others.[20] To test the coming potential conflict among people on this issue, tell them about the themes of this book, and listen to many people's tales of woe in having to deal with the excess poundage of others.

Overweight passengers themselves do not always begrudge the fat hostilities they face and do not necessarily oppose such surcharges as have been tried in spotty ways. In response to a query by a *Chicago Tribune* reporter, one six-foot-two, 350-pound Chicago resident and United passenger assessed the United policy with graciousness: "I can honestly say that I understand the rule and why it is necessary. From the standpoint of a fat flier, I am just as uncomfortable as the poor person who has to sit next to me in coach."[21]

Spreading Fat Suits

Nevertheless, not all "people of size" agree. Airlines have been threatened with lawsuits as passengers have been turned away from boarding because of their size, and legislation is being readied in more than one state to outlaw discrimination against people of "height [short or tall] and weight."[22] Michigan already has a law on its books banning weight discrimination. The Canadian Transportation Agency has ordered Canadian airlines to refrain from charging people with disabilities, including the "clinically obese," extra even when they require more than one seat.[23] Who do you think is going to pay for that "free" extra seat, only the airlines? Come on, costs airlines have to bear have a way of being shifted . . . to whom else . . . their passengers. Ditto for other industries in which people's weight can significantly affect services and products provided. Believe me, the fat wars on several political fronts will, no doubt, escalate.

Health-Care Reform and Fat Discrimination in the Workplace

People's growing excess weight will very likely continue to change management hiring, pay and benefit practices, as well as fuel battles over health-care policies. The unmentioned "800-pound gorilla" in the national health-care debate, reignited with President Barack Obama's inauguration and eventually won by him with the passage of "Obamacare" was and remains, literally, Americans' excess tonnage, which is a not-so-silent killer and an unheralded force behind escalating health-care and insurance costs, as we will see. With health-care costs relating to excess weight being covered by taxpayers, Americans' overweight problems will likely weigh down any health-care system that relies on government funding. Ultimately, a government health-care program will include subsidies that, when provided, will necessarily mean that trim Americans, through the taxes they pay, will cover the health-care costs of the overweight.

The cross subsidies, of course, will reduce the personal costs overweight (and currently trim) people incur for their overeating, which can feed the newly insured people's overeating and weight gain (or so research to be reviewed later finds[24])—unless the government asks overweight people to pay for their government-sponsored health insurance by the pound, which is doubtful.

Doubt the economics? Consider all the evidence presented in later chapters that carries a central message: The price people pay for how much they eat matters in how heavy they are. No doubt, the pending fat wars, which will be organized, to a large extent, around cost shifting among weight groups, can prompt political tensions and personal resentments between the trim and the overweight and between the overweight and the obese—and even among subgroups in the overweight and obese categories of Americans.

As these words were being written, policymakers had passed a law that reformed the country's health-care system in part by denying health insurance companies the right to give their policy holders discounts for healthy behaviors (not smoking and controlling weight), all in the name of equity. The proponents of the prohibition see discounts as a backdoor way of hiking premiums for unhealthy behaviors (smoking and gaining weight), because discounts can be deducted from elevated basic insurance prices.

Of course, if proponents of the health insurance restrictions get their wish, they could be compounding the errors of heavy people's ways, very possibly causing health insurance costs for everyone to go up, thus driving additional Americans out of the health insurance market. To a nontrivial degree, they could be increasing health-care and insurance costs, as well as contribute to the greater consumption of gasoline and jet fuel to haul the added weight and to greater emissions of greenhouse gases.

From Smoking Wars to Fat Wars

Might not the political conflicts between trim and heavy people emerge for much the same reason that conflicts emerged between smokers and nonsmokers? Researchers have long known that smoking causes lung cancer and other deadly diseases. The case for the regulation and heavy taxation of cigarettes was greatly spurred when a connection was made between second-hand smoke and cancer and other diseases. The actions of smokers can force nonsmokers to foot the medical bills of smokers, which can induce more smoking and the deaths of more second-hand smokers. Moreover, nonsmokers who help cover the health-care costs of smokers can incur greater health-care costs of their own and even die along the way from the smoke blown in their faces.

Hence, as we will explain in some detail later in the book, today state governments and the federal government heavily tax tobacco products and the Food and Drug Administration closely regulates them. In some areas of the country (including my home state of California), a pack of cigarettes can cost more than two gallons of gasoline, and cigarettes can be smoked only in designated and, and in some communities, ever-more isolated areas. Many smokers can't light up in their own apartments or even their detached homes, at least not when children are present.

The same arguments for tough regulation and high taxation of smokes can be applied to fat. Smokers can kill themselves in droves on the installment plan, one cigarette at a time, they can also increase nonsmokers' medical problems through "second-hand smoke," which can impose a cost on other people through the country's tax and medical systems. Fat can also kill heavy people on the installment plan, one mouthful at a time. Weight also can (or so it can be argued) have second-hand effects that can be as costly and deadly to trim people as second-hand smoke is for nonsmokers, as the big guy next to me on the Continental flight made me think. He decreased the probability that I and everyone else on the plane could get out safely in the event of a minor accident.

Okay, so the change in the probability of people egressing the plane safely was small, but don't underestimate how politically active antifat interest groups (including the diet and drug industries and weight and nutrition researchers) might use such life-and-death arguments in their pursuit of their "antifat policy agenda." And if you think I am odd in having such thoughts about my reduced ability to egress a burning plane, just ask others around you if they would have had similar concerns had they been occupying a window seat with a 350-pound passenger in the middle.

Moreover, overweight people reduce the chances of others—trim and heavy people alike—to evacuate tall buildings because overweight people can block stairways and slow down people's speed in making their ways down the stairways often designed with the lower weights of people a half century ago—a line of argument suggesting that more Americans died in the Twin Towers on 9/11 than would have died had Americans weighed in on average in 2001 no more than they did when the stairways in the Twin Towers were designed, back in the 1960s. (If you think the problem is trivial, go to a concert and take notice of how heavy people slow the flow of people out of the hall and down the stairs at the end of the performance.) Americans' increasing girths are also causing airports to incur greater costs for wheelchairs; stadiums to increase the width of seats (reducing seating capacities and hiking ticket prices); and ambulance services to reinforce their vehicles and gurneys to accommodate heavier patients.

Fat Taxes on Foods and Drinks

"Fat taxes" applied to high calorie and high fat-content foods and drinks have already been proposed with sufficient frequency that "fat tax" has a Wikipedia entry (see Chap. 8).[25] No doubt, the demand for "fat taxes" will grow as a means of reducing people's eating temptations and their excess weight and of reducing health-care costs. Proposed regulations of calorie and fat content in foods also may surface more frequently. Restaurants could even be restricted on the portions they put on their plates, and patrons might be restricted on where and what they can eat.

Think such controls are too farfetched? One Mississippi legislator has already introduced a bill to restrict restaurants from serving heavy people.[26] Such a bill may have no political traction, but bills at the state and national levels of government requiring restaurant chains (with, say, more than twenty outlets) to post the calories for their menu items, which were instituted in Maine and California in mid-2009, had spread to the rest of the country when this book was competed in early 2011. The health-care reform bill passed in 2010 includes a provision requiring all restaurants in all states to follow Maine and California's example.[27]

Proponents of one variation or another of the fat tax point to the serious health problems that excess weight, especially to the point of severe obesity, cause. The critics respond that a blanket fat tax would unnecessarily and unjustifiably tax thin people who might want occasionally to down a bag of Fritos or a Big Mac. The fat tax, critics tell us, should be directly applied to fat people, and one critic has gone so far as to develop a complicated formula that might cause a mathematician to pause, complete with a provision that lowers the impact of the fat tax for low-income people.[28] However, such an added expression in the tax formula would tend to focus the tax on the wrong people, especially the many trim higher-income *and* lower-income people who go out of their way to control their weight at some personal cost, more so than many heavy lower-income and higher-income people.

I note this proposed version of the fax tax not to advocate for it, but to alert you that my concern about the coming fat war is hardly abstract, pie-in-the-sky, theorizing with no connection to the real world. I am talking about problems and solutions to the country's weight problems that have become contentious and will likely become even more contentious in political circles as people's weights continue to rise and as politicians scramble for new revenue sources, given the continuing rise of government expenditures at the federal level and in many states and communities (and as paternalists and moralists, energized by victories in the smoking policy war, seek to throw their support behind new societal and policy causes). Indeed, economists and nutrition scientists have begun to estimate the impact of various fat taxes on people's weight and health problems, only to find— so far—modest effects, as we will see in Chap. 7.[29] But be assured that the search for more powerful effects of fat taxes continues apace, as we will see in later chapters.

So you think such policy proposals will never work themselves into law because they are "extreme"? Would anyone have thought fifty years ago that smoking in a closed private office would be outlawed today? How about in a car when children are present? Such restrictions are real today, although hardly universal.

Workplace Fat Battles

People of all sizes have always tried to get along in the workplace, but conflicts and tensions are bound to emerge there between trim and heavy people. Weight beyond some level can affect people's productivity and effectiveness in at least some jobs. When so much work must be done in collaborative teams, team members in some workplaces understandably will be concerned about their fellow team members being able to pull their weight, literally and figuratively, because their pay and employment viability will be inextricably linked to group performance.

Also, to the extent that excess weight increases workers' health-care costs and those costs affect employer-provided health insurance, many trim people can be expected to see themselves as subsidizing, albeit partially, the health insurance costs of heavy people and, thereby, the overeating habits of heavy people. With the acquiescence, or even encouragement of trim workers, employers may shy from hiring heavy people (unless they have compensating work skills), resulting in heavy people having fewer employment opportunities and/or receiving lower pay for the same competencies and productivities just to compensate their employers for their health insurance costs not captured in group premiums that are not adjusted upward for weight risks (as is true of most group policies). Nevertheless, research battles and policy skirmishes will likely continue over how much of their full costs are covered by others and how the added costs of heavy people can be recovered without imposing costs on not-so-heavy and trim workers.

Moreover, employers, colleagues, and customers can judge heavy people as less physically attractive than trimmer people, further undercutting the pay of heavy people, research has shown. Like it or not, "beauty" counts in many workplaces, with less attractive people suffering lower pay rates than their better looking coworkers. And fat people are often downgraded in looks for their excess weights.[30] Can you imagine the lawsuits creative lawyers will file in the not-too-distant future?

The future has arrived. Two former Hooters waitresses filed against Hooters for pressuring them to lose weight, even though they were officially in the "normal weight" category (a court case to which we will return in Chap. 8).[31]

At some excessive weight, heavy people may find it very difficult, if not impossible, to secure employment because of their inability to keep up with coworkers, or even to move at all. As mountains of studies continue to indicate the negative impact weight has on workers' pay, we can expect that an "Association of the Acceptance of Fat Americans" (or an organization with some similar name) will emerge, if several haven't already, and call for laws to prevent employer discrimination based on several new attributes, with looks and weight being likely candidates. Such a legislative course can contribute to increased health insurance costs that employers may pass on to trim and heavy workers alike in the form of pay cuts (or just decreases in pay increases) as time goes by. And such expanded antidiscrimination laws can, naturally, induce more employers to favor the nationalization of health care. Through nationalization, the health-care costs employers have to incur for people's excess weights (or fear an antidiscrimination suit) can then be passed on to taxpayers. And you can imagine that taxpayers might have a thing or two to say about their taxes literally feeding further weight gains of the obese.

The Political Dynamics of The Coming Fat War

While I caution about possible governmental control of people's weight, I quickly want to add that the demographic dynamics in the coming fat policy battles will be structurally different than in the past smoking policy battles. Proposals to tax and regulate smoking emerged when the number of smokers in the voting population accounted for less than half the country's adult population and was on the wane, sped up by a string of reports that found that smoking kills. But as reports on the health threats of excess weight have increased, proposals to regulate people's weight have emerged even as the number of overweight and obese people has grown as a percentage of the voting population, which could weaken the legislative success of such proposals (a good or bad thing, depending on your viewpoint and eating habits).

However, some proportion of overweight and obese people are bound to favor tighter regulations and higher taxes on the foods they enjoy just so they will not be as tempted to overeat. In other words, overweight and obese individuals may view government regulation as providing something of the same services for heavy people that the Betty Ford Clinics provide for drug and alcohol addicts: They help control temptations. Moreover, as the battle lines are being formed in the coming fat war, there could be cadres of heavy and trim people who despise fat taxes and the sundry of creative policies that can be concocted, but they might also reason that they could be better off hobbled by government intrusions for all, including the overeating segment of the population, than to have to endure the costs that heavy people can impose on everyone through higher health insurance premiums and higher taxes—and through taking over their private spaces in planes, trains, concert halls, buses, and subways.

Hang on for the Ride

I have an ambitious goal for this book: to examine the varied economic causes and consequences of America's (and the world's) expanding weight. Below are key elements of the arguments to be explored in some depth in the book that aid in understanding the modern growth in excess weight in America and other parts of the world.

Evolutionary Forces vs. Economic Forces

Special attention must be given to the growing conflict during the past century or two between our internal physiology and neurobiology makeup, which evolutionary forces set long ago and which largely determine our eating proclivities today. The problem we face today is that our innate propensity to eat as much as we can and when we can (to be discussed in Chap. 3) has been spurred by the growing efficiency of the domestic food sector, and by the growing efficiency of broader domestic and world competitive markets for a multitude of products that directly and indirectly make calories cheaper, more convenient to obtain, and more easily converted to fat. These competitive market forces that have become global in scope have relentlessly pushed up people's real (inflation-adjusted) incomes and, for stretches of time, forced down the real prices of foods—most notably for calorie-rich and fat-building foods. This is especially true when the lowered time–cost of food preparation is factored into the real or *full* prices of foods, snacks, and drinks (with the "full price" including the money price on the price tag, plus, for example, the labor costs of preparation and any lost future income and mental distress attributable to excess weight).

> One partial but unheralded explanation for the country's growing weight problems is that over the past half century free competitive markets have broken out on practically all points on the globe. More than two billion people in the former Soviet Union and China have been freed from their strict communist economic bondage. In no small way, capitalism has triumphed over all the other "isms." People are fatter because they are freer.

The growth and spread in contemporary obesity rates represents a triumph of economic forces over evolutionary biological forces, a point that economist Dwight Lee has touched on and nutritionists Michael Power and Jay Schulkin have explored in depth but without the emphasis on the market competitiveness that will be the hallmark of the analysis in this book.[32] This is to say, we modern humans have the genes of our long-ago ancestors who much of the time faced down hunger because food was scarce and difficult to obtain. However, we no longer have to spend much energy in our "hunts" for food. All we have to do is load up our supermarket carts with an endless variety of foods and drinks, almost all at histori-cally low *full* prices. The "obesity epidemic," in no small way (no, really in a very large way), is a product of our good fortune. But then, we need to consider the unchecked rhetoric, sometimes loaded with hyperboles, of anti-overweight and anti-obesity forces with skeptical eyes. Many people can profit from people's excess tonnage and from statistics that make people's weight an "epidemic" and/or a "crisis." They could be managing the "fat facts" with a policy agenda, even a "policy crusade," in mind—and, more importantly, with a stake in how the coming fat war is resolved.[33]

Expanding World Markets and Peoples' Girths

In turn, and in no small way, the expansion of trade and specialization to all corners of the globe has been a major hidden or just unnoticed force behind the expansion of people's guts, suggesting that a portion of people's weight gain can be attributed to the downward trend in trade protectionism since World War II. Put another way, the liberalization of international trade—fostered by wide acceptance of Adam Smith's free-market principles—during the last fifty years can be one unheralded cause of the country's and world's weight problems. That is, I had limited seating space on that Continental flight to Houston because of the growing efficiency of factories and farms, as well as the ongoing decline in transportation and tele-communication costs and the build-down in tariff and quota barriers to international trade.

Of course, some modern forces on both sides of the Atlantic *and* Pacific have been at work over decades on people's weight that have caused followers of Adam Smith to shutter, not the least of which have been government agricultural subsidies that have supported the build-up of pyramids of butter, mountains of apples, lakes of wine, and dunes of sugar, all in the name of pre-serving "family farms" and enabling people to buy below-cost foods and pack on below-cost pounds.

> Excess weight is also undermining the military preparedness of the United States, as military-age youth are increasingly unfit to serve. The Pentagon estimates that more than a third of the 31 million Americans aged seven-teen to twenty-four are unqualified for military service. The Pentagon's director of accessions says, "The major component of this is obesity. We have an obesity crisis in the country. There's no question about it." As reported by McMichael (2009).

But, then, there have been a host of other economic forces set afoot that can be connected to America's (and the world's) obesity problems. Americans' midriff bulges were also doubtlessly enhanced with the fall of the Iron Curtain between the Soviet Union and the West and with the collapse of the "Great Wall of Communism," consisting of extensive economic controls that separated China from the rest of the world and prosperity to a degree that the Great Wall of China never did. The collapse of both these barriers—the Iron Curtain and the Great Wall of Communism—freed nearly two billion people to contribute to the world's output and real incomes—and to a reduction in the cost and an increased consumption of calories in America, as well as in the former Soviet Union, China and elsewhere. Not surprisingly, the rise of free-market economics in China has led to a substantial fattening of Chinese, a relatively trim people under full-fledged state economic planning.[34]

Medical Advances and Girth Increases

Moreover, people's weight problems can be partially chalked up to the tremendous growth in medical advances over the last century or so. Now, with those advances available, people can buy more years of life at lower prices with fewer hours of calorie-using work. With the advances in place and with greater real incomes, many people are going to be tempted—as they have been tempted—to use some portion of those extra *potential* years of life to buy life-shortening good times organized around beer, chips and dip, and deep-fried blooming onions.

Medical and pharmaceutical advances have enabled people to redeem their wanton eating ways by popping Lipitor pills and, if necessary, undergoing heart and stomach bypass surgeries. (Moreover, they will soon be able to do so by having a "stomach pacemaker" implanted, which obviates the need for invasive surgical reduction of the stomach as it releases electrical impulses that tell the brain "I'm full," all at a substantial cost, $24,000 per implant[35]). People can, in effect, play the odds attached to poor, calorie-rich eating habits, and do so at lower costs. To make the point personal, when I learned that my taking Lipitor for only a month had reduced my cholesterol score by 35 percent, I couldn't resist telling my doctor, "Dr. Belici, you just gave me a new lease on Outback!" No doubt, I spoke for many Americans. He smiled and replied something to the effect that he and other doctors saw Lipitor as a lifestyle drug as well as preventive medicine.

When gym memberships are widely available at moderate prices and also offer the prospects of easy redemption for wayward eating, we should expect people to once again be tempted to put in their grocery carts the readily available, feel-good cheap foods, the costs of which come in the form of painful curbs in future consumption and painful future exercise regimens, made all the more painful by the packed-on pounds. You might think that people today could resist omnipresent temptations because of the consequential future costs they must anticipate at some level. They can—and many do—at least to a degree. But, again, people today still are pressed to eat whatever they can and when they can by their long-embedded genes of our ancestors, their taste buds and their proclivities to eat when possible, coupled with their limited ability to calculate the future pain from current overconsumption.

The consequences of modern obesity are as legion as the causes. We've already alluded to several, not the least of which has been greater jet fuel consumption for passenger planes and greater gasoline consumption for cars. Consider also the following: The greater demand for gasoline has had the derivative effects of driving up, albeit marginally, the price of gasoline, which has, of course, contributed to a transfer of wealth from the United States to oil-producing countries, several of which are hardly abiding friends of the United States or share Americans' values on human rights and political stability.

Concluding Comments

A theme of this book that weaves through the varied topics covered is that the country's weight problems are in many ways symptoms of our good fortune not available to past generations. We—even with low incomes—are free enough and prosperous enough to get fat, and then some. Diets are difficult because of our abundance (and other reasons to be covered). Indeed, the obesity issue is growing not only for Americans, but also for their pets. Over half the country's 170 million cats and dogs are overweight and nearly a third are obese (as determined by the count of pets that are 30 percent above their "normal weights," as reported by the Association for Pet Obesity Prevention).[36] Would you believe there would be such an association if we were not so well off? The fact of the matter is that so many of the economic and political forces that have improved our welfare have also fed (literally) our weight problems, and the weight problems of our pets.

Let's be straight: The fattening of Americans (and practically all others in the world's advanced economies) is a delicate subject, especially for those at the core of the subject—and especially when using such wording as "fat people" and the "fattening of Americans." But in the analysis that follows, I mean no personal offense by the words I use, regardless of how I characterize overweight and obese people and their problems. I liberally use "fat" in various forms because the core problem facing large people is their fat, or growth in energy reserves stored in their adipose tissue. Few people are concerned with weight gain attributed to growth in biceps and height. I am really concerned with body matter that affects people's health and wealth, and the ties between the two, and then I am extra concerned, as an economist, with the added pounds that impose costs on people who are not carrying the pounds around. Those subsidized pounds encourage excess eating and added medical care costs, and those added pounds will fuel the coming fat policy war that can threaten our individual freedoms of enjoying what we want and when we want it.

Besides, I need to vary my descriptors of weight, often using "fat" and "heavy," just to keep the flow of words from becoming monotonous. And "fat" will lose much of its sting as you read it repeatedly.

In whatever wording I use and wherever the arguments lead, I also don't mean to make moral or even condescending and derogatory judgments about heavy (or thin) people. Many heavy people beat up on themselves enough, even to the point of serious depression and suicidal thoughts.

At a strictly personal level, I am libertarian enough (but, by no means a libertarian ideologue) to take the position, "to each his (or her) own" or "different strokes for different folks," when it comes to weight issues—except when I feel a personal affront or invasion of my space or when I am asked to pay for the costs, directly or indirectly and involuntarily, of the eating and exercise decisions (or lack thereof) of others. Admittedly, I did feel a personal affront when the big guy took the middle seat next to me on the flight to Houston and took over half my seat, diminishing my chances of getting work done on the flight and threatening my safety and that of all others on the plane in the event of a minor accident (not a crash). But then, I hear the retort a clever economist might make: "When you buy a plane ticket, you buy into a lottery. You buy your ticket at the price you do, appropriately discounted by the chance that your space will be invaded and your work will be curbed, at least from time to time. If you want absolute certainty of having a space to yourself, there is a simple solution: Buy a ticket for the seat beside you."

Maybe so. My main purpose in describing the airplane seating scene was not to denigrate the life choices of the big man beside me (and the other big people scattered throughout the plane) but to elevate the myriad points of potential economic and political conflict that can emerge, and have begun to surface, because of the country's growing weight problems. This book focuses on *analysis* of the economic causes and consequences of people's individual life choices. The goal is not to *attack* individuals (although for some readers, my words at times may give the impression that I intend attack).

To all heavy and still-trim people, I say eat all that you want but be prepared to pay the full costs. Understand what those explicit and hidden costs are and how much you would be expected to pay if you covered them all. Consider how people's changing weight is affecting the economy in unseen and unconsidered ways.

It would be a vain hope to expect America's weight problems to go away despite the ever-growing crescendo of public appeals from inspired leaders for all of us to curb our overeating and increase our expenditure of calories through work and exercise. Indeed, there are industries in this country that have stakes in magnifying, if not exaggerating, the country's weight problems and in those problems' continuation and possible expansion. In the end I urge a modest proposal to deal with the country's weight problems, that we make darn sure that public policies and prices of foods and airline seats do not encourage overeating to the detriment of overeaters and the people with whom they must interact.

Chapter 2
Fat Facts

For morbidly obese patients, the Brookhaven Obesity Clinic is the last ray of hope in an endgame of weight gain. The clinic, which has only eighty beds, seeks to rehabilitate not just obese people, but most often the massively and morbidly obese, those whose thighs, with multiple rolls of fat hanging over one another, can be larger than the torsos of some merely overweight people. Even when they are not in the clinic, Brookhaven patients are largely unseen because so many of them cannot even get out in public and, if they could, often choose to remain reclusive, for good reason: They would no doubt feel the constant stares and disapproval of passersby. These patients' personal goals, described in the Discovery Health Channel's two-part documentary, *Inside the Brookhaven Obesity Clinic*, are nothing like those of formerly overweight women featured in Jenny Craig ads, who dreamed of squeezing into their favorite bikinis. On the contrary, Brookhaven patients aim to get down to "only" 350 pounds or to be able to climb a flight of stairs or return to work.

The picture painted in *Brookhaven* is far from pretty. No, it is downright disturbing. The economic costs to society of people's tremendous excess weight are likely . . . well, tremendous, not to mention the personal costs and pain that the obese person suffers in testing the limits of how much weight the human body can endure.

The filmmakers followed several patients, who initially weighed from 400 pounds to close to half a ton, from their attempts to be admitted to Brookhaven through their stays at the clinic, which lasted months. All of the patients recounted lifelong struggles to *contain* their weights, not just to return to some semblance of normal size. And all readily confessed the source of their weight problems: They ate way too much, especially in calorie-rich foods (lots of hamburgers and pizzas, for example).

Several of the patients were bound to wheelchairs when out of bed. One patient, weighing over 700 pounds, had been bedridden for several years. Nevertheless, in the weeks before the filming, the bedridden patient had insisted on double and triple portions for meals at the nursing home where he lived. Another patient, desperately seeking admission to Brookhaven, confessed to eating 15,000 calories a day! That's

R.B. McKenzie, *HEAVY!*, DOI 10.1007/978-3-642-20135-6_2,
© Springer-Verlag Berlin Heidelberg 2012

nearly seven times the recommended maximum calories for an adult male and the equivalent of maybe a dozen of the thickest, greasiest, and sauce-dripping hamburgers that Carl's Jr.®(or any other) hamburger chain can dish out.

Unlike the image of overweight people that Hollywood movies may sometimes portray, there's nothing amusing or jolly about the patients at Brookhaven. In this film, most of them exuded some sadness, loneliness, and desperation, and all recalled profound depression. The 700-pounder lamented the missed opportunities to be with his teenage son at school functions and sporting events to offer support, if only he could have gotten out of bed and his room. Still, he continued to eat more than enough to pack on additional pounds, as he remained bedbound.

Not all the extremely obese applicants to Brookhaven are lucky enough to be accepted. The clinic staff has learned from experience that some patients will not, or just cannot, follow the clinic's required regimen of exercise and diet (sometimes no more than 1,500 calories a day). Also, too many applicants are "recidivists" or "repeat offenders," who lose hundreds of pounds while in the clinic only to return home still obese where they resume their routines of overeating and inactivity, regaining the weight lost, and then some.

One such repeat offender was a former gang member who, weighing close to 600 pounds at the time of the filming, worried whether Brookhaven would give him another chance to lose weight—and to save his life. Brookhaven's director agonized over the young man's readmission, because accepting him would mean one less bed for someone else. The man was admitted, but only after he assured everyone that this time he was serious and committed.

While in the clinic, the patients' home refrigerators and pantries are no longer accessible, which is one reason prospective patients want so desperately to be admitted. They need a physical obstacle between themselves and food as well as some protection from themselves. However, one patient made orders for Chinese takeout through his cell phone for delivery to the clinic late at night, only to gain weight while there and, finally, to be expelled for the last time. The clinic's administrator justifies such expulsions on the grounds that offending patients are "taking a spot away from someone else," which "isn't fair." Brookhaven's resources are scarce, and the clinic has far more applicants than it can accommodate.

I can't help it, but the economist comes out in me: If the clinic faces a shortage of beds, why doesn't it raise its price? You say that is unfair? Suppose at a higher price it could increase the number of patients it serves as it causes applicants to self-select. A higher price can send the message, "Only the *truly* serious applicants need apply." The clinic could waste fewer resources with those who are playing weight games. At the moment, with constrained prices the clinic is simply encouraging repeat offenders. But that's another story.

It's in My Genes

The *Brookhaven* documentary is a powerful visual statement—and reality check—about modern American society and the personal problems very heavy people confront. *Brookhaven* puts a human face on the mountains of mind-numbing statistics that swirl around discussions of the country's growing weight and weight-related medical problems.

Granted, the documentary, taken by itself, paints a greatly distorted picture of the country's (and world's) weight problems; it focuses on the massively and morbidly obese, perhaps largely for cinematic effect, rather than being an even-handed assessment of the weight gain phenomenon. Nevertheless, the film reminds us of the many personal tragedies that lie underneath some weight statistics—and of the economic ramifications—even when the statistics themselves offer, at times, a distorted picture. Despite being unemployed and unemployable, the Brookhaven patients had somehow literally eaten their way to death's doorstep. They had faced in real time all the costs of weight gain, yet they continued to eat and increase the costs they incurred. Lots of Americans are right now, as you read, eating their way to the same doorstep.

What forces were at work that prevented the patients, before entering the clinic, from making the careful cost-benefit calculations economists assume people make? Surely they had enablers (family members, friends, or government). There is no way that people can get that obese relying on their own resources, which are bound to dwindle as they become ever less mobile. And can the Brookhaven patients' problems—and those of all overweight and obese people—really be chalked up, totally or almost totally, to "genetics" or "addiction" (with addictions having likely ties to genetics), as so many observers are inclined to claim or intimate? Genes surely frame our physiological abilities and maybe psychological inclinations, and there are good evolutionary reasons for thinking that people have a propensity or predisposition, in varying degrees, to eat and overeat fattening foods (as we will see in the next chapter), as well as to gain weight from however much they eat. Clearly, as evident with the behavior of smokers, drug addicts, and alcoholics, addiction (again, in varying degrees) is a part of the human condition, if not checked by deliberate decisions to override compulsion (see Chap. 6).

But clearly not all people cede to the temptation to pack in the food and drink and pack on the pounds, at least not nearly to the extent that the Brookhaven patients have done. People vary on all bodily and physiological dimensions—hair and eye color, skin tone, height, and intelligence. There is every reason to believe that people also vary in their genetic *predisposition* or *proclivity* to eat and tendency to add pounds, given the amount eaten, either because of their genes or some derivative inclination toward addiction. Perhaps the patients at Brookhaven reflect the subsample of people who, according to research, have genetic abnormalities that leave them uncontrollably addicted to food.[1] For them, "my genes made me do it" or "I suffer from a food addiction" could be a plausible and reasonable claim that completes their stories—maybe.

Genes clearly play a role in how heavy people are. One study found that twins raised apart are closer in weight than siblings raised together.[2] Other studies have found a higher correlation in the body mass indexes (or just BMIs) of identical twins than fraternal twins,[3] and a "strong relationship" between the weight of adoptees and their biological parents.[4] Finally, other researchers are confident that genes are responsible for as much as two-thirds, if not three-quarters (depending on researchers' assessments) of the weight variation across adults.[5]

But can genetics and addiction be the whole story, even for those admitted to Brookhaven (and similar obesity clinics)? Not likely by a long shot, in all studies of twins, even "identical" twins, the correlation in the twins' weights is not perfect, which is to say there are twins with significantly different weights, partially because "identical" twins are never perfectly identical at the genetic level (they are bound to receive different numbers and forms of their parents' genes) and they always face some (at times, albeit minor) differences in their local environments. Moreover, research does show that people have some self-control over food consumption, although they obviously vary in the extent of their self-control and are more likely to choose "tasty" over "healthy" foods as their decisions become more immediate.[6] And, really, self-control can be developed through the acquisition of skills that enhance self-control; people can influence their destinies on their weights or any-thing else by working hard at developing self-control skills and then working hard on activating whatever skills they have developed.

Finally, genes can't be the whole story for people's obesity simply because virtually all serious health problems can be traced to multiple causes. And if we would combine all of the various genetic explanations for excess weight with all the various environmental explanations, the total effect of all the causes identified by various researchers could be 200 and 300 percent of the observed variation across people and groups.

Genetics alone certainly can't explain why the obesity rates vary substantially across countries and cultures and why there are so many more extremely obese people today than a century ago, or even two decades ago. The spread of extreme obesity, or just obesity, among the masses at all income levels is a distinctly modern problem. Genes change, but only very slowly over hundreds of years, if not millenniums, not over a decade or two, or even five decades. The modern rise in the count of grossly obese people has surely grown too fast to justify slow-moving genetic changes as a plausible explanation for a modern phenomenon.[7] Moreover, there is a good chance that some of the similarities in weights of twins and siblings and parents and their children attributable to genes reflect the common economic and cultural forces the subjects have faced, even when reared apart, as we shall see from other studies in this chapter.

"Food addiction" may explain weight gain for some—even many—people, but it, too, is surely only a partial explanation. After all, people do retain at least some residual control over what and how much they put in their mouths, and we don't need scientific studies to prove it. All we need to do is walk along the row of treadmills at gyms that dot the country or consider all the talk about the relative value of different diets that people adopt with more or less dedication. And through exercising that residual control, people can slow or stop their trek toward Brookhaven's doorstep. For that matter, if people didn't have some residual control over how much they weigh, Brookhaven and many other weight clinics and diet schemes would serve no purpose. For that matter, all weight research would be largely for naught, a waste of resources.

Modern genetic research has begun to support this view, that our residual control over our lives is real, although the control obviously varies across people. British geneticists studied 20,430 men and women to assess people's genetic predisposition toward weight gain, as determined by the number of combinations (or "variants") of identified genes they had inherited and that are associated with obesity.[8] The greater the number of obesity-related variants that a person has, the higher is his risk of becoming obese. The researchers also found, however, that exercise could significantly counter the subjects' predisposition toward obesity. Indeed, one hour of daily exercise can reduce people's risk of becoming obese by an amazing 60 percent, or so the study found.[9]

In reaction to the British study's findings, one obesity researcher made a point that can easily be overlooked in findings of how gene variants affect obesity risk: Our DNA doesn't determine our destiny, at least not fully, a conclusion that might seem imminently plausible from self-inspection. The geneticist added, "The message from this [study] is, if you have a genetic predisposition for some things, you can change your lifestyle and contribute to better health," which, simply put, means that, no matter the strength of our predispositions, most of us have some choice in how heavy we become. Many, many people can say what I can say: I am not as obese as close relatives have been because I chose to avoid their fate by working hard at keeping my weight down. Indeed, their weight fate has motivated me over the years. Real personal *choices* (those which are not determined by externally measurable conditions) are not something science can deal with well, if at all, given that they are subjective and emerge from people imposing their will on their life outcomes.

Instead of always leaning on the refrain, "my genes (or the Devil) made me do it," might there not be powerful unrecognized economic and social forces at work that have reinforced people's genetic tendency to eat excessively and that modify their ability to choose outcomes? Also, might not widespread acceptance of the genetic explanation for weight gain contribute marginally to more of the same, because the social costs of weight gain would then be moderated? We will return to these questions in Chap. 3.

Conspicuous Consumption

The Brookhaven's patients are, figuratively and literally, the tip of a very large weight-growth iceberg. To see in real time the dimensions of people's weight problems, or to imagine where the Brookhaven patients might have been on their paths several years before they went on-camera, take a seat near any shopping mall food court. Watch the shoppers who belly up to the fast-food counters. You don't have to be a demographer, statistician, nutritionist, or economist to get the picture. Any casual count of passersby practically anywhere in the country will surely include people with underarms flapping and butts stretching the limits of spandex.

Even around my home in unusually weight-conscious Southern California (where, because of the year-round temperate climate, excess weight can't be easily hidden under heavy clothes and coats), seriously overweight and obese people are everywhere, some who could be shadows of the Brookhaven patients. In my informal count, at least one out of every eight people who passed my bench in a local mall was clearly obese, not just substantially overweight (as I casually and subjectively define "obese" and "overweight"). The people I counted as obese had stomachs that stretched out like bloated beach balls, if they did not hang like aprons of fat to their thighs under their clothes.

In a mall in Winston-Salem, North Carolina, my percentage estimate of obese shoppers was double that observed in Southern California—and the obese shoppers in Winston-Salem were, as a group, more obese than those I counted in Southern California. If national statistics on the distribution of obese people across the states are to be believed (with, I warn, a measure of skepticism, for reasons to be given), my obesity percentages would have been even higher in malls in Dallas, St. Louis, Indianapolis, not to mention Jackson, Mississippi, the official epicenter of the country's obesity problems. I didn't try to count the merely overweight in Southern California and North Carolina; there were too many of them and much excess weight can be obscured under clothing. The count of normal weight and thin people would have been even lower than any combined count of overweight and obese people (as the data series to be reviewed show).

Amazingly enough, Americans' extreme girth and obesity clinics such as Brookhaven could not have been imagined a century ago, and surely not two centuries ago. Few people in those long bygone eras would have needed Brookhaven-type services, or could have afforded them. Indeed, if weight-related clinics had existed, the likelihood is that they would have been for the malnourished and the outright starving. Back then, the "middle class" (if not the lower portion of the "upper income" class) would have met the modern income standard for the "poverty class." Weight problems were largely the province of the top rungs of the upper-income class who sometimes flaunted their wealth through their added girths, which made excess weight a form of "conspicuous consumption," literally.[10] Lower income classes were trim, for the most part, because they could not afford the luxury of added fatty foods, and they countered any weight gain through the hard physical work required to make a living or even keep house.

A Dated Meaning for a "Human Wonder"

Today, the distribution of the country's weight problems across income classes has reversed, as excess weight problems are disproportionately concentrated among the poor. I saw that point clearly when I took a seat on a ledge outside a Goodwill store to count obese people. Granted, not all people who shop at Goodwill are poor; many are simply frugal people of all income levels who have the time to troll everywhere for good deals. Nevertheless, nearly four in ten shoppers who came out of the Goodwill store were demonstrably obese, even more obese, as a rule, than the obese shoppers in the Winston-Salem mall.

Evolutionary biologists Michael Power and Jay Schulkin suggest that obese people might not have been unknown tens of thousands of years ago (maybe even before *Homo sapiens* had totally forgone their hunter-gatherer ways and settled down to farm), as possibly evident in the four-and-a-half-inch sculpture of the very grossly obese Venus of Willendorf that has been dated to 20,000–25,000 BCE.[11] (For various pictures of the Venus of Willendorf sculpture, go to Google Images and search for her name.) With her grossly protruding stomach all around, humongous breasts falling over her stomach, and extra thick thighs, Venus of Willendorf's body shape rivals those of the Brookhaven patients. Then again, Venus might have been simply the sculptor's fantasy of an idealized female body, as thinness could not then have been uncommon, at least according to scholarly speculation.[12]

Power and Schulkin report that, because of their considerable rarity, obese people in Europe in the seventeenth and eighteenth centuries often earned their livelihoods exhibiting themselves in sideshows along with other human oddities, including the "human skeleton" man (who in one sideshow was supposedly married to the sideshow's fat woman, all for publicity).[13] At the turn of the nineteenth century, Daniel Lambert, who was five feet eleven, was widely recognized for being the "the fattest man in England," which indeed he may have been. At his death in 1809, he weighed 739 pounds (with a waist of 112 inches). But Lambert was not spurned as extremely obese people often are today. He was heralded and, supposedly, widely admired as a "human wonder" and "prodigy in nature" for his unusually massive size, and perhaps because he was able to conduct business in spite of his size. To this day, many pubs throughout England remain named in his honor, according to historians of fat.[14] (For portraits of Daniel Lambert, search Google Images.)

The Malthusian Weight Trap of Old

At the turn of the nineteenth century, those who believed the Reverend Thomas Robert Malthus' *Essay on the Principles of Population* would not have anticipated our modern-day distribution of weight problems across the income classes.[15] The reverend's population theory, grounded in the economic thinking of his day, predicted that workers would be mired in subsistence living that would check population growth (the "Malthusian Trap"). Granted, there were circumstances (war, disease, starvation) that, at times, limited population and decreased the labor supply. The drop in available labor would cause worker wages to rise and, in turn, cause a spurt in a country's population for two reasons: First, people's passion for sex was more or less immutable (except, perhaps, through delaying marriage; Malthus did not marry until 36). Second, higher wages could support larger families. However, a labor supply increase would naturally follow the population growth, and competitive market forces would drive wages back down to approximately subsistence level for the working class. The implication of the Malthusian Trap for our purposes is clear: The same economic forces that held the population numbers in check would also control workers' weights.

> "Portly" once meant stately and was taken as a compliment, a sign of social and economic standing. Now, it's an insult, even though it describes a sizable segment of the population.

True, members of the landed gentry, the nobility, and the merchant classes might lower their workers' wages to gain some economic advantage during population growth spurts, which means the higher-income classes could gain weight because of their sedentary lifestyles and the time and incomes they had to buy food produced by cheap labor. Power and Schulkin point out that "portly" today usually implies a negative characterization, as in "stout," "heavy," or "rotund," but such was not always the case. As late as the late nineteenth century, portly meant "stately" or "imposing": "A portly gentleman was a prosperous gentleman, a person who had succeeded in life. 'Portly' was a compliment when obesity was not common. It's not very likely to be taken as a compliment today."[16] No doubt more like fighting words today.

Population-growth and weight-gain records indicate that Malthus proved to be a good historian, but a poor economic forecaster (although he saw some slight hope for economic improvement over time through the development of institutions, namely property rights and free markets[17]). In the late 1600s, ordinary people enjoyed precious little economic progress and real worker wages remained more or less flat (with only rare and temporary increases in the standard of living). Indeed, until the advent of the Industrial Revolution, poverty was a wrenching, debilitating, widespread, and abiding condition on both sides of the Atlantic and practically everywhere else. Borderline starvation was, in short, the norm for the masses.[18]

But once the Industrial Revolution cranked up to full speed in the mid-nineteenth century, the world's population began to mount, totally shredding Malthus' population predictions, as well as much of the underlying economics driving his population theory (although Karl Marx and Charles Darwin looked to Malthus for inspiration for their own theories). In 1800, the world's population was under one billion, maybe only 800 million. By 1850, it had reached one billion, and by 1900, it had doubled to two billion. All told, per capita income increased close to six-fold during the nineteenth century (as best income can be measured) and increased another eight-fold during the twentieth.[19]

The U.S. population has grown more dramatically than the world's population, attributable in no small way to immigration as well as to decreased infant mortality and increased longevity overall. In 1790, the first census set the country's population at just under four million in the thirteen original states, for a population density of 4.5 persons per square mile. By 1900, the land area of the country had increased three times over, but the population had grown twenty-five times, for a total count of 76 million. In 2000, the U.S. population had nearly quadrupled to 281 million, and a decade later (mid-2010), it was estimated at 310 million (with maybe ten to twelve million more in uncounted illegal aliens) for a population density of eighty-one per square mile. An estimated one person is added to the U.S. population every eleven seconds, net of births and deaths.[20] So much for starvation, pestilence, and wars (and the twentieth century recorded some of the deadliest wars in history) serving to curb population growth.

Contrary to the pessimists of all generations of the last two centuries concerned about the impact of population growth, progress has been substantial in virtually all areas, not the least of which have been health care, transportation, communications, household amenities (plumbing), food, working conditions, consumer goods (and the list could go on at some length, all of which other authors and I have documented extensively elsewhere[21]). Perhaps the best growing evidence of the substantial, accumulative economic, social, and medical progress that humanity has realized can be found in the country's (and world's) weight gain, to the point of serious obesity issues with which this book is concerned. Put another way, had we not experienced the progress we have, this book, and all the obesity research, would not likely have been undertaken.

The Rise of "Full-Figured" Women

As people's incomes rose in the 1800s, workers in America and the industrialized world gained some weight and height, but not as much as might be imagined, considering the six-fold (or more) growth in real per capita income. Weight gain during the 1800s was checked for a very good reason: Worker productivity and incomes increased not only because of the much heralded application of technology to agriculture and manufacturing, but also because people were working longer hours and more days per year as most of the expanding factory work did not have to follow the rhythm of the weather (as did farming). No doubt, longer work days helped to keep workers' weights under some control.

In the late 1700s, before the advent of the Industrial Revolution, Gregory Clark estimates that the average unskilled worker in England probably worked no longer than did hunter-gatherers of 10,000 years before. By 1800, the workday (in London and elsewhere) had risen to ten to eleven hours a day for 300 days a year, for a total of at least 3,000 hours (at least 50 percent greater than the average number of hours an American works today). Evidence also points to work in 1800 being less diverse and more intense than that of earlier epochs. Throughout the 1800s, work in factories and on the farm remained arduous. Workers got more income to buy more food, but many (not all) of them also expended a lot of calories at work.[22]

Surprisingly, solid, carefully collected statistics on Americans' body weights go back only fifty years, no doubt partially because weight was not a prominent, widespread debilitating and life-threatening problem in bygone eras. The evidence on weight gain prior to 1960 is spotty at best, often limited to specific groups of people (school cohorts and military recruits, for example).

In the last half of the nineteenth century, Americans up and down the income ladder may have gained some weight as their incomes rose, but, again, the evidence is not hard data developed from carefully administered surveys of large segments of the American population. The best (but still not very good) evidence of people's weight gains in general comes from historical commentaries and the photographs and sketches of people in clothing advertisements. In the late 1800s, advertisements depicted women who were decidedly plumper (perhaps with dress sizes of 12 or 14) than they are in today's advertisements (often with dress sizes of 4 or lower). Consider photographs of a famous actresses from the late 1800s (any number of which can be found through Google Images) versus photographs of women in contemporary ads in women's magazines.

But of course, images in advertisements are typically the society's ideal rather than the reality. Historians and evolutionary biologists suggest that images of "full-figured" women were prevalent in advertisements a century or more ago because they reflected a different view of female beauty than that today. The extra weight, especially in the hips, may have indicated fertility and the capacity for a woman to handle the rigors of multiple childbirths at a time when birthing was life threatening for both mother and baby and when couples had "excess" children because of the likelihood that several of their babies would die before reaching adulthood, or even childhood.[23] That would also suggest that twentieth century advancements in medical (especially birthing) knowledge and technology might have contributed to the slimming of women in contemporary advertisements (if not in real life). That is, women with slimmer builds might be better able to deal with the demands of pregnancy today than in past centuries.

According to historian Peter Stearns, author of *Fat History*, people's added pounds grew in prominence in the 1890s, leading to increased public discussions of the health problems (for example, heart disease) associated with excess weight and poor diets.[24] Again, solid nationwide data are unavailable, but Stearns points to evidence among military cadets. In the 1870s, West Point Military Academy cadets who were five feet seven inches tall had an average weight of 127 pounds, less than women of equal height today. The average weight among fifteen- to twenty-year-olds attending the Citadel Military Academy was fairly constant before the 1890s (perhaps because of admissions standards), then moved down somewhat in the 1890s, only to return to its previous high level after 1900. By the 1920s, the Citadel's average weight was 10 percent above its level of 1900.[25]

Stearns concludes, mainly from insurance company records, that the average weight gain of Americans of given heights between 1920 and 1940 was about two pounds for the two decades combined. Then, Americans doubled the pace of weight gain with an increase in the average weight of Americans by two pounds a decade between 1940 and 1980. Between 1985 and 1995, Americans, on average, gained more weight than they did in the six decades between 1920 and 1980.[26]

The Growth in Turkeys

The National Center for Health Statistics (a division of the Centers for Disease Control and Prevention, or just CDC, operating under the U.S. Department of Health and Human and Services) got serious about computing a variety of weight statistics for individual states and the country as a whole in 1960, in response to two factors:

- First, there had been a modest acceleration in Americans' weight gain over recent decades.
- Second, a growing number of medical studies connected excess weight to an expanding array of health problems that had been piling up since the turn of the century.[27]

Little did the researchers at the NCHS realize back then that they would document an explosion in Americans' weights over the next five decades. For those readers who like numbers, the details of average weights of men and women twenty to seventy-four years of age, as well as their weights combined, are included in the endnotes and on a Web site for the book in a "Weight Resource Center," which includes a library of charts and tables for all budding "number-philes."

Basically, American men ages twenty to seventy-four had an average weight of just over 166 pounds in the very early 1960s, and then gained seven pounds or so over the next decade, held more or less constant in the 1970s, and then began a relentless rise through the 1980s, 1990s, and 2000s, gaining on average over twenty-eight pounds between 1960 and 2006 (the latest available year for weight data at this writing).[28] American women followed the men's weight-gain pattern very closely, but gained about four pounds less, or between twenty-four and twenty-five pounds on average.

During the forty-six year period, the average weight of American men and women increased

The human body has evolved a highly efficient system for storing energy in "adipose tissues" in the form we call fat. The storage system is so efficient that losing fat can be hard and long work. For example, if a 154-pound, thirty-year-old woman eats a standard-size blueberry muffin (which typically has only 360 calories), the woman would have to spend the following minutes at various activities to burn off the calories in the muffin:

o Lawn mowing	66
o Gardening	66
o Weight lifting	115
o Bicycling (easy pace)	77
o Jogging (5 mph)	33
o Folding Laundry	230

As reported by Cloud (2009, pp. 44–45)

just over 17 percent. In the early 1960s, men weighed an average twenty-six pounds more than women. By 2003–2006, men outweighed women by an average of thirty pounds. The average weight gain for adult Americans of both sexes during the 1960–2006 period was more than twenty-six pounds, equal to about the largest ready-to-cook Thanksgiving turkey you can buy, which they carry around with them spread in varying manners on their butts, in their jowls, and around their waistlines (although some of the weight gain was due to a minor increase in the average height of both sexes).

The BMI Calculator

American's added poundage during the past half-century can be misleading in appraising how much fatter people have become, and it is the fat, not so much the pounds, that is the central health concern. Part of the weight gain can be attributed to the fact that Americans have become on average about an inch taller since 1960.

Health and obesity experts have sought to correct for height differences among people and height changes over time with the Body Mass Index (BMI), a surprisingly old formula developed by Belgium statistician Adolphe Quetelet, who lived between 1796 and 1874. The official calculation might be daunting for non-mathematicians (which is why I have tucked the formula in an endnote[29]), but don't worry: There are many BMI calculators on the Internet into which you can plug your weight and height and compute your BMI with the click of a mouse. Consider using the BMI calculator provided by the CDC (see the link in the endnote or just Google "BMI calculator").[30] I recommend you calculate your own BMI so that you will understand points we make on the BMI's usefulness and limitations in this chapter and the rest of the book.

Almost all weight researchers in universities and health organizations use the BMI to assess the growth in people's excess weight primarily for a good old-fashioned economic reason: It is an inexpensive survey method (compared with all other direct measures of body fat) and statistic to compute. Besides, many health researchers feel confident that the BMI for large populations under study (not at the individual level) correlates tolerably well (but not perfectly, of course) with direct measures of body fat.[31] The World Health Organization has agreed on these BMI classifications, which practically everyone in the weight field employs. If your BMI is below 18.5, you are underweight. If your BMI is between 18.5 and 24.9, you have normal weight; between 25 and 29.9, you are overweight. If your BMI is 30 or above, you are obese; 40 and above, morbidly obese.[32] Some obesity researchers and practitioners add a higher category, "super obese," for those with a BMI of 50 and above (in which practically all Brookhaven patients would fit). (See the nearby box for additional combinations of height and weight that can make you "overweight" and "obese.")

To illustrate how the BMI calculator and classification system works, at five feet nine (the average height of an American male in the early 2000s) and 160 pounds, a person's BMI would be 22.9, or the "normal" (or healthy) "weight" classification. At 169 pounds, the person's BMI would be 25, classified as minimally "overweight." At 203 pounds and a BMI of 30, the same person would be minimally "obese." At 271 pounds, the person would have a BMI of 40 and would be "morbidly obese," suggesting his or her weight could lead to a variety of diseases and could be life threatening. One of the Brookhaven patients, who weighed 730 pounds and stood five feet eleven inches, would have a BMI of 101.8! And, no doubt, he was a high-probability walking heart attack in slow motion.

Judging whether you are "overweight" (BMI > 24.9) or "obese" (BMI > 29.9):

If your height is …	You are "overweight" if you weigh more than … (pounds)	You are "obese" if you weigh more than … (pounds)
5'2"	136	163
5'6"	154	185
5'10"	174	208
6'2"	194	233
6'6"	215	259

As determined by the CDC's BMI calculator.

The Obesity "Epidemic"

BMI data prior to 1960 are necessarily limited. Nevertheless, the available data series, as rough as it is, charts a growth in American weight that tends to validate the proposition that as a population, we have gotten fatter, and so much so to warrant many health-care experts to talk about an "obesity epidemic."

American Weight Before the Twentieth Century

Health economist Lorens Helmchen has found a means of measuring some Americans' average BMIs before 1900.[33] He drew a random sample of 15,000 or so former white Union soldiers who served during the Civil War (1961–1965) from government records. As it happened, to obtain veterans benefits, the former Civil War soldiers were weighed and their heights were measured during their examinations. They also gave other personal data, such as place of birth, birth date, age, disabilities, occupations, etc. on their applications. In other words, the examinations gave Helmchen the data he needed to determine the BMIs of former soldiers at different ages during the late 1800s. He found that the percentage of former soldiers who would have been classified as obese (BMI of 30 or above) for the period 1890–1894 ranged from a meager 3.7 percent for soldiers age forty to forty-nine to 2.9 percent for those age sixty to sixty-nine.[34]

Obese former Civil War veterans by age group averaged 3 percent. That's a small percentage, and is remarkably small, when compared with the average percentage for the same age groups of American white men with BMIs 30 and over in a 1988–1994 national survey (the last years of data available when Helmchen completed his study). The average percentage of white males with BMIs 30 and over was 23.2— *nearly 8 times the average in 1880–1890*. Helmchen also found steady growth in the obesity rate from under 2 percent in 1880–1884 to slightly over 5 percent in 1905–1909. Moreover, he found that the soldiers between fifty and fifty-nine had an average obesity rate in 1905–1909 that was three times the age group's average obesity rate twenty-five years earlier, which means that they had an average annual rate of increase in their obesity rate of 4.5 percent during those 25 years.

The average obesity rate for white men between 1976–1980 and 1988–1994 was several-fold higher than for the former Civil War soldiers. However, the annual rate of increase in the obesity rate between 1976–1980 and 1988–1994 rose at an annual rate of only 4 percent, a growth rate 12 percent lower than for the former Civil War soldiers.[35] This finding led Helmchen to conclude, "[I]n *relative* terms, then, obesity was spreading at least as fast at the beginning of the twentieth century as at the end of the twentieth century."[36] The finding also suggests that economic and other forces behind the modern so-called obesity "epidemic" were set in motion long ago. Those forces may have grown stronger in our recent past, but they have their origins in something other than "modern times" and "fast food," two often-cited culprits of the modern obesity epidemic.

Indeed, in a follow-up study, covering the growth of obesity from the late-1800s to the late-1990s, Helmchen and Max Henderson confirmed Helmchen's earlier finding that the annual rate of increase in the obesity rate (as assessed by the BMI) among men sped up in the late 1800s and early-1900s, only to drop by half from the early-1900s through the mid-1970s. Then, from the mid-1970s, the annual rate of increase in the obesity rate rebounded to its growth rate of the late-1800s. In the 1990s, the annual rate of growth of the obesity rate accelerated, nearly doubling.[37]

American Weight Gain Since 1960

The roots of Americans' weight problems are deep, and the problem accelerated twenty to thirty years ago, evidence indicates. In fact, the country entered the 1960s with a weight problem that has only worsened, according to casual observation and basic obesity data, in percentages of the population, gathered at intervals by the CDC (see the endnote for the data details[38]). In 1960, 45 percent of the population was overweight, a proportion that increased to two-thirds by the time the last survey was undertaken in 2003–2006, and the proportion of the population who were obese increased from 13 percent to one third. More men than women were overweight in all survey periods. However, women have had higher obesity rates than men, although men have been catching up with women over the decades. At the start of the 1960s, the obesity rate for women was 16 percent, substantially higher than that of men at 11 percent. But by the last survey undertaken in the early 2000s, men's obesity rate was 33 percent and women's 35 percent.

Between the surveys in 1960–1962 and 2003–2006, the percentage of over-weight Americans rose nearly 50 percent, and the percentage of obese Americans grew far more rapidly, by two and a half times. Most of this astonishing increase occurred after 1980. The growth rate in overweight Americans decelerated in the late 1990s and 2000s.[39] However, the increase in the obesity rates was slight in surveys done between 2003–2004 and 2005–2006.[40] The annual growth rate was much higher for the obese category than the overweight category, but both categories followed the same pattern.[41] That is, during the 1960–2006 period, the whole of the distribution of overweight and obese Americans along the BMI spectrum shifted substantially rightward, meaning Americans became heavier with the heavier categories growing relatively.[42]

Packing on the Pounds

Casual observation and the available data are stark and undisputed: Americans, taken as a whole, have been packing on the pounds. Also, the weight gains cut across ethnic groups and income classes. Most notably, African–American women had in the 2003–2006 survey an astounding obesity rate of more than 54 percent, more than the obesity rate of African American men (36 percent), Mexican females (43 percent), and white females (33 percent). Maybe more bothersome is that only 18 percent of African–American females in the 2003–2006 survey had healthy weights, half the percentage in the 1976–1980 survey.

Among the twenty-one states reporting obesity rates in 1985, thirteen states had rates of less than 10 percent. The remaining reporting states had obesity rates between 10 and 20 percent. (Twenty-nine states did not participate in the survey in 1985.) None of the reporting states had an obesity rate of more than 20 percent in 1985.

By 1995, all states reported obesity rates of between 10 and 20 percent, but the spread of obesity continued apace. By 2009, only one state had an obesity rate of less than 20 percent (Colorado). Fifteen states had obesity rates between 20 and 24.9 percent, twenty-five had rates between 25 and 29.9 percent, while nine had rates greater than 30 percent (Alabama, Arkansas, Kentucky, Louisiana, Mississippi, Missouri, Oklahoma, Tennessee, and West Virginia). The CDC uses a map of the United States (available at the CDC Web site in the form of a slide show) to show in vivid color the spread of obesity through the states from 1990 (when most of the country is some shade of blue, meaning less than 15 percent of the state population is obese) until 2008 (when most of the country is some shade of red, meaning 25 percent or more of the state population is obese).[43]

In 2009, most of the states with high obesity rates were in the Midwest and South, and states with the lowest rates were in the West. Mississippi was the fattest state in the country with an obesity rate of close to 35 percent; the thinnest state was

Colorado with 19 percent of its population obese. Then, in the most recent survey, nine states had obesity rates of more than 30 percent. Clearly, the South and Midwest are leading the nation in the growth in obesity, but the increase seems to be spreading in all directions.[44]

Children and teenagers have also packed on the pounds over the decades, although the obesity rates for children and teenagers are lower than for adults, understandably (since weight gain is age-path dependent, or weight grows with age).[45] Obesity also has spread considerably among children, although children and teens surveyed had lower obesity rates than adults.[46] In recent years the increase in obesity among children and teens has increased two to three-fold, a somewhat faster pace than for adults.[47] The growth in childhood obesity is troublesome for two major reasons.

Fat women tend to beget fat newborns who tend to become fat children, teenagers, and adults. Fat people tend to add to their excess weights when they flock with fat friends. Weight appears to be "socially contagious," and because of that attribute has been construed as a "disease" in search of a policy remedy.

First, obese children tend to turn into even more obese adults. According to one study of nearly 9,000 participants who were twelve to twenty-one years old at the start of the weight study and who were followed for thirteen years, those who were obese in their youth at the start of the study were seven times more likely to be "severely obese" (or have a BMI of 40 or above, which means they were carrying 8 to 100 pounds of excess weight) in their late twenties and early thirties than were their normal-weight and over-weight counterparts in the study. Fifty-one percent of obese young females and 37 percent of obese young males were severely obese thirteen years later.[48]

Second, obese children have a higher probability of encountering in childhood and adulthood major health problems, not the least of which is high risk factors (cholesterol levels, high blood pressure, and abnormal glucose tolerance) for cardiovascular disease. In a survey of children and teenagers five to seventeen years old, 70 percent had at least one of the risk factors and 39 percent had two. The children and teens also had an elevated risk of developing asthma, fatty degeneration of the liver, sleep apnea, type 2 diabetes, and kidney failure.[49]

Among adolescents, some differences can be seen across various ethnic groups. Obesity rates for whites, blacks, and Mexican–Americans have grown significantly during the past two decades, but more so for girls than boys, and more for black and Mexican–American girls than white girls. Fewer than 15 percent of white girls were obese in 2003–2006, while the obesity rates for black and Mexican–American girls were 20 percent and 28 percent, respectively.[50]

For readers who relish fat statistics, an array of additional facts on fat, or "fatoids," is included in the "Perspective" section at the end of this chapter.

Health Economics of Fat

Anyone who has "people watched" in the malls and on the main streets of the country's cities and towns—as I have done—has to conclude that many Americans are literally eating themselves to death on the installment plan, one oversized meal after another, and with little offsetting movement. Even casual observation reveals the serious side effects of excess weight. Many overweight people have obvious difficulty walking and tire readily, which limits their daily exercise and compounds the negative health effects of overeating. Numerous research studies support the casual evidence, with a variety of researchers making the following claims about weight gains and its effects:

- Excess weight and obesity has been associated with (if not causally linked to) as many as thirty-five diseases, including hypertension; heart disease; cancers of the breast, colon, and prostate; type-2 diabetes; osteoarthritis; gallbladder disease and incontinence, according to the National Heart, Lung, and Blood Institute.[51]
- People with BMIs of 25 or higher experience an increased incidence of heart disease, including heart attacks, congestive heart failure, and angina.[52]
- Obese people are twice as likely as healthy-weight people to have high blood pressure.[53]
- The gain of eleven to eighteen pounds can double a person's chance of developing type-2 diabetes, with four-fifths of type-2 diabetics being overweight.[54]
- A gain of two pounds above the normal weight increases the chance of a person developing arthritis by 7–13 percent.[55]
- Obesity is associated with a higher incidence of asthma and sleep apnea.[56]
- Obese people's heart problems can be caused not just by the fat they carry but also more directly by their high sugar diets, which gives rise to added fat. Researchers at Emory University found in a study of more than 6,000 American adults published in 2010 that those subjects who got a quarter of their daily calories from sugar added to their meals and drinks were more than three times more likely to have low levels of "good cholesterol" in their blood tests than those subjects who got less than 5 percent of their calories by added sugars. At the time of the study, the researchers found that adults studied got about 16 percent of their daily calories through added sugars, up from 11 percent in the late 1970s. In effect, excess sugar is debilitating to the heart independent of the fat that so much sugar becomes.[57]
- Obesity also can lead to complications from surgery and can increase birth defects, as well as the threat of death to pregnant mothers and their babies. In addition, high blood pressure among obese mothers contributes to mothers' pregnancy problems and leads to an elevated rate of Cesarean deliveries.[58]
- Not surprisingly, obese people have a greater incidence of low self-esteem and clinical depression.[59] This is understandable because, according to research, overweight and obese children face "negative attitudes" from their schoolmates and playmates (who view obese cohorts as "mean," "stupid," and "lazy") and

have fewer friends. Obese adults face more difficulty in getting jobs, possibly because of the health insurance costs obese people impose on employers, but also possibly because of the low self-perceptions that obese people developed from childhood.[60]

- In a study of more than 61,000 men and women ages fifty to seventy-one, researchers found that those subjects who were overweight (had BMIs between 25 and 29.9) had a 20–40 percent greater chance of dying within the follow-up decade than normal weight subjects. Those who were obese (had BMIs higher than 30) were three times more likely to die within the decade than all subjects who had BMIs lower than 30.[61]

- A study from the late 1990s found that, overall, obese people have a 10–50 percent greater chance of dying during any given age category from all causes than healthy-weight people, according to research.[62] Indeed, excess weight and obesity together account for more than 400,000 American deaths each year, second only to smoking. Obesity alone has been linked to 112,000 American deaths a year.[63] Moreover, overweight and obese people can reduce their chances of death from heart disease and diabetes by reducing their weight by a few percentage points.[64]

- A large team of medical researchers reported in late 2010 in the *New England Journal of Medicine* on the findings of a study in which 570,000 white men and women, ages nineteen to eighty-four who had never smoked, were followed for an average of ten years. They found that for every five BMI points, the subjects' chance of dying increased an average of 31 percent. More to the point,

  - Women who had BMIs in the overweight range, 25–29.9, had a 13 percent greater risk of dying than women in the normal-weight range, 18.5–24.9.
  - Women with BMIs between 30 and 34.9 had a 44 percent greater risk of dying.
  - Women with BMIs between 35 and 39.9 had an 88 percent greater chance of dying.
  - Women with BMIs above 40 were two-and-a-half times more likely to die than women in the normal-weight range.
  - Men's risks of dying rose in parallel with those of women as their BMIs increased.[65]

- The total medical costs of treating diseases related to obesity (not overweight) and other afflictions, as estimated by one set of researchers, in 2008 was $149 billion (in 2010 dollars), under 10 percent of all medical spending. That year the real (inflation-adjusted) health-care expenditures for obesity, half of which was covered by Medicaid and Medicare, were 50 percent greater than the real health-care expenditures for the obese in 1998. However, when another set of researchers more carefully evaluated the health-care costs directly affected by obesity, they came up with a significantly higher total annual cost figure, computed for 2005 at $188 billion (in 2010 dollars), which was nearly 17 percent of all health-care expenditures in the country in 2005.[66]

- The growth in health-care expenditures between 1998 and 2008 on obesity-related health problems was attributable more to a growth in health-care expenditures per obese person rather than to the growth in the number of obese people. The count of obese Americans rose 37 percent between 1998 and 2006. On average, in 2006, obese people spent 42 percent more on health care a year than normal-weight people (up from 37 percent more in 1998).[67]

What is maddening about covering the scholarly literature and public commentaries on excess weight and obesity is that the evidence on the effects of excess weight is sometimes conflicting, or appears to be so. The dominant themes in the weight literature are almost all negative: Extra pounds of fat are bad for you. They add to people's health problems and shorten their lives. But another line of recent research suggests that while a lot of extra weight is harmful, people with a few— maybe 8 or 15—extra pounds might not be at any greater risk of dying than normal-weight people, and the few extra pounds could have beneficial effects for some, if not most, people.

- Researchers at the CDC found in a survey of 5,000 people that overweight subject had lower rates of death than expected, or did not have "excess mortality," while obese and underweight subjects did.[68]
- In a survey of 9,000 people, Australian researchers drew much the same conclusion, that those subjects who were overweight were less likely to die in their seventies than normal-weight people.[69]
- Another study found a U-shaped curve in medical-care costs across the full BMI range, with underweight adults having medical-care costs as high as severely obese people. That is, medical-care costs fall precipitously for adults as their BMIs approach 20, then level out until a BMI of about 37, after which medical-care costs rise dramatically.[70]
- Medical researchers readily admit to an "obesity paradox" that is hard for them to explain: Obese people tend to die more than normal-weight and overweight people from heart failure. But among patients who have experienced heart failure, those who are obese are more likely to survive their heart failures, with the mortality rate for heart patients falling by 10 percent for every five-point increase in their BMIs. Go figure. The explanation could be that obese patients' extra fat gives them an energy reserve that the body can draw down when the heart has been weakened and/or because the BMI is a poor measure of body fat (with many people who are normal having more body fat than overweight and even obese people)—or some other yet-to-be determined reason.[71]
- And a few extra pounds can, apparently, increase bone density and make people look younger (which can have beneficial labor-market effects that enhance income, as we will see in Chap. 7).[72]

What's going on here? Well, it could simply be that studies involving different groups of people in different time periods and circumstances yield different results. The science of obesity is not exact, to say the least. Another possibility is that the differences in study conclusions is a consequence of an important fact not widely

The Body Mass Index (BMI) may be one of the worst statistics ever conceived, but it is widely used in weight research for a good, old-fashioned economic reason: It is readily available at little cost and everyone uses it, which gives the index research legitimacy. Weight research should be considered with a healthy dose of skepticism. Some of it is misleading and can be designed to further policy agendas.

appreciated: the health effects of fat depend on whether the fat is "subcutaneous," which is fat stored on the buttocks and under the upper arms, or "visceral," which is fat stored around and attached to vital internal organs, which causes "beer bellies." Visceral fat is believed to be the serious killer, for obvious reason: It can impede the functioning of vital bodily processes, heartbeats, for example.[73] Still, might the conundrum be a product of the fact that "fat" can have bad health effects, while being "overweight" can be good for people, because striving to achieve some ideal weight can impose a lot of stress that can be as much or more damaging to health than the fat itself? We will revisit this conundrum and line of argument in the next several chapters when we get serious about the *economics* of weight problems.

Concluding Comments

The late Pat Paulson, a comedian who pretended in the late 1960s to be running for president on the highly rated but somewhat controversial television variety show "The Smothers Brothers Comedy Hour" would hold a mock news conference each week. On one memorable show, a "reporter" asked the comedian to comment on one of the livelier political issues of the day: "Mr. Paulson, so what do you think about the 'population bomb'?"

After pausing, Paulson answered with his customary deadpan drawl: "Look everyone here has two parents, right? Those parents have four parents, with all those parents having eight parents. Backward through time, the parents escalate ... 16, 32, 64, 128, 256, 512, 1,024 and so forth. The best I can figure is that the population has been in rapid decline for some time! I don't see a problem."

Paulson's wry sense of humor, built around twisted thinking, is ageless. His comedic analysis is obviously wrongheaded because it denies the Darwinian theme of all species, not just *Homo sapiens*, having a common ancestry. Moreover, the growth in the *volume* of the parents in Paulson's humorous retrogression is not nearly as great as Paulson's *count* of parents.

Over the eons, people have grown (with ups and downs) in height from three feet when the first hominids walked upright to an average height today for American males of about five feet nine inches and for American females of about five feet four inches. People have also gained weight, partially because of the growth in height and partially because of increasing longevity. Long ago, people didn't live long enough to retire, become sedentary, and gain weight. But, people's increase in weight obviously has other causes.

Still, since Malthus' era, the world's population measured by mass has grown faster than the count of people. Malthus could not have dreamed that in barely 200 years hordes of people—especially those with higher incomes—would be obsessed with losing weight while enjoying little success at doing so, in contrast to his dismal prediction that common folk would continue to live at subsistent standards. How could Malthus have imagined that people around the world would be captivated with the reality television show, "The Biggest Loser" on which the contestants start the show as big as ... well, cows, and the winner takes home a trophy and prize money for losing literally hundreds of pounds—and still leaves the show often times overweight, if not obese? How wrong could a preacher-economist be? In predictive accuracy, he was bad even by the dismal standards of today's economic forecasters.

Readers are wise to be cautious in accepting experts' predictions on the country's weight problems. Malthus, after all, was as wrong as can be. The late population doomsayer Paul Ehrlich was worse in that he dared to predict in the late 1960s in his best seller, *Population Bomb,* that the world would be experiencing mass starvation by the 1980s (a thesis that economist Julian Simon rightly challenged later in the 1960s).[74] True, there are starving people in the world, but starvation is hardly as widespread as Ehrlich dared to predict would be the case (and today's starving populations are usually victims of natural disasters and genocidal campaigns by warring tribes and governments). Most modern experts working more than a half century ago didn't predict the upsurge in obesity in the 1980s and 1990s, or the deceleration in the obesity growth rate in the 2000s (possibly abetted by the advent of the Great Recession). Predicting the future of complex social processes, with weight gain being one, is hazardous.

Exercise caution as well in interpreting "fat" statistics that pervade the media almost daily, some of which are included in this chapter. Be mindful that while the sizable food industry has a host of private incentives to encourage people to eat, and overeat time and again, there is now a sizable antifat industry—including firms and people who conduct weight research, advocate one diet plan or another, or seek government research grants and programs to promote controlled eating and "wellness"—that also has strong incentives to magnify the country's weight problems. The bigger the weight problem as perceived by the public and controlling public officials, both now and in the near-term future, the more opportunities there are for any number of groups to make money through added research grants, diet plans, and surgeries. And do take notice of how so many nutrition and obesity researchers do what they consider to be science, only to use their findings to promote (even in elite scientific journals) one antifat agenda of reforms or another, most notably various "fat taxes" and restrictions on what, when, and where people—not just children, but also consenting adults—can eat. Remember that the fat statistics recited here and so many other places represent very limited information on the particular circumstances under which hundreds of millions of people live, and they say nothing of the life interests of all of those people, which can so often stand in stark contrast with the interests of health experts who make their policy pronouncements.

As I have read a large number of recent reports on the growth in the weight problem, I have been struck by what appears to be disappointment among some weight experts that the trend may have flattened out or, at least, taken a lower growth rate, dashing hopes of keeping the drumbeat of a "coming health-care crisis from obesity" rolling along. When new data was released showing that the rate of childhood obesity in the country might have leveled off after 2004, one obesity researcher reacted, "What I worry about is that people will read these numbers and think we've got the problem solved." He went on to insist that this is "no time for complacency."[75]

Maybe not, but such new findings might suggest caution in adopting an array of radical reform agendas that are grounded in an ever increasing fattening of the country. Moreover, ordinary people can be forgiven for thinking that the media's tendency to pay more attention to "bad" news than "good" news can distort perceptions of the problem.[76] Readers also need to consider the official statistics on people's weights with some caution. Many overweight and obesity data series involve self-reported weights, which can be distorted as people guess their weights or deliberately misreport them.

Studies based on the Body Mass Index should be viewed with at least a healthy dose of skepticism. The index is determined with precision, a mathematical formula no less. Anyone with a BMI equal to or greater than 25 is "overweight," anyone with a BMI of 30 or above is "obese," and anyone with a BMI of 40 or above is "morbidly obese." But why were the BMI cutoffs for overweight and obese set at what they are? Amazingly, many researchers who use the BMI data do so without reporting answers to that simple question, as if the cutoff points are inconsequential, yet they could be very consequential. The cutoff points for the various weight categories are not points at which people's medical, social, and economic problems from their weight suddenly jump upward. Also, the mathematical precision of the BMI belies its accuracy. Here are the problems with the BMI:

- First and foremost, again, like the average weight data, BMI statistics are sometimes based on *self-reported* weights and heights that can be distorted for reasons already noted, not the least of which is that people don't accurately assess their weight and height and then are prone to distort the truth, especially when it comes to their own weight. Evidence indicates that as people get heavier, they tend to underreport the amount they eat and their weight.[77] Moreover, short people inflate their heights, reducing their calculated BMIs. Researchers have found that thin people report only 80 percent of what they eat, but obese people are much worse, reporting only half of what they eat.[78] Data, in other words, do not always emerge from researchers' actually weighing the people in their samples (and "sample populations" need not always be representative of all people in the country).
- Second, the BMI does not measure fat, at least not directly. Muscular, lean people can have BMIs that put them into the "overweight," if not "obese,"

category. My son is a serious weight lifter who can bench press 410 pounds. At five feet seven inches and weighing 192, he has a measured body fat that is trivial (hardly life-threatening). Nevertheless, his BMI is 30.1, which would classify him as "obese," because he is 0.2 point above 29.9. That makes for statistical nonsense. By the same token, I have a good friend who is five feet nine and weighs 156 pounds, giving him a BMI of 23, well within the "normal" weight range. However, in a recent physical, he was told by his examining doctor that he was "obese" based on the "pinch" method of measuring body fat.

- Third, as adults age, they tend to lose muscle and gain fat, about 10 percent a decade after age forty-five, even when they remain the same weight and hold to the same BMI.[79] Does that mean that their healthiness goes down because of the greater proportion of body fat or does their healthiness remain the same when their BMI remains constant?

- Fourth, as people age, they also become shorter (up to an inch), as the cartilage between their vertebrae becomes compacted (not to mention the shortening effects of osteoporosis), which means that if done accurately, people's BMI can rise with their age even when they really have not gained weight or even become fatter (as their average life expectancy has risen over time).

- Fifth, women tend to carry and need more fat than men, especially when breast-feeding. Men and women of the same height and weight will have the same BMIs, even though the women carry more fat, and may need to do so. It is not at all clear that men and women with the same BMIs are equally "healthy" or can anticipate the same longevity, after adjusting for other lifestyle and health issues.

- Sixth, the BMI cutoffs for the "overweight" and "obese" categories were originally set with an eye toward people's achieving "healthy" weights, as BMIs lower than 25 lead to longer life expectancies (or so many people decades ago thought). However, as noted earlier, several studies show that people with BMIs that put them in the overweight category actually are healthier and live longer lives than people with BMIs that put them in the normal weight category.[80]

- Seventh, the accumulation of fat affects various ethnic groups differently. Most notably, Asians tend to have more body fat for any given BMI and greater health problems from accumulated fat than whites, blacks, and Hispanics, which suggests that lower BMI cutoffs for "overweight" and "obese" should be used to classify Asians' weight categories.[81]

No wonder the BMI is not a good predictor of death rates across individuals. BMI is a very rough measure of excess weight and obesity at best, and may give no better indication of the exact extent of the country's overweight and obesity problems than can be obtained from casual observations of people at shopping malls and on downtown streets. But yet, an army of researchers use the BMI statistic in their studies for a simple reason: It is conveniently available at little cost (in Internet-based databases that include literally thousands of subjects and millions of data points that can be downloaded with a few clicks of a mouse) for inclusion in sophisticated statistical analyses (regression equations) that can be repeated with various combinations of variables at lightning speed and sometimes with little thought (other than to get the data to "confess," or confirm hypotheses that can be based on nothing more than conjectures with little theoretical grounding). Besides, everyone else is using it (while figuratively holding their noses over its imperfections and not talking about the imperfections).

Consider the prospect that "weight" just might not be the killer in so many ways that it has been made out to be, simply because many overweight and obese people might have developed diabetes and heart problems had they remained trim all their lives. The count of deaths from weight might be as high as it is because at death a person's weight might be said to be the cause of the heart attack (or whatever), not that it actually *caused* the death in any direct way. Some of what is reported as scientific *causation* may be nothing more than *association* (or *correlation*), which is what makes up so much "junk science." Eric Oliver, a University of Chicago political scientist and severe critic of the practice of obesity science, points out that CDC researchers have not obtained their count of over 400,000 deaths attributed to weight by checking to see if weight was *the* direct causative factor in that many deaths: "Rather, they estimated a figure by comparing the death rates of thin and heavy people using data that were nearly thirty years old."[82] When another team of CDC researchers reexamined the real causes of the people's deaths, they found that weight was a causative factor in only 26,000, 24 percent lower than the counts of deaths attributable to being underweight, as reported by Oliver.[83]

We all need to take to heart Oliver's skepticism over the claimed ties between people's weight and various identified diseases that cause deaths. The point of these words of caution is not that people should gain weight with medical impunity. I've got to believe that beyond some point, weight gain is bound to affect health (perhaps beyond a BMI of 40), which is altogether intuitively plausible (and a point that Oliver acknowledges[84]). We just need to retain some skepticism about the health consequences of weight when people press negative health claims for weight gain at the same time they are pressing a public policy agenda.

Finally, despite all the fuss over excessive weight, people are, on balance, healthier today than forty or fifty years ago. The life expectancy of children born in 2010 is projected to be more than seventy-eight years compared with that of less than sixty-six in 1944 and less than seventy in 1960. The life expectancy today for men and women who have reached the age of sixty-five is 50 percent higher than a century ago (five additional years for men and seven additional years for women).[85]

The increased life expectancy can be attributed in part to reductions in the prevalence of high blood pressure, high cholesterol, and smoking, as well as to lower death rates from cancer and heart disease with the greatest improvements in heavier people—thanks, of course, to advances in modern medicine.[86] And do remember that credible research shows that people who are classified as overweight live longer than people of normal weight,[87] a finding that led one prominent CDC researcher to muse in a *New York Times* interview, "Yes, obesity is to blame for all the evils of modern life, except somehow, weirdly, it is not killing people enough. In fact that's why there are all these fat people around. They just won't die."[88]

Indeed, advances in modern medicine probably have spurred some of Americans' weight gain. The added years of life from, say, blood pressure medications and anticholesterol drugs could have caused people to think, "I know added pounds can elevate my cholesterol score, but I can use Lipitor to offset the added weight. Those pounds might also elevate my blood pressure, but I can curb both my elevated blood pressure and cholesterol with one drug, Caduet." Modern drugs and other therapies, then, might harbor the *potential* for extending life an average of, say, four years but might actually extend life an average of only three years because people essentially use those added years to "buy" more enjoyment from increasing their eating and drinking—and expanding their girths in the process. In fact, research has uncovered exactly this kind of outcome.[89]

None of these cautions overturns a central, undeniable point: Americans as a group have gotten fatter over the last century, especially in the late-twentieth century, with all kinds of economic and social causes and effects. The fattening of America needs explaining. A good place to start is with human beings' evolutionary grounded predisposition to pack on the pounds. That predisposition, coupled with market forces that have raised Americans' real incomes and lowered the relative prices and availability of foods (especially those that we are evolutionarily bound to crave), can be, to a significant extent, potential culprits that explain the fattening of the country.

Perspective

Ever-Growing Fat Facts, or "Fatoids"

The growth in the literature on the country's (and world's) growing weight problems during the past several decades has clearly exceeded the growth in the weight problems themselves. Scholarly and policy studies on the topic are now countless, so large they all couldn't possibly be covered in a single volume like this one without boring readers to death (and many of the journal articles and policy reports are deadly dull). However, for those readers who love data-based observations, a few "fat factoids," or maybe better, "fatoids," can add perspective on the problem (with many of the numbing numbers relegated to endnotes, for readers who insist on knowing the statistical support for generalizations). If your brain has begun to go numb from number-based observations, you can skip this section. For those who are "numberholic" read on through an ever-growing list of findings that help complete the picture of the country's obesity.

- More than a third of American adults, or 71 million, were classified as obese (with a BMI of 30 or above) in 2003–2006. Americans between ages forty and fifty-nine had the highest obesity rate, with Americans sixty and older having the second highest rate and Americans ages twenty to thirty-nine, the lowest.[90]
- Fewer than one in twenty obese people can attribute their weight problems to hormonal, physiological, or genetic *abnormalities*, which is to say that the vast majority of obese people gained their weight from eating too much, attributable to a genetic predisposition of all people to eat as much as their external constraints (income and food prices, for example) permit.[91]

- But then, the physiological effects can affect people's weight in unexpected ways. For instance, stress from personal and work problems can cause the release of the hormones cortisol and adrenaline, which increase the desire for foods that are high in sugar and fat, with the weight gain from stress giving rise to more stress and more hunger-inducing hormones.[92]
- And "nature" does appear to have an impact on people's proclivity to gain weight (which is hardly a surprise). Danish researchers have studied the weights of adoptees, the adoptees' biological parents, and their adoptive parents. The researchers found no correlation between the BMIs of the adoptees and their adoptive parents, but a high and highly significant correlation between the BMIs of the adoptees and their biological parents.[93]
- Paradoxically, many obese people suffer from malnourishment because so many modern calorie-rich foods (sodas and French fries, for example) that contribute to obesity are low in other essential nutrients (for example, calcium and iron).[94]
- Perception of being overweight varies by gender, income, and education:
    - Women are more likely to see themselves as being overweight than men. Whites are more likely to perceive themselves as overweight than blacks, who are more likely to see themselves as overweight than Hispanics.[95]
    - People in higher-income households are more likely to perceive themselves as overweight than people in lower-income households.[96]
    - People with high-school diplomas or more education are more likely to see themselves as being overweight than people who did not complete high school.[97]
    - Parents often delude themselves into thinking their children are less over-weight than their children are, with parents' delusions a possible source of children's weight problems. Compared with parents of young children, parents with teenagers had more accurate assessments of their teenagers' weight problems, but many still underrated their children's weight problems.[98]

- American obesity statistics that have been cited could, in one regard, understate the obesity problem for any number of people because they are founded on Americans' BMIs, not their fat to muscle ratios. Thirty million Americans who have "normal" BMIs (between 18.5 and 25), and "normal" weights could be, medically speaking, obese, given that their body fat to total weight ratios make them unhealthy. They are subject to many of the medical problems that officially obese people suffer, according to a study from the Mayo Clinic, which followed more than 6,000 Americans for nine years.[99]
- Even though black women are more prone to excessive weight and obesity than white women, black women are less concerned about their weight.[100] And overweight and obese black women are more likely to see themselves as being of normal weight than white women in the same weight categories. The difference in weight assessment can help explain why a higher proportion of black women with excessive weights are more likely to see themselves as attractive than white women in the same weight groups. This could be the case perhaps

because black women report feeling less social pressure to lose weight. By the same token, normal-weight black women are less likely to perceive themselves as being overweight than white women. The differences in self-perceptions between black and white women can, of course, partially explain black women's larger sizes.[101]

- Higher-income black women reported self-perceptions of their own weight which were on par with the reported self-perceptions of white women in the same income category, although the black women were still heavier than the white women covered in the study.[102]

- Men are less likely than women to be concerned or dissatisfied with their weights and, accordingly, to feel a need to lose weight.[103] And black men report being less concerned about their weight than white men.[104]

- In the nineteenth century and into the twentieth century, malnourishment was a far greater nutritional issue than excess weight and obesity around the world. Now, the number of overweight and obese people worldwide may be double the number of malnourished people.[105]

- Americans are, on average, significantly heavier than people in many other countries.[106] However, according to the European Associations for the Study of Obesity, a higher percentage of men in Cyprus, the Czech Republic, Finland, Germany, Greece, Malta, and Slovakia are overweight or obese than in the United States.[107]

- Spain, Portugal, and Italy, as well as the Mediterranean islands of Malta, Sicily, Gibraltar, and Crete report obesity rates of greater than 30 percent among children ages seven to eleven. For this age group, England, Ireland, Cyprus, Sweden, and Greece have obesity rates greater than 20 percent, while France, Switzerland, Poland, the Czech Republic, Hungary, Germany, Denmark, Netherlands, and Bulgaria have obesity rates of 10–20 percent. In Europe, the obesity rate among children is accelerating.[108]

- The obesity rate among children ages five to eleven is higher in the United States than in Europe, but countries in Europe, most notably the United Kingdom and Poland, are rapidly catching up.[109]

- Obesity appears to be "socially contagious"; the chances of people becoming obese increase with their having obese friends, family, and even neighbors. Thinness is also socially contagious.[110]

- Sex matters in calories consumed. When college women were observed eating with men at the table in campus cafeterias, the women ate fewer calories than when only women were at the table.[111]

- The heaviness of Americans relative to other parts of the world can possibly be explained by the fact that the average American eats close to a third more prepackaged foods (which tend to be higher in fats, sugars, and salts than home-prepared meals) than people in almost all other countries around the world.[112]

- The problem of losing weight by exercise is not that calories aren't expended in exercise. They are, but with a lot of work, time, and sweat. More importantly, according to academic research, the problem is that people who exercise tend to offset the calorie expenditure from exercise by eating more than they otherwise would and by being more sedate than otherwise when they are not exercising. Unfortunately, exercise can lead to hunger with the stomach literally taking chemical control of the brain, with the chemical pressure to eat growing with exercise.[113]

- In 2010, only 26 percent of American adults ate three or more servings of vegetables a day, about the same as in 2000, according to the CDC.[114]
- Louisiana State University nutritionist Timothy Church and his research team followed 464 overweight women for six months, dividing them into a control group (with the members asked to maintain their normal daily routines) and three exercise groups, with members of each group asked to increase their weekly exercise to different levels, 72, 136, and 194 minutes a week. The researchers found, surprisingly, that the greater exercise did not lead to greater average weight loss when compared to the control group. Indeed, some of the exercising women gained weight, as much as ten pounds.[115]
- One futuristic sounding dieting regiment holds some promise for people losing weight by, get this, getting cold. The body has two types of fat cells, "brown fat" and "white fat" cells, with the latter containing mainly fat deposits and the former containing some fat deposits but many mitochondria, the so-called "engines" of cells that produce energy. White fat stores energy and insulates the body, while brown fat does that and regulates the body's temperature. Brown fat can respond to a drop in temperature fairly quickly, turning its stored energy into heat (which explains why newborns have an abundance of brown fat to protect them against cold until other bodily organs involved in body temperature control develop). Researchers are now looking for genetic ways of turning white fat into brown fat with the hope that the conversion will enable people to lose weight through cold treatments.[116]

- No one should conclude that exercise should be excluded from a weight-reduction plan. Even "The Biggest Loser" program makes exercise a strategic component in its weight-reduction contests, but notice how the exercise on the program is combined with tight constraints on what the contestants eat. The program producers and the trainers work hard to make sure that the exercise regimens don't give rise to uncorked eating at meals. The real moral of the research is that dieters should be aware that with increased exercise regiments, they need to work harder at suppressing the controlling influence of heightened hunger pangs.

Average daily steps taken in ten occupations:

Secretaries	4,327
Teachers	4,726
Lawyers	5,062
Police Officers	5,336
Nurses	8,648
Construction Workers	9,646
Factory Workers	9,892
Restaurant Servers	10,087
Custodians	12,991
Mail Carriers	18,904

As reported by Wells (2010), citing the work of John P. Porcari in *Medicine & Science in Sports and Exercise* (2007).

- A likely source of weight gain (and difficulty in losing extra pounds) can be traced to how little many people move while at work. Weight and nutrition experts recommend adults walking at least 10,000 steps a day, but few jobs require workers to take more than half the recommended count. See the "box" insert in which one study tracked the average daily count of steps taken in ten occupations. Interestingly, when fifty-three workers were able to wear jeans (or other casual clothes) to work, they walked an average of 491 more steps than they did when they dressed more formally for business.[117]

- Cooks interested in controlling their own weight and the weights of their family members and dinner guests need to understand that widely used cookbooks can be an unrecognized source of weight gain, all surreptitiously. For example, along with the growth in obesity, has been a growth in the long and widely used *The Joy of Cooking*, literally—that is, growth in terms of the recommended portion sizes for the ever-changing recipes and growth in terms of the calories embedded in the portions recommended.[118] Word to the wise dieters: Beware of the menus you follow.

- But growth in portion size is, apparently, nothing new, and could have been going on for a millennium or more. Food researchers Brian Wansink, a Cornell University nutritionist, and his brother Craig Wansink, a theologian at Virginia Wesleyan College, evaluated the portion sizes and plate sizes in fifty-two of the most important renditions of Jesus Christ's Last Supper that were painted between 1000 and 2000 AD.[119] Over the course of that millennium, the Wansinks found that the plate sizes on the dinner table in the paintings grew by 66 percent and the portion size of the entrée (which varied in the paintings from fish to lamb to pork) put before Jesus and his disciples grew by 70 percent while the bread portion grew by 23 percent. Much has been made about the increase in meal portion sizes over the last half century or so, which is a source of contemporary weight gain, but as the Wansinks conclude, "[T]he contemporary discovery of increasing portion sizes and food availability may be little more than a 1000-year-old wine in a new bottle."[120]

- A fun study, but the Wansink findings need to be taken with at least some caution. The technology of producing dinnerware over the millennium studied no doubt improved greatly, very likely leading to larger plates because they were cheaper to make. The artists might have painted larger plates because they had no idea what the plates sizes were at the time of the Last Supper (just as most people don't know today). The artists could have been increasing portion sizes for artistic reasons, to make the portions proportional to the larger plates they knew and painted. However, recent research has found that people with larger plates eat more calories than people with smaller plates, and the growth in people's weights in modern times has been attributed to the growth in the sizes of dinner plates.[121]

- But then we really should not be surprised if meal portion sizes began growing as early as 10,000 BC, when humans turned from being hunter-gatherers to farmers. Otherwise, we must wonder why humans made the drastic switch in lifestyles way back then. The prospect of larger portions at meals, as well as greater predictability of meals, must have been a prime reason humans gave up their wandering ways and out-competed those who continued as hunter-gatherers.

- According to the Agency for Healthcare Research and Quality, the number of bariatric surgeries rose in the United States from 13,386 in 1998 to 121,055 in 2004—an increase of 804 percent! The count of such surgeries was estimated in 2010 by the president of the American Society for Metabolic and Bariatric Surgery to be between 200,000 and 250,000 a year, with the direct surgical costs (not including often needed follow-up cosmetic surgeries) to be between $15,000 and $30,000 per surgery.[122]

Chapter 3
Fat Gene

W hy are so many people fat today? A popular answer even in scholarly articles is that—drum roll!—many people eat too much, or as nutrition experts put it, heavy people have had a "positive energy balance" for far too long. Translated from expert-speak: Many people consume more calories than they expend through work and exercise.

Put in even starker terms, many people's positive energy balances have risen because they have failed both at pushing back from their tables and at hitting the treadmill, or just moving. The most exercise some people get is in the heavy lifting of forks full of pasta (or whatever) to their open mouths while sitting on their couches watching, ironically, mostly fit football players beat the hell out of each other or, even more ironically, watching the totally unfit heavies on the popular television program "The Biggest Loser" go through their agonizing paces, pushed to the brink by the contestants' on-camera exercise overlords Bob and Jillian.

If watching television significantly drained calories, there might not be a national or global weight problem, considering how much time most kids and adults in advanced countries spend channel surfing. The Nielsen Company reported that Americans in 2010 watched television an average of thirty-four hours a week (which equals the average workweek), up 1 percent from the year before and 5 percent from two years before, with some of the increase possibly attributable to the recession and sluggish recovery that left many unemployed people with time on their hands and the channel changer in their hands. The time spent watching television in 2010 equals two and a half months of nonstop television watching a year, or nearly sixteen years of an American's expected seventy-eight-year life span.[1] Whew! But the sad news from academic research is that television watching significantly contributes to weight gain. Interestingly, television watching also hikes the risk of death even when watchers don't gain weight.[2] Inactivity is a killer!

No wonder "The Biggest Loser" (which, itself, tempts watchers to remain sedate for yet another hour a week) is perennially swamped by prospective contestants who see their selection for the program as their last chance to get off the trajectory to early death. Yet, remarkably, even the threat of eminent death is not enough to scare the hell out of the would-be and selected contestants into devising their own

R.B. McKenzie, *HEAVY!*, DOI 10.1007/978-3-642-20135-6_3,
© Springer-Verlag Berlin Heidelberg 2012

weight-loss strategies without the supervision and pressure from Bob and Jillian. (And, once they've committed to the show, having their weight-loss struggles fully revealed to the viewing public is apparently no deterrent to participating in "The Biggest Loser" ranch, a modern-day fat farm with every conceivable weight-loss machine.)

The usual explanation for the country's and world's weight gains—"people eat too much and exercise too little"—adds little to our understanding of people's fat problem (when it is a real problem, which often is not the case). We all know that heavy people eat too much and exercise too little; such an explanation is like saying that water entering a bathtub will cause the water level to rise when the tub is plugged. Well, duh!

Besides, most excessively overweight and obese people know all too well—even to the point of having anguished lives—that they are packing excess pounds. Many heavy people may also know that that they eat too many fattening foods—most notably oversized hamburgers and supersized fries and shakes—that carry loads of calories, perhaps far more than they might think. And it is surprising just how calorie laden those All-American, readily available fast foods in fact are and just how little the heavy meals cost per calorie. The "All-American" fast-food combo meal composed of the large burger (most calorie rich), fry, and milkshake that McDonald's sells at $9.98 (at the time of this writing in Southern California) has 2,450 calories (one-third higher than the recommended daily intake for an adult woman) and ninety-one grams of fat (two and a quarter times the recommended daily fat intake). But Chili's large combo meal has McDonald's seem diet quality. Chili's combo selling at $12.70 has 2,840 calories (16 percent more than McDonald's) and 170 fat grams (87 percent more than McDonald's). What is amazing is that the average cost of a calorie in both meals is a meager 0.4 cent! The price of a gram of fat is 11 cents at McDonald's and 7.5 cents at Chili's.[3] This means that a menial worker in California earning the state's minimum wage ($8 an hour) would have to work only two seconds for one calorie at either McDonald's or Chili's and could get more than a day's recommended calories for an hour of work. Of course, some much higher paid professional workers in the state would have to work only nanoseconds for a calorie at either chain. A female worker receiving the average hourly pay of $22 in 2010 could, with an hour of work, buy almost three days of the recommended calories at either restaurant.

Islands restaurants beats both McDonald's and Chili's when it comes to calories in its much larger serving of fries. A full basket of Island fries alone (without burger and drink) contains 2,100 calories, which puts McDonald's and Chili's combos to shame in terms of cost per calorie.[4] During regular meal hours, the Islands' basket of fries costs only $3.69, or less than 0.2 cent per calorie. During happy hour the basket goes for half price, or .09 cent per calorie, which means a female worker earning minimum wage can buy at happy hour her recommended daily calories with less than five minutes of work or can buy more than twelve days of her recommended daily calories with an hour of work. Thank goodness people can't (and don't even try to) live by fries alone.

Fat Evolution

A fundamental and insightful—though largely unheralded—explanation for modern people's weight struggles is found, maybe surprisingly, in evolutionary biology. The eminent nineteenth-century biologist Charles Darwin may have hatched the simplest, most elegant and brilliant idea of all time when he posited that all of life—from grass to trees to flatworms and ants to dinosaurs and on to elephants and we humans—evolved out of some primitive life form (likely a single-cell organism that predates bacteria).[5] Darwin reasoned that primitive life had to be activated in some primordial electrically charged chemical soup, which, he thought when he published *Origins of the Species* in 1859, very likely occurred a very long time ago. Today, the generally accepted estimate for the emergence of primordial life is maybe three to four billion years ago.

> The question that drove Charles Darwin's thinking was this: If human breeders can develop "designer" dogs and pigeons over a relatively short period of time, can't nature do the same through evolutionary forces with species over time, if given enough time?

Even with no understanding of genetics, or the process by which a species' traits are passed from one generation to the next at the molecular level (because genetics had not yet been developed as a thriving science when he published *Origins*), Darwin understood that inheritance must play a role in the evolutionary development of all species.[6] He had a keen interest in the selective breeding of farm animals and pets, for example, dogs, horses, and pigeons, which humans had been selectively breeding for a very long time, maybe thousands of years for dogs. Breeders could select what they considered favorable characteristics of a species (size, color, hair and leg length, plumage, fertility, temperament, intelligence, etc.) in the newborns of breeds and could gradually propagate the desired characteristics until they became common in descendents, which sometimes became "monstrosities" (Darwin's word), as was the case with breeds of pigeons that could no longer fly because of their excessive plumage (or even the almost total absence of plumage).[7] If people could create great variations in various breeds of domesticated animals in fairly short order, Darwin mused, why couldn't nature do the same—if given enough time?

Darwin reasoned that organisms become ever more complex over long stretches of time—maybe 300 million years—through adaptation to their local environments by way of natural variation and random mutations in species' traits (through changes in individual or combinations of genes) and largely nonrandom selection of individual life forms in terms of their procreation of subsequent generations. The Darwinian competitive "struggle" for survival propels organisms forward in their development: "As many more individuals [within and across all species] are produced than can possibly survive, there must in every case be a struggle for existence, either between individuals within the same species, or between individuals of distinct species, or with the physical conditions of life."[8] Those individuals that are more "fit" for their local environments, because of some kind of advantageous "design feature" (resulting from natural variation and genetic mutations) than their competitors will be more likely to survive and to reproduce, which causes the random advantageous features to spread (albeit very, very gradually) through the species over, typically, a multitude of generations by means of inheritance.[9]

According to Darwin, the advancement of species can occur in two basic nonrandom ways, "natural selection" and "sexual selection."

Natural Selection

First, "natural selection": The design feature (humps on camels) can give individuals a greater chance at surviving local conditions (lack of rain) than other individuals within that species or other species. Darwin observed that finches on the Galapagos Islands, which must be descendants of those presumably carried by wind currents the 600 miles from South America to the Galapagos, have different shaped beaks, some long for probing crevices in trees for insects and some stubby for breaking open hard-shelled seeds and nuts. The two types of beaks enable diverging lines of finches to exploit different local food sources. Where local conditions are more or less uniform, only one type of finch might come to dominate, but where those conditions vary, or where food sources require different physical attributes, as they do across the Galapagos Islands, a variety of finches, such as those with differing beaks, can survive and prosper. Indeed, the development of different beaks reduces competitive pressures. The range and amount of tappable food sources expands with the growing diversity in the finch's beak sizes and capabilities (up to the point that additional diversity has no survival advantage).[10]

Needless to say, cheetahs with slightly longer gaits and greater spring in their spines and, thus greater speeds, can feed more of their kids to adulthood, who can then pass on their improved traits to future generations. By the same token, gazelles that improved their quickness and speeds are more likely to escape the cheetahs' clutches, which suggests evolution can amount, over time, to an "arms race" in nature, with the cheetahs and gazelles gradually increasing their speeds (and nimbleness) until they reach some structural limit or their advancement no longer provides any additional survival and reproductive advantage.

For that matter, a multitude of developmental margins exist on which random genetic and trait modifications can aggravate the "arms race." Among these developments are a larger brain that enables a species to outwit both its prey and predators and more efficient fat cells (or, in physiological terms, "adipose tissue") that enable the species to better store energy for leanest times. Such modifications give a species an adaptive—survival and procreation—advantage not available to others, with one improved adaptation after another enhancing the species' "fitness," a code word in evolutionary biology for success, with, again, the key considerations for "success" being survival and reproduction.

Sexual Selection

The second means by which traits—again, improved design features—in species can advance is "sexual selection": The design features that emerge from natural variations and from random genetic mutations can, for whatever reason, make individuals that have them more attractive to the opposite sex. As a consequence, these individuals are more likely to procreate, spreading their traits gradually through the population. [11]

Peacocks could have developed their flamboyant tails because peahens were wowed, or just attracted, by the metallic colored spots on the male's huge displayed tails (possibly because peahens' eyes evolved at the same time as peacocks' tail spots) or because a heavy tail indicated to peahens that these males were stronger and more resilient (and had better genes) than competitors with less flamboyant tails. Why? Because the peacocks with the more flamboyant tails can survive and prosper *in spite of* the encumbrance their heavy tails poses for their survival.[12] Evolutionary biologists theorize that surviving peacocks with flamboyant tails can reasonably be expected to be better fit to their environment than their less endowed competitors—even though peahens do not have any understanding of genetics, or even why they cater to the peacocks they do, which should be expected, given that both hens and cocks have . . . well, pea-sized brains.

Regardless, over time, those peahens that chose peacocks with flamboyant tails reproduced more frequently than peahens that chose peacocks with unadorned, or just less adorned tails, which is a reasonable deduction because peacocks today have massively and excessively adorned tails.[13]

The same selection, arms-race processes were, no doubt, at work on proto-humans, optimizing various traits in the service of survival, such as brain size and fat cells. Why the brains of protohumans began to expand rapidly about half a million years ago (doubling in size from the one-and-a-half-pound brain of *Homo habilis* to the three-pound brain of *Homo sapiens*, or modern humans) is subject today of much debate among evolutionary biologists. *Homo habilis'* brains could have begun to expand because, by walking upright, they freed their hands to undertake more mentally challenging tasks or because they developed language, enabling them to work in larger groups with more complex and challenging social settings, with larger brains having survival value in such settings.[14]

Today, evolutionary biologists acknowledge that the brain size of archaic *Homo sapiens* remained relatively stable until there was an explosion in its size about 500,000 years ago, roughly coincident with the addition of meat to diets and with the development of stone tools.[15] However, evolutionary biologists and psycho-logists and anthropologists are today divided into two basic camps in terms of how evolution has proceeded over the last 10,000 or more years. One camp, which I will dub the "steady staters," appear to have dominated the perspective of modern evolutionary biologists and psychologists for several generations. Steady staters are convinced that not much has changed about human nature and people's mental and emotional proclivities from about 10,000 or so years ago, despite all the cultural, technological, and economic changes over those millennia. Genetic mutations that improve fitness are rare, and it takes long stretches of time for favorable mutations to spread through the general population.

The other camp, the "accelerationists," mainly a relatively small band of anthropologists, is convinced that humans have continued to evolve, perhaps at an ever accelerating rate—*because* of the ongoing evolution of cultural, technological, and economic changes that have had feedback effects on the human genome. Gregory Cochran and Henry Harpending, both anthropologists, open their book on *The 10,000 Year Explosion* with a challenge they accept:

> We intend to make the case that human evolution has accelerated in the past 10,000 years, rather than slowing or stopping, and is now happening 100 times faster than its long-term average over the last 6 million years of our existence. The pace has been so rapid that humans have changed significantly in body and mind over recorded history.[16]

Cochran and Harpending begin their attack on the steady-state view of evolution by pointing to the widely unrecognized but transparently obvious fact that if evolution had stopped or just abated ten-, forty- or fifty-thousand years ago, we would expect people's minds and bodies everywhere on the globe to be the same, more or less. All modern humans' physical and mental attributes would mirror those of our common ancestors who made the trek out of Africa and expanded to all points on the globe. But the considerable variation in racial skin colors, heights, hair colors, body frames, facial features, and even intelligence makes the point that evolution has hardly slowed, much less stopped.[17] To add depth to their argument, Cochran and Harpending cite a mountain of scientific evidence that make their central point, that species, including modern humans have continued to evolve over the last few thousand years or less.

The list of numerous adaptations humans have made in far fewer than 10,000 years (including body size and shape in response to changing weather conditions) could be greatly extended, and Cochran and Harpending have developed an impressively long list of these that took place in fairly short order, given standards of "evolutionary time" (a sample list covered in an endnote).[18] Relatively recent history teaches that culture, economics, and underlying technological advances can change "memes" that can, in turn, impact human's genetics by affecting what traits are sexually attractive and maximize people's chances of survival and procreation.

However, explaining modern weight problems is somewhat easier from the perspective of the steady staters than the perspective of the accelerationists, as we will see. After all, even the accelerationists are not willing to argue that major gene mutations are likely to spread widely across the population in a generation or two, which is the time frame within which people's girths have expanded at an accelerated rate. Both camps, that is, agree that it takes a very long time for changes in the genetics that drive complex bodily functions like eating and gaining weight.

Lucy's Genes and Modern Technologies

Many modern evolutionary biologists and psychologists (maybe a substantial majority) consider it something of an article of faith—perhaps a theoretical premise—that by the end of the Pleistocene epoch, 10,000 or so years ago when humans shifted from hunting and gathering to farming, *Homo sapiens'* mental and physical attributes had evolved to more or less what they are

> We have "Lucy" genes that are slow to adapt and a modern market economy that is evolving very rapidly.

today in size and functionalities. The implication is then pressed with force: We remain today the product of our long-ago past, which is to say we remain trapped, more or less, by our Pleistocene bodies and brains. The human brain, which is crucial to what we want and can do today, took its shape largely in response to the conditions—demands and limitations—that prevailed way back then. Modern conditions play a role, but probably a very minor one (and a modest one at best), in the development of modern humans' mental faculties. The late and widely read Harvard evolutionary biologist Stephen Jay Gould, articulating the steady-state and common view among his contemporary colleagues, made this point succinctly and emphatically: "There's been no biological change in humans in 40,000 or 50,000 years. Everything we call culture and civilization we've built with the same body and brains."[19]

Excess Weight in Evolutionary Terms

According to the static view of evolutionary progress, human beings probably haven't changed much in physical, and especially mental, ways during the relatively short period of recorded history (maybe 5,000 years). Evolution requires millennia for productive genetic changes to pile up and spread through the populations of species, especially a species as complicated as humans. The apparent "evolutionary lag," or the approximately 50,000 years that are necessary for improved mental adaptations to spread throughout the human population, prevents us from having evolved much since we became farmers, only about 10,000 years ago.[20]

As a species, we humans had to evolve some ability to make choices (or control over what we do) at some level because from the dawn of "creation" and through every stage of development, humans have lived among complex physical and social conditions. Humans, even with our large modern brains (cast 10,000 years ago, again), simply could not be preprogrammed to deal by rote or instinct with the myriad modern complex conditions we face. We have not evolved the count of neurons we would need for development of all the mental "software" required to respond in a preprogrammed manner to all combinations of constantly changing local conditions we confront daily (and don't forget that the hominids who migrated in waves out of Africa faced major changes in climatic and terrain conditions to which they had to adapt by the mile and over generations).[21]

Still, a very important point to remember is embedded in Darwin's evolutionary theory: The choices we make today are powerfully framed by how we evolved through long-ago conditions that no longer exist, at least not with the same binding constraints. In other words, many of our "choices" and "behaviors" can be explained by conditions that existed thousands of years ago. These long-ago conditions left their marks on our physical features and mental proclivities. Put another way, living conditions of long ago are hardwired in our brains and etched on our muscles. From this perspective of Darwinian evolution, under which evolution has not had time to affect the human physique and brain since the development of agriculture, our proclivities to fill our forks and to linger eating at our tables remain largely shaped by conditions that no longer exist, which necessarily means our eating and other proclivities may be counter to our individual personal interests today, because those proclivities evolved to deal with conditions that are no longer present and controlling.

> Normal-weight people today have about 40 billion fat cells. Obese people have about 120 billion. And a fat cell can swell at least 64-fold as it stores energy (with the upper limit on the swelling unknown). About 10 percent of fat cells die and are replaced each year.
> As reported for the *Wall Street Journal* by Beck (2010b).

"Lucy" and Modern-Day Fat Problems

Under this largely steady-state view of evolution from the Pleistocene epoch onward, an explanation for modern-day obesity is fairly straightforward. Our common human forebear three or so million years ago—call her "Lucy"—was surely thin (and a little more than half the height of the average modern human).[22] Had Lucy sat next to me on a plane, I could have worked with ease. The big man who did sit next to me on a flight, was, at least partially, as large as he was because of the crosscurrents of ecological forces at work not just on him, but, perhaps more importantly, at work on Lucy and all of her descendants through thousands of generations since Lucy walked the grasslands of Africa. In Lucy's era and far into the future from her short lifetime (maybe two dozen years), being overweight was a highly unlikely problem (at least not a prevalent and lasting one). Securing food was a pressing and persistent issue at hand, an activity that took a lot of energy in miles walked and in frequent struggles to the death with prey sometimes larger than early humans. And then there was the considerable preparation time needed for meals. Lucy and her like had to butcher their kills; all we have to do is select from a range of frozen meat patties.

Our very early ancestors were left with few opportunities to pile on fat or to remain fat for long periods of time. Lucy and her immediate descendants could only eat so much at a sitting, and their food storage techniques, to smooth out feast-and-famine cycles, were unlikely more advanced than those of squirrels and foxes that we observe today.

Lucy and her kin were also likely hampered in their ability to pack on pounds by their short life spans and their small physical size (and by their far greater exposure to the elements and to disease for which they knew no cure—with both types of exposure raising energy requirements). Small animals (squirrels and mice) are typically not able to add fat like their larger counterparts (elephants and buffalos), which means that larger animals, especially carnivores with their protein-rich diets, can go longer without food (their "starvation times" are longer) and are more tolerant of variable food cycles.[23]

An animal's ability to store fat also has survival advantages. Mammals with fat reserves can nurse their offspring, sometimes for months without feeding themselves. Fatter newborns have better survival chances, (newborn human babies are among the fattest of all mammals[24]) and added weight (up to a point) appears to be an important defense against some diseases.[25] Moreover, the rapid expansion of the early human brain half a million years ago likely required a concomitant increase in early human's fat accumulation capacity, as big brains are energy guzzlers (consuming a fifth of the body's calorie intake) and require constant energy guzzling. And the availability of food was inconsistent way back when. Fat, in other words, is effectively an internal "battery" for powering the human brain (as well as other organs) when food is sparse. If humans had failed to fuel their brains with efficient energy reserves in lean times, then surely the brain would not have become as large as it did. The brain and adipose tissue had to develop in size and efficiency more or less in tandem. Along the way, humans had to acquire an ability (*allostasis*) to regulate their physiology to maintain and achieve viability in ever-changing seasonal and local environments, including longer-term climactic changes that affected food supplies. An efficient fat storage system was just such a crucial adaptation, and compared with protein and carbohydrates, fat is a very efficient means of storing usable energy reserves (per gram) that can be drawn down (thank goodness!).[26]

So, Lucy was small. Again, she was only three feet tall, which means the top of her head might have reached a modern human's waistline. She very likely couldn't store as much fat as modern humans because of her size and her yet-to-be fully efficient adipose tissue. But she didn't need as much stored energy as modern humans to power her brain. Her brain (420–500 cm^3) may have been a little larger than a modern chimp's and a third the size of the modern human brain (1,350 cm^3).[27] She also probably didn't have much capacity to assess the impact of her current decisions on her long-term health and viability, including dietary decisions. With a lifetime of not more than a couple dozen years, there was no realistic prospect of a "long term" as we might view it. Lucy's guiding principle for food was likely to have been "eat what you can when you can," and there very likely were few long-run consequences of overeating. The inevitable periods of food scarcity in the near future would take care of any overeating in the here and now, and overeating in the here and now made long-term survival all the more likely. And today, modern humans remain inflicted with an impaired ability to assess the long-term consequences of current decisions taken in sequences, a fact that is evident in academic research and transparent in people's resistance to saving for retirement—as well as in their waistlines.[28]

For Lucy's evolving descendants, the continuing long-ago frequent food scarcities also very likely promoted human preference for sugary and fatty foods because such foods were high in calories, which translated into an increase in survival and more chances for procreation. Those early humans who failed to develop a taste for fatty and sugary foods faded in disproportionate numbers from our lineage, and those who craved them were, on the other hand, relatively efficient food gatherers and high-calorie consumers. We are the progeny of the early humans who loved sex *and* foods high in sugars and fats and who developed highly efficient fat cells (adipose tissue), well adapted for storing energy that, of course, makes losing those stores of fat taxing today. And, to repeat, adipose tissue has evolved to be a far more efficient and expandable energy storage system than any of the internal organs (most notably the liver, which stores quick-release energy readily accessible for fight-or-flight decisions).[29]

As food was scarce and supplies unpredictable, early humans evolved to use their girths, "love handles," and butts as "mobile refrigerators" for storing excess calories gleaned from hunting and gathering. They, as Lucy and her descendant of 10,000 years ago, call her "Eve," had little ability—or need—to assess the future gains and pains from their weight gain. Why develop such a rational capacity to assess future consequences of current eating decisions when it would carry so little utility? This is because, and this is important, the primitive environment and forces of natural selection way back when kept the sizes of people's guts, love handles, and butts in check. When people carried *some* extra weight, they could expend more energy on longer hunts, which probably increased their chances of finding prey, surviving, and procreating.

The added weight also probably made them more sexually attractive, because their girth (up to a point) demonstrated their food-gathering prowess, as well as health and capacity to survive the lean times (or times of so-called "food insecurity"). The little extra weight probably carried the covert message that they had "good genes" that enabled them to develop good hunting and gathering skills, attributes that could have made them "sexy."[30]

Those people who could pack on *some* extra pounds disproportionately became our ancestors, and during the leans times, those who lacked such ability fell in disproportionate numbers from Darwin's "tree of life." They didn't have the butt-based refrigerators they needed to make it to their next meal. Our ancestors with lean genes didn't drop altogether from the human gene pool. Obviously, there remain modern humans who actually have trouble gaining weight, but they certainly retreated as modern humans as the fat gene achieved relatively greater reproductive success.

Yet even in prehistoric times, added weight beyond some point surely became a handicap. Those early humans who dared to get obese did so at some peril from prey and cohorts. The fatter they got, the less able they were to flee and scamper up the first available tree to escape predators. And, the fatter people became (again, beyond some point), the slower they could run to catch game. The obese (and surely the grossly obese) probably risked being expelled from their tribes because their added weight made them worthless as hunters and easy marks for predators seeking energy-rich blubber. Few early humans could outrun their major predators of their era, but the heavy tribe members couldn't even outrun their thinner cohorts, which means they were the stragglers who were picked off by saber-toothed tigers and the like.

> Those ancestors in our long ago past who had the "fat gene" could make it through the lean times and could propagate because they had fat stored on their butts. Those who had the "thin gene" died with greater frequency when times were tough. Modern humans are blessed and cursed by the genes and mental hardwiring that endow them—us—with a proclivity to eat everything we can every time we can, especially sugared and fatty foods.

Under this steady-state view of evolution, we modern humans face a significant problem: Economic forces have altered our physical environmental and our social and economic conditions at warp speed while evolutionary forces have barely touched our genes, tastes, and eating proclivities, leaving them more or less fixed, possibly for the past tens of thousands of years. In a large way (pun intended), we modern humans are Lucy's heirs. We disproportionately have the "fat gene"—or, more accurately, the predisposition to gain weight whenever possible. And, moreover, we probably are cursed with Lucy's and Eve's tendencies, and that of all their descendants, to pay little attention to the long-run consequences of following the prehistoric principle: Eat when you can and all you can.

Having the fat gene is no problem so long as food is scarce and expensive and when predators and diseases impose an upper limit to people's weight gain. Back in Lucy's or even Eve'sday and into the last millennium, gathering food was hardly easy work, but there also was no point in working extra long days to hunt or gather extra food once humans had filled their stomachs and stored a few extra pounds on their backsides.[31] From around 1000 AD (and maybe long before) until 1800 or so, people's workdays averaged three or four hours, about what cavemen put in, according to one economic history authority.[32]

Two reasons for the short workdays are unheralded: First, productivity and wages were low, which means that leisure-time activities easily could be judged as more valuable than work activities because working more produced very little in additional purchasing power. Second, people's means for preserving and storing extra food supplies were simply very limited or costly. Canning and refrigeration are relatively modern inventions, and, incidentally, are unrecognized technological contributors to modern people's weight problems.[33]

Today, the average American line worker need put in only an hour of work to buy at McDonald's or Outback Steakhouse the calories needed for a week's subsistence. The average worker also can store in pantries and refrigerators a mountain of calories, kept fresh in assorted packaging, to be consumed at leisure while watching television after a "hard day" at the office ("hard," perhaps, in stress and frustration but not in physical activity and calories expended).

> "Lucy" and "Eve" used their butts as a refrigerator and pantry. Today, we are blessed and cursed with refrigerators and pantries that can store gobs of food that can easily and continually be transferred to our butts, guts, and love handles.

The prevalence of the fat gene and our ingrained tastes for sweet and fatty foods are a big problem when food is abundant and cheap and can be cheaply stored, readily restocked, and even overstocked with quick drives (certainly not walks or runs!) to the local Costco or Walmart, which, by the way, package their food products in such large portions that running out of food at home is almost a nonexistent problem today in the United States or other advanced countries, even for the majority of poor people. Modern humans find it all too tempting to move food from the storehouses of their pantries and refrigerators to the "refrigerators" they inherited from Lucy, their butts, guts, and love handles. And modern humans have obviously yielded to ever-present temptations.

> People are fat today in part because they have the genes of "Lucy" and the economy of McDonald's (and KFC and Taco Bell and Which Wich). "Lucy" had a successful hunt every time she and her cohorts killed a gazelle that resisted the attack. We modern humans have a successful hunt every time we pass through the doors of a fast-food restaurant with smiling servers greeting us, "Would you like a second or third patty?"

The point here is not that the big man who sat next to me on the plane trip "couldn't help" his massive size. Of course, he most likely could have, at least to some degree. Remember that we also evolved an adaptive capacity, including the ability, to varying degrees, to control our actions—and what we eat. Lots of people control their weight, albeit with more or less difficulty. Perhaps the big man on the plane was among the less than 5 percent of obese people who from childhood have had identified physiological, hormonal, or molecular genetic abnormalities.[34] Maybe he was simply one of the 4 percent of adult Americans who have had to live with a certifiable "binge eating disorder" (traceable to such considerations as loneliness and depression, which could be tied to some traumatic childhood experiences) that makes weight control exceptionally difficult, if not nearly impossible (but, I dare say, not totally impossible).[35] For example, he could have had, throughout much of his life, a thyroid condition that slowed his metabolic rate to a crawl, causing him to gain weight even with limited food intake. But, research shows that such serious medical conditions can't be the whole excuse for all the excessively overweight people. There is simply a mountain of studies (to be reviewed throughout this book) that trace excess weight to a host of environmental, family, and community conditions, as well as economic factors (food prices and income, for example). But such studies do not deny our evolutionary bound *predisposition* or *propensity* to eat when we can, which suggests that our growing weight can, in a major way, be a consequence of a clash between two powerful and ongoing forces—evolution and economics— or so the steady-state view of Darwinism strongly suggests.

Our problem is stark: We have the genes of Lucy and Eve and the economy of Big Macs. The study of modern humans' weight problem ultimately reduces to the triumph of economics over evolution, which means that modern humans need more fortitude to stay thin than did Lucy and her descendents into the early twentieth century. Endowed with Lucy's and Eve's inclination to eat as much as possible at every opportunity, modern humans are faced with a multitude of temptations to do just that. Lucy was programmed to overindulge on calories after every successful hunt. Maybe Eve was less so programmed because she farmed, but heavily programmed nevertheless because she had Lucy's predispositions and was beset with food scarcities that varied radically from season to season and year to year. We are programmed the same way, but we have a successful hunt every time we pass a fast-food restaurant that, unlike Lucy's or Eve's prey, has no ability or inclination to flee or to resist our assaults on its menu.

Of course, all of this expands radically the potential explanations for modern weight problems. We can lay some of the blame at the doorstep of the growing efficiency of modern corporations and competitive markets, and the freeing of international trade through the reductions in government-imposed trade barriers and the globalization of production with advancements in transportation and telecommunications—all of which have increased people's incomes and lowered the prices of fatty and sugary foods.

Concluding Comments

Darwinism reminds us that we humans weren't always built the way we are today, and many of our current abilities and proclivities are the consequence of random mutations and nonrandom selection over the eons. The history of life has been marked by a multitude of mutations at the genetic level that have literally led to the multitude of varied organisms in today's world. Some have little to no choice in their life circumstances, as is apparently the case with amoebas, while others have considerable capacity for choices, as is the case with modern humans (or so I will assert, given that I feel comfortable with the belief that I chose to write this book rather than to do any number of other things).

Many mutations (a third eye, for example) likely have occurred in the lineage of any given organism—humans included. Those mutations that proved to be useless or counterproductive (not "adaptive") faded from the gene pool; those that were useful and productive—that added to our "fitness" (or ability, given environmental conditions at the time)—were selected to remain. The adaptations were, in this way, nonrandom.

The steady-state view of evolution of modern humans provides an easy explanation for why so many people today are fat. The fat gene in almost all modern humans continues to drive us to eat what we can, when we can, with an impaired ability to look down the road and properly assess the pain that creeping weight gain can cause. Many people know they have gained weight, and should lose any number of pounds, but in choosing what to do in the moment, they remain wired to see the food temptations all around them as compelling. The perceived gain from the delicious taste of a banana split right here and now simply overshadows the underappreciated pains of the weight gain over a life expectancy that Lucy and her descendants would dare not waste time assessing with any care.

The more modern view of evolution, which sees abiding interconnections among culture, technology, economics (or forces affecting memes) on the one hand and human genes on the other offers the prospect that people's genetic-based tendency to overeat can be abated, at least somewhat and with some time. As people's life expectancy has increased, then surely they have improved (but not perfected) their ability to assess future gains and pains of current actions, including eating. Survival and procreation can hang in the balance of improved assessments. Moreover, sexual selection is bound to affect the human genome if weight gain impairs fertility and life expectancy, as research indicates. Sexual selection among humans could very well be as powerful a force for the change of the human genome (although at a slower pace) as breeder selection can be in the gene pool of domesticated animals. Maybe the current obesity epidemic will go away—with enough time.

The real question at "ground zero" in the weight-gain phenomenon and policy debate is whether human genes can adjust sufficiently quickly to negate the rapidly mutating cultural, technological, and economic environment that makes eating ever more tempting and affordable. It very well could be that the growth of the culture of excess weight, the technology of food production, and the competitiveness of world food markets have simply overwhelmed any evolutionary potential for our genes to cope with modern food temptations. After all the evidence on the power of modern economic forces at work (covered in coming chapters), what is really remarkable about the contemporary human population is that all of us are not fat—or at least not as fat as we might be, given ever-present temptations to eat what Lucy could not have imagined even in her wildest dreams.

Chapter 4
Fat Economics

At mid-morning in a Panera restaurant in North Carolina, a slew of customers surveys the confections displayed in the pastry bar. Obviously overweight customers—some massively so—with amazing frequency select one of the sugar-coated and cream-filled pastries that carry premium prices, but are surely bargains in price per calorie. Panera's pecan roll has 720 calories and thirty-eight grams of fat; its cinnamon chip scone, 530 calories and twenty-six grams of fat; and even its "reduced fat" apple crunch muffin carries 470 calories if *only* twelve grams of fat (as reported by Panera). Those three items eaten together—if anyone would dare—would exceed the recommended daily calorie intake for an adult female, and their fat content would come close to the *maximum* recommended daily grams.

What economic and social forces are afoot that could bring so many overweight buyers to the Panera pastry bar, and at mid-morning? That is not an easy problem to address. Indeed, it is a highly complex problem. Probably every overweight person at the restaurant has a personal story on how they gained their weight, only to end up (again!) at the pastry bar. But the sheer complexity of the "fat economy" is precisely why the economic way of thinking can be useful in understanding the forces behind the worldwide weight gain problem over the last half century. Economics unravels the puzzle (at least partially), addressing it in reduced form, stripped of the multitude of complexities, as it examines key (and unheralded) forces at work on many people across space and educational and social classes and over both long stretches of time (the last two centuries) and shorter periods (the last thirty to fifty years), with the various forces being more or less isolated from one another.

Naturally, any analysis of the complex and burgeoning "fat economy" will focus on forces that have affected the relative prices of foods—including pastries—that Americans have been able to buy with their rising real incomes. Throughout, we have to pay attention to the *price tags* on groceries bought for home-produced meals and on the *menu prices* at restaurants like Panera, but we can't forget to consider the many economic forces that have affected the *full price* of foods, which includes, most prominently, the labor and time cost of meal preparation.

After all, many customers might not go the Panera pastry bar (repeatedly!) if they could produce the same variety of pastries of equal quality and tastiness in

R.B. McKenzie, *HEAVY!*, DOI 10.1007/978-3-642-20135-6_4,
© Springer-Verlag Berlin Heidelberg 2012

their own kitchens at a lower *full price* (including their time cost) than Panera can, and if they could recreate Panera's social setting, which is possibly as important to many customers as the food opportunities themselves. As we will see, the many economic forces that have shifted food production from small-scale home venues to much larger-scale plant and restaurant venues can go a long way toward helping us understand the country's and world's weight problem. Some of the forces at work are as counterintuitive as they are unrecognized. All the while, many obesity researchers and media commentators continue to lay the blame for obesity on people's loss of control or businesses' excessive greed.

The Economic Way of Thinking

Before the 1950s, economics was staid, chiefly concerned with the subject matter that was central to Adam Smith's work in the late eighteenth century, how markets worked (or failed to work). At the turn of the twentieth century, the then prominent British economist Alfred Marshall was on target when he described the discipline as a study of people in "the ordinary business of life."[1] People's weight in this earlier era was not on many (if any) economists' research radarscope. Weight had little to do with business or markets, or so many economists then seemed to think.

My good fortune is that I came of age intellectually when Nobel Laureates in economics James Buchanan and Gary Becker were in their prime productive years, as they dared to insist that what counts in economic scholarship and commentary is the application of economic *thinking* methods to ever more interesting "non-economic" topics. To their way of thinking, the analysis need not be all that arcane and complicated, or even mathematical, as many other economists tried to make it, and still do with ever more sophistication (and often lesser effect).[2]

Buchanan and Becker (and others) set me on a path that has been a never-ending search for ways to apply economic principles to an ever-expanding array of topics. My career-shaping opportunity came when Gordon Tullock (a brilliant economist who did groundbreaking work with Buchanan and separately) and I teamed up in the mid-1970s to write a book, *The New World of Economics,* on. . . well, the economics of anything and everything (drawing on the burgeoning work of others): voter behavior, presidential elections, panics and riots, lying and cheating, marriage and family (and divorce), sex (the normal stuff, not just prostitution), learning, and dying (and there really is a "most economical way to die," or so we argued).[3] Over the decades since publication of our joint work, I've often told my students that "economics is not a discipline; it's a disease! If you ever grasp the relatively simple way of thinking about everything, you will not be socially acceptable at cocktail parties." Infected economists just can't resist insisting that virtually all topics can be seen through their professional prism. But then Tullock and I never thought way back when to add a chapter on the economics of weight, partially because weight was not then the prominent problem it is today.

University of Chicago economist Steven Levitt and journalist Stephen Dubner have certainly been infected by the economic way of thinking. Moreover, they have accomplished what all of their economist predecessors only dreamed of doing: They have made economics enthralling (if you can believe that) to the masses. Through their two best-selling books, *Freakonomics* and *Superfreakonomics,* they have dared to go where many other contemporary economists had not thought to go, applying economic methods to the incentives faced by school administrators, sumo wrestlers, terrorists, real estate agents, and prostitutes.[4]

In *Superfreakonomics*, they have even reviewed studies of economists who taught seven small-brain capuchin monkeys (four females and three males) in captivity how to trade their allotted "money" (one-inch silver disks) for favored foods, that is, Jell-O cubes, grapes, or sliced apples. The researchers found that when the "price" of Jell-O cubes rose, the monkeys bought fewer cubes and more apple slices and grapes, just as economists would predict. The researchers were then shocked when a trained and enterprising—and horny—male capuchin gave disks to a female capuchin after which they had sex—and after which the female capuchin used the cash to buy grapes, which Levitt and Dubner describe as "the first instance of monkey prostitution in the recorded history of science."[5]

But, the research finding was only surprising because money changed hands. Other animal behavioralists have found that macaque monkeys in the wild have had an ongoing active sex market involving barter for some time. Male macaques groom females, a service for which the females would "pay" with services of their own, sexual favors. The researchers also have found that the longer the males groom the females, the greater the males' chances of getting sex. Moreover, the researchers have discovered that competition determines the female macaques' grooming price for sex. When close-by females are abundant, the males get more sex for less grooming of each female, suggesting that the females are not above competing on "price" for the attention of males.[6]

A small army of economists and I have come to the issue of fat with the same basic question that Levitt and Dubner and their predecessors asked: What can economics, as a way of thinking, add to scholarship and commentary on body weight that specialists in other fields might have missed, not because those in other disciplines are less intelligent, but simply because they address subjects differently, with different mental methods and research inclinations? I also bring with me some protective cynicism about what's afoot in the widely touted "obesity epidemic." After all, many nutritionists and obesity researchers have integrated their science with policy advocacy and legal campaigns, all with requests for more and more supporting federal dollars and expanded research bureaucracies, giving them personal stakes in policy outcomes, as we will see in later chapters.

What is remarkable about the economic way of thinking about everything, including people's weight gain, is that it involves relatively few, simple, and intuitively plausible principles (on which I have elaborated at length elsewhere[7]). Consider this short list of key principles on which almost all economic commentary is founded:

- We economists assume people behave, within limits, purposefully—or *rationally*—with the goal of doing the best they can with their limited or scarce resources, incomes and wealth, or their time, which becomes scarcer and more valuable as income-generating labor market opportunities expand.
- Because people can't do or have everything they want, they must make choices in everything they do, which means that everything has a cost. Cost is simply the value of what can't be done, or the value of the choice not taken. Some costs are salient as indicated by readily available price tags, but many costs are nonobvious or are hidden. Economists are trained to find hidden costs, and they all repeat the mantra, "There ain't no such thing as a free lunch." (If anyone tells you something is "free," watch out).
- If people are out to do the best they can under almost all circumstances, they stand ever-ready to respond to changes in incentives. Incentives really do matter and are powerful forces. The trick is getting them right (even when it comes to weight).
- One of the most important principles in economics is that people respond to price changes in a predictable way: If the price of a good goes up while nothing else changes, people will buy less of the good—and vice versa.[8] This principle—dubbed "the law of demand"—has been validated time and again in theory and practice, and a mountain of academic statistical studies. Just consider the prevalence of sales, quantity discounts, rebates, and coupons; they represent the law of demand at work (and in particular the ubiquity of price-discrimination attempts by sellers).
- One caveat to keep in mind: Different groups of buyers will respond differently—by greater or lesser amounts bought—to given price changes, but they respond nevertheless. A number of the heavy customers at Panera's pastry counter the morning I was there may have been salivating as they considered their choices, giving little thought to the possible weight-gain consequences of their choices, but for economists it's still a good bet that the customers would have been fewer had Panera posted significantly higher prices. If that were not the case, Panera would likely charge even higher prices.
- There are real productive and cost-reducing benefits from specialization of resources such as labor and from scale economies, but specialization and scale economies depend on the scope of markets, and with the computer and telecommunication revolutions over the past several decades, the scope of markets has been extended to the ends of the earth, literally, which, as we will see, has been a contributor to people's weight gain.

Penny Candy No More

In 1950, a mother could give her kid a half dollar and send him off to the corner market for a loaf of bread and the youngster would have had change left over to squander on candy or a soda pop. Nowadays, a kid on the same errand would need a five-dollar bill to buy the bread and have any change left for a treat. From a purely historical perspective, food prices (as in their price tags) have gradually escalated over time, but higher prices may not have deterred people from eating more because the prices of everything else, along with people's nominal incomes (the number of dollars they earn) have outpaced prices. This means that over time people's real (inflation-adjusted) incomes, also have risen. Compared with all the goods and services a family must purchase, food—relatively speaking—may have been quite a bargain, especially in the last few decades. Bargains, the economic way of thinking tells us, drive greater consumption, and when it comes to food, greater consumption often means weight gain.

Cheap Food—In Comparison

Various studies agree that lower relative food prices provide a partial explanation for Americans' enlarging girths over the past thirty to fifty years, although some may quibble about how important a role relative prices have played. Surprisingly, a first look at the data shows that the price of food has risen similarly with those of all other consumer goods. The Consumer Price Index (CPI) tracks the prices of more than 80,000 goods in 200 product categories through monthly surveys of 25,000 stores in major urban areas across the country. Since 1913, the CPI-less food (which is an index for all the counted goods excluding food items) has marched steadily upward, increasing twenty-two-fold by 2010. But, surprisingly, the consumer price index for only food items for the same time period also rose close to twenty-two-fold over the full 1913–2010 span. Indeed, the rise in the CPI-less food and the food price indices have moved so closely together over that long period that you would not be able to distinguish the curves if both indices were put on the same graph for the 1913–2010 period.

Of course, the two price indices—CPI-less food and the food price index—did not move exactly in lock step. The relationship between food prices and the cost of all the other goods that families need or want have to be weighed. *Relative* food prices (or the ratio of food prices to the prices of all other items in the CPI) and not the *absolute* food prices (or the absolute index number) are important in assessing the economic causes of weight gain, especially over short periods of time when the changes in the two price indices diverge. *Relative* food prices gyrated from 1913 to 2010, falling by nearly 30 percent from the end of World War I through the early 1930s, rising again during World War II, trending slightly downward in the 1950s and 1960s, only to jump upward in the early 1970s (an increase very likely spurred by a depreciation of the dollar in 1971 and to the OPEC-induced jump in oil prices in 1973). But since

> The relative price of food dropped during the last third of the twentieth century at about the same time weight gain in the United States accelerated.

the late 1970s, relative food prices have been falling, with some stabilization in the 1980s and 1990s and a slight jump in the early 2000s. Relative food prices dropped fairly dramatically between 1970 and 2000, the very same period when American weight gain accelerated, and then moved up modestly in the first decade of this century.

When Food Costs Less, We Eat More

Clearly, when it comes to food, the law of demand reigns! When food is relatively cheap, we consume more of it, the result of which has been widespread weight gain.[9] More importantly, the rise in the obesity rate during the past four decades can be *partially* attributed to the significant drop in the relative price of food, a 17 percent decrease between its peak in 1975 to its low in late 2000. Then, in the 2000s, as relative food prices rose 5 percent, the rise in the obesity rate for adults slowed and the obesity rate for children may have fallen. Such a responsive relationship between relative food prices and weight gain has spurred weight researchers to take notice.

Economists Darius Lakdawalla and Tomas Philipson found during 1981–1994 that consumers' food consumption increased 0.6 percent when the relative food prices declined 1 percent. Although consumer response is small—the demand is "inelastic" in—it is a response nonetheless.[10] During the same time period, other researchers found that lower relative food prices accounted for 55 percent of the growth in the average adult BMI (Body Mass Index).[11] They tracked lower food prices to technological improvements in agricultural production, which significantly increased the food supply on the market and dropped food prices. In a 2010 study Lakdawalla and his coauthors Dana Goldman and Yuhui Zheng found evidence that the effects on consumption of a 10 percent price drop for a calorie grows with time. Like other researchers, they found that in the short run, a 10 percent drop in the price of a calorie has statistically significant effect although a modest one. However, if the price drop persists for ten years, the 10 percent price decrease in the price of a calorie can give rise to a more than one point increase in the average BMI and to twice that effect if the time frame is made longer.[12]

Obesity researchers centered at Temple University followed 4,600 students from diverse backgrounds and ethnic groups from the beginning of their sixth grade until the end of their eighth grade, or from 2006 until 2009.[13] During the study, half of the students were given instruction on healthy living (covering "nutrition, physical activity, behavioral knowledge and skills, and communications and social marketing"), while the other half were not. At the start of the study, 30 percent of the students in both groups were classified as obese. The student group that received the instruction improved its

> Lower relative food prices can be partially traced to technological advancements and government subsidies in agriculture.

weight control more than the control group, but more interesting are the findings that both groups' rates went down during the time period and there was no statistically significant difference in the drop in the obesity rates for the two groups.[14] One of the researchers told a *New York Times* reporter, "Something is going on in the environment that is leading kids to become less overweight or obese. We need to find out what it is and do more of it."[15]

Perhaps the researchers ought to examine the economic variables that were at work on the kids in their study. One such economic variable could be the *full* relative prices of foods bought, which include foods' price tags, but also their preparation costs and weight-gain costs. Another important variable could be the changes in the real incomes the students' families were earning. After all, two out of the three years in the study period covered the end of the economic boom and the advent of the Great Recession in late 2007, which was declared officially over in mid-2009 (although the unemployment rate remained stubbornly high through early 2011).

In addition to technology, government policies also affect food supply, and in turn, food prices, consumption, and, naturally, weight gain. However, the impact of the full scope of government farm policies on crop prices and weight gain has been mixed. Government subsidies of farm production, in the main wheat and corn, which have depressed their market prices, over the last half of the twentieth century (and before) have fed into greater production and lower prices for a variety of high-calorie processed food products over the decades which have been a factor in Americans' weight gain.[16] Conversely, farm programs that have induced farmers to take land out of production for some crops and tariffs on imported foods that have held up the prices of other potentially fattening food (beef, sugar cane, soybeans, and milk, for example) have muted any weight-gain effect of the subsidy-induced greater consumption of grain-based products.[17] The federal government's induced hike in demand for corn to produce subsidized ethanol, an additive for gasoline, has meant that the proportion of the country's corn harvest devoted to ethanol production rose from 7 percent in 1980 to 39 percent in 2010.[18] This artificial hike in corn demand has definitely contributed to the rising price of corn during the last decade, which has increased the price of corn-based foods (taco wraps and pastries, for example), perhaps contributing to the slower growth of weight gain over the past decade, but also to nutritional deficits and starvation for tens of millions of people in very poor countries who rely on corn-based products.[19] That is, the ethanol policy craze has put the world on a diet, indirectly. On the other hand, agriculture policies have, on balance, been holding up the prices of fruits and vegetables.[20]

More generally, the substantial worldwide rise in relative food export prices starting after 2004 and continuing through 2010 (attributable to, among other factors, increasing food demands in China and India with their rapid development and to relatively greater volatility in weather patterns across the globe) has probably contributed to a slowdown in people's weight gain across the globe and to "food insecurity" and starvation in parts of the globe. When the richest countries of the world pledged in 2009 to subsidize the food purchases of the poorest countries to the tune of $20 billion, the subsidies probably exacerbated rising food prices, especially for the developed countries, which means the subsidies were a force to further slow weight gain in the developed countries.[21]

Lakdawalla and Philipson also found evidence that state sales taxes on food can affect the relative price of food, and in turn, the quantity of food consumed, as the law of demand suggests. Those states that tax food have higher food prices and lower food consumption levels than those states that exempted foods from sales taxes. Consequently, those states that tax food tend to have lower percentages of overweight and obese residents than those states that do not.[22] Of course, it's no big leap to expect obesity rates to be affected by the rise and fall of real sales taxes within states (after adjusting for other forces that affect people's weight gain).

> States that impose sales taxes on food tend to have lower obesity rates.

The rising price of healthful foods (carrots and broccoli) compared with unhealthful foods (hamburgers and pastries) might also explain some of the increasing weight gain and obesity rate. For most of the last half-century, the prices of healthful and unhealthful foods moved upward together, aside for the years between the late-1980s and mid-1990s when the country experienced a jump in weight gain and the obesity rate. Sure enough, researchers have found that during the time period in which the ratio of the price of healthful foods to unhealthful foods rose by close to 50 percent, people consumed more unhealthful foods and became more obese as a consequence.[23] Surprise, surprise!

Contrary to what a lot of people seem to think, the researchers found that the effect of this relative price movement of healthful foods relative to unhealthful foods was meager, explaining less than 1 percent of the growth in people's BMIs and the incidence of obesity from the late-1980s to the mid-1990s.[24] But the minimal effect of the relative rise in healthful foods might be understandable, given the shortness of the time period in which the price ratio rose, only to start declining again after the mid-1990s. People could have been basing their food consumption during the mid-1980s/mid-1990s period on the longer term trend in relative prices, which shows little change in the relative price of unhealthful and healthful foods and little influence of the price ratio on people's pattern of food consumption. Researchers found that the changing relative prices of fast-food and fruits and vegetables between the late 1990s and early 2000s might explain no more than 5 percent of the change in the BMIs and of the weight gains of the groups studied. Other more powerful economic and social forces must be at work.[25]

The important takeaway follows the law of demand: A decrease in the relative price of healthful foods means more healthful foods are bought. But the relative price of healthful foods has not changed very much over enough time to have much impact on the country's weight problems. To see a more dramatic effect, we might just have to wait on a long-term trend of greater technological improvements in the production of healthful foods relative to unhealthful foods. And, as we will see, the meager impact of "price" on food consumption and weight gain may be because the researchers focused on the *price tags* on foods, not on their *full prices*, an important distinction to keep in mind. The relative full price of unhealthful foods could be falling substantially while their relative price tags are falling little to none. Why? The time required to prepare unhealthful foods could be falling more than the time required to prepare healthful foods.

As real food prices have dropped, Americans' real income has grown, providing another explanation for why Americans were consuming, on average, 331, or more than 18 percent, more calories per day in 2006 than in the late 1970s.[26] With no increase in exercise (and only a minor increase in height), those extra daily calories *could* now be adding more than 34 pounds—two good-sized bowling balls—to each and every adult American *each year*! But, of course, not every American is overeating, which means that many have been going above and beyond, packing on several additional bowling balls a year.

Longer Lives Mean Bigger Gains

During the past century, many Americans have enjoyed not only lower relative food prices during some periods, but also increasing longevity and better health. Some weight gain surely indicates many Americans have been eating better and living longer, and people who live longer also have more opportunities to pack on pounds.

> People are heavier because they live longer.

A clear assessment of weight gain among *all* American adults during the entire twentieth century is difficult because data is progressively more elusive as we move back in time. As noted, careful data collection did not begin until the 1960s when the country's weight problems began to be widely recognized as a serious economic, social, and health issue. Moreover, the longer the time period covered by price series, the greater the opportunity for changes in the exact qualities and types of foods consumed.

Nonetheless, we do have a few indications of the growing weight problem. For example, researchers found that between 1890 and 1900, the average BMI of males fifty to fifty-nine years of age rose by 25 percent, with a disproportionate increase in males with higher BMIs.[27] Between 1894 and 1961, the average BMI of males in their forties increased about 10 percent, from 23.6 to 26.0, with a slightly smaller increase for men in their thirties.[28] But much of the weight increase during the first half of the twentieth century shifted many people from unhealthful underweight to progressively less healthful overweight, according to prominent economic historian and Nobel Laureate Robert Fogel.[29]

Moreover, Americans' life expectancy at birth increased from just over forty-nine years in 1900 to seventy years in 1960, an increase of more than 40 percent.[30] This increasing longevity during the twentieth century is very likely a cause of Americans' weight gain because people do tend to gain weight on average as they age, until they hit their sixties. But some of their weight gain also has very likely boosted their productivity and longevity, with both results boosting weight gain.[31]

Since 1960, the increase in Americans' average BMI has been much smaller, 0.9 of a point, and some of this can be chalked up to the increase in longevity. Life expectancy at birth in 2010 was more than seventy-eight years, a gain of eight years since 1960. [32] But as relative food prices dropped from the 1970s through the 1990s, more and more Americans gained unhealthy weight, that is, the added pounds were being progressively concentrated on already over-weight—especially obese—Americans. Since the 1960s, the increase in the average BMI of *obese* adult Americans has been double the average increase for all adult Americans.[33] And researchers will likely show that many heavy people might be living longer lives, but with greater medical impairments. One study found that a twenty-year-old man 2010 could expect to live a year longer than a twenty-year-old man in 1998. However, the extra year will come with more than an additional year with a disease and two years unable to function normally.[34] I suspect that in the near future researchers will be able to link the greater physical problems of longer life with weight gain.

The Great Recession and the Tightening of Americans' Belts

As might be expected, the Great Recession (which officially lasted from late 2007 to mid-2009), like other economic downturns, had an effect on people's spending—and consequently, their weight and health, according to survey reports in spring 2010, but the effects were varied and modest. One researcher "estimated that a one point drop in the percentage of the population employed reduces the prevalence of smoking, obesity, physical inactivity, and multiple health risks by 0.6, 0.4, 0.7, and 1.1 percent respectively. The decline in body weight is concentrated among the severely obese and groups with relatively high risk of early death (males, African Americans, and Hispanics).[35] All the while, public policy makers and com-mentators continued to lament the *growth* in obesity even as the rise in the country's obesity rate began to slow somewhat, and maybe to level off (which means that, if the sluggish recovery continues, any number of forecasts of growth in the country's weight problems may have to be updated).

In recent decades, gym memberships have grown dramatically in step with people's real incomes, but possibly 80 percent of the memberships before the Great Recession were never or rarely used, making them expendable during leaner times. As the Great Recession hit, gym memberships fell precipitously, as much as 25 percent, according to an American Heart Association survey of a thousand respondents. In addition, the survey found that 32 percent of the respondents had reduced their expenditures on preventive health care (e.g., stopped going to doctors and taking their medicine) and 42 percent had reduced their purchases of fruits and vegetables, all to stay within their declining budgets.[36]

Another survey found conflicting news on the good health effects of the Great Recession. First Command Financial Services surveyed a 1,000 adults ages twenty-four to seventy in early 2010 and found:

- 45 percent were eating more frequently at home and spending less on junk food;
- 13 percent were walking and biking more and driving less;
- 10 percent were boozing less, and
- 7 percent were growing more of their own food.

Ninety percent of the respondents said that their recession-induced frugality was making them healthier.[37] But as is so often the case in weight research, not all of the findings about the impact of economic downturns are positive. Analyzing a massive nationwide database from telephone interviews conducted between 1990 and 2007 (before the advent of the Great Recession), economists reported in late 2010 that a 1 percent increase in a state's relative unemployment rate correlates with a 2–8 percent reduction in the consumption of fruits and vegetables and with an increase in the consumption of snacks and fast-food fare, which suggests an economic downturn causes a substitution of unhealthy foods for healthy ones (more so for females than males and for the elderly than nonelderly).[38] In short, recessions in the economy can translate into people's expanded waistlines.

> The Great Recession put the country and world on a diet.

With all the evidence that food prices affect food consumption, we might anticipate the relatively rapid rise in the world prices of food staples (wheat, corn, and rice) during the last half of 2010—an astounding 26 percent—could be expected to have moderated food consumption and people's weight gain at least somewhat, and the more durable the food price increases, the more likely that the higher food prices will moderate weight gain around the world and in the United States.[39]

If food prices were all that were at work in Americans' weight problems, some manipulation of supply and demand would seem to fix the problem. But unfortunately, things aren't that simple. Other forces—some economic, some not—also seem to be at work, although at first glance it may seem a little odd that these hidden and unheralded forces have anything at all to do with weight gain.

The Real Price of Gasoline

Drivers now fret about the high and rising price of gasoline. They often forget (or are too young to know) that the real price of gasoline (measured in 2010 prices) trended irregularly downward from $3.63 a gallon in 1918 to a historical low of $1.37 in 1998, a real-price decline of close to two-thirds.[40] No wonder Americans began buying bigger and more powerful gas-guzzling SUVs during the 1980s and 1990s. Charles Courtemanche, an economist with Washington University in St. Louis, reasons that such a long-term decline in the real price of gas affects weight gain for two principal reasons:[41]

- First, with lower real gas prices, businesses substitute gasoline and other carbon-based energy sources for human power, and as a result, jobs become less strenuous, and workers exert less energy. Also, as gas prices fall, people drive more and walk less, increasing their "positive energy balances."[42] By the early 2000s, only 3 percent of Americans walked to work (down from 6 percent two decades earlier), while 87 percent drove to work and 5 percent took public transportation.[43]
- Second, according to Courtemanche, when gas is cheap, people go out to dinner more frequently as they have more real income to spend on car travel to restaurants and to pay for a meal once they get there. (Cheaper fuel also can marginally lower food costs since the cost of gasoline used in growing and distributing food will be lower.) Between the late 1970s and the 2000s, Americans more than doubled the percentage of their caloric intake from out-of-home sources.[44] And people tend to consume more calories in out-of-home meals than from home-cooked meals because out-of-home meal portions tend to be larger and to have more calories no matter the portion size than those prepared at home (although, as we will see, another study found that portion sizes decreased with a growth in the number of daily meals).[45]

Between 1979 and 2004, the obesity rate ballooned by more than 17 percentage points, and Courtemanche found that cheaper gasoline accounted for 13 percent of the obesity increase (or 2 of the 17 percentage-point increase). Of course, the converse is also true: A rise in the real price of gas can reduce, with a lag of years, weight gain and obesity rates. Courtemanche figures that over five years, a $1 increase in the price of gasoline can lower Americans' average weight by more than two pounds and the country's obesity rate by close to 15 percent. As the obesity rate declines, people's health can improve and result in 112,000 lives saved each year and a $17 billion savings in annual health-care costs, benefits that prompt Courtemanche (and others) to support an increase in gas taxes as a means of pushing up gas prices and pushing down the country's excess-weight problems.[46]

Between 1998 and 2010, the price of gasoline doubled, reaching a peak nation-wide average of more than $4 in the middle of 2008, only to return to an average of $2.73 in June 2010 (with average gas prices back up to $3.11 a gallon at the end of January 2011). Using Courtemanche's estimation methods, this gas price increase could have led to American adults' losing an average of three pounds (compared with what their weight would have been) if the 1998–2010 price increase were to hold for five years. Indeed, the increase in the gas price (along with the increase in food prices) during the 2000s can *help* explain why the obesity rate has been more or less level for men between 2003 and 2008 and for women between 2000 and 2008, although the obesity rate for men and women together was still rather high, at close to 34 percent in 2008, with some indication that the obesity rate was returning to its upward trend after 2008.[47] Keep in mind that in Courtemanche's economic way of thinking, gas prices and people's weight interact together, each affecting the other. For example, he surmises that transporting heavier people makes cars less fuel efficient on average (because big people have to buy bigger cars and all vehicles have to carry more excess weight), increasing the demand for gasoline and pushing up gas prices.[48] In turn, any weight-induced gas price increase can moderate people's weight gain and their demand for large, gas-guzzling cars (although the effect would very likely be small). Why did large SUVs start becoming so popular in the 1980s? Consider two forces at work, falling real gas prices and increasing waistlines. Economists have, indeed, found that people's

> The long-run reduction in the real price of gas in the twentieth century caused people to drive more and walk less— and to gain weight in the process.

weight does put upward pressure on gas prices: The more weight people carry, the higher gas prices tend to be, and the more expensive food tends to be. And both higher gas and food prices together tend to abate people's excessive weight that can, in turn, temper demand for large cars and gas.[49]

Obviously, the price of gasoline, per se, is hardly a direct cause of weight gain. People don't drink the stuff (for long)! But gasoline prices affect transportation costs, which indirectly affect weight gain. Other factors besides gas prices might lower transportation costs as well. The growth in the competitiveness of world automobile markets, with resulting quality and comfort improvements in cars that more than compensate for their higher sticker prices, can be expected to have some of the same effects on weight gain as a decrease in the real price of gas.[50]

As many countries, including the United States, have dropped import restrictions (tariffs and quotas on imports), world markets have become more competitive. Two international trade economists estimate that the U.S. tariff barrier fell from an average of 40 percent of the value of imports in the late 1940s to 4 percent in the early 2000s, resulting in substantial income gains for the rest of the world, as well as for the United States.[51] In addition, the telecommunication/computer revolution from the 1960s onward has enabled firms to produce their goods in lower cost venues and sell them with greater ease anywhere in the world.[52] As a consequence, international trade among all countries has risen dramatically, more so than domestic production. International trade for the United States rose from 6.5 percent of national output in 1960 to 20 percent in the early 2000s,[53] which affected the competitiveness of the U.S. domestic market, as well as the global economies, a force for growing prosperity and weight gain for many.

The documented growing economic freedoms of people across the globe is also a source of greater global competitiveness, higher real incomes, relatively lower real prices of foodstuffs—and a potential nontrivial (albeit difficult-to-measure) source of weight gain.[54] A growing number of "freedom researchers" have found a decisively positive relationship between the "economic freedom index" (devised by the Heritage Foundation) and real per capital income with growing real incomes enabling people to eat more and gain weight. Indeed, when I plotted the economic freedom index for all western industrialized countries against their obesity rates, I got a positive relationship, albeit a weak one.

Still, the more economic freedom people have gained, the fatter we all have become. Chinese have long been noted for being relatively trim people, but they are getting fatter (with the country's obesity rate doubling over just eleven years), and for good reason: They have been allowed to enjoy the fruits of a freer economy both at home and abroad.[55] And people around the world have become heavier because of the freeing of the Chinese economy. Freer markets have broken out everywhere, and the telecommunication-computer-transportation revolutions have made global markets all the more competitive and efficient, which have allowed people the luxury of eating more and gaining sometimes unwanted pounds.

A growth in global economic freedoms can contribute to people's weight gain.

Whatever the reason, when transportation costs are low, people tend to use more transportation rather than their own two feet, and consequently, they can gain weight. When real incomes increase and real food prices fall, more (not all) people eat more and gain more weight. Then, as more people's weight increases, so do the costs of health care and health insurance, which, of course, can have the effect of driving more Americans out of the health insurance market (with the growing ranks of the uninsured giving impetus to the national health-care law passed under the Obama Administration). But never forget that some of our modern weight problems are a product of our good fortune.

Pick a Restaurant, Any Restaurant

Casual observers who have lived through the last three or four decades know that fast-food restaurants have proliferated. Most sizable cities have rows of them in all quarters. Indeed, the count of fast-food and full-service restaurants per person in the United States increased by more than 60 percent during the last three decades of the last century.[56] In 2010, there were nearly twice as many fast-food restaurants in low-income/black neighborhoods than higher income white neighborhoods. By 2010, the typical American lived within a mile of at least one fast-food restaurant.[57] Of course, many Americans can walk out their front doors and find themselves in the midst of a flurry of signs for fast-food joints offering immediate (fatty and sugary) gratification prepared in various ways, all designed to appeal to our "fat genes."

Nowadays, Americans from coast to coast have greater access to a wide variety of out-of-home-cooked meals, and the choices are no longer just among burgers, fried chicken, and pizza. The menus are a United Nations of international cuisines—Thai, Chinese, Indian, Vietnamese, Korean, Mexican, Italian, Persian, you name it—as well as standard hamburger-and-potatoes American fare. More choices suggest a potential increase in real income, albeit unmeasured, but also greater food consumption, especially of fatty and high-calorie foods, as people seek to spend their added "real income" and strike new balances in consumption of everything—across ethnic gastronomical temptations, all the more palatable with added sugar, salt, MSG, and fat.[58] Americans need not go very far—or, more important, walk far—to get relatively more out-of-home meals, more frequently, that include a greater variety of foods with more calories and often served in larger portions.[59] Indeed, they have to walk nowhere. All they have to do is pull out their cell phones, look up local restaurants on Yelp (a smartphone app), and place a home-delivered order of virtually any food they can imagine (even upscale foods that may be no less a threat to weight gain than fast food).

In short, many people are getting heavier simply because they are adjusting very rationally to the ever changing relative prices of all things good and bad around them. In the process, they may be rationally accepting all the discomforts and possible lost days and years of life that might come with their weight gains. In addition, some people might even see themselves as more attractive to themselves and others because they have fuller faces. And some people may see themselves as looking unnaturally and unhealthily gaunt when they are in their healthy-weight range as defined by the CDC or others.

Not surprisingly, increased restaurant density has contributed to Americans' weight gain, and more so for women than for men, researchers have found.[60] From the late-1970s to the mid-1990s, a 1 percent increase in the density of restaurants led to a 0.09 percent increase in the average BMI of adult Americans.[61] More dramatically, U.S. Department of Agriculture researchers have linked increased restaurant density to more than two-thirds of the growth in people's average BMI and obesity rate in the 1980s and 1990s.[62]

Restaurant density may also explain some of the increase in the average daily calories that American adults consumed between the late-1970s and mid-1990s (268 more calories for men and 142 more calories for women) either through additional meals or snacking (not so much through larger meal portions).[63] Calories consumed per day from snacking nearly doubled from the late-1970s to the mid-1990s. During the same period, Americans were eating more actual "meals"—15 percent more, according to one study.[64] Although the calories consumed *per meal* went down by 7 percent for males and 14 percent for females, researchers reported that American adults consume an average of 4.4 meals a day, plus snacks (would you believe!).[65] The researchers conclude that such findings draw into question claims that Americans' weight gain in the 1980s and 1990s was because of increased portion sizes and/or more fattening meals bought at fast-food restaurants.[66]

But then we shouldn't be totally surprised if more meals are linked to fewer average calories per meal. When meals are difficult to come by but amply available intermittently, people will do what "Lucy" and "Eve" and their clans did, eat until they are stuffed, or close to it. But when a meal is readily available at any number of nearby restaurants, people need not consume as many calories at any meal to stave off hunger pains until the next one, which can be "just around the corner." And then why not push back from the breakfast or dinner table early when snacks are readily accessible in convenient, prepackaged, ready-to-eat form (just rip open the bag or carton)? The push-back can encourage its own greater consumption later in a snack, or unscheduled full meal.

All Restaurants Are Not Created Equal

Fast-food consumption grew in dollar value in the United States during the last three decades of the twentieth century by eighteen-fold (while the country's population grew by less than two-fifths).[67] Between the late-1970s and the mid-1990s, Americans increased their calorie-intake from fast-food restaurants from 3 percent of all calories consumed to 12 percent.[68] Out-of-home eating expanded as restaurants of various types sprang up everywhere, but restaurant density is not the same for all types of restaurants or across neighborhoods. Fast-food restaurant density has grown faster than that of full-service restaurants, especially in low-income neighborhoods where weight gain has been more pronounced than in higher income areas.[69] As noted, the density of fast-food restaurants in low-income and black neighborhoods can be close to twice what it is in white neighborhoods (partially because low-income and black neighborhoods are concentrated in densely populated urban centers whereas white neighborhoods are more likely to be in suburban areas where city planning codes or neighborhood covenants may ban restaurants of all kinds).[70]

Not surprisingly, research shows that the more dense fast-food restaurants are in communities (measured per capita or per mile), the greater the obesity rate for young and old alike, but especially for low-income and black neighborhoods.[71] One Canadian study found that for every added fast-food restaurant per 10,000 residents across Canada's major metropolitan areas, the community obesity rate goes up by 3 percent.[72]

> An increase in the density of fast-food restaurants contributes to people's weight gain.

Fast-food restaurants also tend to serve calorie-laden foods, most notably hamburgers smothered in sauces and French fries coated with cheese. Increasingly accessible fast-food led to a near tripling of the calories adults consumed in meals and snacks at these restaurants from the mid-1970s to the mid-1990s, (from an average of 60 calories per day per person to 155), according to one research team.[73] Shockingly, among children, the calories consumed at fast-food restaurants during the same period increased fivefold, according to other research.[74]

No wonder Americans struggle with weight problems. With such an *increase* in average daily calories consumed at fast-food restaurants, each American adult potentially could have gained an average of nearly ten pounds per year, assuming he or she did nothing to increase exercise or reduce calories consumed at home or elsewhere. But don't look to curbs in calories consumed at home during that time period. Although calories consumed in home-cooked meals went down by an average of 203 a day, calories consumed in snacks at home went up by a daily average of 308, for a net increase of 105 calories consumed at home each day, some of which can be expended on the maintenance of more weight.[75] That "modest" increase is enough to add nearly eleven pounds each year, the equivalent of a modest-size bowling ball, to every American adult each year (which likely means greater energy expenditure somewhere, partially in storing and keeping alive the extra fat)! What is amazing is that Americans don't now weigh far more on average than they actually do. Perhaps some of those gym memberships are working to good effect for many (but not all, of course).

The Minimum Wage and Weight Gain

Most economists oppose hikes in the federal minimum wage because in almost all of the more than 200 econometric studies undertaken over the last six decades, hikes in the minimum wage have been shown to have had negative effects on the employment of covered workers, as well as have undercut fringe benefits granted and increased the work demands imposed on covered workers.[76] Some economists have stressed that with the resulting unemployment of covered workers, crime rates go up (since crime is an industry not covered by minimum wages for obvious reasons). These arguments even led the editors at the liberal *New York Times* to advocate in 1987 "The Right Minimum Wage: $0.00" in an editorial by that exact title.[77]

Economists' diligence in showing the detrimental effects of increasing the minimum wage clearly has impacted policy, beginning in the late 1960s. Before then, the real minimum wage (in 2010 dollars) rose steadily upward from its initial level of $3.92 in 1936 (when the first minimum-wage law was signed into law), increasing two and a half times by1968. But then the real minimum wage began to fall irregularly over the following four decades or so, dropping from an all-time high in 1968 of $9.88 an hour (again, in 2010 prices) to $5.83 in 2006 – a decline of 41 percent (before the nominal federal minimum wage was hiked in 2007 for the first time in a decade).

What does the track record of the real minimum wage have to do with Americans' weight gain? More than you might think. The success of minimum-wage opponents likely aggravated, albeit indirectly and modestly, the nation's weight problems in the 1970s, 1980s, and 1990s in two ways.

First, a lower real minimum wage means many menial workers earn less and may have had to shift from eating higher quality, healthier, and higher-priced foods (vegetables and lean meat bought in grocery stores and cooked at home) to lower quality, less healthy, and lower-priced fast foods (hamburgers and fries, again). Such a shift could easily have increased the calorie intake of many minimum-wage workers, especially fast-food workers who grew in number and as a percentage of the working population with the spread of fast-food restaurants. Many fast-food workers get discounts on their meals or can just take what they like when they like. Lower income households tend to eat less healthy foods, but lower income people improve the quality of their diets as their income rises, research shows.[78] But the long-term decrease in real wages can have less effect on the weight of low-income Americans (including minimum-wage workers) than on higher-income groups.

This is because low-income groups spend very little of their tight food budgets on food outside of their homes—less than $250 a year for families of four, as reported in the mid-1990s.[79] Many high-income earners often spend that much in a single family meal at a nice restaurant.

The second way that a lower real minimum wage could have affected weight gain is more indirect. Labor makes up as much as a third of fast-food restaurants' total costs of operations, which means that the drop in the real minimum wage significantly lowered the labor costs for many fast-food restaurants (those that hire a significant number of minimum-wage workers).[80] With cheaper labor costs, fast-food restaurants could slash the real price of their calorie-rich menu items (or increase the calories without a price increase), driving up the demand for fast foods and encouraging a greater number of fast-food restaurants to spring up.

Indeed, with the drop in the real minimum wage many fast-food chains could have had all the more reason to divide their assembly-line food service into repetitive routine tasks that could be handled by ever-more menial workers (those who can only handle relatively simple tasks but are willing to work for the ever-falling real minimum wage). In turn, fast-food restaurants could enjoy a cost advantage leading to their even greater density in communities, especially urban areas and doubly especially, low-income and minority neighborhoods where location restrictions are relatively more relaxed and land prices lower.

In fact, between 1984 and 2006, a $1 drop in the real minimum wage gave rise to an increase of 0.06 in the average BMI of American adults (when the BMI averaged 25.8 for all American adults), researchers report. The full decrease in the real minimum wage accounted for 10 percent of the change in the BMI between 1970 and 2006 (during which time the average BMI rose from 25 to 25.8). The causal link shows up across income classes and for both sexes, but the weight-gain effect of the real decline in the minimum wage is greatest for the most obese Americans.[81]

Again, low-wage workers were not alone in feeling the weight-gain effects of a diminishing real minimum wage. Higher income Americans have increasingly patronized the dense and various restaurants, fast-food and otherwise, as real prices of calories on their menus have fallen along with reduced labor costs and technological improvements in fast-food assembly lines. Of course, the flood of legal and illegal immigrants into the United States has enabled many restaurants (not all by any stretch) to prosper, and grow their customers ever fatter, as some restaurants have been able to pay below the established minimum wage, knowing that illegal immigrants have good reasons not to report their employers for labor-law violations.

Weight gain and obesity can, in turn, drive up health-care and health insurance costs, if research is to be believed. As the decline in the real minimum wage has negatively affected American's weight and health, it also has contributed to a rise in health-related costs, even causing some Americans to remain uninsured, a point we have made before and will return to repeatedly. One survey of 2,500 heart attack victims found that a third of the victims had eaten at least once a week at fast-food restaurants in the months before their heart attacks (with the potential of their fast-food habits increasing the likelihood of their having heart attacks), but a fifth of the victims were back to eating at fast-food restaurants six months after their heart attacks.[82]

Reversing the argument, we can surmise that the increase in the nominal federal minimum wage from $5.15 an hour (where it had been stuck since 1997) to $5.85 an hour in 2007 and then in two more steps to $7.25 an hour in mid-2009 (a 41 percent real increase over the two-year period) may be expected to lead to relatively higher fast-food prices, some minor (yet-to-be-determined) average weight loss (or some slowing in Americans' weight gain), and possibly a decrease in health-care and health insurance costs (through, for example, fewer heart attacks)—with the reduction in medical costs possibly increasing the rolls of the insured (and, hence, a weakening of the case for national health insurance).[83] And higher fast-food prices have been linked to lower body weight through their negative impact on the consumption of fast foods and their positive impact on the consumption of fruits and vegetables.[84] If research on the link between fast-food dining and heart attacks is telling, then the series of jumps in the federal minimum wage enacted in 2007 should give rise to higher relative prices of fast-food meals, a reduction in their consumption, and (with a time lapse) to fewer heart attacks.

Women's Place Beyond the Kitchen

Women have always worked, but until recent decades, their workplace opportunities outside the home and farm and in business (especially at professional levels) have been limited with their workplace wages significantly lower than men's, leaving women to be responsible for home-cooked meals and other household and child-rearing tasks. But mother at home minding the children and stirring the pot is largely a scene from the now distant past. With labor-saving home appliances simplifying housework and with antidiscrimination laws (marginally) affecting employment, women's participation in the workplace has steadily grown from 34 percent in 1950 to 43 percent in 1971 to more than 60 percent today.[85] More women are now earning college degrees and using them to enter the job market. Before 1980, men earned a majority of college degrees, at which point the earned degrees were evenly split between men and women. But in 2010, women earned close to 60 percent of all college degrees, prompting talk of a newfound "gender gap" and a shortage of males (and dates for women students) on campuses, which has often resulted in favoritism toward male applicants to obtain a gender balance in enrollment.[86]

Working outside the home has become increasingly necessary for women, given the growing laxity of divorce laws, the increase in divorce, and, subsequently, the risk of relying on a husband's support through the child-bearing and rearing years. Working outside the home has become relatively more profitable for women, too. The annual median earnings of women working at least thirty-five hours a week has risen from close to 60 percent of men's annual median earnings in 1960 to 77 percent in 2008 (according to the way in which the U.S Census Bureau computes the gender wage gap, although the actual wage gap remains a matter of contention among economists).[87]

If Mom can earn a progressively more competitive wage at the office (or at the plant), her time in the kitchen can progressively become a costly (even losing) proposition as the cost of a home-cooked meal progressively rises. Instead of the chicken stewed all day on the stovetop, the family understandably opts more and more frequently for prepackaged frozen chicken fingers or chicken dinners at the nearby restaurant. Time and money may be saved, but not calories, as processed and prepackaged foods as well as restaurant menus tend to be more calorie-rich than home-produced meals without processed ingredients. In one study of 990 children ages eight to twelve, researchers found a positive relationship between the time children's mothers spent at work and children's weight and BMI. For every five months mothers worked, their children gained on average one pound beyond the weight gain of the children's classmates whose mothers did not work. The children's weight gain attributable to their mothers working was most pronounced in the fifth and sixth grades.[88] The early childhood weight gain attributable to mothers working can, of course, lead to eating habits that, in turn, lead to continued weight gain later in life.

But sending Mom home to cook isn't the overarching solution to America's weight problems you might think it would be, as the effect of women's higher relative wages explains no more than 10 percent of the rise in obesity in the late twentieth century, according to one set of obesity researchers (at least according to the study just covered, plus one other study completed in the early 1990s).[89] This suggests that the major causes of people's weight gain must lie elsewhere, not so much in "women's workforce liberation."[90]

Breastfeeding and Weight Gain

There may be a more direct way in which women's growing employment outside the home is affecting the country's weight problems, especially for infants and children—the prevalence of bottle-feeding over breastfeeding. In 2010, three-fourths of mothers of newborns start out breastfeeding, with only 43 percent of mothers breastfeeding after six months at which time only 13 percent of babies are exclusively breastfed. The breasting rates for African-American mothers are much lower.[91]

Breastfeeding, which provides partial protection from adolescent and adult obesity,[92] and many other health benefits,[93] is obviously more difficult for women who work and place their children in child care centers or even with family members. Even if mothers begin feeding babies at the breast, many supplant breastfeeding for the convenience of bottle-feeding once they return to work, which is often within several months (if not a week or two) after delivery.

Not only can milk formula be more calorie rich than breast milk, bottle-fed infants can be given more milk than they would receive from the breast. Physiology of mother and baby limits breast milk—even when a mother pumps and stores her breast milk for later use—while bottle milk is limited only by the family budget and the price of formula.[94] Except in bygone eras when wet nurses were not uncommon and today when a mother goes to the trouble to pump her own milk, only the child's mother can feed a breastfed baby. But the convenience of bottles and the plentitude of infant formula allows anyone—relative, home visitors, caregivers—to use a bottle to feed or comfort (and fatten) a crying baby.

> People's weight gain can be partially attributed to the emergence of women's liberation during the last half of the twentieth century.

In addition, there is a good evolutionary reason why women tend to gain weight during pregnancy: They can draw down their stored fat as they produce breast milk. When babies are bottle fed, mothers no longer have the imposed diet that breastfeeding provides. Consequently, mothers, who got used to consuming more calories during pregnancy, may not lose the weight they gained and may even pack on extra pounds after delivery.

Also, out-of-home care not only can, but does, affect a young child's weight gain, or so researchers tell us. The earlier infants are placed in child care (whether in child care centers or with relatives) and the more hours the child spends in out-of-home placement, especially child care centers, the heavier they are at ages one and three.[95] In Washington State, from the period 1990 to 2002, the proportion of children in licensed child care centers more than doubled, with the child care for children of low-income parents being subsidized by the state in order to allow parents, mainly mothers, to work.[96]

Babies typically lose some weight a few days after birth, but bottle-fed babies tend to lose less weight and to regain the lost weight sooner than breastfed babies.[97] Bottle-fed babies also tend to begin eating solid foods earlier than breastfed infants and toddlers, which potentially can lead to greater weight gain—and then heavier children and heavier adults.[98] At twelve months of life, bottle-fed babies and toddlers are heavier than those who are breastfed, research shows, by between 1.3 and 1.4 pounds (which equals 5–8 percent more weight for year-old babies in the "healthy weight range" of seventeen to twenty-six pounds), with no difference in height.[99] Bottle-fed babies are heavier still at three years of age.[100]

Breastfeeding offers not only some protection against excessive weight gain, but also added health benefits and the accompanying savings in health care costs later in life. If 75 percent of mothers breastfed while in the hospital and 50 percent thereafter, as the U.S. Surgeon General recommends, the health-care costs for infants associated with only three infant diseases (otitis media, gastroenteritis, and necrotizing enterocolitis) would have been $3.6 billion lower in 2001 (more than $4.4 billion in 2010 dollars), according to estimates.[101] But that is the least of the health-care cost savings linked to healthier weight gain that could come from more prevalent breastfeeding.

The popularity of breastfeeding has gone through a major cycle between the 1940s and today, no doubt buffeted by changes in cultural attitudes, medical

Bottle-fed babies tend to gain more weight that breastfed babies, and the more hours babies spend in child care the heavier they become.

research, levels of support for breastfeeding mothers, and vigorous advertising campaigns from formula companies. In the late 1940s, almost all newborns were breastfed, but with the refinement of infant formula, those numbers were cut in half by 1956 and in half again by 1967, when only 25 percent of mothers breastfed their infants at all. In 1982, breastfeeding was on the rise again, with 62 percent of mothers breastfeeding their infants. In 1998, 62 percent of mothers breastfed their infants while in the hospital,[102] and more recent surveys showed, as noted, 75 percent of newborns were breastfed in 2010 but only 66.3 percent in 2003.[103]

Although breastfeeding of infants, at least initially, has risen in recent decades, the duration of breastfeeding may be short-lived once mother and baby are home following ever-more-brief birthing stays in hospitals and especially after the mother returns to work. As noted, only slightly more than four in ten mothers continue to breast feed six months after the births of their babies and nine out of ten are then relying to some degree on formula milk (although the percentage of mothers still breastfeeding at six months in 2010 was up nearly half from what it was in 1998). Formula may actually prevail over breast milk as the food of choice in babies' first years of life. The link between women's opportunities in the workforce and fewer babies receiving the health benefits of breastfeeding may also apply in another restricted sense: Had fewer women entered the workforce during the last forty or fifty years, or had workplaces become more "breastfeeding friendly," breastfeeding could very well have grown by more than it did, affording even more children protection against obesity.

Of course, sending Mom home from the office to breastfeed is no more a solution to America's weight problems than sending her home to cook dinner. Women's contribution to their households' economic well-being and the greater economy is clear. Yet bottle-feeding has had some influence on the population's weight gain, and we can see the link between women in the workforce and an increase in bottle-fed children who may be at risk of becoming obese adults (who then confront an array of health problems that can lead to depression, which can have feedback loops on weight gain, as we will see in the next chapter). No one can say exactly how much weight Americans may have added because of the growth in the workforce participation of women during the last fifty years. What we can do is speculate that maternity leave, which allows women to take leave from their jobs to care for their newborns, and greater overall support for breastfeeding can have important economic advantages: an increase in the prevalence and duration of breastfeeding and reduction in future health-care and health insurance costs, which can increase the number of people with health insurance, I remind you.

But then, it might also have been the case that had the divorce rate not risen so dramatically from the 1960s through the early 1980s (because of cultural and legal considerations), there might well have been more breastfeeding, less weight gain by infants over the past few decades—and fewer obese adults today.

Fat Mamas, Fat Babies

Even before birth, economic forces are very likely affecting people's weight. Heavier women give birth to heavier newborns. No one should be surprised if the weight of pregnant women correlates strongly with their babies' weight at birth.[104] And we should also not be surprised that the more weight women gain during pregnancy, the greater the weight of their newborns. A duo of health economists from Columbia University and Children's Hospital Boston have studied these issues by looking at the data for more than a half million pregnant women who gave birth to more than a million babies between the start of 1999 and the end of 2003.[105] Their central finding is intuitively plausible, "a consistent association between pregnancy weight gain and birth weight."[106] Indeed, they found that women who gained fifty-three or more pounds during full-term pregnancies doubled the chance of their babies' weighing more than nine pounds at birth over women who gained only eighteen to twenty-two pounds.

> Heavy pregnant women tend to give births to heavy newborns who tend to become heavy children, teenagers, and adults.

However, the increase in babies' weight relative to the weight gain of their mothers seems modest. The researchers found that for each 2.2 pounds expectant mothers gained during full-term pregnancies, their newborns gained on average one-fourth of an ounce. This means that women who gained eighty pounds during pregnancy (no longer a rare occurrence) would likely give birth to babies that weigh on average about seven ounces more than the babies of women who gained twenty pounds during pregnancy. But those seven ounces represent a 6 percent weight gain for a seven-pound baby.

You might think that a baby's weight is potentially and fully genetic based—dependent upon genes received from her parents. To control for the influence of genetics, the researchers simply assessed the weights of a sequence of babies from the same mothers, with their central conclusion undisturbed: the greater the weight gain of mothers during different pregnancies, the greater the weight of their babies.[107] Moreover, the heavier the newborns, the heavier are the children at age nine, and the more risk factors they have for heart disease and immune system disorders.[108]

These findings suggest a cyclical process that's making us fatter. Women are getting fatter before they get pregnant, and for all the economic reasons enumerated. The heavier women gain progressively more weight during pregnancy because of these same economic forces at work, and then give birth to even heavier babies. The heavier babies complete the "fat cycle" by becoming heavier children, teenagers, and adults, and the cycle repeats and escalates.

Quit Smoking, Gain Weight

Smokers who seek to kick the habit face a duel challenge: overcoming nicotine addiction and not gaining weight in the process. Nicotine dulls the senses of smell and taste, suppressing appetite and inhibiting weight gain. Smoking increases the body's metabolism, burning additional calories (as much as 200 calories a day for heavy smokers), and reducing calories stored as fat. Smokers who quit often gain five to ten pounds mainly because their appetites improve and metabolisms slow.[109] As smoking becomes less popular and more expensive, through cigarette taxes, weight gain can be expected to follow.

The law of demand applies to cigarettes as well as all other products, even addictive ones: When the price goes up, smokers curb their habits, at least somewhat, and some even quit.[110] Although smokers are not likely to be highly responsive to price increases in cigarettes, they can be expected to respond somewhat (or else what's the point of antismoking campaigns and higher cigarette taxes?).

Moreover, cigarette price increases can deter many prospective buyers from ever taking their first puffs, and the prospect of progressively higher future cigarette taxes and ever tightening restrictions on smoking can add to the curb in current and future smoking. How much smoking is reduced depends on just how high the *full* price of cigarettes goes, or is expected to go.

During the last decades, several forces—not just rising prices for packs of cigarettes—have been driving up the *full price* of smoking.

- First, average state taxes on a pack of cigarettes have risen dramatically, more than three-fold at the state level just between 2002 and 2009. Federal taxes on cigarettes also more than doubled in 2009, rising to more than $1 per pack,[111] and cigarette taxes, as noted, have been shown to curb smoking through raising the price of smoking.[112] Most smokers can now reasonably anticipate states' trying to balance their budgets in the future off of their puffs (smokers have become the social pariahs of our age, partially because their political influence declined with their numbers).
- Second, since the 1960s, pervasive information campaigns have warned people of the health risks that go with smoking. Practically everyone now knows smoking increases the risk of lung cancer, respiratory disease, and early death (with average longevity of smokers cut by as many as eight to ten years).[113] These more widely recognized *risk costs* of smoking have increased the full price of lighting up.
- Third, information campaigns have stigmatized smoking as being an indulgence that only stupid people do, which has increased the *social stigma*—translated, *cost*—of smoking.
- Fourth, smoking has been gradually banned across states in restaurants, workplaces, and other public places (even outside of buildings close to doorways or on beaches). The difficulty in finding a convenient, comfortable place to smoke further increases the full cost of smoking.

- Smoking restrictions over time have become only tighter and taxes only higher, which can lead many smokers to reasonably expect these curbs and bans to become ever more troublesome into the future. In some states people soon might not be able to smoke legally in their own homes or cars, if children are near, because of the widely publicized and nontrivial health effects of second-hand smoke. In 2010, Santa Monica, California, banned smoking within the city limits in all open-air public places, including beaches, playgrounds, and outdoor patios of restaurants.[114]
- Finally, we have noted how tobacco companies have had an incentive to hold their cigarette prices down to hook new buyers whom they could tap for added sales and revenues often for their lifetimes. As the government shows signs of continuing to raise cigarette taxes and to tighten smoking restrictions, tobacco companies can reason that they have less reason to suppress their prices, or, rather, they have a stronger incentive to increase prices to tap revenues from today's addicted smokers as best they can. In other words, higher cigarette taxes can boost cigarette prices by more than the imposed taxes (which is one reason economists found tobacco company prices and profits were rising in the 1980s and early 1990s at the same time their stock prices were falling).[115]

Any expectation of further increases in the full cost of smoking will cause some smokers to quit today, and other nonsmokers to suppress any urge to start. The long-term demand for smokes can be more responsive to price changes than might be expected of an addictive good, which means that higher cigarette taxes imposed today might have a "double whammy" effect on weight gain: Smokers who quit are likely to gain weight in the near term and so are nonsmokers who never experience the appetite suppression of nicotine in the first place. People who never take up smoking will tend to have a higher trajectory of weight gain than would have been the case had they picked up the habit.

As the full price of smoking has increased substantially during the past forty years, the prevalence of smoking in the United States has been cut in half. In 1965, about 40 percent of American adults smoked. In 2007, fewer than 20 percent smoked, which, if the research is to be accepted, surely led to some weight gain for Americans.[116] Paradoxically, the campaign against the "smoking epidemic" of the 1960s and before has been partially responsible for the "obesity epidemic" of the last third of the twentieth century. The reduction in health-care costs and deaths from smoking has been traded, albeit partially, for a rise in health-care costs and deaths from excess weight. In short, some uncountable number of deaths from fat over past decades can literally be laid at the feet of the success of the antismoking campaigns.

> The antismoking campaign of the past half century contributed to many people's weight gain. The count of people dying from obesity has gone up in part because the count of people dying from smoking has gone down.

No one to my knowledge (at this writing) has figured out whether health-care costs and deaths have, on balance, gone up, gone down, or remained the same from the crosscurrents of the smoking and obesity epidemics of five or more decades. What we do know is that health-care costs and deaths from obesity have been on the rise, and deaths from fat is now the leading cause of preventable deaths among Americans (at least the way obesity experts count, or rather "guesstimate," preventable deaths from weight, a subject of some controversy, as noted in Chap. 2).

Medical Technology and Weight Gain

Improved medical technologies for dealing with the health consequences of weight gain can be partially responsible for people's weight growth precisely because they reduce the future health costs of overeating. Two economists have found that better treatments for diabetes, which is a nontrivial health problem associated with, if not caused in part by, excess weight, have led to increases in people's BMIs.[117] Again, the law of demand applies to eating—if the *full* cost of overeating is the focus of analysis. If the cost is lowered, either currently or prospectively, people will naturally gravitate (at the margin) toward eating more.

> Many medical advances that ease the long-term pain of weight gain can encourage weight gain.

As odd as it may seem, new and improved medical treatments for problems associated with excess weight—including heart disease—may actually be found in future research to aggravate these weight-related health-care problems as economists would predict. Similarly, new and more effective diets, because of their implied reduction in the *full* price of overeating (extended into the future), will likely one day give rise to weight gain, at least for some groups of people. How can that be? Again the law of demand will be at work. The development of laser removal of tattoos has been a force behind the rise in the popularity of tattoos, because the laser technology lowers the lifelong commitment to tattoos. The development of safer cars has contributed to more unsafe driving, as measured in one study by the increased fatalities among pedestrians.[118] The imposition of state laws requiring children and teenagers to wear helmets when riding their bikes has had the intended effect of reducing fatalities from bike riding, but such laws have also had the unintended effect of reducing kids' bike riding, which could have increased risk taking by kids when they bike and could be a contributing factor in the weight gain of youth.[119] Similarly, many people can be expected to take greater chances with overeating knowing that their weight problems can be relieved more readily and with less pain with the new and improved treatments and diets.

Technological Advancements: Plentiful Food in No Time

All these sundry forces—decreasing real food prices, rising incomes, women's lib, smoking cessation, and the like—have contributed in some way to Americans' growing waistlines.[120] But these contributions are small when compared with what could be a major culprit—technology. What's really changed in the way Americans eat is the ease and speed of food consumption—often accomplished in no time at all.

Economists David Cutler, Edward Glaeser, and Jesse Shapiro stress that the effects of economic forces like the real minimum wage, gas prices, and excise taxes are relatively small, individually explaining no more than low double-digit portions of the growth in America's excess weight and obesity rate since the 1970s. These researchers have found:

- Portion sizes at meals did not change very much in the 1980s and 1990s (indeed, calories consumed in home-cooked dinners likely declined). The growth in calories consumed came from more meals, an average of 4.4 meals a day at the turn of the twenty-first century, and from more snacks taken between meals.
- People did increase their time spent watching television (an additional twenty-two minutes per day) during the last quarter of the last century, but that is a little over half the increase during the previous decade, 1965–1975 (forty minutes per day), which suggests that weight gain might have been greater in the 1960s than in the 1980s, which was not the case.
- The percentage of workers in "highly active" jobs did fall, but only by 3 percentage points (from 45 to 42 percent of the labor force in the 1980s), hardly enough to account for the pervasive weight gain, especially since gym memberships and exercise equipment purchases were growing as people took on more sedentary jobs.

Yet, all the while, excess weight and obesity rates jumped upward.

Food price declines and household income inclines also do not seem to be the most significant cause for increased weight. Cutler, Glaeser, and Shapiro acknowledge that income gains can cause weight gain, but income and weight (and weight gain) over the last several decades appear to be inversely related. Low-income groups have gained weight in spite of no or limited real income increases during the last quarter of the twentieth century, and low-income groups have gained more weight than high-income groups. During the last several decades of the twentieth century, the relative price decline for food has been modest at best, and researchers have had a hard time finding a significant decline in the prices of unhealthful foods relative to the prices of healthful foods, as noted (aside from a ten-year stretch between the late 1980s and the mid-1990s).

What's to explain, then, all the weight gain in recent decades? What's been missed?

Cutler, Glaeser, and Shapiro "propose a new theory of increased obesity that has as its premise reductions in the time cost of food. This [time–cost reduction] has allowed more frequent food consumption of greater variety, and thus higher weights."[121] Dramatic technological advances in manufactured foods during the last half century have overcome critical problems in producing ready-to-eat and almost-ready-to-eat foods for home meals and, more importantly, in producing out-of-home meals. Among these advances are:

- Controlling the atmosphere in plants,
- Preventing spoilage from microorganisms, and
- Preserving flavor and moisture while foods are distributed and then held in pantries and refrigerators until needed.[122]

These and other advances have shifted food production from individual homes to manufacturing plants with all their benefits of specialization of labor and economies of scale, lowering the combined time cost of food preparation, all the while increasing the variety and quality of meals served in homes and restaurants—or in city parks, for that matter. And as time costs decrease, we eat more—it simply takes little to no time to fix a meal or snack.

Grandma's devices to peel, core, cut, mash and otherwise prepare foods for cooking are all but foreign to today's home kitchen, replaced with the one necessity—a microwave oven. Developed in the 1940s, the microwave has spread throughout homes and restaurants since the 1970s, reducing snack and full meal preparation to a matter of minutes. Many foods are specially manufactured and packaged so they can be stored in the freezer and zapped in the microwave—no preparation needed.

Ease of preparation can drive our food preferences and choices. For example, French fries were not widely consumed in the home or even in restaurants before the 1950s, Cutler, Glaeser, and Shapiro point out, because making them was too labor intensive. Potatoes were largely eaten baked or mashed. But with the development of potato processing equipment in plants (where potatoes can be washed, peeled, cut into fries, and even partially or fully cooked at the rate of billions per day), the full price of French fries dropped precipitously, which is a good reason they are so much more widely consumed today (and constituted nearly half of the vegetables children in the United States ate by the 1990s[123]).

At least some of people's weight gain can be chalked up to equipment improvements in processing plants and food distribution systems, and not just to the greater efficiency in preparing the fatty fast-food fare at McDonalds and other restaurants and then eating the food on the fly (with an added reduction in the time cost of eating the fast food). But there, too, technological advancements in transportation have sped the delivery of partially and fully processed foods from tractor-trailer truck to restaurant to the stomachs of a growing (and fattening) customer base. And need we forget that insulation technology has made home-delivered pizzas (and fried chicken and moo goo gai pan) a multibillion-dollar industry, seductively accessible via smart phones with which a person may order his fondest (fatty) delights with a few keystrokes. Want a pizza or a Thai noodle bowl at your office desk or next to you on the couch, touch, again, the Yelp icon on your iPhone and then hit send! A mountain of calories will soon be on your doorstep, delivered with a smile.

Farm technology has obviously improved between the early 1970s and early 2000s, a span when American farmers increased their total output enough to provide every American with an additional 500 calories per day, and they accomplished that feat with far fewer farmers and less land under cultivation.[124] Competition among farmers, no doubt, depressed the price of farm products, which has contributed to food processing and distribution industries' ability to provide consumers with more calories in greater variety and at lower prices.

Remember: We are talking about the *full* price (including the value of food preparation time) of food here. Although the actual price (as stated on the tag or label) a consumer may have paid for many foods may have risen during the past three or more decades, the *full* price dropped even as quality and convenience increased. And for these reasons, the decline in the full price of food is far greater than is suggested by price index measures. Although both the CPI and food price indices rose by about twenty-fold between 1913 and 2010, the Cutler/Glaeser/Shapiro line of argument suggests that the *full* food price index (if it could be constructed with reasonable accuracy, which it cannot be) probably increased far less than the CPI-less food. In short, the *relative full* price of food was, in all probability, much lower in 2010 than in 1913.

Technology is the main culprit in the overweight and obesity problem for Americans, as well as people around the world, and Cutler, Glaeser, and Shapiro point to an array of evidence to support of this claim:

- Quick, easy, and tasty snacks have made Americans fatter because snacks—chips and dip and ice cream—require little to no time to prepare and eat. Foods with extensive time costs in home preparation are not a significant source of people's greater calorie intake.

- Farmers' foodstuffs spend more time in food processing plants on their way from field to market in order to reduce the time cost of food consumption. In turn, as food processing has increased, so has our food consumption.

> People's weight gain can be partially attributed to technological advancements that have reduced meal and snack preparation time.

The larger the amount of food processing across food categories, the greater the increase in consumption between 1970 and 1999.[125] Consequently, the farmers' share of food revenues during this time has dropped dramatically across many product categories. Even in vegetables and fruits, the share of consumer expenditures at grocery stores going to farmers declined from 34 and 33 percent, respectively, in 1982 to 19 and 20 percent in 2004.[126] Branded foods (chips, for example) tend to be more heavily prepared than unbranded foods (broccoli). The degree of branding is highly correlated with greater calories, and consumption of branded foods has grown relatively to unbranded foods. Some of the increase in calories consumed can be chalked up to incentives food preparation firms have to brand their foods and capture their preparation and branding costs.[127] Put another way, had marketers not found ways to improve the efficiency of the branding of foods, especially processed foods, we Americans could be a little less heavy.

- Low-income consumers have reaped the greatest time–cost savings from prepared and highly processed food because they have always had to spend more time preparing their own meals. High-income groups eat a greater percentage of their meals out, fully prepared, than low-income groups. Economic thinking tells us that the group benefitting the most from the reduced time costs of high-calorie processed foods will be the group that consumes more of these foods, and as a result, will gain the most weight. This is exactly the pattern of food consumption that Cutler, Glaeser, and Shapiro (and any number of other obesity researchers) have found. Also, since women do most of the cooking of home-produced meals, they benefit more from the time–cost savings in prepared foods than men, which should be expected to show up in women's relatively greater weight gain. Again, this is what Cutler, Glaeser, and Shapiro (and others) have found to have been the case.[128]

- Government intervention in food production can drive up food costs, and drive down weight gain and obesity. In fact, Cutler, Glaeser, and Shapiro found that the greater a country's food price controls (holding up food prices) and the tighter government food regulations, the higher the food prices and the lower the growth in obesity rates.[129] Government price controls and quality and safety regulations can increase the cost of food production and impair the development and implementation of technological advances in large-scale plant-based food preparation.[130] In turn, some of the time savings in food preparation (and the lower full price of food) can be lost. The deregulation movement that began with the Reagan Administration in the 1980s and continued during the following two administrations, could be an unsuspected, albeit indirect, cause of the America's weight problems. It follows that if President Barack Obama remains true to his goal to reassert government controls over the economy, with more intensive regulation of the food industry, the real prices of foods can move upward and marginally affect the nation's excess weight and the obesity rates, which is to say that a government regime of greater food regulation can have a greater impact on the country's weight than a fitness campaign (depending on how stringent the food regulations are).

> Government food regulation can drive up the relative price of food and drive down people's weight.

- Cutler, Glaeser, and Shapiro's investigation of the link between the price of a McDonald's Big Mac and a country's obesity rate clearly focuses the effect government policies can have on weight gain. They found that countries with the highest priced Big Macs—as a result of various government imposed market restrictions (food laws, import tariffs, special food taxes, and land-use controls restricting restaurant locations)—had the lowest obesity rates.

- Of course, it's a good bet that any environmental regulations that disproportionately affect agriculture and food processing (e.g., restrictions on chemical runoffs from fields and subsidies for ethanol production) can put downward pressures on weight gain, according to this line of argument and supporting evidence. Proponents of curbs on global warming also can be unwitting advocates of curbs on global obesity, because tighter restrictions on, for example, CO_2 emissions can raise the price of gasoline and many food prices (especially meats, since release of methane gas by cattle is a major greenhouse gas); higher prices for both gas and food can work to curb people's appetites for out-of-home, prepackaged and processed foods and snacks that tend to be relatively high in calories. And if their efforts prevent a rise in global temperatures, they will also be preventing increases in the growing seasons (especially in northern regions of the world) and greater food production.

Concluding Comments

The lesson learned: The law of demand rules in televisions and cars—and in food! An array of statistical studies consistently has found that decreases in the price of food encourages eating. Ditto for calories and ditto for pounds of weight. If the price of added weight goes down, many people will "buy" more pounds and gain more weight. The reverse statements are just as solid propositions about human behavior.

When the *full* price of any product is considered—especially food—the law of demand is all the more on full display. The *full* price of food includes a high time–cost component that has radically reduced the time we need to invest in gathering and preparing food, and thus, economic principles predict that we will buy more food (and eat more calories) even when the *price tags* on food remain constant or move upward in lock-step with the prices of other goods. And for more than a century, we have been doing exactly that.

People have been gaining weight because calories are now, more than ever, cheaper to come by, but not so much by lower price tags but lower *full* prices. People simply don't have to go very far to gather food by the cart load or the take-out-bag load.

And do remember our evolutionary past and our hardwired inclinations to eat when we can and as much as we can. As Southern Methodist University economist Dwight Lee, my good friend and coauthor on other books, quipped when we were bantering about themes in the fat literature, "Yes, thousands of years ago when our ancestors took days and weeks to slay a wildebeest on the plains of Africa, they had a successful hunt. Today, we have a successful 'hunt' every time we push open the doors of a KFC or pass a vending machine."

People can now multitask, eating while driving and working as never before. And they can spend little to no time preparing their meals. Place an order at the drive-up window and go. Pop open a bag of French fries, throw them in the microwave for a couple of minutes, and munch away. Never in the history of humankind has gaining weight cost so little and taken so little time. Getting fat centuries ago was hard work; now it's child's play—and practically irresistible. Armed with the law of demand, we can range widely for unsuspecting explanations for weight gain—from the decline in the real minimum wage and the real price of gas that boosted restaurant density and consumption of high-calorie fast-food meals to the tectonically rapid shift from home-based food production to the large-scale economies operating in food processing plants, restaurants, and restaurant chains that deliver increasing varieties of calorie-packed foods in a matter of minutes to the typical American.

Applying the law of demand to the food industry, we can venture a variety of deductions. For example, we can deduce that the management control systems that McDonalds and other fast-food chains, as well as Walmart and Costco, have refined to improve the quality and efficiency of meal production can be partially blamed for people's weight gain. As large scale food distributors have instituted management-control efficiencies that have shown up in greater quality and variety of foods and as those distributors have become ruthless negotiators for lower prices for their customers, they have reduced the relative full price of foods and increased consumption.

Of course, even as efficiency improvements in food production and delivery play a role in people's weight gain, they also explain some of the growth in people's weight-related health problems and the corresponding dramatic rise in medical and health insurance costs that very likely have priced many people out of the health insurance market.

Why in 2010 were there nearly fifty million Americans without health insurance? Consider as a partial cause the workings of the law of demand, which has meant that people have done what comes more or less "naturally": they have gained weight as the relative *full* price of various foods has fallen and the opportunities to eat have increased. They have increased their medical costs, which has fed into higher health insurance premiums, which have induced many Americans onto the rolls of the uninsured.

Of course, the law of demand, applied to food and weight, works worldwide, too. The efficiency in international commerce, whether founded on technological improvements or growing competitiveness of all markets, has contributed in varying degrees to weight gain and health-care and health insurance problems worldwide.

Despite human beings' neuronal limitations, the economic way of thinking makes understanding the truly complex problems of excess weight and obesity manageable. Moreover, the cost of future weight-related health problems is a component of the current full price of overeating, an insight that allows us to speculate that medical advances (or the prospects of medical advances) to deal with future weight-related health problems can lower that full price, allowing more people to relax about overeating, knowing that medical advances will fix their problems. Similarly, new and improved, and less painful, diets can have the same effect, which, interestingly, can increase the need for people to go on diets.

But we've hardly exhausted all economic-based explanations for excess weight, most of which are based on the assumption that people are *rational*. [131] I know, it's now fashionable for psychologically oriented scholars to deride economists for assuming that people are rational at all, much less as rational as economists assume.[132] Duke University behavioral economist Daniel Ariely is surely right when he states that "life is complex, with multiple forces simultaneously exerting their influences on us, and this complexity makes it difficult to figure out exactly how each of these forces shapes our behavior," implying that economists are mistaken to assume that people are capable of making the very precise rational calculations that the economic way of thinking requires.[133] Indeed, Ariely and other behavioralists insist that people are "predictably irrational," captured by an array of decision-making biases: "availability bias," "optimism bias," "status quo bias" or "inertia bias," "representativeness bias," "relativity bias," "loss-aversion bias," "anchoring bias," "planning bias," and the list goes on.[134] We need not go into the nature of the biases here; the point is that people's decisions are heavily flawed. I can only agree that some of the country's weight gain has been due to flawed decision making, rather obvious, don't you think?

But, frankly, I have to wonder how analysts who firmly believe that people are pervasively (if not completely) irrational can expect to hold a decent rational discussion with their readers concerning people's pervasive irrationalities, which, ironically, they seem intent on doing in their *reasoned* scholarly studies.[135] Why advise people to reduce their plate (or bowl) sizes and why recommend "fat taxes" (which behavioral economists and psychologists have done), if people are incapable of considering the advice or responding to the higher taxes—and their implied incentives? Is there not at least a partial contradiction in the critics' arguments?

Granted, people are imperfect decision makers, and asking people to consider the future costs of current food intake may strain many people's mental capabilities. But if people cannot consider the future consequences of their current food purchases with some tolerable level of rationality, then it seems to me that the modern "battle of the bulge" is truly a lost cause; no amount of education and anti-obesity campaigns or higher prices spawned by "fat taxes," which we take up in Chap. 8, could change people's behaviors. Yet, obesity campaigns are heavily weighted toward informing ordinary people of the short- and long-term consequences of their eating habits, suggesting that the backers of such campaigns believe people are far more rational than critics of economics, including behavioral economists and psychologists and some obesity and nutrition experts, might think. Advocates of "fat taxes" must believe that the law of demand is applicable to anti-obesity campaigns. Otherwise, why use special taxes to drive up the price of fatty foods if the law of demand has no rational foundation or if incentives don't really matter?

Well, I will leave a full discussion of the behavioralists' criticisms of conventional economics to another book of mine.[136] Here, we do need to consider, starting in the next chapter, the extent to which weight can be rational and irrational, addictive and contagious, which will help us understand why people often go through boom-and-bust diets. In short, there is more fun to be drawn from the economic way of thinking about the country's and world's weight problems.

Chapter 5
Fat Addiction

I n a medium-sized Mississippi River town, a greyhound racetrack and casino hug the river bank, where hordes of Midwestern Americans looking for some weekend fun pour into the lounge and buffet restaurant before the afternoon races begin. Many diners who push their trays through the all-you-can eat smorgasbord are overweight or obese, selecting platefuls of fried chicken, prime rib, mashed potatoes and gravy, and slabs of cake and pie a-la-mode for dessert. The one-price-fits-all deal encourages the petite and overweight alike to pile on the food and return for seconds or thirds lest they not get their money's worth. No one seems embarrassed if they overeat, for here, as in many places across the country, "birds of a feather flock together," and so do people of weight.[1]

Clearly, there's more to weight gain than economics. Culture (or a set of shared values and behaviors for relevant groups) plays a role, and some of the rise in excess weight and obesity can be chalked up to social norms and values passed along from one generation to the next. Overweight black women are more likely to believe their weight is "about right" than are overweight white women, and can feel encouragement from black men who are more inclined to prefer heavier women than do white men.[2] Heavy parents and kin tend to beget heavy children, and obese preschoolers are more likely than their trim classmates to be obese teenagers and adults, or so research shows.[3] Heavy people tend to congregate in groups and to be concentrated in identified states and regions of the country, for example, in the South, where tradition and culture favor more calorie-laden foods.[4]

Researchers studied the weights of 12,000 adults over a thirty-two year period and concluded that an individual's chances of being (and/or becoming) obese increased by 37 percent if the spouse were obese, 40 percent if a brother or sister were obese, and 57 percent if a friend were obese. And as with the racetrack aficionados crowding the buffet, people tend to eat more when they dine with family and friends than with strangers.[5]

Moreover, the gender of people's eating partners affects how much they eat. Researchers secretly observed 460 college students as they ate meals in their campus cafeterias and found that women students ate 100 fewer calories when they had meals with men students than with women students, while men students'

R.B. McKenzie, *HEAVY!*, DOI 10.1007/978-3-642-20135-6_5,
© Springer-Verlag Berlin Heidelberg 2012

intake of calories was unaffected by the gender of their eating partners.[6] As "heavy" becomes a cultural norm, driving more weight gain, overweight can be a communicable disease. Choices made in the immediate cultural context seem perfectly rational (in large measure), even though the long-term effects are not beneficial for the individual or for society at large. The *full* price of overeating declines relatively as heavy becomes the group or community norm.

Consider an American high school in which Jim and Julie are the sole fat teenagers. Feeling the social pressures of weight gain, the pair might have a tough time making the cheerleading squad, getting a date, or being elected class president (without seeking to compensate for their physical size with genuine intellectual superiority and/or fabricated jolliness or congeniality). Research does show that heavy people face serious negative social and economic pressures (stigmas and discrimination) all around, in education, employment, and health care, for example. This can cause some heavies to do what comes naturally when they face stigmas, eat more and add more excess poundage and hold off seeking health care and remedies for their overeating, and then group with others who are doing the same things.[7]

But, if everyone in the high school is heavy and growing heavier, the personal and social pain (cost) endured can be moderated, or even fall. Jim and Julie's classmates will simply have fewer opportunities to discriminate against them or other heavy teens by choosing normal-weight people for cheerleaders, dates, and class presidents. As Jim and Julie pay lower costs for their weight gains, they are all the more likely to continue their same lifestyle choices and gain more weight. In other words, social acceptance can lower the social and economic costs for their weight gain, which can beget more of the same, and so on, round and round. Of course, this can mean that heavy people are damned if they do and damned if they don't: They can eat more because of any overweight stigma (and possible accompanying depression), but then they can eat more when the stigma is relaxed.

Economic forces, such as the real minimum wage, gas prices, and improved food production can cause weight gain on their own, as we have seen, but the lower social cost of weight gain compounds the problem. An individual's incentive to curb excess eating and lose weight can be undercut as his or her family and friends gain weight, which can cause more weight gain. America's (and the world's) weight gain over the past half century could have been, to a degree, self-compounding, with people gaining weight because others around them, near and far, have been gaining weight, all for reasons that have economic (cost/benefit) foundations. This is to say that reductions in the price of high calorie meals can have a snowball effect through time, with the snowball still rolling on its own self-propulsion as I write.

No one should conclude that weight gain can be an ever-mounting vicious cycle. Weight gain is self-limiting, as it must ultimately be.[8] Beyond some point, weight gain can impose ever greater health-care costs, becoming more salient as weight-related health problems mount over time, which can, eventually, check people's decisions to continue eating with abandon. Then, there is the ultimate check on weight gain and obesity: death by fat (and associated problems), literally on the installment plan. At this writing, over 400,000 Americans were dying from excessive weight and related health problems each year (at least, that is the Centers for Disease Control and Prevention's estimate, although the researchers' procedures may be exaggerating deaths attributable directly to fat itself, as noted in Chap. 2); for the first time, annual deaths from excessive weight (as estimated) have risen above those from smoking.[9] But then there is an inherent link between deaths by puffs and death by fat: As fewer people die from smoking, more people must be dying from other causes. And, as we have seen, the decline in smoking has fed (pun intended) the growth of the overweight and obese population, and, in turn, the increase in deaths by fat (some of which are directly attributable to the cessation of smoking). And, of course, cessation of smoking can compound the self-propulsion of the snowball effect noted for lower prices of calorie-laden meals.

"Hand Over the Chocolate, and No One Gets Hurt!"

A popular bumper sticker, "Hand over the chocolate and no one gets hurt!" spoofs the very real fact that for many people foods of various sorts are addictive. Certain foods may temporarily suppress many people's appetites, only to increase their appetites for the consumed foods over time. Certain pleasurable foods, such as chocolate, for instance, can release chemicals in the brain, creating good feelings or euphoria, or "highs," similar to those that arise from consumption of alcohol or heroine, although at a far lower intensity. "Chocoholics," seeking to repeat the pleasurable experience, feel compelled to eat more candy more often. An addictive good can create a dependency on the chemicals released in the brain as well as those in the addictive substance itself, which in turn fuels greater and greater consumption.

More on the chemistry of the brain in a moment, but at this point the critical *economic* attribute of addiction is this: The greater the good's addictiveness, the more current consumption will drive ever more future consumption. As consumption begets consumption, even a small price decrease in an addictive good today can elicit greater consumption over time. Over the long run consumers can be highly responsive to current price changes in addictive goods—or the demand can exhibit a greater elasticity (to use econ speak) than might be thought, as Nobel Laureate Gary Becker and his University of Chicago colleagues Michael Grossman and Kevin Murphy found to be the case for cigarettes.[10] This can be the case because a reduction in the current price can lead to more current consumption, but then the greater current consumption can have, again, a snowball effect, growing consumption over time, which offers another economic explanation for the country's growing weight problems. To the extent that foods are addictive to some people, even small changes in food prices can lead to relatively large changes in people's weights through time. And as we have seen, the *full* price of food has gone down during the last several decades for a number of reasons, including reduced food preparation time. And, need I add, the cessation of nicotine addictions can beget food addictions.

The Brain Chemistry of Addiction

The evolutionary forces that have endowed human beings with a desire to eat what they can and when they can have also conveniently placed the key sensory organs involved in eating—smell, taste, sight, hearing, and touch (the lips and tongue)— very close to our brains. As a flood of information bombards the senses (which can happen in the modern food court), the brain can work directly, quickly, and reactively. The brain and key senses are well situated to maximize our chances of finding food and enjoying what we find, with built-in reward systems. There might be no food addiction if all fatty and sugary foods offered the neuronal reward of raw cabbage. Our brains aren't stupid; they are built to cause us to react much like Pavlov's dog. All they need is a little reward that our neurons can interpret as pleasure to get us to return to the favored food—and those buffet lines—time and again, and again.

The mechanics of addiction are certainly complex and can be activated in varying degrees through a number of physiological routes. And researchers in the hard sciences have begun to show with scholarly clarity that chemical responses in the brain and stomach to images of various foods and then to the consumption of them trigger us to eat—and overeat. Indeed, the stomach seems to have a brain of its own, which neuroscientists dub the "gut brain" (or more formally the "enteric nervous system") which has 500 nerve cells (as many as a cat's brain) throughout the digestive system and which communicates in a two-way fashion with the brain.

Neuroscience research is hampered by the substantial costs of brain scans, which can run from hundreds (for functional Magnetic Resonance Imaging, fMRIs) to thousands (for Positive Emission Tomography, PETs) of dollars per scan, which is why neuroscience research typically involves small counts of subjects, often twenty or even fewer subjects.[11] Nevertheless, Columbia University obesity researchers showed ten obese and ten healthy-weight women pictures of cakes, French fries, and other high-calorie foods while monitoring the activity of their brains through brain scans. They found that in the obese women, the images evoked very strong responses in the area of the "midbrain" where dopamine (the "desire chemical" that is involved in sexual responses) is generated, as well as in the area involved in planning rewarding activity, presumably, in this case, eating what they saw. The obese women reacted similarly when they heard the words "chocolate brownie," but not when they heard "cabbage" (which is hardly a surprising finding). The nonobese women did not respond nearly as strongly.[12] Other researchers have shown through brain studies that many people could be obese because they have few dopamine receptors, causing them to have to eat more food than normal-weight subjects just to obtain the same feeling of pleasure that normal-weight people would get from eating less.[13]

In a sense, people can use food, especially fatty and sugary foods, to "self-medicate," to bring on "highs" that can vary across individuals (and all very legally!). Many people, including researchers, think that people need a "sweet" taste in order for many foods to give them their dopamine fix. That may not be the case. Neuroscience researchers at Duke University have bred rats that cannot taste sugar in their foods. Nevertheless, their dopamine neurons would go into overdrive when given sugary foods, apparently because the stomach and intestines can detect calories per se and can send the brain chemical signals that effectively say, "feed me and let the dopamine flow!" A similar dopamine flow was not detected when the "taste-less" rats were fed food with artificial sweeteners and no calories. That is to say, the rats, and maybe humans, can get their highs from energy alone, or the stomach's chemical signals can compound the feeding message of the taste of sugared (and fatty) foods.[14]

Fortunately, the highs people get from food are far lower than what they can get from street drugs, which generally means that it is less painful for most people to lose weight than to kick drug habits. Nonetheless, addiction can make corrective policies difficult to find in the case of food (especially sugared and fatty foods), given that there must be thousands of foods that they can use for self-medication.

In another study, neuroscience researchers observed the brain scans of thirteen obese and thirteen normal-weight subjects when they actually smelled and tasted chocolate or strawberry milkshakes. Obese subjects had strong neuronal activity in the emotional centers of their brains regardless of whether they had recently eaten, but normal-weight subjects had similar reactions only when they were hungry.[15]

Weight gain also can be related to the digestive system's ability to alert the brain stem (the primitive or "reptilian" brain) and hypothalamus (which regulates vital body functions) that enough food has been eaten, researchers have found. These signals are weak in obese people but much stronger in normal-weight subjects. Fat cells release leptin, a chemical signal that tells the brain to shut down on eating (a fact not known before 1994), but obese subjects tend to have an overabundance of leptin, which, paradoxically may cause the leptin receptors in the brain's "satiety" center to become "leptin resistant" and ignore the signals.[16] (A similar situation occurs with type 2 diabetes, in which abundant circulating insulin creates a reduction in insulin receptor activity.) Translated, many obese people may have to eat more to achieve the same level of self-medication as normal weight people.

All of these physiological differences between obese and nonobese people can be at work in the varying degrees of addiction to food or other things they may develop. Addictions can be mainly people's attempts to recover and amplify the pleasurable experience, or "high," they experience when they consume certain things. People differ in how addicted they become because of the differences in the reward they experience – due to differences in the actual flow level of brain chemicals and the sensitivity of neuronal receptors.

Modern brain research is remarkable for the sophisticated machinery used to improve our understanding of how the brain works. We now know a great deal about which parts of the brain do what—control an arm or an emotion—and we know much about how neurons communicate. But neuroscientists also have bucked up against the limits of what they don't know and perhaps can't know, beyond the mechanics of the brain's operations. For instance, neuroscientists really don't know how an image of some food is recreated, with more or less precision, in our *minds*. Yes, they know that dopamine elicits a mental image and a sense of "euphoria," but such is what subjects report and is not directly observed in the brain except in terms of changes in neural activity (although we should not be surprised if advancements are made from ongoing brain research that now involves several disciplines, not the least of which is economics).

Similarly, neuroscientists can't say (at least not now) exactly how the chemical stew in the brain leads to value assessments that can extend into the future. They don't have a clue as to how real people make decisions, other than pointing to activation of various parts of the brain and to the chemicals that are involved. People could be making sophisticated cost-benefit calculations, and some research does suggest that cost-benefit calculations, including risk expectations in financial decisions, are being made at the neuron level.[17] Perhaps one of these days, neuroscience will be able to offer better explanations for how images, memories, and calculations are made. Until then, we need some way of thinking through people's likely decision-making processes, informed and constrained by what we now know about the brain. The economic way of thinking can provide such a framework—a scientific complement to what we know about human decision making from neuroscience and evolutionary biology and the boundaries of those abilities. The economic way of thinking, and the rational decision making it implies, sheds at least some light on why people eat what they do, and why they may end up paying the consequences of excess pounds or even obesity.

Rational Addiction

Some people are fully born with their addiction (or propensity toward addictive behavior) for nicotine, alcohol, food, or whatever, according to neuroscientists and geneticists. But not everyone is so addictive from birth. Many, perhaps most, people (no one knows for sure how many or what percentage of people) will show signs of becoming addicted to whatever through life experiences (choosing to take their first puff, shot, or hit). Are people in this latter group behaving in a way that is not rational, or worse, "irrational?" Or could the economic way of thinking be at work with these people, providing them with a very rational route to addiction (on top of the chemical route) that can afflict anyone? After all, people have to make their consumption decisions within certain constraints—"external" constraints such as available incomes and resources and "internal" constraints such as limited bodily resources and defined bodily processes. Other disciplines may offer a variety of good explanations for addiction (or just overeating), but at the core of the economic approach is the presumption that people have at least some control over what they choose and do, at least at some point. Granted, as people become progressively more addicted to a substance, they lose a measure of control (by definition), but that hardly means that *everyone* everywhere loses *all* control.

Simply put, the economic, rational explanation for addiction starts with a recognition that the gains from consuming any addictive (fattening or otherwise) good are quite close at hand, if not immediate, while the consequences—pains or costs—are realized over time, sometimes in the distant future. Consequently, people can be expected to downplay or poorly evaluate (discount) the future costs because of the pleasure of current consumption.

For purposes of illustration (and only to illustrate the more general point), consider a cost-benefit calculation set in dollar terms: Someone might reason that a $1 chocolate truffle will give at least $1 of value when eaten at the time of purchase, but he also may recognize that the treat will add several ounces of fat, contribute to a chocolate addiction, and cause weight gain over time. For purposes of illustration (only, again), let's say the added pounds from eating the chocolate lead to $3 in health-care expenditures (or lower wages or social ostracism, or whatever) over time. Still, the rational person will buy and eat the truffle only when he calculates that the benefits of eating it and the $1 spent for it today are worth more than the additional $3 in future costs, which will be appropriately discounted for the time delay (which lowers the current assessed pain of the costs). In this sense people can be "rationally addicted" to whatever (foods, alcohol, and street drugs), as Becker and Murphy conjectured in one of their many important articles.[18] Once addicted, of course, the chocoholic (or "hamburgerholic") might lose significant control of her rational capacity, but before taking the first bite, she can rationally weigh all the costs and benefits of consuming the first truffle and all subsequent truffles into the future. From an economic point of view, the person will consume the first unit if all evaluated costs going forward are assessed at less than the current benefits from consuming the first unit, and they will not consume the first unit if the assessed future costs are greater than the current benefits.

People may not seem to make complicated cost/benefit calculates before deciding to eat a chocolate truffle, or any other addictive good.[19] But all of us, knowing full well that certain food choices are going to add to our waistlines, decide to eat or not eat the offending food based, to some extent, on when we think we will have to pay the piper, and how much the piper may demand. As rational beings, how we deal with an addictive good, such as chocolate, depends on how urgently we need that truffle—or our "discount rate," in econ-speak. The greater the urgency, and the longer the time lapse before paying the negative consequences, or the higher the discount rate, the lower the assessed cost of indulging in truffles and the greater the resulting addiction and weight gain.

In numerical terms (and, again, for illustration purposes only), if the costs of eating the $1 truffle are not incurred for ten years and the person's discount rate is 20 percent, the assessed value today of the $3 in our supposed future health-care costs will be just under 50 cents. The rational person will buy and eat the chocolate, and suffer the consequences of the addiction and added weight, if not obesity. There's a net payoff. However, if the person's discount rate is 5 percent, the assessed value of the $3 in future costs today is $1.84. In that case, the rational person will not buy and eat the chocolate today and will avoid the chocolate addiction and resulting weight gain. There's a net loss in value.

Okay, people aren't computers, but they can still make rough and ready decisions, and develop rough and ready heuristics for making such rough and ready cost/benefit calculation. The point is that people can bring whatever rational capacity they have to bear on their eating and weight-gain decisions, all of which can be influenced by their discount rates (which, admittedly, can be affected by their body chemistry that, in turn, is influenced by what they eat).

Why Little Education and Excess Weight Go Together

The general rule for eating foods that are addictive is this: The greater a person's urgency (discount rate) for eating any addictive food, the more likely they will eat the food and the greater the likelihood that they will gain excess pounds and become obese. Obviously, people differ significantly in how addictive foods are for them, how urgent their consumption, and how high their discount rates are. Otherwise, we might wonder why so many slim people coexist with so many fat people, even in the same household and same daily environment (and even among so-called "identical" twins).

People with high discount rates will be inclined to spend their money on things that give pleasure now, not tomorrow. They prioritize needs and pleasures in the here and now rather than those that may not pay off for years or decades to come. For example, people with high discount rates tend to spend less on education because the costs are clear and close at hand while the payoff is not so clear and in the future. On the other hand, those with low discount rates will invest in additional years of education because the payoff in higher future income more than compensates for their current sacrifice.

Accordingly, economists have surmised—or predicted—that weight gain and obesity will tend to be inversely related to the amount of education people have, at least in societies like the United States where food temptations abound (not so much in backward societies where serious food shortages force people to live at subsistence levels). People with high discount rates will tend to have less education but also have greater risk of food addictions and the related weight gain and obesity. In fact, the increase in weight gain and obesity has been disproportionately concentrated in lower-income and lower-educated groups, but not (necessarily) because low income and little education are the core cause of weight gain, and not because these groups are less rational than others. Rather, low incomes and low education levels, as well as food addictions and excess weight, can all be the consequence of the same force—a high discount rate (which can have physiological and sociological foundations). That is, low-income and less-educated people suffer from having urgent needs for immediate gratification and impaired assessments of the future costs of weight gain (perhaps partially because of their expected limited lifespans), which holds down their incomes and pushes up their weights.[20]

In addition, people with little education tend to earn less, which can force them onto unhealthy lifetime diet tracks. Moreover, heavy people can suffer from lack of encouragement to go after more education, which can force them to remain in low-income cultures of weight gain.

Of course, the tie between little education and excess weight is hardly perfect. Exceptions abound on both ends of the education spectrum: well-educated professors who are heavy, and little-educated janitors who stay trim. What is at stake here is the *tendency* of little education and excess weight to move together across large groups of people.

The "Me Generation," Discount Rates, and Weight Gain

For any noted social problems, psychologists often point to preference and attitude changes. Much has been written of the emergence of the "me generation" and the "narcissism epidemic," which has left people, children and adults alike, feeling more entitled to getting now what they want when they want it.[21] Translated to economic themes in this book, many people could have gained weight during the last several decades of the last century because their "discount rate" used to evaluate the future costs of weight gain could have risen. That is, many people's weight gain over recent decades can be chalked up to greater urgency for gains today relative to pains tomorrow, and years into the future—or people's assessed current value of the future costs of weight gain has retreated relative to the assessed value of current food consumption.

In concrete terms, the discounted costs of current and future weight gain from downing hamburgers and fries (or beer and ice cream) could have declined over the decades relative to their current consumption value, a point that can help explain why hamburgers have gone from single to triple patties and fries have gone from small to supersize at many fast-food restaurants and why people, rich and poor alike, now eat out more often. "Me worry? Pass the mayo, ketchup, and salt—and hurry!"

What *could be* the best evidence that the urgency of current consumption, or the discount rate, has gone up for many, in the United States? Two statistical series are worthy of consideration: First, the decline in the personal saving rate (as measured by total personal savings as a percent of disposable income), and second, the rise in the household debt burden (household debt divided by disposable personal income) over the last five decades.

Political leaders and pundits across the political spectrum have widely decried Americans' saving rate, which increased irregularly from 1960 until the mid-1970s, only to fall off in the late 1970s, rise again through 1982, and then precipitously decline in the 1980s and 1990s, going below zero after 2004. The savings rate rose somewhat, and maybe temporarily, during the Great Recession.[22]

Not surprisingly, household debt has grown with the fall in household savings. Household debt was close to 35 percent of disposable personal income in the early

1950s, only to double by the mid-1960s and then to plateau until the early-1980s. From the mid-1980s until just before the advent of the Great Recession, the household debt ratio soared, reaching above 130 percent in 2006, after which the debt ratio declined as households curbed spending to adjust to the income realities of the Great Recession and as homeowners in droves began to walk away from their homes that increasingly were no longer affordable and were worth less than their mortgages.[23]

The decline in the saving rate between 1982 and the early 2000s and the expected concomitant rise in household debt during much the same period has, no doubt, many explanations, not the least of which is that during the period of the savings-rate decline and debt increase, Americans' equity in the stock market and in their houses, not counted as "savings," was generally on the rise, the particulars of which could sidetrack us here.[24] However, there is still room for the paths taken by savings and debt to be explained by an increase in people's discount rates. If the discount rates were on the rise, then the value of future consumption fell relative to current consumption. People can feed their current consumption demand by saving less and incurring more debt—and getting fatter in the process.[25]

I find the foregoing line of argument somewhat satisfying. After all, businesses—especially restaurants—have worked to persuade consumers to buy now and pay later. But, admittedly, like so many other economists I worry about explanations for economic phenomena—weight, for example—that rely on proposed fundamental changes in people's preferences, with discount rates being an integral component of preferences. Preference changes can be too easy of an explanation, which can cut off search for explanations that are founded on changes in people's circumstances, a theme that Nobel Laureates George Stigler and Gary Becker warned against in a classic article decades ago.[26] One such line of argument can point to the decline by half or more in real interest rates (nominal interest rates minus the inflation rate), which happened in the 1980s and 1990s and into early 2000s (where the real interest rates actually became negative), and in the growth in the availability of credit (and credit cards), which encouraged people to spend more and save less and incur more debt to finance the current expenditures.[27] The greater availability of credit at lower real interest rates (made possible, in part, by the growth in the securitization of all forms of debt, including credit card debt), of course, could have induced people to eat more, especially on high calorie meals at restaurants of all sorts. Indeed, through the continuing growth in the interconnectedness of world financial markets during the last third of the twentieth century, the growth in savings in China and other Asian countries could have been a contributor (albeit a marginal one) to the growth in Americans' girths.

The Economics of "Cold-Turkey Diets"

Some people, especially those who have highly addictive propensities, may have to go "cold turkey" to beat their addictions, Becker and Murphy have argued.[28] If they try to change their food choices in "baby steps," as many nutritionists recommend for practically everyone, even a small amount of the addictive food can compel greater consumption. Each bite fuels another, and another, defeating the dieting goal. Under such conditions, crash diets make economic (and nutritional and health) sense for addictive foods, which is why we hear so often of people going from gross overeating to tightly constrained under-eating, such as participants on "The Biggest Losers."

Of course, when food is addictive, people often cycle through significant weight gains and losses. To lose weight, people have to have a significant "negative energy balance"—they have to take in fewer calories than are needed for weight maintenance. But when food is highly addictive, the number of calories must be even fewer. Consider the potential real-world problem that an obese person must face: Seriously overweight and suffering from food addiction, Charlie needs 4,000 calories a day just to maintain his basic bodily functions and all his extra fat cells. To reach a normal body weight, he goes on a crash diet that allows for no more than 1,500, or even 1,000, calories a day. Once Charlie reaches his goal, he can increase his calories to 2,000 a day for weight maintenance at a normal level. But for Charlie, who is strongly susceptible to food addiction, an increase in calories can drive greater consumption, and a return to his former overweight state. The general conclusion: The greater the addictiveness of foods to people, the greater the weight gain and the greater the potential for weight cycling (when reaching a normal weight is an earnest goal).

Although this relationship has not been scientifically investigated, to my knowledge, I will be surprised if future research does not support such a hypothesis. Clearly, people who go to fat farms and who resort to bariatric surgery (or "stomach stapling") understand in a very deliberate or rational way the problem of weight cycling and the need to erect barriers (which translate into greater costs) to the playing out of addictions. Then again, some people might dispense with commitment to hold the line on eating for periods of time because holding to the commitment can impose ongoing stress, which can be debilitating physiologically and can undercut their productivity. I have a good friend who is a world-class neuroscientist, who is substantially obese, and who readily posits a neurochemical explanation for his weight cycling. He has found that his scholarly productivity has been greater when he has relaxed on his weight control (during which time he has gained an average of eighty pounds) than when he controlled his eating (during which he has lost the eighty pounds gained during his "up-cycle").

The Economics of Procrastination on Diets

Weight cycling is common for a related reason—procrastination, or postponing paying the costs of weight loss. Consider Jim, who stands six-feet-one and weighs a normal 180 pounds. Jim and his wife Lorraine take a Caribbean cruise to celebrate their tenth anniversary, and Jim returns home carrying an extra five pounds—and not in his suitcase. Jim may reasonably figure that his minor weight gain is of little or no consequence (even if he can't stop thinking about the lobster they enjoyed more than once on their vacation and as he searches for where he can find something comparable nearby). Besides, Jim has read that lobster is a good meat choice (if you can afford it). He has also been told that a *few* extra pounds can have no adverse effects, and might even have positive ones, in terms of health and longevity.

After six months, Jim is still carrying his "post-cruise weight"—maybe even a pound or two more—but Lorraine has stopped nagging him about it. At his height, he hides the extra pounds well, and his golfing buddies and officemates haven't seemed to notice. Jim reasons that the personal, social or health-care costs—if there are any—of his weight gain are way off in the future, and at forty-two, he has plenty of time to return to any recommended "normal weight."

As for now, Jim and Lorraine have become regulars at a lobster restaurant that he has discovered in town. Jim can accurately evaluate the pleasure he enjoys from eating, which is sizable, but he may not be quite so accurate in his assessment of the future costs of his current eating habits. As George Akerlof, another Nobel Laureate in economics, puts it, "Present costs are unduly salient in comparison with future costs, leading individuals to postpone tasks until tomorrow without foreseeing that when tomorrow comes, the required action will be delayed yet again."[29] In effect, Akerlof is saying what everyone knows (including economists, when they step outside their theoretical worlds), that we might be rational, but our rationality is limited by our brain power and the perceived need to use our limited neurons to fine-tune decisions of limited consequence. We simply take notice, and act on, some things more than others, and some things that are right in our face—literally, food in the here and now—are more readily considered and weighted than some things—costs, for example—that have to be imagined with more or less clarity because they are off in the future. Put another way, we can over-discount future consequences (known in behavioral econ-speak as "hyperbolic discounting").

Jim feels little urgency to get serious about losing some weight because his food indulgences don't seem to dramatically affect the numbers that spin by each morning when he steps on the bathroom scales. Even though Jim knows he has been eating more than he should, he correctly notes that any *given* level of excess calories taken in has diminishing returns in terms of added weight. Some of Jim's excess calories are being used to maintain the excess pounds he gained on the cruise and afterwards, which can be reason enough to increase the calorie intake.

As the winter holiday season approaches, Jim decides he can postpone the pain and suffering of a diet until summer, which diminishes his assessed (discounted) personal costs today of the diet and, in turn, assuages his guilt for overeating at his mother-in-law's Thanksgiving dinner. Besides, if he doesn't pig out, he might insult the cooks.

Jim's diet (successive) procrastination—and that of thousands of others—fuels America's weight gain problem: Jim and his fellow procrastinators continue to add pounds as they reduce the assessed social, personal, and economic costs of being overweight and as they delay the inevitable, serious diets.[30]

And don't forget, some procrastination may have a good effect, buying time while people gather more and better information on weight gain.[31] For example, procrastinators who have deferred losing the extra ten to fifteen pounds have recently learned what Jim was told, that those few extra pounds could be good for their health and longevity. Some procrastinators, who have gained more than a few extra pounds, can heed with all due speed the negative lessons learned from their weight gain and correct the errors of their eating ways. But food addictions may capture others, complicating the solution to their weight gain. And as more overweight people procrastinate, the numbers of overweight people also balloons, and by sheer numbers they can lower the economic and social consequences of being overweight for others. Weight gain for a group of friends or community or even country can be a proverbial snowball.

As spring arrives, Jim and Lorraine make plans to join her family at the beach in early July. Only half teasing, Lorraine makes a few unkind comparisons between large ocean mammals and Jim's paunch, reminding him that he should start that diet and lose a few pounds in the next four months before vacation. But with the truncated time line, Jim's personal (discounted) costs of getting serious about weight loss have grown progressively, which provides him with a good reason (or quasi-rational foundation) for yet another round of procrastination. Why not wait until after the vacation and then start the diet and exercise routine? No need to make himself miserable while trying to relax at the beach.

Still, Lorraine's comments remind Jim that his weight gain is becoming all the more transparent to himself and others. He notices that he is a bit more winded than normal when hiking up the big hill at the golf course, and he isn't looking forward to enduring a few pot shots from Lorraine's brother, a marathon runner, at the beach in July. As the personal, social, and health consequences of his growing weight gain loom ever closer, Jim is able to evaluate them more accurately, and makes a precommitment to start a diet the day he and Lorraine return from vacation. Jim sets his goal, figuring he can return to his normal weight in about sixteen weeks.

Jim's setting a deadline for himself (including a date on which his goal weight is to be achieved), Akerlof argues, is a productive approach because it forces him to increase his assessment of future costs relative to immediate costs, truncating his procrastination (or at least lowering the probability of his continuing to procrastinate).[32] By making a precommitment to his deadline, Jim gives definition to "failure" (a perceived "bad") and, thus, increases the psychic costs of rolling off the diet wagon.

Will Jim keep his precommitment and be successful? Quite possibly, as the weight he has gained over the past eighteen months is relatively modest. But like all dieters, his pledge will come under growing pressure as he begins to lose weight. Initially, as Jim reduces his intake of calories, he will drop pounds as his body converts fat stores to energy just to feed the rest of his excess fat. But as Jim progressively loses more weight, he will likely notice that his new reduced-calorie diet yields less and less weight loss.

Being a (quasi) rational human being, Jim will realize that the rewards he is reaping from his weight loss are diminishing. To get off the weight loss plateau, Jim will have to reduce his calories even more. Jim's pain of refusing dessert, foregoing a second (or third) glass of wine, and passing on his favorite lobster dinner is immediate even as the consequences of shucking his diet become more remote in time. Jim, like many rational dieters, may take a respite from his commitment to lose weight—a commitment made in the ever more distant past. And once Jim goes off his diet, the consequences of his food addictions (lobster dipped in butter) will take hold and his weight will rebound. Then, as the numbers on Jim's bathroom scale spin round to some critical mass, a precommitment to a diet will again appear rational.

Thus, cycles of weight gain and loss can stretch into Jim's future, and economic theorists have found significant cycling in people's weight as they go on and off diets (under conditions of imperfect decision making) and gradually gain weight as they age and go through their weight-gain/weight-loss cycles, which has been documented to be a human tendency.[33] The danger Jim faces with the advent of cycles is that he may simply observe their historical records and give up. With that may be the start of massive weight gain and all the health-care problems associated with obesity. Other researchers have found that some foods filled with fat and sugar—cheese, chocolate, but especially a variety of items on the menus of fast-food restaurants—affect addictions through changes in brain chemistry. For example, researchers at the Scripps Research Institute studied three groups of rats. One group was given a healthy diet, the second group was given limited access to high calorie and sugared junk food, and the third group was allowed to eat whatever fast food given to the point of obesity. They found that the brain adapts easily to its diet, which is the problem. [34] As one of the researchers Paul Kenny noted, "When the animal overstimulates its brain pleasure centers with highly palatable food, the systems adapt by decreasing their activity. However, now the animal requires constant stimulation from palatable food to avoid entering a persistent state of negative reward."[35] The researchers found that the obese rats would not return to healthy diets when their junk food was taken away. Moreover, the rats would even continue to eat the junk food when faced with electrical shocks to get at it, which, in the minds of the researchers, demonstrates that food addictions and drug addictions "are based on the same underlying neurobiological mechanisms."[36]

The Special Challenges of Food Addictions

Food challenges our rational decision making because unlike most other consumer goods, food is essential for life and has to be acquired (purchased) continually. A cost-benefit analysis of many goods—large-screen LED televisions, comforter covers, and barbeque grills—is fairly easy to make. Such purchases are infrequent and expensive, which justifies careful evaluations, and the purchase of a large-screen is made independent of the next television set, which may not be bought for several years. All one has to do is look at the sticker price and consider the set-up and repair costs and weigh the full estimated price against the imagined value of watching various televisions programs in the years to come (over and above the benefits of sticking with the current set).

These calculations, of course, are not always easy, which is why many buyers may study various models carefully over several months before making the purchase. But compare those decision-making problems with those of selecting foods, often "small" decisions that have to be made frequently, if not fairly constantly, and that affect future food-buying decisions. And to the extent that food is addictive, food-buying decisions made today can compel decisions made tomorrow. Food-buying decisions can become very complex and, thus, potentially very costly, which can cause people to throw up their hands and cast caution to the winds. Why? People may judge that it's better to suffer the consequences of some bad food-buying decisions to avoid current decision-making costs. After all, the complexity of reading labels for sugar and fat content and counting calories requires time, right here and now, often on every trip to the market and at every meal or snack (or at least when products change, which is frequently for many foods). Indeed, by forcing food producers to pack progressively more nutrition information into their labels, they may have caused many buyers to absorb less nutrition information as the font size of the print on the labels has fallen and as their brains short circuit with too much information, increasing the cost of careful decision making.

In contrast, street drugs, alcohol, and cigarettes, are not necessary for life (until, perhaps, a full-fledged addiction sets in). Many people can appraise the current and future costs and benefits of drug addiction, weigh the balance, and never take the first hit, which can, if ever taken, lead to life-paralyzing consequences. Food is different. We can't escape consuming food for more than a few (maybe only two) weeks, if we want to avoid death. All people must subject themselves to the threat of becoming addicted to some type of food, which is reason enough why we might find food addictions more common than drug, alcohol, or tobacco addictions and why there are more obese people among us than drug addicts.

Public interest campaigns for smokers to "kick the habit" can be more effective than similarly intense campaigns for people to put down their forks and push back from their dinner tables. Smokers can go "cold turkey," never smoke again, and live to tell the tale. Not so with food. At some point, a person must consume some food, which, for some individuals, may introduce the threat of a food addiction once again. Also, as people deny themselves foods, the high eaters experience from consuming some additional food can become progressively more intense, making food temptations all the more powerful and the dieters' resolve all the weaker.

Generally, people need fewer calories as they age, because their basal metabolism—the energy required to stay alive (which, for most people, comprises 60–75 percent of the energy consumed)—declines with age to varying degrees.[37] This means that the energy intake required to maintain a normal weight declines in a difficult-to-predict pattern through people's lives. A twenty-five-year-old may consume 2,200 calories a day and maintain a slim figure; however, that calorie intake can add to the waistline of a forty-five-year-old whose basal metabolism has declined (as well, perhaps, as his physical activity).

In addition, the excess calories at age forty-five can fuel a food addiction, which can lead to perpetuating weight gain as the years go by, making dieting all the more difficult with age. Low-cost and easily accessible foods are no less tempting to the twenty-five-year-old than the forty-five-year-old, but that's part of the problem. People have to acquire progressively greater fortitude to resist food temptations (and addictions) as they age to avoid weight gain, which means that weight gain can be all the more probable. That is, an "upward drift in weight" can be built into our physiology and the progression of greater and greater temptations to eat that come with changing economic forces through our lives.[38]

Finally, one of the special problems with food is that it is typically bought in relatively small but repeated purchases (by individual items or, at most, by the grocery cart) and ingested in smaller doses at meals and in snacks with time lapses in between. On any hot summer day, Jill can't resist a box of mini-sized ice cream bars advertised on sale at her local grocery. Unpacking her bags at home, she can rightfully reason that eating one bar can have a small, maybe inconsequential, effect on her weight gain. Besides, she decides, she will compensate by skipping dessert tonight and adding a couple miles to her run this week. Her decision reprises a now familiar problem: The benefits of downing the ice cream bar are immediate, while the costs of skipping dessert and running more miles are set off into the future and are currently discounted. As the future arrives, however, those costs loom larger. As her husband and children are enjoying the ice cream bars for dessert that evening, Jill finds it harder to stick to her decision to abstain—why not have just one more and then that will be it for the week. And as for running extra miles—Jill can reason that she can add those miles any time, no big hurry. At any moment, Jill can easily and rationally postpone her decision to compensate for eating the ice cream, and she may find that her constant cost-benefit analysis through time can lead to weight gain. To overcome their short-term rational tendencies, people have to substitute longer-term perspectives, which can challenge human being's limited rational capacities.

Depression, Suicide, and Overeating

For many people, some mental illnesses can impair rational thinking. Indeed, it often does, especially when the illness is based on a chemical imbalance or electrical malfunction in the brain that undercuts, or destroys, neuronal function. After all, the brain is clearly a chemical and electrical communication system, electrified Jell-O, as it were.

Mental illness—depression, for example—has many causes, and is considered to be an affective disorder that can be genetically based, but that can be precipitated by stressors—a traumatic life event, the death of a child, for example. Stress can bring on various physiological changes in the brain that affect different people (depending on their race and gender) in different ways, depending on the nature, severity, and duration of the stressful events. Depression may lead some people to become gaunt while others become heavy.[39] The weight gain among people suffering from depression, or other mental illnesses, is easier to explain using economic principles.

Depression often brings about a drop in the release of serotonin and dopamine in the "pleasure center" of the brain. Food (and, for example, other addictive things like sex, nicotine, alcohol and street drugs, or even an activity like shopping) can restore serotonin and dopamine levels, thus relieving fully, or just somewhat, the depression, albeit temporarily (in much the same way, but with far less force, that wine or cocaine can). In addition, the drop in dopamine and serotonin also stimulates the release of a stress hormone which can induce great psychological pain, sense of loss, and the full blown symptoms of withdrawal. Many depressed people can end up gaining weight because, as research shows, the brain is hardwired to respond to chemical deficits by sending signals that produce cravings for foods— often ones that are fatty and sugary—that will enable the brain to rebuild its chemical balance. However, when the imbalance involves an excess rather than a deficit in key chemicals, the brain works to divert most of the excess nutrients to other bodily functions—including fat storage.[40]

Depressed people—or those with severe food addictions—must engage their higher reasoning ability with much more force to control or lose weight than they do to gain it. Indeed, they have to use their higher reasoning ability, concentrated in the more recently developed frontal cortex of the brain, to override their brain-induced craving to eat, originating in the more primitive parts of the brain that are directly in the line of fire of sensory stimuli—sight, taste, smell, touch, and sound—that come from foods. Yet, the strongest brain connections in the frontal region, where cold cognition and reasoning are processed, run from the lower, more primitive areas. In a sense, emotion and limbic drives of hunger and craving will almost always trump reason in people who are genetic addicts. That's why telling people in stark (and maybe exaggerated) terms about the consequences of their natural eating proclivities may help them overcome their primitive responses to food sensory information. It's probably not a bad idea to tell people, whether depressed or not, in the booths at Outback Steakhouse that its "Bloomin' Onion" (a battered and French fried onion) has 1,551 calories and eighty-three grams of fat. Such a fact, accompanied by details on the adverse health effects of the purchase (with exaggerations used freely), may cause people to engage more fully whatever rational capacity they have (no matter how impaired) than they would otherwise.

Of course, weight and depression can worsen each other interactively. Depressed people can pack on additional pounds as they seek to self-medicate with food. Their added weight can result in weight-related problems such as poor health, underemployment, and social isolation, causing them to become more depressed, and then to eat ever more to relieve (temporarily) the symptoms. Mental health can have many of the same interactive effects on weight gain that addictive foods can have. In a study of more than 5,000 young adults (eighteen to thirty years of age), those subjects who reported the highest levels of depression at the start of the study gained the most weight over fifteen years, with the added pounds concentrated around the waistline.[41] This study did not find that the added weight increased the subjects' depression, but other studies have indicated the bidirectional and feed-back-loop effects: obesity fuels depression, and depression possibly contributes to some subjects' weight gain.[42]

In 2006 (the latest year of available data), there were an estimated one million suicides worldwide and more than 33,000 in the United States, with an estimated ten to twenty attempted suicides in the United States for every fatal suicide. The actual count of suicides in the United States rose between the middle of the twentieth century and the first decade of the twentieth-first century, but the actual suicide *rate* (suicides per 100,000 Americans eighteen and older fell by 17 percent, or from a rate of 13.2 in 1960 to 10.9 in 2006). American males kill themselves at a substantially higher rate than females, and the suicide rate by age group peaks in the seventy-five to eighty-four year age category at 27.9 per 100,000 in 2006.[43]

Researchers estimate that all types of depression, including the various forms of bipolar and major depressive disorder, affect twelve million women (or 12 percent) and more than six million men (or 7 percent) in the United States (but the gender gap in depression could be partially a matter of men and women's monthly hormonal cycles and a difference in the willingness of women and men to report mental illnesses).[44] Moreover, cases of depression are disproportionately concentrated among middle-aged people and the low-income—groups in which weight gain also has become more prevalent in recent decades.[45]

However, our arguments on the links among depression, suicidal inclinations, and excess weight are merely suggestive, hardly conclusive, and would apply to certain types of individuals. As noted, depression and suicidal leanings can affect people's weights differently, and likewise, excess weight affects people's mental and physical health in a variety of ways. To say the least, more research is needed, but we shouldn't ignore the likely effects of mental health on people's cost-benefit assessments of overeating, and then, all the evolving economic and social forces that affect mental health. The economic way of thinking provides a way to assess how these forces affect the way that people judge the benefits and costs into the future that emanate from their current eating decisions.

Concluding Comments

The worldwide weight gain and obesity epidemic is not simple. Hundreds of millions of people throughout the world, living under widely varying circumstance, have serious weight problems, and each has his or her own reasons for eating to excess. Some may link their weight gain to the depression they faced in the wake of divorce or the death of a loved one. Others may have relocated from an exercise-conducive environment, such as Southern California, to an area where weather restricts outdoor activity, such as hot and humid southern Texas or frigid and snowy northern Maine. Still others may have gained weight because they suffered a debilitating accident, discovered a love of pasta and cream sauces, or because their car simply became a more comfortable and affordable substitute for walking.

Or maybe the improved technology of a large-screen, surround-sound, high-definition television seductively led some to spend a lot more time on the couch than in the gym.[46]

And, unbelievable as it may sound, a few people may have intentionally set out to gain excess weight. The *New York Post* reported in early 2010 that Donna Simpson, who at the time of the news report weighed 600 pounds and couldn't move more than twenty feet without resting, was eating the calories of Olympic swimmers—12,000 calories per day—in an effort to become the "world's fattest woman," as recognized in the *Guinness Book of World Records*.[47] Wow!

Taken by itself, the Donna Simpson story is hardly worth mentioning, but it does convey a broader point: Many people gain weight for reasons that are simply bizarre (by the standards of "normal people," me included), but they also gain weight for reasons that are as varied as the local economic and social conditions individuals face. Some married people may gain weight simply because, having "bagged a spouse," they no longer have to compete on attractiveness scale in the mating market. (As an aside, this line of argument suggests the prediction that weight gain during marriage might vary across states according to how difficult getting a divorce can be. That is, the more difficult divorces are to come by, the greater the weight gain after marriage, after adjusting for other weight-gain factors.)

I know, you are thinking that there is a simple explanation for why people overeat, develop food addictions, get fat, and go through repeated cycles of weight loss and gain: People are simply not rational. They eat without thinking or without considering with any precision the costs and benefits of eating and overeating. No doubt, there is some truth, and scientific evidence, that people are simply not always very good at assessing costs and benefits, especially when the costs and benefits extend into the distant future.[48] And evolutionary pressures probably have restricted our assessment abilities, mainly because our long-ago ancestors didn't live very long and followed a straightforward rule: "Eat when you can, and damn the future consequences because tomorrow may never come." Again, we *Homo sapiens* evolved to reduce the risk of starvation, not the risk of obesity.

I grant you that many people today might be fat because they are more or less irrational (or non-thinking) when it comes to filling their grocery carts and putting their forks down at their dinner tables or closing up bags of chips while watching television in half comatose states. Undoubtedly, people are less rational than economists often assume, implicitly or explicitly, and people's inclination to assess accurately the costs and benefits of their consumption decisions can change with the importance of the decisions.

Still, the economic way of thinking is most useful in considering how people will tend to behave regarding food, no matter how addictive it is, when there are changes in economic and social circumstances. Research documents that people will buy more food and become heavier when food's relative *full* price declines. We can add that people will risk becoming overweight from food addictions when they can delay or avoid the consequences—that is, incur all the costs—from overeating. The reality is that heavy people's overeating is often "subsidized" by others who suffer costs because of heavy people's girths. Had the big man who sat next to me on the flight to Houston (see the start of Chap. 1, if you skipped it) been required to compensate his seatmates—the trim lady on the aisle and me—for taking extra space (our space), perhaps he would have gained less weight over the years. As for Donna Simpson, she supports her $750-a-week grocery bill by charging people to watch her eat through her Web site. We have to wonder if she reaches her goal weight of a thousand-plus pounds, whether she (and family members and other enablers) will be able to cover her grocery bill for weight maintenance, plus all of her future health-care costs and the expense of caring for her daughter (who was born in 2007, at which time Ms. Simpson set a record for being the heaviest mother in the world at 532 pounds).

Similarly, few (and maybe no) employer-based health insurance policies include an added premium (penalty) for being overweight, mainly because many states outlaw price discrimination on group policies. Consequently, healthy-weight employees may have to cover the increased health insurance costs of heavy colleagues, which, according to one study, amount to an average of $150 a year for each healthy-weight employee,[49] with the lifetime costs imposed by sedentary individuals running possibly more than $3,300 (in present dollar values).[50] This means "the costs of the overweight couch potato's unhealthy decisions are imposed on the gym rat who diets carefully and watches his cholesterol."[51]

If heavy employees had to pick up their full health insurance tab through their working careers, perhaps many of them would not have run the risks of food addiction—or just chocolate or chip addiction—years ago. Bringing the costs closer at hand, and lowering their discount rate, may have prevented some obesity. And the research record is pretty solid: Group health insurance policies that do not penalize people for excess weight have been a partial cause of weight gain during the past forty or fifty years.[52] The effect on firms' overall cost structures very likely has been muted, however, because employers simply hire fewer overweight and obese workers precisely because of their higher health insurance costs, as we will see in the following chapter. The lower demand for overweight workers lowers their wages and forces them to cover their added medical-care and health-insurance costs indirectly.

When we consider how evolutionary forces have more or less hardwired human beings to eat when they can, and even beyond what they need at the moment, and when we consider the growth in people's real incomes coupled with the temptations and opportunities to eat more, tastier, and varied foods, the issue of why there are so many overweight and obese people is not nearly as perplexing as why there are so many trim people.

Economic forces very likely have played significant roles in the country's weight gain over the last half century, and one advantage of devising economic explanations is that they potentially can lead to corrective policies. As we recognize that food production has shifted from small-scale inefficiencies of individual homes to the economies of scale possible in food processing plants and restaurants, we can apply the law of demand to understand that the *full* price of consuming many meals and snacks has declined. And more meals and snacks, added weight, and all the attendant health-care problems have followed. This analysis harbors the suggestion that "fat taxes" (and other curbs in food productions and sales) may help reduce Americans' waistlines and the country's health-care costs. However, no consensus exists for fat taxes as the solution to the weight gain and obesity problem (at least, not at this writing).

Conceivably, research might also show that people will curb downloads of music to their laptops and MP3 players when prices go up and will, consequently, develop fewer hearing problems over time. Should we, therefore, tax music downloads? And fat taxes will tax trim people who have worked hard at controlling their weight as well as fat people, imposing the costs of the latter on the former.

With lower relative food prices (and especially unhealthful foods), people's welfares might be greater even when they gain weight. As noted in Chap. 2 some excess weight gain can be good for people (in the sense they will, on average, live longer), and they might lead longer lives with excess weight simply because their concessions on their weights mean they endure less stress from always trying to resist food temptations and always trying to meet some weight goal set by others.[53] Excess weight can debilitate, hike health-care costs, and even kill, but so can stress. Stress also can partially defeat dieting efforts, because the body, in response to stress, releases cortisol, a protein that stimulates insulin production, and in turn, encourages the body to convert foods into stored visceral fat, especially around the waistline. And excess visceral fat has been linked to heart attacks through its influence on the buildup of cholesterol in the veins of the heart. [54]

Many people may simply prefer to spend their incomes on more food intake and weight gain than any other alternatives, even when the health-care costs are considered. In other words, people can be expected to strike new balances in their purchases across products as the full prices of weight-inducing foods fall and their availability rises; and many (not all) people can be expected to seek a new balance between the problems associated with weight gain and the problems associated with fighting temptations to overeat. While a large swath of people might gain weight, some variations in weight gain can be expected simply because people have varying physiological responses to the sight, smell, sound, touch, and (lastly) taste of food, which drive their urges and addiction to eat and then determine when to stop eating.

As the old adage goes, "Different strokes for different folks," which might cause some people to pause on advocating "obvious" solutions to the country's and world's weight problems. Personally, I've always found it interesting how heavy people can be heard condemning smokers, and vice versa.

I understand that a lot of nutritionists insist that people are consumed with irrationalities, but I repeat a theme taken up before: If such is the case, you have to wonder why the nutritionists then spend so much time and energy telling people what foods are bad for them if they didn't have some remaining rational capacity to make better choices. Why even go to the trouble of explaining to people how and why people are so darn irrational, if they—researchers and listeners alike—were as irrational as they say? Go figure.

Central to the policy debate surrounding solving the weight gain and obesity problem, of course, are the very real economic consequences of weight gain, which are many and important. We discuss those in the following chapter.

Chapter 6
Fat Consequences

In the mid-1990s, a teenager from northern California—let's call her Melanie—became in death the poster child for the end-game many obese Americans, especially children, could be playing.[1] Melanie was thirteen when she died in her Walnut Grove, California, living room (near San Francisco). Many teenagers die each year, but Melanie's death made front-page news because she was only five-feet-three-inches tall but weighed 680 pounds when her heart failed. The coroner linked her gross obesity to the cause of her heart failure from an external examination only (that is, without undertaking an autopsy).[2]

Even more shocking, Melanie died in apparent squalor with empty food containers and uneaten, rotting food scattered about her corpse. Dried feces were trapped between the folds of her fat and her clothing and surrounding fabric were stained with her urine. Multiple bedsores covered her body, and according to one report, insects had been dining on her flesh.[3]

Melanie's mother was prosecuted for felony child abuse at the time of Melanie's death. The National Association for the Advancement of Fat Acceptance (NAAFA) immediately came to the mother's defense, with the head of the organization fervently arguing, "Well, I am supporting her because the media is making a circus out of this case. If this child had weighed 120 pounds and everything else had been equal, this story would not have made it to Page 30 of the newspaper, let alone Page 1. It is making front pages because the media has picked up on the fact that this is about weight. They would not be prosecuting this woman if the child hadn't weighed so much. Now the prosecutor is saying that weight is not an issue, which is so obviously a lie—the issue *is* fat."[4]

The Walnut grove police detective who had been the first to arrive on the death scene did, indeed, deny the case was about the girl's weight: "A lot of news reports have focused on the weight of Melanie, but that doesn't matter at all. She was lying in her own filth. It wouldn't matter if she was thirty years old or fifty or eighty or if she weighed two pounds or 5,000 pounds. This case is going to trial because of the conditions the girl was living in."[5]

What is remarkable about the interchange is that the detective claimed that the girl's weight was not an issue in the case. How could it not be? Why would it not

R.B. McKenzie, *HEAVY!*, DOI 10.1007/978-3-642-20135-6_6,
© Springer-Verlag Berlin Heidelberg 2012

be? And just as remarkable, the NAAFA spokesperson insisted that the issue of the girl's weight should not be an issue in the single mother's prosecution. The spokesperson argued that single parents can't make their children keep their rooms neat, can't keep them from eating when the parents are away at work, and can't make their children go to doctors and nutritionists for help, especially when the parents can't lift them—and when the children are too heavy to walk out the door.[6] Yet if the mother—single or married—had been enabling her daughter to drink martinis at will, to the point of extreme intoxication, on a daily basis, would the mother not have been prosecuted for child abuse or endangerment, regardless of the home's conditions?

Of course, Melanie's mother probably should have controlled Melanie's eating early on. By the time she was eight years old, Melanie weighed 237 pounds, four times the size of the typical child, according to trial testimony. A dermatologist testified that the child's bedsores had to have been in the making long before death and would have required months of hospitalization to heal. Moreover, he insisted that Deborah must have known the seriousness of her daughter's medical condition because "... there would have been a terrible odor from this little girl's skin."[7]

Melanie's mother was convicted of misdemeanor child abuse in early 1998, which means the judge faulted her for "passive misconduct," not active abuse. The judge also reasoned that the mother "knew or could have known that her conduct or failure to act was likely to produce great bodily harm or death" to her daughter.[8]

Melanie's tragic story dramatizes in the extreme the many consequences and potential legal issues of weight gain in this country and the world. Excess weight—even far less than Melanie was carrying—can kill, and is rising as a cause of death. But short of death, the overweight and obese confront weight-related medical problems, which drive up health-care costs for themselves and for health insurance companies, costs they can, under some circumstances, pass on to everyone in higher premiums. No one should be surprised, however, if members of NAAFA and others argue that Melanie's heart failure had nothing to do with her weight. Such an argument seems a stretch, although an important caution should be made against assuming that the deaths and health problems of heavy people always have a direct causal link to their weight and not to other factors, their genes, for example.

Gross excess weight has direct tragic consequences for individuals' emotional and economic well-being as well, costs that can't be easily shifted to others. Gross obesity can debilitate people physically and emotionally, causing more overeating, which, when addictive foods are involved, can spiral into ever more eating, and even affect heavy people's working lives. Weight gain then can become a form of a "contagious disease" within whole social groups and communities, as some weight experts have argued (maybe in fits of enthusiasm for magnifying the country's weight problem and pressing for food and drink policy reforms). Melanie's weight would have, very likely, made her unemployable had she lived to adulthood. Excess weight well below Melanie's is bound to affect people's employment opportunities because of stigmas as well as the debilitations and limitations of weight and added health-care costs. How can morbidly and grossly, or just, obese people be expected to support themselves physically and financially (aside from charging Web site visitors for the opportunity to watch them chow down thousands of calories in a single extended sitting, as Donna Simpson has done in her quest to be the world's fattest woman)? And if they can't support themselves, then who should support them?

Melanie's case also raises the question of who can or should be held legally (and morally) responsible for people's weight, the obese, their enablers, or in the case of children, their parents and caregivers? At what weight (or BMI) should responsibility be assumed and by whom? Employers can't now discriminate in employment and pay because of workers' age, gender, religious affiliation, or sexual orientation without violating a variety of civil rights laws. Should the obese be included in the list? (Michigan thinks so. That state already has a law on its books against weight [and height] discrimination.)

Are heavy people paying the "full freight" for all the personal and social costs associated with their added weight? If so, what should be done about their weight, if anything? Should heavy people's costs be borne by other trimmer people who incur their own costs associated with controlling their weight? Are there public policies that harbor the potential for improving the distribution of all the personal and social costs associated with excess weight?

Such questions raise the specter of an escalating "fat war" in politics over fat taxes, food regulations, discrimination and also in the courts over fat people's human rights and whether the Americans with Disabilities Act (ADA) applies to excess weight. Make no mistake about it, the debate over whether obesity is an ADA-protected disability has already been joined. Google "obesity and ADA" to see the multitude of hits, and consider the seriousness of the policy and legal combatants. The exact nature of the economic, environmental, social, and health-care consequences of excess weight, however, will surely shape how these debates play out.

The 800-Pound "Gorillas" in Our Midst

The basic statistics on the fattening of America over the past half century reported earlier are stark, which can be briefly summarized here for emphasis. More than two out of every three Americans are now overweight (at least, as "officially" so classified). Over a third of them are obese, two and a half times the obesity rate in 1960 and more than ten times the obesity rate at the turn of the twentieth century. The country is now rearing the next generation of obese adults with an ever-expanding count of obese teenagers, children, and even babies. No doubt, a few will end their lives as Melanie did (and, hopefully, none of them will try to take Donna Simpson's "crown" for being the fattest woman—or man—in the world). Without question, the country has gotten fatter to the point of triggering nontrivial consequences that will likely inspire future policy and legal battles, even if the official government statistics overstate or misstate (perhaps for political purposes) the country's weight problems (as critics have argued[9]), which is likely (given all the problems the weight statistics have, which I've noted).

This quick review of summary weight statistics may appear somewhat over-blown due to measurement problems and BMI cutoff points that have been set artificially low (as critics argue, noted in Chap. 2), yet the statistics remain worrisome. The general upward statistical trend in excess weight is supported by our casual observation of people who pass us by in malls, airports, and especially along fair midways. There are a lot more budding Melanies than there were one, two, or five decades ago. Weight statisticians now predict, if current weight growth continues, half of the American population will be obese by 2020 and three quarters will be overweight, only a decade into the future.[10] There might very well have been fewer Melanies, or budding Melanies, decades ago simply because their enablers would have had to incur higher costs. Economic constraints have a way of controlling the eating predispositions of heavy people and their (negligent, sometimes parental) enablers. People's low incomes combined with high prices for fattening foods can contain weight gain, and weight gain can lower heavy people's real incomes and raise the full prices of the food they eat.

Contrary to what many overweight and obese people might want to think, only a minor percentage of excess weight can be chalked up to genetic *abnormalities*. If all the weight gain in recent decades were a matter of genetics, why aren't black Africans as heavy on average as black African Americans? Or how could human weight-controlling genes, which took millennia to evolve, have changed so much in America (especially relative to the rest of the world) over the last half century or less? The stark facts are this: An overwhelming percentage of the country's added weight can be attributed to the obvious—overeating, encouraged by cheap, fatty, and sugary out-of-home meals that many Americans choose not to resist because the choices are immediately available (at home and work) and time-saving. We've learned that the growth in the country's weight problems can be attributed to specialization and traditional considerations, like lower real *full* prices for foods and higher real incomes that, in turn, can be attributed to technological advancements in food production, processing, and distribution. We've also learned that unsuspected factors are at the root of some of the weight gain, for example, the reductions in food regulations, the freeing of world markets, and the growth in television screen sizes with ever greater definition, number of cable channels, HD-DVR players and recorders—and on and on.

Granted, given our evolutionary past, modern humans may have a *predisposi-tion*, felt with more or less urgency across individuals and ethnic groups, to eat as much sugary and fatty food as possible and whenever possible. But such a predis-position is different from a genetic disorder or abnormality that causes people to lose so much control of their eating that they have no real choice in the matter, absolving them of all personal responsibility for their weight. Yet modern economic forces play upon human's eating predisposition, contributing to people's weight problems and making dieting all the more difficult. Considering these forces, some average weight gain over the decades is hardly unexpected and certainly no (or little) contemporary average weight gain would be surprising.

But the 800-pound gorilla in our midst is the magnitude of our weight gain and the varied personal and societal consequences of people's added pounds. And, like any other problem, solutions to the problem depend on a clear understanding of the problem. Moreover, many of the reports on the country's weight problems are either founded on or inspire policy agendas that can be a major source of political conflict ahead as reformers seek to control in various ways everyone's eating proclivities to abate the weight problems of some.

The Big Haul

Between 1960 and 2006 (the latest year of available data), American adults (twenty to seventy-four years of age) gained an average of more than twenty-six pounds (the weight of the largest turkey that can be purchased at Thanksgiving). In other words, adult Americans weigh collectively *three million tons* more today than they would have had they stayed as "trim" as they were in 1960 (and there were plenty of overweight and obese Americans in 1960). Three million tons in total weight gain is equivalent to:

- Twenty-four *billion* – yes, *billion*! – four-ounce deep-fried Twinkies, close to fifty times the annual production of Twinkies.[11]
- More than 120,000 empty seventy-five-foot, eighteen-wheel tractor-trailer trucks that, if put end to end, would stretch, via the shortest road route possible, from Los Angeles to St. Louis, Missouri.
- More than thirty-seven million 1960-equivalent American adults—or 7.5 million of the fabled 800-pound gorillas.

And these calculations do not include the pounds added by the 100 million or so overweight kids, teenagers, and seniors seventy-five years old and older. If their extra tonnage were added to the total, the lineup of tractor-trailers would draw up just short of the Capitol in Washington, D.C.

Hauling around the equivalent of seven to eight million 800-pound gorillas in our cars and planes (over and above what we were hauling in 1960), adds a tremendous drag on the nation's transportation system and undermines the fuel efficiency of vehicles that transportation manufacturers have been struggling to increase over the decades. Auto manufactures have reduced the weight of cars, replacing steel parts with lighter-weight plastic, to improve fuel efficiency, but consumers have put the weight right back in their cars through the spreads of their backsides.

Indeed, for every pound increase in Americans' average adult weight, gasoline consumption goes up by thirty-nine million gallons a year, according to transportation engineering research.[12] So, Americans' average twenty-six-pound weight increase between 1960 and 2006 burned an additional 1.1 billion gallons of gasoline, enough to fuel two million passenger cars for a year. And the 2006 increase in fuel consumption due to added weight was 21 percent (or 200 million gallons) more than the calculated increase for 2003.[13] You can imagine that the projected weight gain of Americans over the next decade will add to the country's fuel demand and negate somewhat any improved fuel efficiency of automotive and other forms of transportation, which can be cause enough for some politicians to advocate that car manufacturer work harder to raise the average fuel economy of their fleets.

Granted, these calculations provide only rough estimates (for only two out of many modes of transportation), which, in all fairness, must be viewed in a wider context. The added fuel consumption for the added weight amounts to a minor fraction of Americans' total annual fuel consumption, which was 137 billion gallons in 2008 (close to four billion gallons less than that consumed in 2007, before the full force of the Great Recession set in).[14] The increase in Americans' average weight increased annual fuel consumption by only 0.8 percent. Not much proportionally, but keep in mind that American drivers aren't very sensitive to price increases and the responsiveness of gasoline suppliers is not all that high either, given the delays in adding refining capacity (or, in "econ-speak," the demand for and supply of gasoline are "inelastic"), and a very small increase in demand can spur a disproportionate increase in the price at the pump. For example, energy economists estimate that gasoline prices in North American may increase as much as five times the percentage increase in demand,[15] which means that a 0.8 percent increase in demand can drive up prices by 4 percent per gallon, or about 10–12 cents at today's prices. Of course, when fuel prices go up because of added weight, trim people also pay the higher prices, which is a nontrivial concern for economists when the added excess weight is, in various ways, subsidized directly or indirectly through government policies (whether in the form of farm subsidies for fatty foods or through subsidies for weight-related health-care costs, which research has shown can cause people to get all the fatter[16]).

The good news (if you can call it that) is that rising gasoline prices may prompt more people to walk or bike instead of drive, eat at home more often, and, consequently, lose weight. The nearly doubling of the price of gasoline between 1998 and 2010 could result in as much as three pounds of weight loss per American adult, a loss that can, in turn, lower health insurance costs, along with deaths from excess weight by more than 100,000, using another researcher's econometric model.[17]

The bad news is that at $3 a gallon, a 12-cent increase in a gallon of gas can (roughly speaking, again) lead to an increase in annual gas expenditures by Americans of over $16 billion.[18] Again, that increase may not sound like much, but recognize that the demand for gasoline because of weight gain will contribute to the world demand for oil, which can feed the coffers of oil-producing countries, a number of which are hardly peace-loving friends of the United States and the civilized world. And note that none of these calculations takes into consideration the added fuel consumption needed, for example, to grow and produce the food heavy people demand to maintain their weights and then add more pounds in coming years.

All those extra twenty-six-pound turkeys that Americans have been carrying around with them also take a toll in jet fuel consumption. Researchers report that the eight-and-a-half-pound increase in average weight of Americans in the 1990s caused airlines to consume an additional 350 million gallons of jet fuel in 2000, at a cost of $275 million, which added to the losses of the American airline industry.[19] Americans' weight gain could now be causing airlines to burn more than a billion gallons of jet fuel each year than they would have had to burn had Americans remained at their 1960 average weight (although such an extrapolation can be taken as only a rough estimation). Weight gain could very well be partly to blame for higher airfares, fees for bags, and the elimination of free meals on flights.

Global Warming and Weight Gain

Human activity, many scientists say, has significant environmental effect and is an unheralded culprit in global warming. As people have added tonnage to their stomachs and backsides, they require more gasoline and jet fuel to move around the country and the world—a billion more gallons of gasoline and a billion more gallons of jet fuel per year based on our weight gain since 1960.[20] The added body weight also needs more calories just to keep the added fat fed, which requires additional fuel to produce food and transport it to market (and calories for human consumption are energy-intense to produce). And of course, with added fuel consumption comes added emission of greenhouse gases.

Environmental researchers estimate that a world population with a 40 percent obesity rate requires the use of 19 percent more food energy just to maintain the weight. They conclude, "greenhouse gas emissions from food production and car travel due to increases in adiposity [fat tissue] in a population of one billion are estimated to be between 0.4 giga tons (GT) and 1.0 GT of carbon dioxide equivalents per year."[21] With the actual world population rapidly approaching seven billion, the greenhouse gas emissions resulting from the greater fuel consumption could be several times greater. Thomas Robert Malthus, the population theorist of the late eighteenth century mentioned earlier in the book, never thought that global warming could be one of the natural checks (in addition to famine, pestilence, and war) that could put a brake on population growth.

> People's added weight is increasing fuel consumption and the emission of greenhouse gases, which can be threatening the survivability of polar bears.

Can you not see how this line of argument can fuel intense political conflicts over how to constrict Americans' propensity to overeat, and thereby reduce the price of gas and food, undermine the financing of the political foes of the country, and save the arctic ice shelves and polar bears?[22] You are a skeptic about the tie between weight and global warming. No matter. Can't you imagine how the line of argument just laid out can be exploited by advocates of greater controls on people's eating?

Medical Costs of Excess Weight

The link between being overweight or obese and ill health—even death, in Melanie's case—has been clear to medical and nutritionist researchers for decades. Medical research has causally linked excess weight and obesity to thirty-five (or more) diseases, including hypertension, heart disease, various cancers (breast, colon, and prostate), type-2 diabetes, osteoarthritis, gallbladder disease, and incontinence. More recently, obesity has been linked to impaired brain function and the incidence of dementia and Alzheimer's disease among the elderly.[23]

In fact, other researchers have found through brain scans of ninety-four people in their seventies who were not afflicted with brain diseases, that overweight (not yet obese) subjects had 4 percent less brain tissue in critical areas than their normal-weight counterparts. The lead researcher characterized the finding as "severe brain degeneration" with the implication that weight can affect cognitive functions. Obese subjects in the study had 8 percent less brain tissue, a deficiency that could affect their self-control over their eating, which means that weight has another potential feedback loop, leading to greater excess pounds because of weight's effects on the available working neurons.[24] The brain tissue was lost in four areas of the brain: the frontal and temporal lobes (involved in planning and memory), the hippocampus (involved in long-term memory), the anterior cingulate gyrus (involved in executive functions and attention), and the basal ganglia (involved in movement and coordination).[25]

In computer terms, the overweight and obese subjects had less internal random access memory (RAM) to work with. Presumably, the loss of brain "RAM" is gradual over decades, with the pace and extent of loss dependent on how overweight people are and for how long they have carried added pounds. (Again, some care needs to be taken in assessing these findings. People can become obese partially because of the missing neurons, or excess weight can cause loss of neurons, or both. And then, there may be only an association between obesity and a lower count of neurons, with both conditions caused by some other genetic or environmental force.)

Treating obesity-related diseases in 2005 racked up $188 billion (in 2010 dollars) in medical costs, or nearly 17 percent of all medical spending, economists estimated in 2010.[26] And the costs are rising. That year the real (inflation-adjusted) health-care expenditures for obesity, half of which were covered by Medicaid and Medicare, were 50 percent greater than the real health-care expenditures for the obese in 1998. Rising costs do not go unnoticed among government oversight agencies and health insurance companies, of course. The Congressional Budget Office (CBO) found that health-care costs for all obese Americans in 2007 was 38

> People's added weight is increasing health-care costs and health insurance premiums and driving many people from the insurance market.

percent higher than for normal-weight Americans. For morbidly obese Americans the extra expenditures was 93 percent higher, which is why insurance companies shy from insuring heavy people and why employers discount the pay of their heavyweight workers, a consequence to which we will return later in the chapter. The CBO found that the gap in medical expenditures between normal-weight Americans and obese Americans was continuing apace in the 2000s.[27]

Bring on the Reinforcements

America's excess weight crisis is never more real than for paramedics sent to rescue progressively heavier people with equipment designed decades ago for lower "peak loads." Melanie's extraordinary weight—nearly eleven pounds an inch and more than four times the average weight of American women—must have strained the carrying capacity of the coroner's van, as well as the support capability of the medical examiner's table, not to mention the backs of the rescue and medical teams.

Paramedics frequently encounter people who substantially exceed the 350-pound peak load for rescue gurneys. In one dramatic rescue in 2007, firefighters-turned-construction-workers cut off the front of an upstairs bedroom in a home to extricate a 900-pound man and, with the help of a forklift, removed him from his bed and carried him off for medical care on a flatbed truck. The thirty-three-year-old man had not left his bedroom for the previous four years because he could not get through the doorway. To shield the man from onlookers, the firefighters covered the heavy man with a blue tarp.[28]

> People's added weight are causing paramedic teams to reinforce at added expense their ambulances and gurneys to accommo-date their greater peak-load problems.

To handle heavier patients, communities across the country are dramatically upgrading their ambulances, gurneys, and examining and operating tables—all at a higher cost, of course. Replacement gurneys and operating tables these days can accommodate 1,000 pounds, and sometimes even 1,600 pounds. Gurneys with the latter capacity have a mattress a foot wider than the normal gurney and a place to attach a winch to aid moving the gurney into an ambulance and through emergency room doors.[29]

Such heavy-weight gurneys come at a hefty cost. Columbus, Ohio, thought its eighteen gurneys at a cost of $5,000 each, designed to hold 650 pounds, would do for decades to come, only to realize in 2010 that emergency calls from patients weighing far more were on the increase. The city planned to buy thirty-four additional gurneys with hydraulic lifts that would support up to a half ton, each costing $10,000.[30] (To see what a super-sized gurney looks like, see one captured in a *New York Times* report noted in the following endnote.[31])

Of course, larger, heavier gurneys call for ambulances to match. Standard ambulances (accommodating patients up to 400 pounds) in Omaha, Nebraska, have cost between $190,000 and $200,000, but the city will be spending an additional $20,000 per replacement ambulance for upgrades to carry much heavier patients. The upgrades include a winch, wider doors, re-enforced floors, and larger patient compartments to accommodate the larger gurneys and the patients on them.[32] Columbus, Ohio, spent $6,000 in 2010 on each ambulance to accommodate larger patients, mainly by installing winching to pull larger patients into the ambulances.[33] An ambulance service in Western Australia spent $300,000 for an ambulance that can carry patients up to 1,100 pounds. The vehicle includes a hydraulic lift (much like those that are common on large delivery trucks) to take the patients from ground level to the bed level of the ambulance.

Facing a growing obese population and a tenfold increase in calls to transport obese patients, an ambulance service in Oxford, England, upgraded one of its ambulances designed for heart patients to carry people weighing up to a 1,000 pounds, at a modest added cost of $7,700.[34] Not surprisingly, to serve substantially obese patients, ambulance companies have to use three to four times the manpower and incur two-and-a-half-times the cost of assisting normal-weight patients, which explains why they have begun adding surcharges to serve these patients. In 2009, a Topeka, Kansas, ambulance service got the city council to approve a hike in its fees from $629 for normal-weight patients to $1,172 for patients who weigh more than 500 pounds.[35] In a real sense, large patients will be paying by the pound, which, of course, can cause many people to ask, "Why?" with many others asking, "Why not?"

Hospitals in Britain have spent hundreds of thousands of additional pounds for "super-size" gowns wider than small cars, special equipment to measure and weigh obese patients, re-enforcements for their operating tables, and reconstruction of doorways to accommodate wider gurneys and obese patients.[36] Hospitals everywhere are buying bariatric crutches and wheelchairs, with and without motors, for patients weighing up to a half ton.

One Texas-based hospital architectural firm reports that it must include many design features to accommodate hospitals' growing population of obese and severely obese patients and visitors. For example, a majority of its projects must now:

- Make patient room doors two feet wider (using two doors as opposed to the previous one) at one-third greater cost,
- Avoid the installation of wall-mounted toilets, which can't hold the weight of floor-positioned toilets, a change that reduces the flexibility of bathroom designs,

Of course, heavier patients lead, inevitably, to back strains for paramedic and hospital staffers with hospital administrators reporting increases in disability absences for back problems among nurses and orderlies who have to work with large patients. Also, heavier patients lead to larger corpses, which have required hospital morgues and coroner offices across the country to purchase larger and sturdier examining tables and storage bays, and install winches and cranes to maneuver the bodies.[37] Naturally, "super-sized" coffins are becoming ever more popular, or rather necessary. Goliath's Casket in Indiana now regularly builds coffins twice the size of its once standard models and reports building one casket for an obese man from Alaska that was seven feet wide. Some crematoria are sometimes unable to handle large patients, while others are revamping their ovens and applying surcharges for cremation of the obese.[38]

The federal government mandates that car manufacturers install seatbelts, but only to fit a 215-pound male. Most major companies—Ford, General Motors, Chrysler, Nissan, and Honda—add eighteen to twenty inches beyond the government's required minimum length and then provide extenders. But the heavier the person, the more uncomfortable the seatbelt may be, and extenders add risks of upper body injury in crashes. Eighty-three percent of normal-weight people report using seatbelts all the time, but only 70 percent of extremely obese people report doing the same. That is, as the BMI goes up, seatbelt use goes down, adding yet another risk factor of injury or death for obese people, and for ambulance and hospital personnel who must deal with the wreckage and carnage on the country's roads.[39]

Can you not imagine how anti-obesity advocates will (and have) argued that the country needs to put policy brakes on people's food choices and eating habits for the same reason as taxes on alcohol and cigarettes, to reduce all the social and private costs from people's weight gain?

- Equip a fourth to half of patient rooms with overhead lifts at a cost of $7,500 or more per bed,
- Provide sturdier beds, stretchers, wheel-chairs, and dialysis chairs that can increase equipment cost by more than half,
- Insure that at least a fifth of the chairs and couches in hospital waiting rooms can hold up under bariatric patients and visitors at one-fourth greater costs,
- Plan for larger CT and MRI scanners,
- Increase the floor area for showers by close to 40 percent, which can increase the cost of shower stalls by close to half, and
- Install dialysis washer boxes in almost all intensive care units partially to control skin infections of obese patients.

As conveyed in a personal communication (January 24, 2011) by Sean Wilson of Beck Architecture, LLC (Dallas, Texas).

Super-Sizing Everything

The growth in people's weights is, of course, leading to a major super-sizing not just of medical-related equipment but of virtually everything—clothing, furniture, and public seating. "Plus sizes" for "full-figure" or "mature" women have become euphemisms for extra large sizes. Men's clothing have been gradually scaled upward with added Xs, as in XL, XXL, XXXL, and XXXXL, a size labeling system that has given way at many clothiers to simpler large-size indicators, as in 2XL to 8XL.

One enterprising journalist, Abram Sauer for *Esquire* magazine, became concerned that after aging and gaining weight, he could still fit into pants labeled as having a 36-inch waist. He also found that he could, at one store, actually fit into pants with a 34-inch waist, that is, as labeled. Puzzled, he got a tape measure and found that stores had begun to account for men's weight gain with "vanity labels," or those that indicate a size that may actually be several inches smaller than the true measurement of the garment.[40] At H&M stores, Sauer found pants labeled as having a 36-inch waist measured 37 inches, but that was only a start. Gap 36-inch-waist pants actually had waists of 39 inches, and Old Navy, waists of 41 inches! Sauer understandably observed, "I enjoyed many of these pants, as I mentioned, but I'm still perturbed. This isn't the subjective business of mediums, larges, and extra-larges—nor is it the murky business of women's sizes, what with its black-hole size zero. This is *science,* damn it. Numbers! Should inches be different than miles per hour? ... Multiplication tables don't yield to make us feel better about badness at math; why should pants make us feel better about badness at health? Are we all so many emperors with no clothes?"[41]

> People's additional weight has called for wider stadium seats and larger coffins.

Plus-Size Growth

> Clothing designers have begun to use "vanity sizing" to delude heavier customers into believing that their old sizes still fit.

The clothing industry has always been dominated by women's fashions, which are now beginning to adjust in a major way to provide style to over-weight women. Women's clothes are notorious for varying across designers and for given sizes moving up to fit larger women over the decades. That is, a current dress today sized as a 12 could very well have fit a women who wore a size 14 two or three decades ago. Moreover, spandex is a common fabric in women's clothing, tops and bottoms, and flowing garment construction is designed to make excess weight less apparent. Muumuus are back in "fashion" but not for style purposes, conventionally considered.

Over a third of American women are obese, but only 17 percent of women's clothing sales by dollar volume are in plus sizes (size 14 or larger).[42] The disproportionately low sales could be attributed to women downsizing, as in squeezing into smaller sizes on the presumption that extra tight is stylish and that their diets would work. The relatively low plus-size sales could also be attributed to the fact that plus sizes have gotten progressively larger, but also because plus-size women are disproportionately in lower-income groups where style, especially high-priced high fashion, may not be an affordable priority. But fewer clothing options for heavy women could also be a reason for lower sales in plus sizes. Heavy women buy less because there is less variety from which to choose. Designers have traditionally focused their attention on trim to skinny women, and limited retail space prohibits stores from carrying the full range of sizes required today. Large women may also be reluctant to try on clothes in the dressing rooms of stores catering to much trimmer women.

But the market condition appears to be improving for plus-size women. Women's clothing stores are awakening to the economic reality that has come with the fattening of the country—there are profit dollars to be made by the spread in extra full-figure women. Forever 21 (with its plus-size Faith 21 clothing) and Target (with its plus-size Pure Energy clothing line) are adding larger sizes to their racks, increasing the clothing options that have been offered for decades by plus-size women's stores such as Lane Bryant and the Forgotten Woman. In the twelve months ending in 2010 (a year of continuing recession in sections of the country and a year of sluggish recovery in the overall economy during which retail sales continued to be anemic), retail sales of plus-size clothing *rose* by 1.4 percent, while overall retail clothing sales *declined* by 0.8 percent.[43]

In past years, fashion shows and print clothing ads were reserved for bone-thin models. But in 2010, media reports abounded on the success of full-figure models strutting their stuff in print clothing advertisements and down the elite fashion runways reserved exclusively for designer clothing for large women. In recent years, high-fashion women's clothing designers Jean-Paul Gaultier, John Galliano, Elena Miro, Mark Fast, and William Tempest used full-figure women in their shows held in the four fashion capitals of the world, Paris, New York, London, and Milan (changes that have been painful for some designers tied to the usual thin models).[44]

It's easy to see why clothing designers and stores have moved to serve the hordes of heavier women. The market is there ready to be tapped, and it's growing (pun intended). Certainly heavy people deserve as many clothing choices as anyone else, but from the economic way of thinking, an unintended consequence may emerge as the fashion industry shifts to cater to heavier people. In so far as the fashion industry's marketing decisions lower the *full* cost of weight gain by expanding clothing options, greater weight gain can be expected. Again, the law of demand lives! Designers who find creative ways to camouflage people's weights very likely will boost their business, to the extent that their camouflage designs lower the full cost of weight, encourage more eating, and discourage people from curbing excess weight. This is to say that clothing designers who have sought to be a solution to weight gain can contribute (albeit marginally and inadvertently) to the problem.

Wider Bottoms

Clothing is hardly the only sector of the American (and foreign) economy that has been affected by the weight-gain problem. The furniture industry has had to offer "plus-size" and "oversize" chairs and sofas of all sorts, naturally with reinforced frames that can accommodate men and women 500 or more pounds.[45] Oversize-Furniture.com offers a full line of chairs and sofas with extra wide bottoms (up to forty-four-inches wide for arm chairs) to fulfill its professed mission, "To bring joy to people and confidence to shoppers" (that their furniture will not collapse under them).

Theater and stadium seats have had to be widened to handle the broader backsides of concert attendees, moviegoers, and sports fans. When the new Yankee Stadium opened in 2009, it had much the look and feel of the old stadium, but with 6,000 fewer seats primarily because the new seats were wider.[46] The New York City Center ripped out all of its seats, which were seventeen-to nineteen-inches wide, in 2010 to replace them with seats nineteen- to twenty-two-inches wide, an increase of 10 percent or more, all intended to improve the center's competitiveness in attracting larger theatergoers.[47] And heavy people have acquired market power that firms in hot pursuit of profits and survival dare not ignore, but which can make the problem all the worse.

Disneyland shut down one of its most popular attractions, "It's a Small World," for ten months in 2008 to give the magical water ride a fresh coat of paint. But the refurbishment also provided an opportunity to address another problem. Over the years, as ride passengers—children and adults alike—grew heavier, the boats were sinking deeper in the water, often scraping the bottom of the waterway (and wearing down the fiberglass on the boats' bottoms) or even getting stuck in mid-ride. To reduce the repair problems, Disney "imagineers" had begun letting boats leave the starting ramp with unfilled seats. During the 2008 shutdown, Disney rebuilt the boats with wider seats to carry heavier passengers, which allowed for fuller loads (with pun intended).[48]

> Businesses have imposed "surcharges" for heavy customers for the damage they can do to furniture.

Just as this book was being sent to the printers, the Federal Transit Authority proposed raising the assumed average weight of city and intercity bus passengers by 17 percent, or from 150 to 175 pounds per passenger. If adopted (which it surely will be), the higher average weight will mean that fewer passengers will be allowed on buses. The higher weight standards can be expected to show up in greater costs for more buses and bigger buses making more trips, which can make bus travel less fuel efficient with more pollutants emitted.[49]

Would you believe that obesity is now hitting nail salons? Obese women have been causing wear and tear on manicure/pedicure lounge chairs, which are made for women weighing up to 200 pounds and can cost $2,500. With their repair bills going up, Natural Nails in DeKalb County, Georgia, tacked on a $5 surcharge to the normal $24 manicure/pedicure charge for overweight women. You can imagine the coming legal war over such surcharges for overweight patrons. The store manager told a television station reporter, "Do you think that's fair when we take $24 [for manicure and pedicure] and we have to pay $2,500? No." The customer, who protested to the store and eventually got her $5 returned, reacted, "I was humiliated. The word has to get out there that these people are discriminating against us because of our weight. You can't do that."[50] Let the lawsuits begin.

Fat Biases

Really heavy people face social stigmas, disadvantages, and rejections on all sides—at work, in social gatherings, in schools, and even in doctors' offices and hospitals—that are as large as they are, according to surveys of thousands of overweight people and those who encounter them.[51] Negative reactions to the obese may be subtle discrimination or blatantly rude and hurtful comments, not something anyone wants to applaud (especially for the few who can't help being otherwise), but such problems are real for heavy people. And the economic reality to remember is that discrimination and unkind comments add to the costs incurred from being heavy and could be a check on people being heavier than they are. This means that as heavy people form social "enclaves" of like-weight people, they shelter themselves, albeit somewhat, from the full costs of their weight, which can reduce the pressure for them to control their weight.

Workplace Fat Prejudices

In a survey of more than 2,200 overweight and obese women, a quarter of the respondents reported that they were discriminated in some way in employment because of their weight, such as being denied a job. Fifty-four percent reported episodes of weight prejudice on the part of coworkers (e.g., pejorative comments), and 43 percent reported incidents on the part of their employers (e.g., denied a promotion).[52] In another survey of over 2,800 adults, researchers found that self-reports of workplace discrimination (denied jobs and promotions and wrongful termination) rose dramatically with weight, and overweight and obese women were more likely to *report* workplace discrimination than overweight and obese men (with emphasis on "report" because women may have a greater sensitivity to discrimination or just a greater inclination to tell others about their discriminatory encounters).[53]

The negative "vibes" overweight and obese people detect appears to have validity in surveys and hard statistics. In one survey, 28 percent of teachers reported that they thought becoming obese was the worst thing that could happen to a person; 24 percent of nurses reported being repulsed by obese patients. Moreover, parents provide less college support for their overweight children than they do for their trimmer children.[54]

Medical Fat Prejudices

Heavy people's weight apparently can also affect the amount and type of medical care they seek and receive. Only 18 percent of 1,200 doctors surveyed said they would have weight management discussions with their substantially overweight patients, but 42 percent said that they would have such discussions with mildly overweight patients, which means more than half the surveyed doctors would shy from such discussions with even mildly overweight patients. Only a third of surveyed primary care doctors reported that they felt responsible for their obese patients' weight management. Seventeen percent of surveyed physicians reported a reluctance to provide obese women with annual pelvic exams, and 83 percent reported reluctance to provide the exams when the women were at all hesitant. And surveys do reveal that the reluctance of women to have pelvic exams or just to seek medical care of all kinds rises with their weight, perhaps because of their own impaired self-images and the apparently very real negative judgments these women receive from many of their nurses and doctors.[55]

More than half of 620 American doctors viewed obese patients as unattractive (if not ugly), according to two other surveys. A third considered their obese patients as "weak-willed, sloppy, and lazy," attributing their excess weight largely to sedentary lifestyles and overeating.[56] Surveyed medical-care professionals in Britain and France held much the same negative views of their obese patients, with 30 percent of the French doctors viewing their obese patients as lazier and more self-indulgent than their trim patients and attributing the excess pounds to lack of self-control.[57] Indeed, such antifat attitudes seem to be prevalent among doctors, nurses, medical students, dieticians, and fitness professionals all around the world.[58] And just ask doctors, nurses, and medical administrators who regularly deal with severely obese patients and you are bound to hear comments about how severely obese patients "grow things" between the folds of their excess poundage.

Fat Pictures

Obesity also stunts educational attainment, apparently. A Swedish study of 700,000 men found that the obese men in the group were less likely to go to college, even after adjusting the statistical analysis for the men's intelligence and the social and economic positions of their parents.[59] Similarly, surveys in Britain and the United States found that obesity seems to have undercut how far both overweight and obese men and women have gone in school.[60]

The overweight and obese also suffer social rejection and isolation, even more so than those with physical disabilities. In one study, men and women were shown six pictures of potential sexual partners. The pictures included an obese partner, a healthy partner, and partners with four different disabilities: One potential partner was pictured in a wheelchair, another was missing an arm, another had a mental disorder, and the last one had a history of sexually transmitted diseases. Both men and women ranked the obese partner last in terms of sexual desirability, although men were significantly more negative on the obese partner than were women (which could be one reason women may spend more on weight-related health care than men).[61]

In a similar study, overweight and normal-weight subjects were shown pictures of one healthy person and five people with disabilities—one without a hand, one in a wheelchair with a blanket, one with a facial disfigurement, one holding crutches with a brace, and one obese. Both the overweight and normal-weight subjects, adults and children alike, judged the healthy person as most attractive. The adults ranked the obese person second to last in attractiveness, while the children ranked the obese person least attractive.[62] The researchers had found in an earlier study that the stigma children held for their obese peers had grown over the previous four decades even though the subjects making the rankings had become more overweight along with the general population of children.[63]

> Heavy workers confront an array of workplace and social stigmas.

In a study of women's dating advertisements, men were less likely to respond to ads from women who admitted to being obese than to ads from women who admitted to having drug problems (again, a potential cause for the difference in medical care expenditures of men and women).[64]

In the media, overweight people are disproportionately the butt of humor and ridicule in sit-coms, which a variety of studies have documented.[65] Weight-related comments are often reinforced with bursts from laugh tracks. Even print and television commercials for various weight-loss plans and schemes may intentionally (or maybe, at times, inadvertently) portray overweight and obese people negatively through "before" and "after" pictures depicting the heavy person with a sad expression and lackluster appearance before the promoted weight-loss regime only to be followed by a radiantly smiling face and flattering hair and makeup after the pounds are lost. The ads often carry the none-too-subtle suggestion that weight is a matter of self-control, and a snap—with the purchase of the advertised diet plans and products.[66]

Even friends and family members are not above making weight-related put-downs and inflicting prejudicial treatment upon the heavy among their ranks.[67] No wonder overweight and obese people report a higher level of loneliness, which rises right along with their BMI (although the evidence is somewhat conflicting), with another potential feedback loop with the higher loneliness leading to greater weight.[68]

Just as excess weight brings social stigmas, losing weight can, apparently, reduce their effects, overweight and obese people report. In a survey of patients *before* they had bariatric bypass surgery (in which the size of the useable stomach is reduced to curb appetite and food intake), 87 percent reported being denied jobs because of their weight, 90 percent felt that their coworkers stigmatized them, 77 percent reported being depressed on a daily basis, and 84 percent reported that they avoided going to public places. (Of course, they might not have been seeking the surgery had they not faced such personal and social problems.) Fourteen months *after* their surgery and weight loss, they all reported lower incidence of weight discrimination.[69]

Overweight people at all levels face real social and personal pressures, an obvious conclusion from the mountain of survey findings and statistical research, and these pressures take their toll on the self-esteem of the overweight and obese—especially the grossly obese. Bouts of depression may follow, and episodes may become more frequent and severe as weight gain rises. Low self-esteem and depression feed weight gain, and a destructive feedback loop emerges.

But we must remember that it's not just the trim people who hold unflattering prejudices against heavy people. Because weight prejudices are spread so widely in the populations and because so many people are overweight and obese, it must follow that many heavy people also harbor strong unflattering prejudices against people in their own weight categories.

You can imagine how the statistics covered here on the social, medical, and workplace problems faced by heavy Americans will likely work their way into calls for weight discrimination laws and into policy debates over whether government should control how much people eat and weigh.

Fat Workers, Slim Wages

It is hard to imagine how the multitude of negative attitudes toward heavy people would not have labor-market effects, not the least of which can be fat-related restraints on the market demand for overweight and obese workers. *If* added weight makes heavy people less productive or adds to their medical-care and insurance costs, then the economic value of heavy people to firms will be undercut with a concomitant reduction in the labor-market demand for heavy workers.

The reluctance of some employers to hire heavy workers was reported in a *Newsweek* magazine poll of 202 hiring managers. Fifty-seven percent of the respondents said that unattractive prospective job seekers would have a harder time finding a job than attractive job seekers, with excess weight being a factor in "unattractiveness." *Newsweek* also found, "Two thirds of business managers said they believe some managers would hesitate before hiring a qualified job candidate who was significantly overweight."[70]

Note that not everyone needs to share the negative attitudes toward heavy people for market demand for them to decrease. If only a significant portion of hiring managers share the negative attitudes (and very likely few hiring managers actually seek employees *because* they are heavy), then the labor-market demand for heavy people will be impaired, and it really doesn't matter if the negative attitudes are justified or not. Not surprisingly, the restriction on the labor-market demand will grow with increasing weight *if* and *when* added weight truly undercuts workers' productivity, lowers customers' buying experiences, and adds to their health-care and insurance (and maybe other business) costs. Regardless of whether workplace stigmas toward overweight and obese workers are justified or not, the resulting decrease in demand for such workers means that both employers who believe the stigmas and those who do not can get by with paying overweight and obese workers less than normal-weight workers—at least for a time.[71]

> Heavy workers pay by the pound for their excess weight in terms of lost employment opportunities and wage penalties.

Coworkers' attitudes may also affect the labor market for overweight people. If nothing else, trimmer workers might fear that their own health insurance premiums will go up when heavy people are hired, especially when there is no premium differential for excess weight. When health insurance premiums are the same for all people regardless of weight, the additional health-care costs that heavier people incur *can be* (but as we will see, are not necessarily) spread across all who are insured.

Trimmer workers might also worry that the impaired productivity of heavy people can hike their firms' cost structure, putting their firms at an impaired (albeit slightly) competitive disadvantage – and putting all workers' jobs at greater risk in the process. A firm that hires heavy workers may be pressed to compensate trim workers for the added job risks with added wages and other fringe benefits in order to get the trimmer workers to continue to work with heavy people (or just support the hiring of heavier workers).

Of course, the added compensation for trim workers will translate into an added cost for hiring heavy workers, a consequence that can further decrease the demand for them. The concomitant restricted demand might be expected to show up in lower real wages and fringe benefits paid to overweight and obese workers.[72] Of course, it might be that no one—not trim (or trimmer) workers, managers, and owners, not to mention heavy workers themselves—in firms really wants to discriminate against heavy workers in employment opportunities and in any and all forms of compensation (wages, fringes, and time off). They might rightfully consider such discrimination repugnant, even when justified on economic grounds. But there are at least two expected market forces that will press firms to discriminate against heavy workers *if*—or *when*—they are less productive and impose unusual health-care and insurance (or other) costs on their firms:

- First, as already noted, in some (certainly not all and maybe not even most) occupations heavy workers may increase firms' costs to the point of making them uncompetitive vis-à-vis firms that do discriminate and that, as a consequence, can charge lower prices (or offer higher product quality and service for the same price). Firms that don't discriminate can be forced to contract their operations as more firms with more competitive cost structures expand.

- Second, and just as important although less widely appreciated, when managers hire heavy workers in significant numbers (say, in proportion to their representation in the general population) knowing that they will add to their firms' costs without compensating productivity increases, their firms' profit streams into the future will necessarily be less than they could be. You can imagine that top managers whose annual compensation is heavily dependent on bonuses tied to firm profitability will feel real pressure to trim their workforces—and keep them trim—when and where weight makes a difference in firm productivity and costs. The firms' impaired future profit streams will necessarily depress the firms' stocks below what they could be (because current stock prices will tend to reflect the present discounted value of the future profit stream). Moreover, savvy entrepreneurs can be expected to see that "money is being left on the table" by the firms' antidiscriminatory employment policies toward heavy people and can be swayed by the depressed stock prices to buy out these nondiscriminating owners. The entrepreneurs who take over the nondiscriminating firms can then shift their new firms' hiring policy toward trimmer workforces, pushing up the firms' future profit stream and hiking the firms' stock prices. That is, such entrepreneurs can do what comes naturally to them: buy low and sell high, pocketing the capital gains in the process, which will tend to approximate the cost savings.

Okay, markets might not operate with the precision suggested here, fine tuning firms' labor-market demands to account for the added pounds of their workers, pound by pound. In any number of occupations (bookkeeping, cooking, maybe selling, even jobs in the executive suites of many firms, for example), worker weight might not depress worker productivity at all, or by consequential amounts. In other occupations (security guards and sumo wrestling, for example), added weight (up to a point) can be an occupational advantage. No problem. The point is that *when* added weight adversely affects worker productivity and hikes worker health-care costs to significant (meaningful) extents, the economic way of thinking suggests the *direction* of labor-market demand and compensation outcomes that should be investigated statistically to complete the argument. And beyond some point, weight must create economic problems that have market consequences, or else all the broad-based talk about the "obesity epidemic," "obesity crisis," and even "obesity pandemic" is nothing more than ... well, talk.

"Beauty" in the Workplace

Fortunately, economists have developed a sizable cottage industry trying to figure out how worker attributes affect the levels and forms of worker compensation. It's common knowledge that workers' age, work-related experience, gender, and educational attainment affect compensation. But far less discussed is the relationship between worker attractiveness and compensation, although worker "beauty" has been given growing attention in the economics literature over the past two decades. Indeed, according to a widely cited study, "plain" workers suffer, on average, a wage penalty of 5–10 percent when compared with "average-looking" workers. "Good-looking" workers receive a wage premium of just under 5–10 percent when compared with average-looking workers, which means that plain workers earn somewhere between 10 and 20 percent less than good-looking workers, with worker "beauty" positively affecting the wages of both men and women.[73] And as work experiences increases, the wage premium for attractive workers can grow more rapidly than unattractive workers, or so widely cited labor-market research shows.[74]

Moreover, taller workers apparently receive a wage premium of about 10 percent over their shorter counterparts.[75] Good-looking tall workers are, accordingly, in privileged market positions, which could explain why actors and actresses, CEOs and successful politicians tend to be taller and better looking than average.[76]

The wage premium for beauty and height may not all be solely and directly due to those personal characteristics per se. After all, researchers have found that after adjusting for such factors as education and work-related skills and experience, height doesn't seem to matter in terms of worker career compensation.[77] However, economists suggest that better-looking and taller students in high school and college (and earlier in life) may get more attention and encouragement from their teachers (and friends and family) to develop their work-enhancing social skills and their "human capital" through extended education. And according to one study, better looking high school students are more inclined to go to college. They may be more socially accepted by, say, their high school peers, which causes them to participate earlier in clubs and sports, which can affect their career paths, an intuitively plausible point which research has supported.[78] In other words, beauty and height can feed into higher earnings paths for attractive and tall workers through their impact on workers' other attributes that are honed early in life.

If beauty and height can affect worker wages, why not weight, at least beyond some BMI level (say, beyond a BMI of 37 when, according to research, obesity-related medical-care costs escalate exponentially[79]) and in those occupations where weight impacts firms' costs and revenues? Weight might serve to depress wages in several ways:

- First, weight can, and apparently does (as noted earlier), affect perceptions of worker attractiveness, with any assessed unattractiveness tending to align the heavy worker's wages with the wages of those assessed to be equally unattractive for other reasons.

- Second, excess pounds can make overweight and obese people look shorter than they are, with heavy people's wages declining in line with other workers who *appear* to be equally tall (or equally short). (After all, *perception* of height, not actual height, can be all that matters.)
- Third, weight can undercut worker confidence and self-esteem, affecting overweight and obese people's desirability as workers, undercutting their wages, and with these various connections playing out in labor markets.[80] Surely all the reported negative attitudes toward heavy people must translate into their having to work harder to override justified or unjustified negative attitudes, which means they can have less time and energy to spend developing their work-related skills that can make positive contributions to their firms' bottom lines.
- Fourth, the added health-care costs caused by added pounds can raise the health insurance premiums of overweight and obese workers, which effectively lowers their take-home real wages (but only when insurance premiums are not adjusted for weight-related health risks, as we have seen).
- Fifth, any impaired productivity of overweight and obese workers (both through impaired physical ability or cognitive function[81]) can decrease their value to firms, which can undercut their wages, just as lack of education and experience can undercut worker wages (because of the impaired productivity vis-à-vis other workers). And weight must, beyond some point, undermine worker productivity in some jobs that require movement, agility, and endurance. Overweight and obese workers can narrow the range of their employment opportunities, which can undercut their real wages.

Fat, Productivity, and Wages

As might be expected, research findings on the impact of weight on worker wages are not uniform. The various studies include different groups of workers, over different time periods, and with different attributes, differences that must be integrated into statistical models to tease out the added costs of added weight on heavy people and their employers and the effects of those added costs on heavy people's wages. One review of nearly a hundred studies on the economic effects of weight found:

- The incremental costs to all parties—heavy people, firms, and larger society—of morbidly obese people are far higher than for moderately obese people, with the magnitude of the added costs affected by gender. The total added costs (dominated by medical costs) for obese women are nine times the added costs of overweight women. The total added costs of obese men are six times the costs of overweight men.[82]
- The productivity of workers goes down as weight goes up.
- Similarly, workplace absenteeism (due mainly to incremental medical issues) goes up with weight.
- The probability that workers will suffer a disability that affects their work goes up with greater excess weight.

- The heavier workers are, the shorter their life expectancy and the shorter their working careers (because of the onset of weight-related chronic health conditions), which helps to explain why heavy workers tend to retire earlier than normal-weight workers.[83]

Fat Wage Penalty

Understandably, a number of studies have found that obesity typically imposes a wage penalty, especially for white females. One such study found that body fat is unambiguously associated with decreased wages for both males and females among whites, and that evidence indicates that fat-free mass (FFM) is linked to increased wages.[84] Another obesity research study concluded, "[W]eight lowers wages for white females," with sixty-five pounds of added weight on women associated with a wage reduction of 9 percent, which "is equivalent to the wage effect of roughly one and a half years of education or three years of work experience."[85] In their review of economic studies that test the impact of weight on worker wages, researchers found that the annual wage penalty for women workers ranges from less than 2 percent to 15 percent, while the annual wage penalty for men is small ($75 a year) to nonexistent. (No one has yet been able to explain this gender-based difference, other than pointing to the substantially higher weight-related medical expenditures of women relative to men).[86] Yet another study found that both men and women suffer a weight-related wage penalty, but their findings suggests that the penalty for women might be a consequence of how their weight affects people's assessments of their attractiveness (since the wage penalty kicks in before their BMI reaches the overweight category).[87]

Another longitudinal study found that obese workers suffered a wage penalty for at least the first two decades of their career, while another found a decidedly differential effect of body mass on wages of men and women. For every 1 percent increase in women's body mass, they suffered a 0.6 percent decrease in their family's income and 0.4 percent decrease in the "prestige" of their occupation.[88] Indeed, a theme in the research is that obese white women tend to suffer the greatest wage effect, while in comparison, white men and black men and women either suffer a lower wage reduction or no wage reduction from their extra weight.[89] In addition, the greater the excess weight, the lower is self-esteem, and the lower the self-esteem, the lower are worker wages, especially for white women, or so research has found. In other words, weight can depress wages through its impact on self-esteem, as we may expect, although the effect on wages is relatively small, 1–2 percent for all obese workers (and less for overweight workers).[90]

Other researchers have found that the wage penalty of excess weight, which they figure can reach nearly $6,500 a year (in 2010 dollars), can be chalked up mainly to the fact that heavy people have higher annual health-care costs unless their firms' group health insurance premiums do take excess weight into account. That is to say, when workers who have higher medical costs do not pay for those costs in higher health insurance premiums themselves, the premium costs are spread across all the workers insured. As premiums increase, firms simply take the added health insurance costs out of the hides of overweight and obese workers through reduced compensation packages (as would be expected from the economic way of thinking). Stanford researchers found that when firms provide group insurance and do not adjust worker premiums for weight-related health risk, workers on average lost $4.56 an hour in 2010 prices, for a loss of annual income of $9,120 in 2010 prices.[91]

When workers' firms do not provide group health insurance policies and workers must buy their own individual health insurance policies (with the policy premiums presumably adjusted for weight), overweight and obese workers suffer no wage penalty. This finding suggests to the researchers that weight did little to nothing to undercut the productivity of overweight and obese workers whom their study covered (which, of course, might not hold up with other groups of workers in different jobs).[92]

In short: You can't fool Mother Nature, and you can't fool markets. Labor markets will tend to take account of the negative effects of worker excess weight, when there are significant negative effects. The greater the excess weight, the greater the wage penalty, although women tend to suffer a greater penalty than men.

The Gender Fat Wage Gap

The persistent but gradually narrowing gender-based wage gap (with full-time working women earning 80 percent of their men counterparts, as estimated in 2009[93]) that is widely recognized could be rank discrimination, but very likely not all of it is because on average, heavy women's weight-related medical costs are generally greater than men's. However, it needs to be stressed that there is a good economic reason for women suffering a higher wage penalty for their obesity than men: According to one study, the added annual health-care costs incurred by obese women above the annual medical-care costs of normal-weight women is more than three times the differential in health-care cost for obese and normal-weight men.[94] The relatively greater added medical-care expenditures of obese women can be an unrecognized, albeit partial, explanation for the widely lamented wage gap between men and women. If the research is to be believed, wide adoption of group health insurance policies that have a weight-risk premium penalty could be a force that further narrows the wage gap.

Readers should keep in mind that weight doesn't matter in some occupations, and many studies do not focus their analyses on the impact of weight only in occupations where weight really does indeed matter in consequential ways. The wage penalty on overweight and obese workers in those occupations where weight really matters is very likely greater than reported in the above studies.

Nevertheless, can you not see that the variety of findings on wage and employment discrimination can activate any number of political groups to work for weight discrimination laws and opportunities for legal entrepreneurs to go after firms with deep pockets? Might legal suits be hotly pursued especially if the advocates' (and attorneys') labor-market discrimination arguments on behalf of heavy people are complimented with findings that for all too many heavy people, their weight is not a matter of choice (and, hence, not a matter of personal responsibility), but rather is a consequence of their luck (or, rather, bad luck) in the draw of genes, which makes their weight a medical affliction?

Concluding Comments

Words of caution are in order regarding the various statistical studies (and especially media reports on them) of the effects of weight, especially the wage penalty. Statistical assessments of the wage penalty for weight are instructive; however, don't assume the dollar estimates of wage losses attributable to weight can be taken with the precision with which they are offered, sometimes to the second or third decimal place for an hourly wage.

The penalty estimates are, at best, rough and ready and are most useful in proving the efficacy of the economic way of thinking applied to weight problems and showing the direction of worker wages as their weight rises. Data categories of "overweight" and "obese" are broad, containing people with differing job requirements and with wide variations in how much of their weight is muscle and bone. Researchers are effectively grouping "oranges and apples and bananas" into categories, "overweight" and "obese." Some heavy workers may be well qualified for their jobs, and their excess weight may have inconsequential effects on their productivity and, for that matter, their health-care costs. Including these people in studies can mute the potential estimate of the effect of excess pounds for other people in jobs where weight does indeed affect worker productivity and health-care costs.

Moreover, we should expect overweight and obese people to self-select into occupations where their weight has a minimal effect on their productivity and, thus, where their weight-related wage penalty is minimal, which, again, tends to mute the measured effects of weight on wages. Moreover, many people who expect to gain weight over their careers (say, because of family weight patterns) might choose college majors in subjects that have tight labor markets—say, accounting—so that they can offset some of their expected weight-related wage penalty by valued "human capital" (a tie-in that could suggest that for some people weight and reported income could be positively related, to the confusion of obesity researchers).

The adverse wage effect of weight may cause some workers to settle for second- and third-best jobs that, if they weren't carrying the excess pounds, they might not accept. The wage-weight penalty can morph partially into job dissatisfaction, which many studies don't try to assess. Of course, some of the weight-wage penalty can show up in other components of workers' full compensation packages, for example, in cuts in fringe benefits and time off with pay and in reductions in respect they garner from bosses and colleagues (as overweight and obese workers report they confront).

In short, don't be surprised that the full and real weight-wage penalty is, in reality, greater than what all the econometric studies in the world estimate. Also, if you change the workers studied in different industries, occupations, locations, and time periods, the wage-penalty estimates are likely to vary.

Still, a lot of econometric studies support the economic way of thinking about the impact of weight in the labor marketplace: Weight does matter in many workplaces. The big surprise would be if researchers found that weight (especially for workers with BMIs above 37) never mattered in the terms of employment when it seems to matter in the attitudes among many people (including many heavy people) toward excess weight.

Similarly, we are wise to consider but also to remain somewhat reserved in accepting, for example, studies suggesting, albeit tentatively, that weight can impair brain function in our elderly years (if not before) through a reduction in the brain's neurons. Two notable problems arise:

- First, extra weight could be driving the neuron loss, as researchers (and media reports) have suggested, but the elderly overweight and obese people just as easily could have gained their extra pounds because they were missing the brain tissue all their lives, leaving them with less self-control of their eating (less resistance to modern ever-present temptations to down inexpensive, calorie-packed foods).
- Second, weight gain and neuron loss may not be causally connected at all. Some third physiological force (genetics and environmental particulars, for instance) could be at work, pressing subjects to overeat and depleting their neuron base. Nevertheless, we should keep a mind's eye open toward the prospects that weight gain and brain tissue loss could be interactive and that weight gain can impair mental functions that, in turn, contribute to more weight gain.

Despite these red flags, take to heart two overarching observations:

- First, people, especially young people, would be foolhardy to presume anything other than that labor markets can be hard taskmasters. Market forces can punish people in terms of compensation and other job attributes to the degree that excess weight undermines productivity and increase health-care costs.
- Second, the problem of excess weight throughout the world often has real costs—some substantial portion, perhaps, afflicting the overweight themselves, their families and friends, but many affecting the economic well-being of all of us.

Certainly, Melanie paid a heavy cost (literally, no pun intended) because she gave up decades of her life. As noted in the chapter, overweight and obese workers who pay the same health insurance premiums as their coworkers should understand that the absence of a health insurance risk premium for excess weight will likely show up in a narrowing of their job opportunities and/or a lowering of their real compensation.

Still, the rising costs of accommodating heavy people in many aspects of life—medical care and entertainment, for example—could be spread to others through higher taxes than would otherwise be necessary. And, the spreading of such costs can be a source, albeit of marginal consequence, of additional weight gain. One of the problems of nationalized health insurance ("ObamaCare," for example) is that the imposed taxes spread over the citizenry to cover the costs of the program might not be weight adjusted, for purely political reasons (there are a huge number of heavy voters), which can show up in more weight gain since people can impose their health-care costs on the broad taxpaying population. And research does support this view: Extending health-care coverage, private or public-provided, but especially public-provided, to the uninsured (perhaps thirty to forty million people under the national health-insurance program pressed by the Obama Administration) is likely to be a force for weight gain among the newly insured. Covering the uninsured by private health-care insurance increases their BMI by an average of 1.3 points, by public health-care insurance by an average of 2.1 points, a finding that caused authors to muse, reasonably (from the economic way of thinking perspective), "[B]y insulating people from the costs of obesity-related medical care expenditures, insurance coverage extensions create moral hazard in behavior related to body weight."[95]

Health-care researchers have made much of the impact of the growth in obesity on Medicare expenditures. However, by the extension of the potential moral-hazard problem associated with the spread of health-care coverage, the extension of health-care coverage to tens of millions of elderly and poor Americans in the late 1960s through the creation and explosive use of Medicare and Medicaid programs over the last several decades *could* be an unheralded source of the country's weight gain during the last third of the twentieth century. Those two government programs simply made overeating and weight gain personally less costly and, hence, more affordable for many elderly and poor Americans.

The spreading of the added health-care costs of more people with greater insurance coverage can be a force that can add fuel to the coming "fat (policy and legal) wars," to which we can now turn. Understandably, many trim people (especially those who work hard at remaining trim) might be expected to vigorously oppose making tax (or premium) payments for health-care costs that induce heavy people to pack on even more excess tonnage and, thus, to need more health care, the costs of which feed back into even higher taxes (and premiums) for trim people.

However, the new national health-care law of 2010 has one provision that harbors the prospects of curbing firms and their workers' health-care and health insurance costs with the right kind of incentives. The new law (under the "Safeway Amendment") allows employers to provide discounts on group health insurance premiums of up to 30 percent by 2014 (and up to 50 percent with special approval) for workers who join wellness programs or meet company-specified health goals (as measured by, say, weight, blood pressure, or BMI).[96] The discounts obviously offer workers incentives for healthier eating. However, they also offer companies and their insurers opportunities to penalize workers for unhealthy eating and for excess weight gain and the attendant health-care costs.

How's that? As explicitly allowed by the new national health insurance law, insurers can raise their premiums for *all* workers with appended "discounts" (equal to or above the increase in the premiums) for healthy living and weight. Those workers who do not control their weight to meet the insurance standards are effectively penalized, albeit indirectly and maybe surreptitiously, which means they will then have a heightened incentive to control their weights and in other ways live healthier lives. The result of the weight loss can be long-term reductions in group health insurance costs, or so it can be argued. However, no one should be surprised that supporters of the rights of heavy people will see through this provision of the law and seek its nullification in the courts and the halls of Congress on several grounds (as reflected in the commentary of Harold Schmidt, a fellow at the Harvard School of Public Health):

- First, "these incentives hold people responsible for things beyond their control" (which is to suggest that all, or a substantial majority of, heavy people can't control their weights and that people who live healthy lives should be held responsible for behaviors beyond their control, the unhealthy behaviors of heavy people).
- Second, because poorer people are more likely to be obese, the poor face a "double whammy": "They may need to make higher insurance contributions and suffer the consequences of being obese" (which is to say that other people should suffer the "double whammy" of the costs they incur to remain healthy and the costs of the unhealthy behaviors of others).
- Third, "If your aim is to use money as an incentive to promote better health, does it make sense to give premium discounts to people who are already healthy" (an argument tendered with no recognition that healthy people don't have the extra medical costs that unhealthy people incur and impose on the health-care and health insurance system).[97]

Let the policy and legal battles begin.

Chapter 7
Smoking War

T he 1950s is a memorable decade for a particular reason beyond the idyllic portrayal of those times in the movie *Grease* and the television series "Happy Days". Of course, as the movie and TV series idealized, the 1950s was a decade in which mom and pop diners dominated the restaurant industry, especially in small-town America. It was a time that gave "cool" its original meaning (which was tame by today's standards of "cool"). James Dean's ducktail hairdo in *Rebel Without a Cause* and John Travolta's pegged pants in *Grease* were the rage for teenage boys in the 1950s, as were Olivia Newton-John's bobby socks and crinolines worn in *Grease* the fashion for teenage girls. Bee-bop and doo-wop music dominated the airways, as did hula hoops the playgrounds and "sock hops" high school gymnasium floors.

But what probably sets the 1950s apart from the 2000s in forgotten memories is ... You guess ... No, you missed it. The answer: ashtrays! How easy it has been to forget them, even though in the 1950s and 1960s, they were omnipresent. Every home and every business—every office and cubicle—had them, and not only cheap, minimally acceptable bowls, but frequently expensive, substantive molded works of art in glass and pottery to accent all décors. Ashtrays had to be everywhere convenient lest ever-present smokers flick their ashes wherever they happened to be (as they did) or, worse yet, stomp out their butts on the carpet or linoleum. Even so, cigarette burns on floors were not uncommon in hallways and lobbies. Smokers seemed to be an inconsiderate lot, oblivious to how their puffs permeated other people's clothes and draperies, not to mention their lungs. And smokers thought nothing of dropping cigarette butts on the ground anywhere, as if no one would notice.

In the 1950s, nonsmokers really had to accede to the wishes of smokers who were ubiquitous on guest lists and among business associates. In 1950, close to one out of every two American adults smoked regularly (males nearly twice as numerous as females), averaging nearly a pack a day. The top two brands, Camel and Lucky Strike, had combined sales of nearly 180 billion cigarettes a year, or about sixty packs for every man, woman, child, and baby in the country![1]

R.B. McKenzie, *HEAVY!*, DOI 10.1007/978-3-642-20135-6_7,
© Springer-Verlag Berlin Heidelberg 2012

Movies and television series of the 1950s were filled with smokers, who owned the airways in more than obvious ways. Back then, you dared not ask a smoker to go elsewhere to smoke. For that matter, you dared not chastise others for blowing smoke directly into your face. Smoking was close to a God-given natural right. Nonsmokers had to leave the room if they wanted fresh air.

But since the 1950s, ashtrays have all but disappeared from public buildings and even homes, a casualty of the "smoking war" (or more accurately, the "antismoking war"), which the smoking opponents have won pretty darn decisively, almost to the point of total surrender on the part of smokers and their suppliers, derisively demonized as "Big Tobacco." Yes, smokers can still be spotted, but they have been largely marginalized as social outcasts, and packs of cigarettes now can cost more than meals at fast-food restaurants thanks to heavy taxation at every level of government. Nonsmokers have usurped (or maybe retaken), for the most part, the rights of smokers to the airwaves. (You're right, President Obama has been photographed puffing away, but he profusely apologized soon after he was "caught" on camera, with his apology plastered all over the Web.[2])

Today, a new social policy conflict is gaining momentum—a war against fat— and the antifat forces appear to be using the antismoking forces' playbook. First, you organize research programs designed to show a variety of serious personal medical problems and longevity threats from excess weight. Next, you show that people's weights adversely affect the health and wealth of others through one form of social transmission or another. After that, you create a "crisis" or "epidemic" climate through a steady, widespread stream of media reports concerning research that links excess weight to an ever-expanding array of health, personal, and societal problems and to ever-mounting costs affecting everyone. Be sure to freely allow and encourage rhetorical exaggerations among pundits and public officials on high and in the media. In the smoking war, the battle lines were drawn in "old media," print, radio, and television. In the coming fat war, the battle lines will likely form in "new media," certainly the Internet, which has already been in heavy use, but also social networks, such as YouTube and Facebook. The combatants in the fat war will, naturally, do what they can to manage their Google relevance, or the likelihood that their statistics and arguments rank high on search engines.

The antifat playbook also encourages using economic reasoning to justify government controls and taxation of food production, as you demonize food suppliers for their fraudulent sales pitches and for taking advantage of virtually "innocent" victims of their genetic malfunctions and primordial proclivity to eat as much and as often as they can, especially high-energy sugary and fatty foods. And finally you seek government programs to inform a major segment of a presumably ill-informed public of all the negative consequences of excess weight, only to be followed (when the information efforts prove ineffective) by campaigns to secure ever-tightening regulations and ever-increasing taxes designed to solve the array of documented weight-related health, personal, and societal problems.

Like the antismoking forces before them, opponents of fat draw upon a number of economic arguments that are tagged "market failures" to justify government intrusions into the economy. After the conflict has run much of its course, you announce firmly that "the debate is over," followed by a litany of favored policy remedies for the core contention, in this case, fat.

Free-Market Failures

From the writings of the venerable Adam Smith in the eighteenth century, economists have touted the virtues of free-market, competitive economies. In free (or tolerably free) competitive markets, businesses' hot pursuit of profits and buyers' hot pursuit of personal gains offer strong incentives to innovate and produce cost effectively. With both pursuing their own gain (as they define gain), buyers and sellers can be induced to serve all others and, following Adam Smith, can be led by an "invisible hand" to serve the broader "interest of the society," so long as competitive market checks remain in place and the government does its job of protecting people's lives and property, administers a system of justice, and provides a few public goods (such as roads, designed to expand the scope of markets and to facilitate and intensify competitive market forces).[3]

> The past antismoking war is important to the study of the coming antifat war because anti-obesity policy proponents appear to be following closely the very successful anti-smoking playbook in pressing for "fat taxes" and food controls.

For those who worry about free markets being motivated by greed, the late long-term free-market intellectual Milton Friedman assures all, "What kind of society isn't structured on greed? The problem of social organization is how to set up an arrangement under which greed will do the least harm; capitalism is that kind of a system."[4] Friedman would insist that socialism and communism, not to mention America's system of government bureaucracies, are every bit as driven by "greed" and the self-interests of the people in those systems as are entrepreneurs and consumers under capitalism, although their antagonists and protagonists might say otherwise. Both Smith and Friedman would also insist that greed can be, and is, a force for a great deal of good in the world—*so long as it is properly contained by morality, law, competitive markets, and so long as people pay their own ways in whatever they choose to do (which is to say they cannot shift their costs to others)*.

Friedman's pronouncement doesn't mean that there is nothing for government to do. Indeed, like Smith, Friedman muses, "The existence of a free market does not of course eliminate the need for government. On the contrary, government is essential both as a forum for determining the 'rules of the game' and as an umpire to interpret and enforce the rules decided on."[5] But Smith and Friedman worried that shifting economic activity from the market arena to the political arena would not suppress greed at all but create more mischief as politicians cloaked their greed in noble talk about "society's welfare" (as they constrict individual choices). After all, politicians and government workers are drawn from the same pool of humanity as those who work in markets, and the competitive constraints on the expression of unbridled greed in political arenas can be less intense than the competitive constraints in market arenas. This can be especially problematic when voters only go to the polls every several years and then have little incentive to become and remain informed on policy issues, as public choice economists maintain they are.[6]

Pay Your Own Costs

Nonetheless, economists following in Smith's and Friedman's footsteps—even Smith and Friedman themselves—have justified (limited) government involvement in the economy through taxes and regulations so long as the intrusions are in accord with one of the more fundamental "rules of the game": *The government should keep you from hitting (or, in other ways, harming) me, while it keeps me from hitting (or, in other ways, harming) you.* If the government carries out that function, then not only will the government have a large and productive role to play in the economy, but also, fewer resources will be wasted in counterproductive redistributive fights.

Applied generally to the smoking and fat policy wars, this principle means that the government should prevent you from imposing on me some (or all) of the costs of what you produce, sell or buy, and consume, and it should give me equal treatment. In econspeak, the government has a duty to prevent both of us, and all others, from imposing "negative externalities" (or "negative external costs" or "negative spillover effects") on each other, and all others.[7] The economic reasoning is straightforward: If either of us as *producers* can impose some of our production costs on others, we will be able to sell our goods at lower prices and can encourage greater and excessive consumption (remember the law of demand). And some of what consumers buy will have higher total costs (those costs incurred in production plus those "externalized" to, or imposed on, others) than the values consumers assign them, a clear loss of welfare.

> The first economic role of government is to keep each of us from harming the other without agreed-upon compensation.

Similarly, if *consumers* can impose some of their costs in consuming goods on others, then they will, again, buy more of the goods than otherwise, and the total cost of some of the goods consumed will exceed their total value. In both cases, the market is not *efficient*—or is *inefficient* or *suboptimal*. But instead, when producers and consumers are forced to incur their own costs of production and consumption, the general welfare of all improves. When the market is efficient (costs and values more closely align), more resources are available for producing higher valued goods and services.

Pollution is the classic example in which the prevalence of external costs— through the emission of, say, CO_2 into the atmosphere—can make market outcomes inefficient or suboptimal. The polluters impose some of their production and consumption costs through smoke released into the atmosphere (or chemicals released in streams). Members of the larger society feel those external costs as, because of smoke pollution, they are forced to paint their houses or seek relief from respiratory problems more frequently than otherwise. The same argument can be extended, as it has been, to "sound pollution" and "odor pollution." Few economists would have a problem with pollution controls, although they might quibble over the extent and forms of the controls, favor market-based solutions (selling "rights to pollute"), and warn that the political process could potentially use pollution control powers to serve special interests and to harm the general public.

Those suffering the direct effects of pollution are not the only ones who can favor government controls; even polluting firms themselves can favor such measures. Individual firms might pollute only because competition forces them into it. They might like to be socially responsible and pay the costs to curb their pollution, but doing so would put them at a distinct disadvantage in the marketplace among firms that do nothing to abate their pollution. As a result, all pollute when, possibly, all would prefer a world in which no one polluted (or all polluted less). The firms might have to incur greater abatement costs because of government-imposed pollution controls, but they all don't have to suffer the lung and environmental problems (including the possible long-term effects of global warming) that unchecked pollution can bring. Indeed, no one should be surprised if many polluting firms are big supporters of antipollution campaigns, and they have been (with Walmart and BP being two of the more prominent large corporate supporters of environmental controls, at least in words for BP before its disastrous Gulf of Mexico oil spill in 2010 and, apparently, in deeds of clean-up after the spill).[8]

If this "externality" line of argument justifies government intrusion into the economy, then for the sake of consistency in argument, not to mention economic efficiency, chosen government policies should not themselves encourage offending polluting parties to impose more costs on non-offending parties. Moreover, government policies should not impose costs on non-offending parties just to correct the decision making of the offending parties. Otherwise, government policies themselves can aggravate the problems of external costs, and economic inefficiency. Under the externality line of argument for government intrusions, few can, with a straight face, recommend government subsidies for tobacco farmers or, maybe worse, for cigarette manufacturers. The subsidies can lower the price of smokes and encourage smokers to blow more smoke in nonsmokers' faces, and can encourage previous nonsmokers to take up the habit. The subsidies and the greater health-care costs from greater smoking can increase "external costs" through higher taxes on everyone. This is to say that government taxes should target the offending policies. To the extent they don't, or can't, they can aggravate the problem.

Fraudulent Dealings

Market economies are founded on mutually beneficial exchanges between buyers and sellers, with the expectation that people get what they pay for, or are told they are getting. Outright fraud in the form of misinformation, misrepresentation, omission of information, disinformation, and failure to perform as promised can lead to market inefficiencies, as people on both sides of trades use resources to make sure the parties deliver what they promised, or they just don't trade at all, missing the potential added value of the of the nonconsummated exchanges. If people can't trust one another, government can establish laws and enforcement agencies to penalize fraud, thus potentially elevating trust and improving market efficiency. Such government intrusions hold the promise that private resources will be freed to produce more real goods and services than otherwise. Put another way, fraud can be construed as a form of theft, since people don't get what they pay for, and government needs to control fraud for the same economic reasons it needs to control theft.

Information Problems

A free market economy is predicated on the presumption that people are tolerably well informed on what they want and on the qualities and characteristics of the goods and services they buy, or at least can acquire tolerably good information on such matters at tolerable costs. But consumers can never be perfectly informed about their preferences and the available goods. Economists generally, and even Friedman, have been willing to give government an educational and informational role in the economy, but Friedman and his libertarian-leaning followers worry that government's role might go too far and morph too easily into controls on what consenting adults can buy and sell. Friedman and other economists (especially Friedrich Hayek[9]) might ask, "Can politicians and government bureaucrats, and even researchers, be expected to make better decisions for a multitude of individual consumers than the consumers can make for themselves?" After all, consumers have access to very detailed and local and personal information—not the least of which are privately held subjective evaluations—that politicians and their agents have little hope of obtaining, much less comprehending, simply because there are so many consumers in different circumstances and with different needs and wants.

Still, a case can be made that certain classes of consumers might benefit from governmental controls. Young children, for instance, are generally judged to lack the competence to make good decisions for themselves, and sometimes need protection from their parents regarding what they, the children, can consume. Similarly, people who have limited mental capacities might also need protection.

Also, some sellers and buyers are not, and perhaps cannot be, equally informed about the deals that are made in purely free market settings, making them vulnerable to exploitation from those who are more informed. The health-care industry is an example in which such "asymmetric information" can distort market trades. Doctors can know a great deal about the values and consequences of the procedures they perform and the pills they prescribe; their patients may know little to nothing about the values and consequences of what doctors do to them or give them. A case can be made that by monitoring and regulating some goods and services involving asymmetric information, informed government agents can *potentially* enhance consumer welfare. I emphasize "potentially" because many government agents base their interventions on research findings, and as science writer David Freedman documents thoroughly in his widely read book *Wrong*, research is often not right and far too often (maybe half the time in medical research) is just plain wrong or contradicted by subsequent research findings.[10]

For example, one set of researchers might find that caffeine is good for your heart, while a following research team finds the opposite. Exercise can cause weight loss because calories are burned. No, exercise can cause weight gain because it stimulates appetites. Then there is much research that is simply fraudulent or is guided by special interests on one side of some policy conflict or another. Obesity scholars Paul Campos and Eric Oliver in separate books press that the war on fat is being driven largely by misleading statistics.[11]

Everyone has a healthy skepticism about the findings from medical research funded by drug companies. Perhaps everyone should have a similar skepticism toward the findings of government-sponsored research, since political agendas and the need to keep funding flowing can distort researchers' work. Research comes now from every direction, so much so that real and self-anointed experts have some latitude in picking their "poison," or rather picking the information to which they pay homage, at least that is David Freedman's argument (and Milton Friedman would likely agree).

The point is, information and education programs create another potential battle line in the coming fat war. As with the smoking war, policy debates will rage concerning what and how much information government and food producers should provide consumers to persuade them to adopt healthier (and thinner) lifestyles and food choices. After all, most obese adults could rationally be making choices that suit them just fine (a fatty steak for a few hours or days off their life expectancy). Another question will be whether the information provided is worth its cost. Should a billion-dollar information campaign be launched if the weight-loss effects are inconsequential or barely consequential?

Pervasive Irrationalities

Economists have historically assumed that market participants are rational, fully capable of making finely tuned consistent choices in their own personal interests (whatever they may be, including helping distant others or helping themselves and their families), always appropriately discounting the costs and benefits for risks and time delays. But a new cadre of economists has emerged in force over the past two or three decades who have challenged conventional economists' basic rationality premise. Through surveys and laboratory experiments, they believe they have demonstrated fairly conclusively that the overwhelming majority of people are pervasively irrational, so much so that they are "predictably irrational," to use a phrase Dan Ariely, a Duke University behavioral psychologist, has used for the title of his widely read book.[12] People simply can't make the finely tuned cost/benefit calculations conventional economists say they can. They are subject to an array of decision-making "biases," which generate a plethora of errors, not the least of which is the inclination to avoid a loss rather than receive a gain of an equal amount. As noted in Chap. 4, people can simply make a host of decisions (relating, for example, to smoking and eating) that they understand, at least on reflection, are not good for them, not only in the long run, but even in the short run, or so behavioralists argue.

Such extensively (if not fully) irrational people need to be "nudged" by a host of potential decision-making changes that ultimately they will consider good for them. Markets fail to achieve a respectable level of efficiency in many sectors of the economy because the people in them make far too many decisions that they subsequently recognize as being wrong. Consumers need paternalistic guidance from others, "choice architects," who, from research, learn how to structure people's alternatives so that they make improved choices, or make more welfare-enhancing decisions.[13] This line or argument, while appealing, is contestable, as it will be in our discussion of the coming fat war. Are the proposed "nudges" right ones, based on truly sound and lasting research findings? Might they be found to be wrong at some future date? Might the nudges be inflexible across people who face different circumstances, which means that they harbor the potential of doing more harm than good over time as conditions change?

Who is going to choose the nudges? I've always wondered if behavioralists would favor nudging as government policy if I were the appointed "choice architect" to devise the nudges (with one option I might consider being no nudges at all)? My guess is that key behavioralists would be horrified at my selection, or many others who do not share their political proclivities.[14]

These are just a few of the potential *market failures* that have formed the foundation of policy skirmishes in the antismoking war and are appearing with greater frequency in the coming fat war. Now, let's return to see how these lines of arguments have been used, directly and indirectly, in the smoking war. (Chap. 8 draws out the parallels in arguments between the two policy conflicts that have marked our times.)

The Smoking War

Most people who came of age during the 1950s had to know at some level that smoking could not be good for them. Omnipresent smokers' nagging coughs were a constant reminder that inhaling pollutants, one cigarette after another, damaged the lungs. Frankly, I don't remember a classmate in my North Carolina high school, whether bound for college or for the textile mills, who didn't understand that there were potential health problems from smoking (although experts today tell everyone that the world of the 1950s was filled with totally duped smokers). Still, in their quest to be seen as cool, teenagers defied their parents and coaches (my high school coaches, as did many others, prohibited smoking on the grounds that it undercut stamina). Nevertheless, sneaking smokes behind the woodshed was good sport during the "happy days" not portrayed on the large and small screens.

Big Tobacco's Big Stall

Tobacco companies and their executives had to know (or at least suspect) in the 1950s, if not before, that cigarettes were addictive to people in varying degrees, or why else would they have directed their advertising campaigns so often toward young people? Why else in the 1950s and into the 1960s did they have pretty girls in short skirts roam college campuses at the start of the fall terms with trays of cigarette packs that they passed out as freely as they could? Like street drug dealers, tobacco companies must have understood (even if they never undertook research on the health effects of smoking or never looked at their own companies' medical research) that their giveaways were an investment in hooking customers for decades, if not their lifetimes, making their freebies a paying proposition. Nevertheless, they publicly continued to deny that cigarettes, or any substance in them, were addictive, even in testimony before Congress as late as 1994, six years after the Food and Drug Administration had declared nicotine to be an addictive drug.[15]

At the same time that teenagers and adults were dead set on emulating the Marlboro Man (or any number of movie stars who chain-smoked their way through scenes), research studies were bolstering the battle of ideas on the ill-effects of smoking. In 1950, Morton Levin, director of Cancer Control for New York State, published the first major study in the *Journal of the American Medical Association* linking smoking with cancer, finding that smoking doubled people's chances of getting lung cancer.[16] Other researchers reported in the same issue of *JAMA* that nearly all (or 96.5 percent to be exact) of the nearly thousand lung-cancer patients surveyed had been moderate to heavy smokers. [17]

1964: The Year D-Day Comes for Big Tobacco

D-Day in the smoking war arrived in 1964: U.S. Surgeon General Luther Terry, heeding the advice of a select advisory committee that had been at work since 1957, officially made the causal link between smoking and cancer.[18] His report also drew ties between smoking and chronic bronchitis, emphysema, and heart disease, and linked the amount of smoking with greater risk. "Average" smokers had a nine to ten times greater chance of getting lung cancer than nonsmokers did, the report said. Moreover, "heavy" smokers' risk of coming down with lung cancer was more than double that of average smokers, with the heavy smokers' risk of lung cancer estimated to be twenty-four times that of nonsmokers.

In light of such devastating evidence, the country entered a half century of smoking policy conflict with the two sides adopting close to religious stances.

The Surgeon General's office issued a report on the adverse consequences of smoking and smoking promotions almost every other year after 1964, finally declaring nicotine to be addictive in 1988.[19] On the other side, tobacco executives repeatedly denied they ever had knowledge that tobacco (or any substance in tobacco, nicotine, for example) was the least bit addictive or was a potential carcinogen.

In 1994, the top executives of the country's seven largest tobacco companies all repeated the same refrain at the start of a House subcommittee hearing: "I believe that nicotine is not addictive," to the total disbelief of most people who watched their stonewalling on television.[20] Videos of their testimonies still remain readily available on the Internet. Of course, they might have freely confessed to the addictiveness of tobacco, or nicotine, were they not afraid that such an admission might only encourage the legal pickpockets' intent to glean millions—no, billions—from tobacco companies' very deep pockets. Indeed, lawsuits, claiming real and imagined damages, were already being filed all over the country with occasional but growing success.

Koop's "Militant Army"

One of the more prominent and forceful antismoking warriors was C. Everett Koop, appointed Surgeon General by Ronald Reagan. Koop gathered an army of supporters who pressed for partial, and later complete, bans on smoking with almost religious zealotry, bolstering their arguments with a constant flow of substantive reports on the health harms from smoking. They *knew* smoking was bad for smokers and nonsmokers alike and was just plain wrong for everyone, period. Everyone? They argued that the state should protect smokers and would-be-smokers, especially children and teenagers, from their personal failings. Moreover, Koop's "militant army" would not rest until everyone was protected from "second-hand smoke," which they said, had many of the same debilitating health effects of smoking itself, albeit in muted form. "Involuntary smokers"—bartenders and restaurant patrons—suffered from smokers' lighting up with abandon.[21]

Further, smokers required more medical care, pushing up health-care demand, which translated into rising health-care and insurance costs for everyone. So what if smokers lived shorter lives and died fairly quickly from lung cancer, the health-care cost they inflicted on the health delivery system was obvious; the health-care cost not incurred (and the social security benefits not received) in years not lived because of smoking was not so easy to quantity or visualize (although researchers have found that smokers drain fewer social benefits over the course of their shortened lives across all welfare programs than longer-living nonsmokers[22]). Any Friedman-type arguments that people should be left "free to choose" to harm themselves slowed the antismoking crusade only marginally.

But, it should be added, many pro-smoking consultants and think tanks were paid handsomely for pressing their losing cause, and you can bet, they wanted the smoking war to continue. One of the more interesting policy proposals tendered inside the pro-smoking forces was that any added revenues derived from cigarette taxes should go to study the health effects of smoking, not because new harmful effects would be uncovered, but rather because the rich revenue stream might actually slow the movement to ban smoking. Smoking proponents reasoned that antismoking groups and researchers would have strong self-interest to keep the funding flowing and, therefore, would curb their efforts to squash smoking altogether. Earmarking tobacco taxes to research would be just the thing to entangle antismoking efforts with tobacco sales, revenues, and profits (although the American tobacco lobby never adopted the strategy).[23]

The pro-smoking lobby was, nevertheless, fighting a decidedly uphill—and ultimately futile—battle. But their efforts did likely slow moves to ban smoking, and may have contributed to governments' becoming more fiscally dependent on cigarette taxes paid by the minority of people who simply would not, and maybe could not, break their habit. Clearly, smoking became widely recognized as the leading cause of preventable deaths in the country—or, as the Centers for Disease Control and Prevention dubbed it, the "leading killer"—which it continued to be until very recently. As late as 2008, 443,000 deaths were attributable to voluntary and involuntary smoking, and hundreds of thousands of children under eighteen months suffer each year from lower respiratory tract infections because of second-hand smoke (among a catalogue of other smoking-related health problems).[24] About 20 percent of American adults now smoke and many do so in the privacy of their cars or in isolated places apart from crowds.[25]

Needless to say, the antismoking advocates and silent supporters won the public relations and policy battle, although they had to work hard for every incursion they made on smokers' rights. In 1958, the Gallop Poll found that 44 percent of adult Americans believed that smoking caused lung cancer; by 1968, 78 percent believed it did. In 1965, Congress required cigarette manufacturers to place the familiar warning that smoking causes cancer on the sides of every cigarette pack. In 1969, Congress banned all cigarette advertisements on television from 1970 onward. [26]

The Tightening Grip of Tobacco Controls

Over the past six decades, state and federal taxes on cigarettes have been greatly increased, both to curb consumption and to pad state treasuries. In 1950, only 40 states and the District of Columbia taxed cigarettes, and the state tax per pack ranged from 9 to 45 cents (in 2010 dollars). In mid-2010, all states taxed cigarettes at an average of $1.45 per pack. The federal per-pack tax was $1.01 in 2010 (up from 39 cents per pack in 2009), for a total state and federal tobacco tax of $2.46 a pack, when the price of a pack of cigarettes averaged $5.33 across the country (not including local, community tobacco taxes and not including any general state and local sales taxes that might apply). New York City had the highest combined state/local tobacco

Smokers tend to incur more health-care costs than nonsmokers while they are alive. However, smokers' life spans are an average of eight to ten years shorter, which means that many smokers soak up fewer health-care costs than many longer-living nonsmokers. Smokers certainly receive fewer social welfare benefits, such as Social Security, than nonsmokers because those benefits depend on how long people live, which means smokers can, on balance, be less of a drain on the country's social welfare safety net than nonsmokers.
Viscusi (1994).

excise tax of $5.85 a pack.[27] In many areas of the country, governments make more from cigarette sales than do the tobacco companies.

The CDC has estimated that in 2006 the country's medical-care costs relating to smoking were $11 a pack (in mid-2010 prices), suggesting that smokers could be imposing some portion of their smoking costs on others through added taxes and medical-care costs and, hence, are smoking more than "optimum," or more than they would if they had to cover all costs of their habits.[28]

In 1973, smokers were first relegated to seats in the back of airline flights. In 1987, smoking was banned on all domestic flights of less than two hours. Three years later smoking was banned entirely on all domestic flights. Smoking, once common in restaurants, was at first disallowed except in restaurant bars.[29] Then, in 2006, Surgeon General Richard Carmona declared, "I am here to say the debate is over. The science is clear. Secondhand smoke is not a mere annoyance but a serious health hazard that causes premature death and disease in children and nonsmoking adults." He stressed that secondhand smoke exposure raises the risk of heart disease among nonsmoking adults by 25–30 percent and accounted for 46,000 premature deaths from heart disease and an additional 3,000 premature deaths from lung cancer.[30]

He added, "Smoke-free environments are the only approach that protects nonsmokers from the dangers of secondhand smoke." So what if freely consenting adults were willing to gather in the same place with no prospect of others "smoking" involuntarily. Consequently, smoking has been banned in all parts of restaurants and, for that matter, all public and private businesses, in twenty-eight states, with four more states allowing smoking only in stand-alone bars.[31]

Indeed, in many parts of the country, smokers may not light up around entrances to buildings and even in many public parks. In early 2011, the New York City Council voted to ban smoking in its 1,700 parks and along fourteen miles of the beaches within the city.[32] Smoking bans are even being enforced for apartment buildings where smoke can drift among apartments and give rise to "involuntary smoking." Several states are in the process of preventing people from smoking around children, even considering smoking bans for parents in their own homes when their children are present.[33] Moreover, in 2010, the Food and Drug Administration, which Congress has delegated the authority to regulate cigarettes as a drug, "test drove" proposed new dramatic, if not ghastly, labels for the fronts of packs of cigarettes, (which can be found on the FDA's Web site[34]).

Concluding Comments

The antismoking forces have won the smoking war hands down. To no small degree, smoking has moved from being the thing to do in sophisticated society to something only stupid, uneducated, and low-class people do—or the hopelessly addicted. Smokers have become social pariahs even as they have become a signifi-cant revenue source to fill government budget gaps and to cover public expenditures that have nothing to do with smoking, like parks and playgrounds.[35] Between 2002 and 2010, forty-seven states, the District of Columbia, and several territories raised their excise taxes on cigarettes a combined 100 times.[36] Given the current depen-dency of states and local governments on cigarette revenues, the state has a clear conflict of interest, as do researchers who are dependent on grants funded with tobacco revenues. Governments and many researchers have an interest in making sure that they don't kill the "goose" (smoking) that is laying golden eggs annually. We just might not see the count of smokers falling much further for two reasons. First, smoking is something some people love to do, even with the health risks. Second, with so much red ink flowing through state budgets across the country, states may now need tobacco revenues as much, maybe more, than smokers need their cigarettes. States can be expected to work all the more intensely to make sure that they do not raise their taxes on cigarettes so high that the fall in the count of smokers lowers their cigarette tax revenues.

Today, ashtrays are so rare in homes that it seems odd that they were once ubiquitous (and sometimes pieces of art). If businesses have ashtrays, they now tend to be outside of their entrances, mainly available for smokers to snuff out their smokes before entering the buildings. Nonetheless, antismoking groups have an interest in keeping the antismoking drumbeat going; many of their livelihoods are dependent on their not winning the smoking war, not totally at least. As we will see in the following chapter, in the coming fat war anti-obesity groups may also face similar conflicts of interest if they follow the policy path that antismoking groups have charted and end up taxing all the sugared and fatty products that cause people to pack on the pounds. As in the smoking war, there's a good chance that heavy people will end up being marginalized as burdens on larger society (more than they already are). They may end up paying more than their way through life, through lower market wages and then through taxes on sugared and fatty foods targeted at them, but imposed on the heavy and trim alike, with much of the acquired tax revenues used for government and special interest purposes far removed from improving Americans' waistlines and health.

Chapter 8
Fat Taxes, Bans, and Discrimination

E veryone has a fat person story. Start discussing the economic implications of the weight and obesity crisis, and people (sometimes including heavy people) will not hesitate to relate a real-life experience of how some bloated fat person penned them to the window in their airplane seat (in much the same way I opened the first chapter) or prevented them from passing comfortably through a narrow corridor or stairwell. They will talk about their surprise at watching grossly obese shoppers loading their grocery carts with calorie-laden snacks while shoving honey buns and sodas at their already overweight children (or even infants). And they will lament having to pay for checked bags on air flights when obese people were able to board without an added dollar.

Such are the now faint marching songs for a brewing "fat war." At the present time, the media has caught only the refrains from researchers and pundits who lament Americans' growing waistlines and the attendant medical-care costs, and advocate an array of policy reforms (from lame to draconian). The resentment toward really heavy people—sometimes tame but sometimes simmering—rarely surfaces in public forums, perhaps because people have an innate desire not to be hurtful toward the afflicted and because pundits and political leaders have not yet really moved to broadly impose the types of taxes and bans on sugared and fatty foods and drinks that have been imposed on cigarettes. True, sugared and fatty foods are covered by state sales taxes, but such taxes are designed to raise tax revenues, not to discourage excessive eating.

But once political leaders get serious about antifat measures, the battle howls from what now may be only a "silent minority" will likely erupt everywhere. It's one thing to tax and ban cigarettes, which are not necessary for life, but quite another to tax and ban things that are as American as . . . well, apple pie—and the untold number of products that are as calorie-rich as apple pie. The coming fat policy war could look a lot like the past smoking policy war, but a lot more intense simply because food and drink at some level are essential to life. Taxes and bans on cigarettes are restrictions on a product no one must have, and in the smoking war, the ammunition hit directly and exclusively the offending parties—smokers—not

R.B. McKenzie, *HEAVY!*, DOI 10.1007/978-3-642-20135-6_8,
© Springer-Verlag Berlin Heidelberg 2012

nonsmokers. But tax and ban certain food products, which everyone consumes, trim and heavy people alike, and everyone pays to control the excesses of some.

In the smoking war, cigarettes and a handful of other tobacco-packed products, with fairly tight demarcations, were the offending products. In the coming fat war, there are a gazillion products that are more or less fattening, which invites political skirmishes at every level of fattiness among products that may be targeted for taxes and restrictions. And it should get messy since some healthy foods (avocados and olives, for example) are loaded with calories. Imagine the gold mine the coming fat war will be for politicians and lawyers, and governments strapped for cash.

Another major political difference between the past smoking war and the coming fat war may intensify the battles. As the smoking war was progressively engaged with ever-tighter taxes and bans on smoking, the smoking population was less than half the adult voting population—and it was gradually contracting. But the overweight and obese population currently constitutes, potentially, more than two-thirds the voting population, and may grow (in numbers and weight-related problems) to as much as three-quarters of the population if recent trends are extrapolated to 2020, making the political dynamics complicated and the outcomes hard to predict.[1] The anti-obesity crowd can only hope that a sizable number of obese people will favor government taxes and controls to contain their wanton ways, while their opponents—for example, members of Americans Against Food Taxes[2]—will enlist many trim people who oppose government food intrusions on principle or who simply want to be able to consume fatty and sugared foods at untaxed prices and who have little fear of gaining weight.

The Equivalence of Policy Wars

The tactics of the antismoking war are visible in the beginnings of the fat war, or the widening policy war over what to do about the country's weight gain problems.[3] Many of the arguments used to curb smoking are directly applicable to curbing people's food and weight gain choices. Over the next several decades, this new policy war could produce similar outcomes to those of the antismoking war— higher taxes on a growing array of fattening foods and drinks and tighter controls on people's food and drink choices through regulations on what the food and beverage industries can produce and advertise. Let us count the similarities in the antismoking war that has been largely won and the coming fat war that has yet to be fully engaged.

Fat Fatalities

From a sequence of research studies, smoking opponents have been able to assemble a growing list of debilitating and fatal diseases linked to smoking. Lung cancer is mentioned most prominently, but several other respiratory and cardiac diseases also raise concerns and have fortified the case for society to protect smokers from themselves. Antismoking researchers and advocates have been able to point to $97 billion in annual medical costs directly related to smoking (while rarely, if ever, mentioning that those costs amount to less than 1 percent of GDP and are largely covered by the smokers themselves, not by society at large).[4]

In similar fashion, excess weight, especially to the point of gross obesity, has been linked to a diverse and growing list of debilitating medical problems, not the least of which is that heavy people's impaired mobility exacerbates their weight and health problems. As if by rote, experts frequently repeat that obesity can cause or contribute to (or just be associated with), at least thirty-five serious medical problems, the most prominent of which are diabetes and heart disease. Just like smoking, obesity also can even cause respiratory problems.

Indeed, obesity has been linked to more medical problems than has smoking, a list that has lengthened in recent years (see Chap. 2 for the original thirty-five listed health problems). Researchers have now tied excess weight to loss of brain tissue (and impaired cognitive function) in the elderly and to the early onset of dementia, as well as being a factor in automobile injuries and deaths due to heavy people's relatively greater reluctance to wear seatbelts. In August 2010, the *Los Angeles Times* reported that the percentage of white girls, ages ten and below, who had experienced the onset of puberty in the form of breast development had more than doubled between 1997 and 2010 (from 5 percent to 10.4 percent), which researchers attribute to their increased weight. Body fat, apparently, contributes to an increase in the release of the hormone estrogen, which promotes breast development.[5] Now, researchers tell us that when drinking, heavy males become more aggressive, an effect less frequently observed among trim males or among trim and heavy females.[6]

> Fat is now reputed to have overtaken smoking as the nation's number one killer.

The health-related effects of excess weight, of course, take a toll on medical costs. The Centers for Disease Control and Prevention (CDC) currently estimates the annual medical-care costs for 2008 attributable to excess weight to be $147 billion, nearly two-thirds higher than medical costs attributable to smoking (but still just slightly more than 1 percent of GDP). The data point is often given, I should add, without any indication of how much of those costs the afflicted heavy people cover themselves and without any suggestion that the total costs might seem small, given the array of serious health problems attributed to weight. The presumption is that the total health-care costs related to weight are imposed on the general public (if there really is any increase in the *lifetime* medical-care costs from obesity, which might not be the case since excess weight can shorten life).

If a case can be made on medical-cost grounds for controlling smoking, cannot a case also be made for the control of what people eat and of how much they weigh? Anti-obesity groups think so, and the CDC is leading the campaign against obesity. Lamenting the increase in the number of states with obesity rates of 30 percent or more (from zero in 2000 to three in 2007 and to nine just two years later), the CDC reworked a rallying cry it has made in earlier reports:

> Obesity is a complex problem that requires both personal and community action. People in all communities should be able to make healthy choices. To reverse this epidemic, we need to change our communities into places that strongly support healthy eating and active living. Given the magnitude of this problem, past efforts and investments have not been sufficient.[7]

To add urgency to broader anti-obesity efforts at all levels of government, the CDC then notes that seventy-two million adult Americans are obese and incur on average $1,429 more in annual per capita medical costs than do normal-weight Americans. Once more, the CDC suggests (with maps in a PowerPoint slide show) that obesity is spreading across the states like plagues in our distant past.[8]

Antismoking advocates have stressed, gaining battle points and recruits to their ranks, that smoking is the nation's number one cause of "preventable deaths." The count in 2009 was 443,000, even when the percentage of self-identified smokers is less than half that of 1950. The CDC continues to trumpet with force the full scope of the "burdens of tobacco use," including medical costs and lost productivity, as if there has been no progress in that policy war and as if, again, the rest of society, not smokers, bear all costs—reason enough to seek ever tighter controls and higher taxes.[9]

With a similar sense of urgency, in 2001, then Surgeon General David Satcher proclaimed weight gain in the United States to have reached "epidemic" proportions, even though people's weights had not then reached what they are today. He also delivered a call for remedial government action in words reminiscent of his predecessors' clarion calls to curb smoking:

> Overweight and obesity may not be infectious diseases, but they have reached epidemic proportions in the United States. Overweight and obesity are increasing in both men and women and among all population groups. In 1999, an estimated 61 percent of U.S. adults were overweight or obese, and 13 percent of children and adolescents were overweight.
>
> Today there are nearly twice as many overweight children and almost three times as many overweight adolescents as there were in 1980. We already are seeing the tragic results of these trends. Approximately 300,000 deaths a year in this country are currently associated with overweight and obesity. Left unabated, overweight and obesity may soon cause as much preventable disease and death as cigarette smoking.[10]

In early 2010, the CDC estimated that obesity had overtaken smoking as the leading cause of preventable deaths in the United States, and with excess weight being the leading cause of preventable poor health among Americans[11]—and do note that the CDC makes no real mention in its press releases of the fact that its count of deaths directly attributable to excess fat is a crude, indirect estimate, not a count of people who were necessarily killed by fat, as distinct from diabetes and heart attacks, for example, that could have occurred regardless of whether many of the victims were fat, trim, or in between.

Official pronouncements that the country faces an obesity "epidemic" or "crisis" can be expected to become ever shriller as the percentage of the adult population with BMIs above 25 or 30 continues to spread across the states. The agency has graphically portrayed this trend with maps, color-coded for the percentage of obesity, that get ever darker (with dark orange identifying states with an obesity rate between 20 and 30 percent and dark red for the nine states with obesity rates above 30 percent).[12]

> The country's considerable weight problems have morphed into an "obesity epidemic," or so health-care officials assure everyone.

Although most proposals at the national level to abate the country's weight problems currently tendered seem innocuous enough, you can bet that opponents of government intrusion in the food industry will raise doubts about the cost effectiveness of such proposals. Pointing to the government intrusions in the smoking war, they are likely to raise concerns that even more onerous policies will be proposed as informational and educational efforts fail to achieve the CDC's goal of no state with an obesity rate of 15 percent or higher (a goal that very well could have been chosen to assure failure). Be assured, however, the proponents of expanded government intrusions into the food and beverage industries will also look to the smoking war to justify their proposals; expanded government intrusions in the tobacco industry ultimately were effective tactics to curb smoking. The same success can be achieved in the food and drink industries, or so the proponents might think.

Second-Hand Fat

A powerful argument made for taxing and regulating smoking was that smokers "externalize" their smoking costs to others through "second-hand smoke." People who have to work and play in a haze of cigarette smoke are effectively smoking, perhaps unwillingly and unwittingly, as they breathe in the exhaled fumes (and nicotine) that smokers find so intoxicating, and eventually debilitating. Antismoking advocates have made much of the fact that as many as 120 million Americans have been "involuntary smokers," and Surgeon General Koop made second-hand smoke a prominent issue in his Campaign for a Smoke-Free America. It's one thing for smokers to harm themselves; it's another to harm others (without compensating them for doing so).

At one time, there was no counterpart to "second-hand smoke" in the policy battle over the country's weight problems. Obviously, people can't puff their excess weight into the lungs and eyes of people around them, impairing their life expectancy. But studies have revealed a form of "second-hand fat," which antifat groups will likely infuse, as some already have, into their campaigns to control people's eating habits.

Excess weight and obesity may not have all the markers of an "infectious disease," as one Surgeon General has attested, but they may be "socially contagious." In a 2007 report, researchers who followed 20,000 subjects over thirty years concluded that weight gain is transmittable, in some ill-defined way. As noted earlier in the book, after controlling for a number of factors that can affect weight gain (age, for example), the researchers found that:

- Subjects who have friends who are obese have a 57 percent greater chance of becoming obese within two to four years of the friends becoming obese (during which time the subjects gained an average of five pounds).
- Subjects with obese siblings have a 40 percent heightened chance of becoming obese.
- Subjects with obese spouses have a 37 percent increased chance of becoming obese.
- Subjects have a greater chance of coming down with obesity (so to speak) by being a friend of a friend of someone who is obese.[13]

Obesity researchers have argued that friends and family members tend to adopt the same social norms toward excess weight, researchers explain. But weight contagion also has potential economic foundations: When the number of heavy people in a group increases, the personal and social cost of being heavy can decrease. Thus, applying the law of demand, group members can be expected to add excess pounds. Indeed, some (to date, unknown) portion of Americans' continuing weight gain can plausibly be chalked up to the feedback loop—and the "negative externalities" or "spillover effects"—from eating habits and of weight gain by way of the law of demand. Because everyone is getting heavier, we all have less incentive to control our weight. We all may want to control our weight, but we are locked in a predicament that economists call the "prisoner's dilemma" in which people, making their decisions separately or uncooperatively, end up in the worst of all worlds, one in which everyone is inflicting costs on everyone else, just as polluters do (or so it can be, and has been, argued). The negative externalities can also come in the form of higher medical bills, poor self-images, higher taxes to pay for upgraded bariatric rescue and hospital equipment, higher health insurance premiums, higher taxes to cover higher Medicare and Medicaid expenditures, and/or lower real wages and/or fringe benefits. As polluters might favor controls on their emissions, so might heavy people favor controls to curb weight contagion, which can then reduce their own and friends' and family members' weight, or so the argument can be made.

> Officials assure us that "second-hand fat" can kill just like "second-hand smoke."

Obviously, cigarette smoke can drift through the air, infecting the lungs of innocent bystanders, as all forms of pollution can, which is justification enough (even for free-market economists) for controlling smoking. It's no big stretch for obesity foes to use similar economic analytics, as they have. To take a vivid illustration, food aromas can float through malls, into shoppers' noses, and onto their olfactory receptors, increasing the likelihood that more people will indulge in whatever smells good. As explained in an earlier chapter, smells can dull the capacity of people to make reasoned decisions because the sensory information goes to the lower, primitive or reactive parts of the brains before they ever get to the higher, reasoning part.

You can bet that Cinnabon counts on the delectable aroma of its cinnamon pastries, freshly baked several times a day, to reel in mall shoppers. Indeed, Cinnabon places its bakeries in malls for a good reason, to make sure that the smells of their baked goods spread with intensity.

Smoking can kill innocent people but so can fat. Heavy people, especially when they pay extra to sit in exit rows, can reduce the probability of everyone exiting a plane in the event of survivable accidents. Because of their impaired mobility, heavy people can also impede people's movement down stairwells of tall burning buildings, decreasing the likelihood that all "innocent bystanders" will get out alive. Many stairwells in older buildings were designed so that people with the average weight of the 1960s or before could go down them side by side, which is less possible today. Researchers have learned from interviews with 9/11 evacuees from the World Trade Center that obese evacuees slowed the egress of others from the collapsing Twin Towers (as did people with any number of other disabilities). This means that fewer people might have died on 9/11 in the Twin Towers had people not gained as much weight as they had since the towers were erected (given that survey reports suggest that egress from the buildings was slowed by heavy people).[14] The message is clear: Weight can kill innocent others, just as second-hand smoke can kill innocent others.

Cigarette fumes, in econ-speak, are "negative externalities" because they impose costs, physical disabilities, and a higher risk of death from various preventable diseases on innocent bystanders. Then, the heightened medical-care costs of smokers and bystanders can increase the demand for health-care services and raise their prices and insurance premiums for everyone. In addition, the added medical-care costs tied to smoking can raise Medicare and Medicaid expenditures, which may require higher taxes. The argument can be easily reversed: Controls on smoking can reduce medical-care costs and insurance premiums as well as ever-growing state and federal deficits. Drawing directly on the tried-and-true law of demand and economic arguments to control pollution, antismoking advocates make the case that smokers are not bearing the full cost of their habit; they are smoking "too much," or more than they would if they had to pay all costs themselves. This is to say that unfettered smoking markets are "inefficient." Smoking controls not only save lives, but they force a better allocation of the country's (and world's) limited resources, fewer resources going into cigarette production and medical care (the costs of which are not covered by the smokers themselves), leaving more resources to produce other things—more food, for example.

Again, it's no big stretch to apply the same line of argument to food and drink. Control what and how much people eat and drink, and medical costs and health insurance premiums will fall. Government budget deficits can be reduced as weight becomes progressively less contagious. Sure, heavy people might have to pay higher prices for their favorite fattening foods, but these government controls will be doing the overweight folks a favor—checking their temptations to eat and overeat and reversing social contagion as their friends and family members lose weight, or so the policy argumentation can be developed, as it has been, overtly or covertly.

In short, much of the ammunition for the coming battles over weight-control policies comes from solid economics (with some stretch marks): Market distortions are causing people to weigh more than they would want if they had to pay all of the costs of their excess weight. But some of the policy drive is nothing short of paternalism: "We knew what was good for smokers. The policies adopted over the last five decades worked to curb smoking, and smokers and their family members and friends have thanked us. We know now what is good for heavy people. They also will thank us in the end, if they are not with us in the beginning."

The Devil Made Me Do It

People in democratic societies cherish their freedom to make their own choices, however misguided they may sometimes or often be. For the most part, we make our own decisions and suffer the consequences, good or bad. Much of free-market economics is founded on the presumption that people should be, and can be, held responsible for their behavior. Given the right incentives, people can be expected to do what is best for them. The late Milton Friedman had the ability to state the fundamental principles of free-market economics in a straightforward, easily digestible, if not seductive way. For example, he wrote with his wife Rose, "There is no place for government to prohibit consumers from buying products the effect of which will be to harm themselves." Elsewhere, he mused, "If the government is to try and ban private consumption of alcohol and tobacco, it must surely ban such activities as hang-gliding, skiing, rock-climbing and so on. Where should it stop? Rugby? American football? Ice hockey?"[15] (With all three sports now increasingly recognized for their high incidence of injuries, especially concussions.)

> Many people who decry unhealthy and risky behaviors of others have unhealthy and risky behaviors of their own.

Good question, but Friedman's question missed a growing problem at the time—eating. I dare say that when Friedman made his comment, he probably didn't dream that arguments against cigarettes would be used within a few short decades against honey buns and hamburgers.

Frankly, I empathize with Friedman's position. I have always been amazed at the extent to which hang gliders and heavy people have been in the vanguards of antismoking campaigns. For example, former Surgeon General C. Everett Koop, one of the more forceful crusaders against smoking, has never been morbidly obese, but neither was he the paragon of a fully healthy weight person while in office (according to the current weight standards). To me, pictures of Koop at the time he was leading the antismoking campaign (which can found by searching the Web through Google Images) shows evidence of more than a few extra pounds around his midsection.[16] But Koop was never alone as an overweight smoking protester. Just go to Google Images and search for "smoking protesters," and you will find plenty of sign-carrying antismoking street marchers who have spare tires more inflated than Koop's.

In my way of thinking there was an important element of "the pot calling the kettle black" in the smoking war. But maybe not for all. Perhaps, when Koop's picture was taken and when the antismoking protesters blocked traffic intersections, there was no recognized inconsistency between some protesters' words and weights. When the antismoking campaign was gathering steam in the early 1960s, the country's weight problems had hardly reached the "epidemic proportions" evident on street corners today. It's likely that few of the smoking protesters knew that their growing extra pounds would add to their own health problems and the country's health-care crisis (or, potentially, to global warming, as some might argue today). Moreover, in linking the risks of smoking with those of hang gliding, Friedman was really worrying about how smoking controls could be the proverbial camel's nose under the tent, with the threat of more controls to follow. And in the coming fat war, the now transparent successes of the antismoking campaigns will fortify the many arguments for controls on food choices. In the emerging fat war, we can see more of the camel's head and are perhaps living through Friedman's worse fears in an area of risk taking that Friedman did not anticipate. What's next?

Proponents in the coming weight war are today honing their arguments, if for no other reason than to counter Friedman's and other free-market proponents' objections, in part by seeking to demean or just discredit the messengers. And Friedman and Ronald Reagan have faced a rhetorical beating over the last few decades, as advocates for expanded government have used the country's and world's financial and housing crises, followed by the Great Recession, in recent years as the best evidence yet of the intellectual bankruptcy of the free-market ideology that Friedman and Reagan espoused. Even Judge Richard Posner, a law and economics scholar who honed his free-market leanings at the University of Chicago, cites the Great Recession as a grand example of market failure, and former Federal Reserve Chair Alan Greenspan, a self-professed lifelong "libertarian Republican," has confessed to being partially wrong in his presumption that markets can, and will, everywhere regulate themselves.[17] Indeed, the "obesity epidemic" can be touted as more strong evidence that markets left to their own devices can lead to outcomes that are welfare—and life—destroying. How? There is good evidence, covered earlier in the book, that a nontrivial source of the country's and world's weight problems has been this outbreak of economic freedoms and competitive markets on a global scale.

So, the Great Recession, and all the problems from which it emerged, and the obesity epidemic will form commentary battle lines in the coming fat war. Free-market advocates will stress, as they have stressed, that the Great Recession was largely government induced through an easy money policy that went on too long, tight regulations of banking that encouraged the development of nonbanking institutions that leveraged their meager capital to the hilt, and government encouragement for banks to make low-to no-down-payment mortgages to people who would not have been deemed worthy decades earlier. Free-market advocates can also be counted on to insist that rather than being a case of market failure, the obesity epidemic can be cited as a triumph of capitalism. We should count our blessings.

Who will win this ideological battle? I don't have a crystal ball, but I wouldn't lay money on free-market advocates. A similar set of conflicting arguments was laid out in the smoking war, and the Friedmans of the world, along with "Big Tobacco," lost hands down. Their loss in that war will be used against them in the coming fat war, especially since proponents of government intrusion in people's food decisions will rely, as they have relied, on other arguments that have passed economic muster and that harbor the potential for greater market efficiency.

Proponents of food and drink controls will press another favorite line of argument against government intrusions in individuals' consumption decisions: personal responsibility, or the notion that people should be, and can be, held responsible for their behavior because they will do what is best for themselves. One of the strongest arguments pressed in the smoking war was that the usual economic presumption about personal responsibility does not hold with cigarettes. Tobacco, or substances in it, is addictive, varying in intensity among people. Those who happen to be highly addicted to cigarettes can be captured by the smoking habit, even when they are fully aware of the dire medical, personal, and social consequences. They need to be protected from the consequences that they may not appreciate and foresee and do not, and cannot, deny.

Similarly, the overweight must be protected from their weight-related health problems, and everyone must be protected from the costs that heavy people can inflict on the people around them and the general population.

New York Times business columnist David Leonhardt offers a preview of this policy stance. After noting how obesity has become the country's most serious health problem, he observes how and why additional incentives for people to control their weight are not likely to work: "It's also worth noting that the obese, as well as any of the rest of us suffering from a medical condition affected by behavior, already have plenty of incentives to get healthy. But we struggle to do so. Daily life gets in the way. Inertia triumphs." But I can't help but challenge Leonhardt on the fact that we "already have plenty of incentives to get healthy."[18] If we did, would we not choose to be healthier than we are? "Inertia triumphs"! Does it really? Okay, he is taking literary license, but that would be no problem if Leonhardt did not then offer a framework for his own reform path, grounded not so much in individual responsibility as in collective responsibility, with no argumentation or evidence for the shift in responsibility being productive of his own political agenda.[19]

Leonhardt declares that the problems he identifies "are beyond the control of any individual." Really? For *all* (or even a major proportion of) heavy people who can be seen from street corners? If that were such a valid blanket assessment, then why aren't all, or almost all, people fat? Have not many trim people proved him dead wrong; they've worked to control their weight. As have other proponents of intrusion, Leonhardt relishes the fact that some forms of "fat taxes" would have the blessing of none other than Adam Smith who wrote, "Sugar, rum, and tobacco are commodities which are nowhere necessaries of life, which have become objects of almost universal consumption, and which are therefore extremely proper subjects of taxation."[20]

Strong evidence indicates a range of foods and drinks, especially sugary and fattening ones, are addictive in varying degrees. Even when foods don't fit a strict definition of "addictive," evolutionary arguments can be posed that people have long-standing proclivities to favor certain foods and to eat whenever they can as much as they can (see Chap. 3). People, in short, are not everywhere and always in full control of what and how much they eat. Indeed, some people may have little or no control.

Throw in all the "decision-making biases" and failings that behavioral economists and psychologists press, and you can see the makings of a fairly long policy battle for controls that, advocates will maintain, can enhance market efficiency—and the welfare of heavy people. And some of the overweight are likely to take their places in the front lines, fighting for regulations on everyone's choices so that they also will be prevented from yielding to food temptations. Governments at all levels can provide the services of restraint for heavy people in all income sectors that Betty Ford Clinics provide for high-income alcoholics and druggies.

"My genes made me do it," or did they?

You can imagine how this line of argument can be pressed on fairness grounds: Many rich people go to fat farms and pay good money for weight controls. Government controls can be seen as leveling the playing field. That is, government antifat policies can be seen as a means of providing the same fat-farm services cost effectively for not-so-rich Americans. The argument can be framed as a win-win policy course for everyone, fat and trim Americans alike. With food and fat controls, fat and trim people will not have to deal as often and to the same degree with the "negative externalities" that can come with heavy people crowding into other passengers' seating space on airplanes and with additional weight-related medical-care costs spread across the general population, rich and poor alike, through higher taxes and health insurance premiums. A form of this externality argument worked well for the proponents in the smoking war, which is all the more reason for it to be used continually, in various forms in the coming fat war.

The Policy Battle Lines in the Fat War

The coming fat war will be fought on several policy fronts that range from the unobtrusive and more or less uncontroversial reform proposals—information campaigns on how people can make better food choices and architectural redesign of staircases so that they will be used more often—to the highly intrusive and controversial reform proposals—taxation of some fattening foods, outright food bans, government-provided rescue and hospital bariatric (or obesity) services, requirements for wider seats on airplanes and in sports arenas, laws against weight discrimination in workplaces and public accommodations, and for workplace accommodations for heavy people. As the fat war evolves, don't be surprised if the policy trail follows the one worn bare in the smoking war, with ever-tightening controls on people's freedom to choose what and how much they eat.

At this writing the Food and Drug Administration is pushing for graphic new labels for packs of cigarettes with pictures of the feet of corpses on the front. Would anyone have imagined forty years ago such an escalation of the antismoking war on the label front? Care to bet against a similar labeling requirement for Twinkies or Big Macs forty years into the future?

We might also not be surprised if, along the way, many food providers, from manufacturers to fast-food restaurants, are gradually demonized to one degree or another for victimizing their customers, especially young people, by withholding information on how their products are calorie rich, can be addictive and life-impairing, and by using seductive ads that induce and seduce people to pack on far more pounds than they were (mis)led to believe they would. "Big Food," a catch-phrase already widely used in commentaries on the country's weight problems (just Google the phrase), could replace Big Tobacco as public enemy No. 1 on the policy hit list, with governments at all levels seeking to recover, via taxes and class-action suits, their past medical-care expenditures on overweight and obese citizens who have been too poor (made poorer by their excess weight) to cover fully their own weight-related medical-care costs.

Who would be caught off-guard if key heads of fast-food chains are paraded before some congressional committee where good sport will be made of the executives' claims that they had no knowledge that their menu items could be fattening. Of course, fast-food executives may have learned from the smoking war that they might as well confess to being responsible for the weight gains of their customers, although such confessions may put their companies in legal jeopardy. There's money to be made in the country's excess flab. We have to imagine even at this moment, the lawyers who chased class-action suits against Big Tobacco, seeking enormous settlements for the health problems of their smoking clients, are retooling their arguments to be used against Big Food. The anti-obesity forces are bound to see Ronald McDonald as an easily caricatured symbol of the country's weight problems. Colonel Sanders will not likely be allowed to rest in peace, as anti-fast-food groups seek to tie the country's current weight problems to the billions of greasy chicken thighs his company has served.

Without much doubt, McDonalds and KFC, among hundreds of large restaurant chains, will be beefing up their stable of attorneys to fend off the growing array of legal challenges to the weight consequences of their menus. Big Food will also have to dramatically increase their lobbying staff and their political contributions just to blur the line of demarcation between "healthy" and "unhealthy" foods and to suppress some of the more oppressive efforts to have them foot the bill for the proposed menu of remedial diet and exercise programs, efforts that will drive up the prices of their menu items (and have some effect on people's weight reduction even if government restrictions are never passed). Politicians could very well lambast Big Food executives for greedy marketing efforts that have been inflicting untold harm on America, as were the executives of Big Tobacco.

But there is no shortage of greed to go around. Much of the $246 billion that states won in class-action suits against Big Tobacco did not go to fund antismoking campaigns as promised, but was diverted to a multitude of other initiatives.[21] If there is that much money to be extracted from tobacco companies, might there not be an attempt to extract even more from the fast-food industry that has annual sales of more than $120 billion from 200,000 locations in the United States (nearly fifty times U.S. tobacco sales), not to mention all the other levels of the food industry who will also be defendants?[22]

As the policy battle unfolds, any number of kind words might be offered to heavy people as a group, because no one will want to heap pain on people, some of whom might already be suffering under the load they are carrying (besides, few politicians will brave offending two-thirds—and a growing portion—of the population). Yet, heavy people are unlikely to emerge unscathed from the battle, as many news reports on policy proposals will be accompanied with pictures and videos of very heavy people waddling through sidewalk traffic (their faces not shown, of course, as is now a common practice in news reports and documentaries on people's excess weight). With an array of food choice constraints and taxes slapped on everyone, many trim Americans will surely want to shift the blame for people's excess weight from Big Food to Big People who can't push back from their tables or resist the snack shelves in grocery stores.

> Who should shoulder the blame for the country's weight problems? Big Food or Big People?

Doubt the growing resentment among trim Americans toward heavy Americans? Ask your trim friends how they appraise the fairness of their having to pay extra for their twenty-pound checked bags (or carry-on bag on one airline) while heavy people pay no additional fee for the extra fifty to a hundred (or more) pounds they carry on wrapped around themselves.

The Information and Education Battle Lines

People cannot consistently make good, responsible choices if they don't under-stand the nature and consequences of their choices. That's why free-market advocates from Adam Smith to Milton Friedman have little problem with governments' efforts to provide education and informational services (at least up to some level and with some parental choice). Even Friedman was clear on the potential valuable role of some publicly provided education and information (at least up to some ill-defined level). He wrote with his wife Rose Friedman, "Insofar as the government has information not generally available about the merits or demerits of the items we ingest or the activities we engage in, let it give us the information. But let it leave us free to choose what chances we want to take with our own lives."[23]

When a potentially controversial and divisive policy course is proposed, advocates generally organize their initial steps around providing more education and information (as was the case at the start of the smoking war) and extending what government may already be doing about the issue. The CDC has done just that, tendering a range of educational and informational suggestions that various levels of government and consumers should undertake. None of these have the sting of new taxes and regulations, nor would they seem to raise fierce objections that might end the battle before it has begun. Specifically, the CDC recommends that the federal government promote weight reduction through, among a modest list, "empowering parents and caregivers" and "providing healthy food in schools." States can encourage the development of "farmers' markets." Communities can encourage breastfeeding. And individuals can "eat more fruits and vegetables."[24] (The CDC's full list of recommended nudges toward healthier eating can be found on the CDC's Web site.[25])

Recommendations have already surfaced for constructing multistory workplaces with stairs that are clearly visible, which may encourage more workers to use them, expend more energy, and perhaps lose weight. In one study, only 13 percent of the people observed in workplaces used stairs when they were hidden or remotely located. But in workplaces where the staircases were visible, and at times an architectural design feature, 43 percent of observed workers climbed the stairs. When "motivational signs" for taking the remotely located stairs were placed near elevators, stair usage rose 34 percent.[26] Likewise, proposals to increase the number of parks and playgrounds and miles of bike and jogging paths abound across the country. [27] In 2010, the U.S. Senate passed unanimously the Child Nutrition Act to help schools meet new nutrition guidelines and provide more funding to cover the school meal costs of additional poor students.[28]

These policy suggestions and accompanying initiatives (such as First Lady Michelle Obama's anti-obesity campaign under the banner of "Let's Move") are hardly divisively controversial (but most first ladies' efforts are generally tame, lame, and ineffective, as was Nancy Reagan's "Just Say No!"). Indeed, they seem tame and, for the most part, unobtrusive—and maybe of little consequence in terms of actually changing many people's energy balance. Opponents of government intrusion might rightfully worry about what comes next. The smoking war started out with educational recommendations and warnings that were followed by controls on cigarette ads directed at children that, in turn, led with time to high taxation of cigarettes and spreading bans on where and when people can smoke.

The "Libertarian-Paternalists" Battle Line

> How will the "choice architects" be chosen to devise all the "nudges" to move people toward healthier lifestyles?

Behavioral economists and psychologists believe they have demonstrated beyond any reasonable dispute that people are not the fully rational calculating machines that economists assume they are in their models. Indeed, behavioralists contend people are replete with decision-making frailties, not the least of which is being unable to accurately assess the costs and benefits of street drugs, alcohol, tobacco, and food, especially over long stretches of time. They effectively ask, "If people had the decision-making powers economists ascribe to them, would we have so many drug addicts, alcoholics, cancer-riddled smokers, and overweight and obese people around? Grossly obese people are living proof of the fallacy embedded in the economists' models," or so it might be inferred from behavioralists' arguments.

University of Chicago behavioral economist Richard Thaler and Harvard University behavioral legal scholar Cass Sunstein make no bones about it. The conventional economists' rationality premise is "false—obviously false. In fact, we do not think that anyone believes it on reflection."[29] As noted in Chap. 4, behavioral economists believe that carefully structuring available choices can improve people's decision making. "Choice architects" can "nudge" people toward better decisions and outcomes than they would experience on their own. Similarly, Duke University behavioral psychologist Dan Ariely insists, rightly, that economists' usual assumption that people are rational, and perfectly so, leaves no room for suggested improvements in decisions and behaviors. On the contrary, an assumption that people are so irrational that they are "predictably irrational" leaves a great deal of room for him and other researchers to improve hordes of other people's behaviors either through nudges or "new methods, mechanisms, and other interventions [what Ariely might agree are forms of 'nudges'] that would help people achieve more of what they truly want"[30] (which they assume they can determine). Presumably, the behavioral economists could apply such interventions to "nudge" people toward better food choices and weight control—what the behavioralists divine people "truly want."

Sound a little paternalistic? Thaler and Sunstein would agree; nevertheless, they assure their readers that they favor only "libertarian paternalisms," which ultimately allow people free (or almost free) choice over what they do—or eat and drink. Besides, there are times and circumstances in which someone must structure the array of choices in some way, to achieve some objective, for the benefit of the people who are served. For example, food offerings in cafeterias must have a structure (an "architecture"), and how the foods in school cafeteria lines are presented may influence children's eating habits. Indeed, researchers at Cornell University have found (among other things) that

- If nutritious foods (for example broccoli) are put at the front of school cafeteria lines, sales rise by 10–15 percent;

- If cereal bowl sizes are reduced from eighteen to fourteen ounces, the average cereal serving goes down by nearly a fourth;
- If salad bars are repositioned from the wall to right before the cashier, sales of salads increase threefold, and
- If an express healthy checkout line is introduced, sales of healthy sandwiches doubles.[31]

Thaler and Sunstein ask, "Would anyone object to putting the fruit and salad before the desserts at an elementary school cafeteria if the result were to induce kids to eat more apples and fewer Twinkies?" They maintain that no coercion is involved and argue "that some types of paternalism should be acceptable even to those who most embrace freedom of choice."[32] But, again, the crucial question is, "What's next?"

Granted, the alignment of foods on an elementary school cafeteria counter might not, by itself, raise the hackles of free-market devotees, and in this example we are dealing with children who have underdeveloped decision-making powers (or more undeveloped than adults). But can we accept handing over to governments, and their frail human agents, more sweeping power to arrange people's—adults' as well as children's—choices? Would not these "choice architects" also be beset with all the human mental frailties that Thaler and Sunstein say people have? (And I've written a book in which I've pointed to any number of problems with their arguments, which could be attributed to their own human mental frailties, or maybe it is just me.[33]) But the point is, the choices of choice architects will not be laid down without considerable controversy over what constitutes correct choices (or just correct structures for the choices of so many others).

More problematic is the fact that choice architects would most likely be selected through the political process, which would mean those chosen would not be endowed with the savvy and research skills of Thaler and Sunstein. If choice architectural schemes are set in some centralized location, like capitals of the country or states, will the choice architects know enough about the people's needs and "what they truly want" (to use Ariely's words) and the local environmental constraints to make better choices than people who are the object of their paternalism, libertarian or otherwise? The worry is real because the country is large, the economy is huge, and there are more than 310 million people to "nudge" one way or another in a gazillion different choice settings.

Food controls and taxes can be a slippery policy slope.

Moreover, people—even children—are not the robots that the behavioralists might imagine. Sure, if fruits are placed at the start of school cafeteria lines and schools are required to offer healthier fare, it very well could cause school children to eat healthier—when they are at school—but no one should count on the healthiness of children's daily food intake to rise in line with how they change their eating propensities at school. They could easily satisfy their appetite for sugar and fat satiated foods before and after school from a thousand and one sources, which is bound to mute the effectiveness of such school-based nudges. We have to wonder if any *net* gain in healthier eating will be worth the billions of dollars required to subsidize school food budgets (and according to reports, the Child Nutrition Act could require close to $5 billion in added federal spending[34]). My guess is that self-appointed "choice architects" do not know the *net* worth of their proposed nudges, because they've not run the numbers (from my reading of their works), and really can't before the social experiments la grande are tried.

And mind you that free-market types will rightfully worry that the choice architects will not likely be as libertarian as Thaler and Sunstein profess they are. Many people far removed from the libertarian end of the political spectrum will likely want and seek the powers that go with being choice architects for everyone else. "Libertarian paternalistic" candidates for posts of choice architects might not do any better in the country's polling booths than do libertarian candidates for Congress or the presidency.

Nudging people to eat better and contain their weights may be all well and good, but the fat war has already moved beyond proposals to provide people with better information and education to proposals to designate "experts" who are given the authority to structure and restructure people's food choices. And no matter how innocent or minimalist a reform proposal appears, there will be people who can, and will, oppose the proponents at every step of the way. Few would object to Thaler, Sunstein, and Ariely advising school principals on a voluntary basis, but, if they and other behavioralists want to dictate their favored nudges, they need to understand those are fighting words and positions to many others. The fat war will have been joined, and the conflict might be uglier than the smoking war, given the breadth and depth of the country's weight problems.

No matter, in late 2010, Congress passed legislation, pressed by Michelle Obama and signed by President Obama, on a House vote of 264 against 157, that effectively makes the Secretary of the U.S. Department of Agriculture the chief "choice architect" of nutrition standards for school lunches and school vending machines across all schools in the country. The standards would mandate all schools to serve more vegetables, fruits, whole grains, and low-fat dairy products. Of course, the bill was opposed on fiscal grounds (it would add to the federal deficit) and on paternalistic grounds ("the federal government has no business setting nutrition standards and telling families what they should and should not eat," one congressional opponent lamented).[35]

The Fat-Tax Battle Line

Obesity researchers, who lament the growth in obesity and weight-related health problems, sometimes excuse heavy people for their weight, saying things like: "Heavy people's excess weight is a consequence of their genes." "They are addicted to food." "They obviously make irrational eating decisions." "They are not able to control themselves when food is about." "They are the victims of the marketing campaigns that lure them into eating way too much of what they shouldn't, and know they shouldn't." In general, "Their excess weight is not their fault," at least not for the most part.[36]

Then, pressed for solutions to the problem, obesity researchers and weight control advocates propose a contradictory economic solution: taxes on the offending fatty and sugary foods. If a person's excess weight is not his fault, if he (or she) has no rational capacity to weigh the costs and benefits of overeating, if marketing campaigns have manipulated him into making poor economic decisions, then how could slapping a tax on food and drink possibly be expected to have any effect on this poor irrational soul?

But then, people who make claims that people's weight is not their fault may only be saying that, under their circumstances, people are heavy because their assessments of the benefits of eating have been greater than the assessed costs of gaining weight. If so, taxes can work to reduce their eating and drinking and their weights, as the economic way of thinking predicts. Fat taxes can raise the prices of the targeted food and drink, reducing their consumption (in line with the law of demand). Kelly Brownell, director of Yale's Center for Eating and Weight Disorders (and who would not be described as trim[37]), has made this line argument for more than a decade in pressing for a tax on sugared beverages, and he is now convinced that the imposition of some form of fat tax, most likely on sugared beverages, is "just a matter of time."[38] In fact, proposals for some sort of "junk-food tax" or another abound in state legislatures across the country. Brownell's proposed sugared beverage tax is representative of many of these proposals, and his argument can be replicated with little variation for proposed fat taxes on a range of other high-calorie goods, from triple-decker hamburgers at Carl's Jr. to café lattes with three doses of vanilla syrup at Starbucks.

Most recently, Brownell has teamed with his colleague Thomas Frieden to make the following supporting arguments for a one-cent tax per ounce on sugared beverages, which has been proposed in New York State and supported by the state's governor and by New York City Mayor Michael Bloomberg (who, as noted, wants a tax on sugared sodas and other drinks in his city even if the tax is not applied elsewhere in the state)[39]:

- Studies have shown that the growth in people's weight can be tied to the growth in consumption of sugared beverages.
- During the 2000s, the intake of calories per person in the United States from sugared soft drinks increased 30 percent, with the sugared beverages replacing healthier beverages (juices).
- The increase in the consumption of sugared drinks can be partially attributed to their greater affordability (relative to, say, fruits, vegetables, and fruit juices).
- The consumption of one additional can of soda a day increases children's chances of becoming obese by 60 percent.
- The increased consumption of sugared drinks has increased medical-care costs imposed on taxpayers through higher Medicare and Medicaid expenditures.

- Higher tobacco taxes have effectively undercut cigarette consumption through higher prices, which suggests that fat taxes can be equally effective, if not more effective.
- Brownell and Frieden estimate, through their own statistical analysis, that a 10 percent increase in the price of sugared beverages can be expected to decrease consumption by at least 7.8 percent, rising to as much as 15 percent for major soda brands, which they tout as strong evidence of just how effective their fat tax will be. Other researchers have found that a 20 percent increase in the price of sugared sodas will result in reduction in adult's daily calorie consumption by 37 calories and in children's by 43 calories. These calorie-intake reductions can, according to researchers, be expected to reduce the weight of adults by 3.8 pounds and of children by 4.5 pounds over the course of a year, with the potential for reducing the obesity rate among adults by 3 percentage points.[40] Brownell and Frieden write, "Such studies—and the economic principles that support their findings—suggest that a tax on sugared beverages would encourage consumers to switch to more healthful beverages, which would lead to reduced caloric intake and less weight gain,"[41] a finding that other researchers have strongly contradicted.[42]
- If the proposed New York tax is enacted, sales of the targeted sugared beverages will fall by 13 percent. *If* a similar tax is imposed across the country and *if* people partially replace their sugared beverages with healthier drinks, reducing their calorie intake per year from sugared beverages by 8,000, the result will be an average weight reduction for the country of more than two pounds, which can lead to a reduction in the nation's medical-care costs (and, by way of extension, an increase in the affordability of health insurance).
- A tax of one cent an ounce for sugared drinks sold can generate annual revenues of $1.2 billion in New York alone, which can be used to fund government programs that encourage healthier eating and drinking.
- In New York, polls show that maybe no more than a third of surveyed people favor the proposed fat tax, but the approval jumps to 72 percent of surveyed people when they are told that the additional revenue would be earmarked for obesity-control and prevention programs.

Brownell and Frieden make strong points, but no one should expect narrowly targeted taxes, which reduce consumption of the targeted drinks (or foods), to result in weight losses in line with the reduction in consumption. Notice the "ifs" attached to the proposal. True, some people may shift some of their drink consumption to healthier drinks, but an undetermined number may also switch to untaxed drinks that may be no healthier than the targeted sugared beverages. Some people may switch to, say, lemonade, which can have more sugar and calories per glass than sugared sodas do per can (depending on the "sweet tooth" of the person making the lemonade), or some may also move marginally to wine, which has at least as many calories per ounce as sugared beverages.

Oops, I know you are thinking that wine has been taxed heavily for some time and carries a much higher price than an equivalent amount of soda, but that does not disturb my point. A new special antifat tax on sugared beverages can still raise the price of those beverages *relatively* and lower the price of wine *relatively*. Even though the higher price of sodas remains below that of wine, the law of demand will still be at work (because the law of demand works with *relative* prices, not *absolute* prices). People can be expected to move from the then *relatively* higher priced sugared beverages to the even higher priced but *relatively* lower priced wine. The total calories consumed from drinks may go down, but any reduction in calories downed from fewer sugared beverages can be at least marginally offset with calories from more wine or other drinks and/or foods consumed than otherwise. And if wine is the substitute of choice, other obvious health and societal problems may ensue, not the least of which could be a greater incidence of driving under the influence.

Okay, the incidence of drunk driving might be affected in only a minor way, but still the prospects of the effects must be considered, if the economic way of thinking that Brownell and Frieden employ works in real life the way and to the extent that it is supposed to work for sugared drinks. Fat-tax proponents can't tout the "good" effects and ignore the "bad" ones. Given the complexity of the entanglement of prices across goods and drinks, it's a good bet that fat-tax proponents can't anticipate all the derivative and largely hidden effects of their tax proposals. You can imagine that in the coming fat war there will be battles over what the *net* effects are, if they can be determined with any reasonable precision. Who would have thought in the full heat of the smoking war, focused as it was on the ill effects of smoking, that decades later anyone would be concerned with how the success of the smoking war has contributed, albeit marginally, to the "obesity epidemic" that, in turn, is motivating the fat war. For sure, one thing always leads to another, often by surprise.

Fat Controls

Medical researchers for the international consulting firm McKinsey & Company have surveyed people's weights throughout the world and have found that those who fret about the "obesity epidemic" in the United States have overlooked the larger fat fact that the world faces an "obesity pandemic," given that people's weights in most countries have been rising along with the weights of Americans (although the obesity rate in the United States remains several years ahead of the next closest "competitor," Mexico). They have estimated the total obesity costs in the United States at $450 billion in 2010. Never mind that almost all of those costs were incurred by private individuals (through either higher prices for plus-size clothing and lower wages), these researchers insist that some costs are imposed on the nonobese, which justifies their demand that governments around the globe appoint "obesity czars" who will administer an array of new and extended governmentally imposed food controls. Their trimmed-down list of policy changes to deal with the "obesity pandemic" includes the following:

- Unspecified subsidies for people's purchases of fruits and vegetables funded by taxes on sugared drinks;
- Regulations limiting the density of fast-food restaurants (or any other restaurants deemed to be a part of the world's fat menace);
- Bans on advertisements for large portions;
- Taxes on foods that are high in fat, salt, and sugar;
- Bans on ads for foods that are high in fat, salt, and sugar at all times or at some times during the week (for example, "early morning weekend hours"), especially on food ads directed at children, and an ad ban proposed for the entire world by the World Health Organization as this book was about to go into production[43];
- Incentives to discourage driving in towns and to encourage walking;
- Incentives to encourage children to walk and firms to provide workplace weight management programs.

These researchers exude confidence that their proposed policy agenda will have the intended effect, all of which will be welfare enhancing for people around the world. Of course, they also recommend government subsidies to make medical checkups and nutrition counseling "convenient." Interestingly, this team of researchers obviously believes incentives matter, given the array of government-developed incentives they recommend, but they are totally mum on incentivizing people by making them responsible for the consequences of their own weight gain.

> Inducing people to shift from sugared sodas to diet sodas can give rise to weight gain.

Unexpected and Unintended Consequences

Moreover, fat-tax and fat-ban proponents need to be careful because they might not like all of the indirect consequences of what they wish for. If only sugar-based sodas are taxed, consumers might move to diet beverages, which have potential health problems of their own (although research studies have conflicting findings). Researchers in separate studies have shown that drinkers of diet sodas are more likely to be overweight than drinkers of sugared beverages. One study found that drinking one to two cans of diet soda a day increases a person's chance of becoming overweight or obese by 54.5 percent, a two-thirds greater chance of becoming overweight and obese from drinking one to two cans of sugared beverages.[44]

Yes, many overweight people might turn to diet sodas to control their weight, which suggests that the diet sodas might not be *causing* all of the added weight of those who drink the diet beverages. However, the diet drinks themselves could be causing the weight gain through any number of routes. People might feel better about drinking more diet beverages than they would feel about drinking sugared beverages, and their drinking more beverages may induce more eating. Again, the artificial sweeteners used in diet drinks could also artificially stimulate appetite,

Fat taxes on sugared sodas, or other products, might be ineffective in controlling people's weights because there are a thousand and one substitutes by which people can get their sugar and fat fixes.

with the Web currently alive with studies that connect through association appetite with artificial sweeteners. Moreover, research that followed 2,500 adults for nine years and reported in early 2011 found an association between consumption of artificial sweeteners and "vascular events" (strokes and heart attacks). Indeed, after controlling for a number of other likely causative factors, people who drank one diet soda a day had a 48 percent greater risk of having a stroke or heart attack.[45] At this stage, we can't be sure artificial sweetener is a true *cause* of the identified medical problems, but the findings are probably no less solid than the findings of other research that points to an association between downing sugared sodas and a number of medical maladies. My guess is that both sugared and diet sodas affect different people differently (which is hardly a daring bet since so many things in life and research are like that, which remains a strong argument for giving people the freedom to live their lives as they wish).

Sugar and Fat Fixes

At bottom, reformers must remember a point made briefly earlier in the chapter: People who are inclined to become overweight, if not obese, may simply seek a more general "sugar and fat fix" rather than specific foods – sugared beverages or triple hamburgers. And there have to be a thousand and one ways people can get those fixes. One of the reasons Brownell and Frieden found the demand for sugared beverages to be as "elastic" (or responsive to price) is that there are simply so many options available for people to obtain their more fundamental need for sugar and fat. That is, when sugared beverages are taxed and their prices rise, people seek their sugar fixes in a host of other available and untaxed drinks and foods. Indeed, their econometric work might be a strong indicator of how ineffective, not how effective, their proposed fat tax will be.

And don't forget that when the government raises the prices and lowers the profitability of targeted goods, entrepreneurs can be expected to move into action to create new and "improved" goods outside the target's specifications to escape taxation. A savvy entrepreneur will do well to furnish people with their sugar and fat fixes at relatively lower prices.

Fat taxes just may not be an effective solution to Americans' growing waistlines, according to other studies. As is so often the case in medical research, studies contradict one another. In one study, the effect of a fat tax is substantial. In another it is nil. We've covered studies finding consequential, if not substantial, effects. Consider the polar studies. Using household expenditure data from 1990 through 2006, three economists predicted that a 1 percent increase in states' soft-drink tax would produce only a 0.003 reduction in the average BMI, or from 27 to 26.997. The rates of overweight and obese people in the country would decline by a meager 0.01 and 0.02 percentage points, respectively. For low-income groups, the impact of the higher soft-drink tax is a little greater, but still barely consequential, 0.01 of a BMI point.[46]

Another clinical study of more than 800 subjects found that a reduction of a hundred calories a day from drinking sodas was associated with the loss of just half a pound over eighteen months. [47] You might recall that in Chap. 2 we cited the finding that even if a 100 percent tax were applied to all fatty and low-nutrient foods (which is hardly likely to be enacted), the country's average BMI would fall by no more than 0.2 point, or by much less than 1 percent.[48] In another study involving analysis of two large data sets, these found "*no evidence* that, as currently practiced, either [a soda tax or a ban on vending machines] is effective at reducing children's weight" (emphasis added).[49]

Fat taxes are also the slipperiest of policy slope—if they are to work effectively, they cannot remain narrowly focused on a few foods and drinks, which elevates a real problem. And experimental research does show that if you tax a range of available "unhealthy" food choices (raising their prices by as much as 25 percent) and leave "healthy" food choices untaxed, consumers can be expected to switch from unhealthy food to healthy foods.[50]

So where do you stop? If sugared sodas and candy bars are taxed, why not lattes and hamburgers? What about movie popcorn (the large tub can have over 2,000 calories when smothered with butter)? Twinkies? Real butter? Fatback and bacon? Bread? Peaches? Guacamole? Olives? Tartar sauce and salad dressings? Tax the latter two categories of condiments and you can discourage people from eating fish and salads.

The issue here is not solely a matter of the exact effects of taxes; it is more fundamental: Do we want to give people in the seats of political power the additional authority to decide where to draw the line between fattening foods, which should be discouraged, and healthy foods, which should be encouraged? Drawing that line involves real, abiding, and august power, both political and economic because foods and drinks are so varied and prominent foundations of people's welfares, as they determine their welfares.

Moreover, go too far with taxation of food and drink and you ultimately can undercut significantly people's real incomes, especially those of the poor and near poor. As their income is lowered, these groups actually may move down the food pyramid to less healthier and more fattening foods. You can imagine the protest that producers of the targeted goods will make on "fairness" grounds. A registered dietician from Kentucky, according to a report, has already protested: "This is the most ridiculous idea I've heard. . . (I don't) care to be penalized for indulging in ice cream now and then." Another protester fretted about the unfairness of junk-food taxes: "I am not about to raise taxes on a single mom scraping by on a low-wage job."[51] Imagine what the single mom, especially the trim ones, might say and then imagine other heated arguments from the food producers and restaurants them-selves: "There are a multitude of causes for the country's weight problems, and there are a multitude of high-calorie products and foods. Why pick only on us? I smell a political rat." And why pick on food? It's hardly the only thing people buy that carries risks of bodily injury and deaths. Again, consider hang gliding, surfing, skiing, mountain climbing, football, horseback riding, staying up late, and the list can be extended ad nauseam. Does anyone detect the prospects of a slippery downhill policy slope?

Although people make such proposals with the best intentions, we should never forget the "law of unintended consequences" that could be at play in the fat war. The actual effects of fat taxes are likely to vary across the broad swath of the taxed population, with some people losing weight and others gaining it. If such a mixed outcome occurs, where is the welfare improvement, at least at the level fat-tax proponents tout?

"Two'fers"

Brownell and Frieden and others favor fat taxes because they offer a "two'fer," two gains from one tax. The tax will both curb consumption of the targeted unhealthy goods and provide revenue to subsidize healthy food and drink. Consumers will have a double reason to improve the healthiness of their diets. Such could be the case, although don't forget those unintended consequences.

A tie-in between a fat tax and a "healthy subsidy," however, has problems that both proponents and opponents apparently have overlooked (at least they haven't written about them). Research has found that a subsidy for healthy foods can reduce people's total expenditures on healthy foods, which means that consumers can, and apparently do, use their released real incomes to buy unhealthy foods (for example, chips and dip).[52] Also, as the fat-tax rate goes up and up, the progressive curb in consumption of the offending foods and drinks can, beyond some point, lead to lower total revenues—that necessarily means lower subsidies for healthy foods. And don't forget that there is no natural starting and ending point to the healthy subsidies. If we subsidize broccoli and orange juice, why not baby carrots, tomatoes, and milk (whole, 2 percent, 1 percent, or all milk)? Does anyone want to allow politics to work its magic on which products get subsidies (and which are taxed)? Do you see a political and bureaucratic catfight in the making, as well as a gold mine for politicians seeking campaign contributions?

No doubt, politicians love to tap new revenue streams, especially if the justification is to do good for society, but they also love to access new revenue streams to benefit their particular constituents—and the needs of their campaign coffers. The tobacco settlement with the states was intended solely for antismoking campaigns, but major chunks of the $200 billion-plus payoff have been diverted to any number of uses that have nothing to do with curbing smoking (parks, swimming pools, for example).[53] Should we not expect some of the same with the proposed fat taxes, especially if the taxes are raised enough to have a significant effect on the country's weight problems?

Regressive Fat Taxes

Finally, even Brownell and Frieden recognize one very powerful argument against their fat-tax proposal: The tax will likely be regressive, perhaps excessively so. Obesity is disproportionally concentrated among the poor possibly because they tend to have high discount rates (greater urgency for current consumption with little consideration for future costs, as explained earlier), little education on nutrition, and need to buy low-priced fatty and sugar foods with their limited incomes. And fat undercuts people's employment opportunities and wages, a force that encourages weight gain and that pushes people into the poverty classes.

Accordingly, poor people will pay a greater percentage of their incomes in fat taxes than higher income groups. But their response to this fact is unlikely to alleviate the sting: ". . . the poor are disproportionately affected by diet-related diseases and would derive the greatest benefit from reduced consumption; sugared beverages are not necessary for survival . . ."[54] If that were an acceptable argument, we can justifiably tax poor people at higher rates because they get most of the welfare and unemployment benefits. Then why not make all taxes that dispropor-tionately help the poor regressive, for consistency in political philosophy, if nothing else? Moreover, their higher taxes can deny poor people real income to buy the after-tax higher-priced healthy foods and can, thus, cause poor people to buy even more unhealthy foods because they are cheaper. But then there is a worse problem. Why tax the trim poor, who restrain themselves, to correct the wayward ways (if they are that) of their heavy poor cohorts?

Another problem that emerges with fat taxes that did not appear in the smoking war can't be emphasized often enough: tobacco taxes directly affect the offending parties—smokers—but fat taxes apply to everyone—fat and skinny alike—who buy the targeted product. Nonsmokers do not pay cigarette taxes because . . . well, they don't buy cigarettes, but yet they are relieved of the second-hand smoke problems. But imposing fat taxes on certain foods means that trim people, poor and rich alike, will have to pay higher prices for the goods they want—even after incurring any costs associated with controlling their weights. Many people may stay trim while drinking calorie-rich Cokes all day, but only by watching their calories in meals, desserts, and snacks or by expending lots of calories on runs and biking trips. And don't forget there are many "poor" people who are highly educated (in universities we call them "graduate students" and lecturers in the humanities!).

Can anyone claim that it is fair to tax people who are not in the targeted group, especially if they are poor? Why should everyone be forced to suffer because of the behavior or misbehavior of the few—or really the many in this case? Besides, the tax applies to everyone just because the proponents don't like people being over-weight and having the health problems they do. Well, I understand the proponents' concerns about the grossly obese, but they give every indication that they want to curb the weight of practically everyone whom they have classified as merely overweight, or who don't meet their standards of healthy weights (which seems to be a BMI of below 25). But studies suggest that having a few extra pounds can

Fat taxes can be "regressive" because they will hit the poor harder than the rich—whether trim or fat—and fat taxes can contribute to weight gain among the poor.

reduce health problems and increase in life expectancy; so, can anyone assure us that a fat tax is really in the interest of everyone who is overweight or even obese? I suspect not, because it's almost a certainty that the fat-tax proponents don't know the multitude of details of the lives of the hundreds of millions of people their policy prescription will affect, and for good reason: They simply don't have the brainpower to learn about, absorb, and use the multitude of details, and most of those details involve subjective evaluations that can be known only by the people who have them, a point Friedrich Hayek made with force in his writings.[55]

Fat Bans

As an aside, even Mayor Bloomberg's modest proposal to ban the use of food stamps (now tagged as SNAPs, for Supplemental Nutrition Access Program, with the food funds distributed in the form of electronic benefit transfer [EBT] cards) within New York City for sugared drinks may have very little effect on food-stamp recipients' weight. Food stamp recipients generally have incomes from welfare, work, and black-market sources. Their money incomes and food stamps are virtually interchangeable: Recipients can use cash or food stamps to purchase food, more or less with ease. Food-stamp recipients can use their food stamps for sugared sodas and their cash for other things, or for additional food and drinks after they run out of food stamps. If you deny the recipients the right to use their food stamps to buy sugared drinks, they can use their food stamps for allowable food items and their cash for sugared drinks.

Bloomberg is apparently unaware that food-stamp recipients can now turn in their food stamps (or EBT cards on which their allotted food subsidies are encoded) at stores' checkout counters receiving cash in return, and then turn around and use the acquired cash to buy sugared drinks (all perfectly legal under the rules of the food-stamp program). Because the proposed soda restriction would reduce the value of food stamps (albeit marginally) for some, more recipients can be induced to sell their food stamps to non-food-stamp recipients at a lower price than otherwise (in the black or just gray market)—with the food-stamp recipients using the acquired cash to buy the sugared drinks they want.

Also, many food-stamp recipients are well positioned on the city's perimeter to simply walk across the city limits and buy all the sugared drinks they want with food stamps. Then there will be entrepreneurs who will save the food-stamp recipients the hassle of cross-border travel. These entrepreneurs can sell sugared drinks inside the city for food stamps, and then take their bank of food stamps outside city limits to replenish their stocks of sugared drinks for resale inside the city.

Most food-stamp recipients might buy slightly fewer sugared drinks in the process because they are slightly more inconvenient (more costly) to purchase, but don't expect their consumption of sugared drinks to go down by more than a minor amount, if at all. Then, recognize that low-income people, who may not be as stupid as proponents of such bans assume, can use their food stamps to get their sugar fixes in a multitude of other ways from drinks and foodstuffs not subject to food-stamp bans. And, don't forget also that any substitution of diet soda for the sugared variety, which the ban may prompt, could simply backfire and induce weight gain, because artificial sweetener can increase people's appetites. Mayor Bloomberg's proposed trial ban might be rightfully expected to affect the weights of low-income city residents by no more than nanograms and could have the perverse effect of increasing their weight, if they are induced by the ban to switch to diet sodas. But we will see. Thank goodness he has proposed the ban as an experiment.

Efforts on the West Coast to micromanage food choices also may have dubious effect on obesity. Out of professed concern for rising obesity among children and under the banner of "food justice," the Board of Supervisors in San Francisco followed the example of their counterparts in Santa Clara County, California, and passed an ordinance that would ban the inclusion of toys in kids' meals at fast-food restaurants (most notably Happy Meals at McDonalds) within the city, unless the meals passed stipulated nutritional requirements (fewer than 600 total calories for both the food and drink, with less than 35 percent of the calories coming from fat). The ordinance, which takes effect in late 2011, also requires all restaurants to provide fruits and vegetables in all meals for kids.[56]

One San Francisco supervisor justified the bans on the grounds, "From San Francisco to New York, the epidemic of childhood obesity in this country is making kids sick, particularly kids from low-income neighborhoods, at an alarming rate. It's a survival issue and a day-to-day issue," only to add later in the newspaper report, "It's astronomical how much it's going to cost if we don't address it. It's incredible the crisis that's going to hit us."[57] Fortunately, San Francisco Mayor Gavin Newsom vetoed the toy ban on the grounds that the supervisors had "gone too far" and because the city had once again become the butt of late-night television mockery.[58] Not giving up, San Francisco supervisors were working to override the mayor's veto.

Stay tuned because McDonald's Happy Meal has become a symbol, if not a major cause, for all that is wrong with American fast food and the growing weight problems of the country's children, mainly because, according to the editors of *The New York Times*, the Happy Meal, with 640 calories, contains half the recommended daily calories of inactive children ages four to eight, all pressed on gullible children and their parents by high-powered and omnipresent Happy Meal (and other McDonalds) ads that have made McDonalds the most popular restaurant by far for children.[59] The Center for Science in the Public Interest has joined with a mother of two from Sacramento, California, (and child nutrition advocate) Monet

Parham to sue McDonalds, asking the courts to make Happy Meals less appealing to children by forcing the chain to remove the toys from Happy Meals. Why, you ask? Ms. Parham asserts, "Because of McDonald's marketing, [her daughter] Maya has frequently pestered Parham into purchasing Happy Meals, thereby spending money on a product she would not otherwise have purchased." But why doesn't Ms. Parham just refuse to take her children to McDonalds: because if she doesn't, then her children "pout" and generally become disagreeable.[60] The editors of *The New York Times* seem to agree that the case has at least some merits because parents must "push back against the [McDonalds'] relentless tide of marketing aimed at their children."[61]

As this chapter was also being finalized in late 2010, Los Angeles city leaders considered restricting the number of fast-food restaurants (defined as an eating establishment that doesn't have table service for a limited menu range).[62] The proposed restrictions would apply to South Los Angeles, a forty-square-mile section of the city with predominantly poor and black residents, where 45 percent of all eating establishments were fast food, a substantially higher percentage than in other parts of the city. The proposal didn't set a quantitative limit on count of fast-food restaurants, but it might as well have. If passed, the new ordinance would require a cumbersome and lengthy approval process, with the mayor's signature required. Such a restriction would surely increase the relative cost of establishing new fast-food restaurants that, in turn, could jack up the prices at all fast-food restaurants and lengthen their lines and increase the time cost of buying fast food in the targeted area.

Understandably, the California Restaurant Association vigorously opposed the measure, pointing to the number of needed entry-level jobs that fast-food restaurants brought to the area and the count of millionaires fast-food restaurants had made from the ranks of the poor. They might have also questioned the measure's efficacy.

With all the scary talk in support of the various bans, you have to wonder about the efficacy of the ban on kids' weight. Surely the toy in kids' meals influences only a portion of the kids-meal purchases; the effect on sales could be minor even if parents and fast-food restaurants do nothing to circumvent the intent of the ordinance. And parents and kids have many ways to do just that. Parents and their children can adjust their behavior to circumvent the ban by going outside South Los Angeles for fast-food meals or outside the city limits for their Happy Meals or upgrading their Happy Meals to more calorie-heavy Big Macs. Alternately, the fast-food restaurants can adjust by simply lowering the price of their kids' meals and then selling their toys separately. For that matter, restaurants can give the toys away to every child who goes through the restaurant, with possibly the unintended consequence of more children eating more meals at fast-food restaurants. Alternately, fast-food restaurants that have been providing toys in their kids' meals can include another treat that doesn't match the ordinance's definition of "toy." For that matter, they can use the funds that would have been spent on toys to redesign their kids' meals box or bag to make it a functional toy or educational game. The point is that fast-food restaurants can do a lot of creative things to circumvent the law.

In the case of any restriction on the entry of new fast-food restaurants, the growing demand on existing fast-food restaurants can, for example, cause them to expand their facilities, increase the number of order registers (including drive-through order stations), adopt any unused technologies to increase the speed of drive-through service, add some limited table service in order to escape the definition of "fast food" in the city ordinance, increase the availability of home delivery, and reduce the sizes of their tables to pack in more customers. Non-fast-food restaurants can accommodate residents' demand for high-calorie meals that can't be satisfied at fast-food restaurants by inserting higher calorie meals of their own. Perhaps there will be some net reduction in calories consumed in the targeted area, because of the added costs and inconvenience imposed by the restrictions, but no one should expect the restriction to have anywhere close to the effects advertised by the restrictions' supporters. And, of course, fast-food restaurants can be expected to locate new restaurants on the border of the targeted city district, reducing the distance residents of the targeted district have to go to get their fast-food fix. The added restaurants on the border will reduce the travel costs for their fast-food fixes for those residents just outside the targeted district, increasing their consumption of fast food. This means that if there is any weight loss inside the targeted district, it can be partially offset by more weight gain in the areas of the city that surround the targeted district.

As noted, we also have to wonder about the fairness of such bans. True, the restrictions on restaurants and toys might discourage a few parents from buying their heavy children high-calorie meals, but such an achievement is sought by denying *all* parents and *all* of their children—whatever their weight, exercise routines, and diets—the right to a meal (with toy included), fast-food or otherwise, they decide they want. San Francisco's and Los Angeles' city leaders might not also be aware that some parents—even targeted low-income black parents—might use occasional trips to McDonalds, Burger King, or Carl's Jr. as rewards for healthy eating and living at other times of the day or week.

Mother Nature and Mother Market

These are only a few of the multitude of fronts on which the impending fat war will be waged. California and Connecticut early on required restaurants with more than a specified number of locations (twenty in the two states mentioned) to post the calories for all menu items on separate cards that could be given to customers on request. The new national health care program, passed in 2010, now requires all restaurant chains in the country with more than twenty outlets to post the calories for each menu item as served (not by some different "portion" size) alongside the items on the menus themselves and on menu displays above the order counter, following the lead of California, again.[63]

In early 2011, the U.S. Department of Agriculture was readying regulations that would require grocery stores to include in their labels on forty of the most popular cuts of meat (beef, pork, lamb, and chicken) the total calories, calories from fat, grams of fat and saturated fat, plus details on the protein, cholesterol, sodium, and vitamins in various cuts of meat.[64] At the same time, in early 2011, the efficacy of the required calorie labels for fast-food restaurants was being drawn into question by scholarly research. Nutrition researchers centered at Yale University and New York University followed nearly 500 New York City teenagers before and after the city required fast-food restaurants to post the calories for their menu items in mid-2008 to assess how the mandated labels influenced the teenagers' knowledge of the calories of fast-food items and then food choices. They used teenagers from Newark, New Jersey, which did not have mandatory labeling, as a basis for comparison. They found that while New York teenagers became more aware of the calories they were downing because of the labeling mandate, the labels did not significantly affect their food choices, that is, did not affect the calories consumed. The researchers found that the parents of teenagers were more aware of the calories for menu items. However, even when parents were involved in the teenagers' food choices, the calories consumed were unaffected by the labeling. One of the lead researchers on the study interjected, "[I]t is important to understand that labeling is not likely to be enough to influence obesity in a large scale way. Other public policy approaches, as well as the efforts of food companies as other actors, will be needed."[65]

Of course, there will be beefed up public awareness campaigns to get more people to eat healthier and to exercise more, such as First Lady Obama's current "Let's Move" campaign.[66] But don't be surprised when the tame (which some advocates of taxes and bans might see as almost spineless) education campaigns fail to make a significant dent in America's weight problem, they morph into more command and control measures. Many of these control measures already have been proposed around the world and are gaining support in the United States, as discussed. Such tentative information and control measures have caused legal scholars in the United States to up the ante in the festering fat war. Their proposed fairly radical "performance-based regulation[s]" for restaurant chains to abate obesity, with a focus on childhood obesity, will hardly be voluntary, given the "substantial financial penalties" proposed for failing to cooperate.[67]

The U.S. Department of Agriculture has greatly expanded the use of food stamps, from just 17 million in 2000 to 42 million Americans in mid-2010 with, apparently, two goals in mind: first, making the distribution of food stamps a "stimulus" for economic revival (with, supposedly, $1 in food stamps generating $1.73 in greater national income) and, second, using food stamps as a means of influencing people's diets (for example, by giving discounts of, say, 30 percent, for the purchases of fruits and vegetables), a program direction, you can bet, that is not going to be cheered by the corn and wheat industries. [68]

Surely the food industry is already building its war chests and aiming at policy makers in state capitals and Washington. The food industry is unlikely to take kindly to the claim that it alone has a "moral" responsibility for everyone's weight problems. After all, others are freely doing the buying, and others—most notably parents—are in a better position to determine what they and their children eat. Researchers may assert the moral high ground in a debate (which may be intended to put their policy proposals beyond the dispute of mere mortals), but they should not assume the moral high ground simply by their asserted claims. If food and drink producers are giving their customers what they "truly want," are they in the moral low country, simply because researchers don't agree with the customers' desires? Okay, researchers may be smart people, but are they smart enough to divine the choices of hordes of people whom they do not and cannot know, especially when they live—and eat—in far more comfortable circumstances?

But then those who would wage a war on the food industry on moral grounds might resist an inconvenient truth: The real economic effects of their proposed controls on food-chain producers will fall in large measure on those whom they would like to protect—the average Joe and Jane, who come in all shapes and sizes. Restrictions on producers are bound to affect market supplies, which affect the price and quality of the food and drink people buy. Go after producers and, no matter the veil, consumers stand in the line of fire. You can't fool Mother Nature and you can't fool Mother Markets, although reformists would like everyone to believe that they can do both. No way.

As the conflict heats up and control proposals become ever more serious, there will be the inevitable battle of words, literally, over what constitutes "food," not to mention "fast food," and what is "healthy" and "unhealthy." The standards for "overweight" and "obese" will be recognized for what they are, political variables designed to press policy agendas.

Fat Discrimination

Who would have thought that Hooters restaurants—known for their chicken wings and beer but more so for their big busted petite female waitresses in tight shiny orange shorts—would be on the legal frontline of the coming fat war? Clearly, Hooters is in the business of offering their largely young adult male patrons a chance to ogle women who would not likely give many of them the time of day if the men were not there to place orders. The waitresses' good looks and sexual appeal is known in retailing as the firm's "unique selling proposition" (just as everyday low prices is Walmart's unique selling proposition and the "happiest place on earth" is Disney's). And if Hooters were to offer its same fare of food (which few would praise) served by heavy waitresses in muumuus, it's a good bet that its business would collapse. The women who apply to work as waitresses at Hooters understand the business model, wouldn't you think?

Nevertheless, that does not always appear to be the case. Two former waitresses at Hooters in Roseville, Michigan, have filed separate suits in 2010 under that state's weight antidiscrimination law. One of the waitresses, twenty-year-old Cassandra Marie Smith, maintains in her 2010 complaint that she was recruited to be a waitress while dining at Hooters in 2008.[69] At the time she started work at Hooters, the waitress stood five feet eight inches tall and weighed 145 pounds. During the next two years, she received "high marks" on her performance evaluation and was promoted to shift leader, according to her lawsuit. In the spring of 2010, even though she had reduced her weight to 132.5 pounds (which means she had a BMI of 20.1), she was for the first time "admonished, disciplined, and counseled by Hooters supervisors . . . about the fit of her uniform and advised to join a gym in order to lose weight and improve her looks so that she would fit better into the extra small-size uniform she was required to wear."[70] The only other available sizes were extra, extra small and small. She was put on "weight probation."

According to her complaint, the disclosure of her weight probation to coworkers and customers was humiliating, which effectively meant that she had been "constructively discharged because she was unable to meet the Hooters' discriminatory and illegal requirements of a 'Hooters Girl.'"[71] She claims that Hooters violated Michigan State statute on both gender and weight antidiscrimination.[72]

The two waitresses could, eventually, have a court decision on their side along with a cash award (if the case isn't settled in advance of a trial). After all, Michigan's antidiscrimination law seems clear under the Elliott-Larsen Civil Rights Act of 1976 (as amended as late as 1992), which prohibits ". . . discriminatory practices, policies, and customs in the exercise of those rights based upon religion, race, color, national origin, age, sex, height, *weight*, familial status, or marital status . . ." (emphasis added).[73] In short, businesses in Michigan can't discriminate in height or weight, or any combination of the two, at least as I read the law. Similarly, businesses may not discriminate on weight in hiring and service decisions in San Francisco; Birmingham, New York; Santa Cruz, California; Madison, Wisconsin; Washington, D.C.; and Urbana, Illinois.[74]

But who can believe that discrimination by height and weight, as well as appearance overall, isn't rampant in Michigan and, for that matter, everywhere else? Consider an obvious and prominent example of height discrimination in Michigan: The Detroit Pistons, a professional basketball team, surely takes height, and even weight and gender, into consideration in selecting players. A five-foot-four-inch (female?) guard would surely have to be exceptional not to be dismissed out of hand if he (she?) tried to walk on the court at a preseason training camp. Heavy people would surely have a tough time being accepted into professional dance troupes, such as the professional dancers on the hit television program, "Dancing with the Stars". Most model agencies work mainly, if not exclusively, with thin models (although, as noted, there has been a recent rise in the use of full-figured women in ads and on runways).

Hooters clearly seeks to sell beer and wings partially by elevating the arousal of its male customers. Seasons 52, a new restaurant concept spreading across the country at this writing, offers an upscale faire with no menu item having more than 475 calories. The chain clearly discriminates in selecting servers based on weight. If it didn't, it's hard to understand why *all*, or practically all, of the servers at the restaurant I have patronized several times in Southern California have been trim (and young and fairly good looking). At the very least, heavy (young) men and women in the population of Southern California are not fully represented on Seasons 52 serving staff in proportion to their representation in the population. Indeed, there would certainly be a disconnect between the wholesome food image at the core of the restaurant's business model and servers who would be viable candidate for "The Biggest Losers" television program, or even would just have substantial spare tires around their waists.

Many men and women seek trim people for mates, while others seek heavy mates. According to surveys, women generally seek male partners who are three to four inches taller than they are, and men seek women shorter than they are, and both sexes tend to see obesity as a turn off in the so-called "mating market," according to surveys.[75] Clearly, anecdotal and scientific evidence suggests that people everywhere discriminate on the basis of weight, and understandably. Even heavy people do so. Some deliberately choose other heavy people; others choose trim people; and some are "switch hitters" on weight, depending upon time and circumstances. It's hard to believe that even Hooters waitresses, as a group, don't discriminate from time to time on the height, weight, and appearance of dates and life partners, and maybe even on how they treat their customers.

Many people—even many heavy people—don't want to be around, much less work with, heavy cohorts. We have noted that a sizable percentage of surveyed people view very heavy people as a group in derogatory terms, not the least of which is "lazy."[76] Beyond some weight gain, heavy people tend to incur progressively more health-care costs, have more frequent and longer bouts of absenteeism from work, be less productive, and have careers and lives shortened by their excess pounds. Even many Hooters waitresses are likely to prefer that their employer seek only trim and pretty waitresses. Why? Because such an employment policy can be good for their income and job security.

Of course, weight per se might not be the direct cause of discrimination. The real discriminatory factor might be appearance, with weight being one of several factors comingling in various proportions across people in determining their acceptable, if not desirable, level of appearance. Hooters might rightfully claim, as it has, that weight is not really the company's central concern; the company's unique selling proposition, its franchisable image, is the attractiveness (or maybe, more bluntly, sexuality) of its frontline workers—its waitresses. If the courts give the entertainment industry an exemption from weight discrimination prohibitions on the grounds that looks, including weight, are central to its unique business proposition, you can imagine that Hooters could claim that its waitresses are entertainers in that the waitresses strutting their stuff in the restaurant aisles are as crucial to satisfying their customers as are dancers and singers strutting their stuff on stage.

While Michigan is (at this writing) the only state with an explicit weight antidiscrimination statute, such laws might spread rapidly across states, given the continuing growth in overweight and obese people, who may experience the stings of discrimination but who have the growing political power of votes, which can cause them to press for weight antidiscrimination laws. You can imagine their case: Any number of credible studies reported in this book have found that heavy people suffer wage penalties and missed opportunities for advancement at work.[77]

However, many heavy people don't necessarily need explicit weight antidiscrimination state statutes or federal laws to seek court-based remedies for what they believe are instances of weight discrimination. The former Michigan Hooters waitresses have claimed that they have been subjected to both weight *and* gender discrimination on the understandable grounds that the company's weight restrictions apply mainly, if not exclusively, to female servers. The standards don't apply (at least not with the same force) to the cooks, busboys, and managers. In 2010, the CEO of Hooters was the focus of an episode of the television realty show "Undercover Boss", in which the heads of medium to large companies take on disguises to work with frontline workers. The Hooters CEO was trim, but the manager of one Hooters restaurant the CEO visited was huge, well into the obese weight category (and he was also shown talking with and treating his female waitresses in grossly demeaning terms, which very likely was the reason he was no longer working at Hooters when the showed aired). Moreover, studies have shown that heavy female workers suffer much greater wage penalties than their male counterparts.[78]

One can also easily imagine heavy African-American and Latinos (and maybe other ethnic groups) claiming employment and service discrimination on racial grounds, since, as groups, they include large concentrations of heavy people. Weight restrictions can be viewed (reasonably or unreasonably, depending on your perspective) as having strong racial biases. Moreover, the country has a growing record of court cases affirming the antidiscrimination prohibition against people with documented physical, mental, and emotional disabilities. Indeed, under the Americans with Disabilities Act (ADA), businesses must make reasonable efforts to accommodate people with various certified disabilities. Many weight researchers and activists now claim that excess weight is a disability, if not a disease, that should be covered explicitly under the ADA. Who would be surprised if the number of weight discrimination lawsuits rapidly escalates in the not-too-distant future?

Admittedly, from all outward appearances, the treatment of the Hooters waitresses in Michigan is particularly hard to defend on weight grounds. After all, at least one of the waitresses was very trim, only 1.6 BMI points from being classified officially as "underweight." But then, we shouldn't rush to judgment. Weight is, again, hardly the only consideration in determining waitresses' appearances. Appearance can depend on how the two waitresses were carrying their weight, which means exactly how the shorts fit. For that matter, the Hooters manager may have wanted to dismiss the waitresses for reasons other than weight, or how tight their shorts were (or for what they did or did not reveal). The manager may have simply used "weight probation" to encourage workers' with inappropriate attitudes toward their coworkers and customers to move on. Who knows? We just can't say without knowing far more details of their cases than can be acquired and reported here. Both Hooters and the former waitresses need their day in court.

What we can do here is point out three serious economic problems with making weight discrimination illegal that must be weighed in the emerging weight war. First, it is abundantly documented that at least beyond some weight (fat) level, heavy people tend to incur escalating medical-care costs, to be absent from work more often, and to be less productive than their trim coworkers. One might like to think that weight antidiscrimination laws will force business owners with deep pockets to cover the added costs of their heavy workers. Transparently, many owners of businesses, large and small, are at all times struggling to survive. You have to wonder why even the "rich" business owners should be required to pay the costs of heavy workers when their weight was not a consequence of their employment.

Moreover, if employers can't discriminate against heavy people, then the weight antidiscrimination laws can force firm owners to raise their prices, which means that their customers, trim and heavy alike, rich and poor alike, will have to cover some of the costs of workers who have not controlled their eating. Alternately, heavy workers' added cost burden to their firms can be imposed on all workers—again, heavy and trim alike, low-wage and executive workers alike—through higher health insurance premiums applied to all workers. When firms are teetering on the edge of survival, the added cost burdens of retaining heavy people (without paying them discriminatory wages and fringe benefits) can further undercut all workers' job security.

Second, legal restrictions against weight discrimination (in the form of a heightened threat of lower wages and job losses) can effectively lower the *full* cost of people's weight gain incurred through time, just as surely as the provision of health insurance coverage to all workers does without a risk premium for excess weight, which has been shown to induce weight gain.[79] Firms can be forced to pay heavy workers comparable wages to trim workers, regardless of their differential costs and productivities. But don't forget, the law of demand applies with force to eating and weight gain: Lower the cost people have to bear from overeating and weight gain, and the more people can be expected to eat and the more weight they can be expected to gain. In short, weight antidiscrimination laws and regulations can make the country's (and world's) weight problems worse. That is, the count of overweight and obese people can be expected to rise.

Third, weight antidiscrimination laws are designed to curb the power of businesses to determine the fate of heavy workers. However, such laws don't mute economic power: They simply shift decision-making power from businesses to others, heavy people and prospectively heavy people who will then have the legal right to impose the costs of their excess eating and weight-gain decisions on others. Has justice, fairness, or economic efficiency been improved by such a shift? Not necessarily, in my book.

Nevertheless, a number of court cases have already been filed and sometimes with judges and juries siding with employers. For example, a security guard for the Cincinnati Correctional Institution was dismissed in 1995 for his morbid obesity, after his employer tried to get him on a weight-loss program and required him to meet the physical tests for his job that others had to meet. The guard claimed that his obesity was a protected disability under the ADA. The appeals court ruled that the claimant had not provided evidence that the employer viewed the plaintiff's morbid obesity as causing a substantial limitation of a "major life activity."[80] In another weight-discrimination case a court held that morbidly obese plaintiffs, charging weight discrimination on promotions, failed to show a connection between plaintiffs' obesity and a "physiological disorder or condition."[81]

At other times, courts and juries have sided with workers who claim weight discrimination, under the legal theory that weight is a legally protected disability. For example, in 1993, an attendant who had worked off and on at a Rhode Island state facility providing care for the mentally retarded applied to be rehired when she was five-feet-two-inches tall and weighed 329 pounds, which gave the attendant a BMI of 60.2, 50 percent higher than the bottom limit for morbid obesity of 40 (Cook v. State of Rhode Island). An examining nurse working for the state agency found the attendant to be fit for her anticipated care duties, but the state agency turned her down for reemployment anyway on the grounds that her morbid obesity would impair her ability to evacuate patients in cases of an emergency. Nevertheless, the jury didn't buy the state's argument and found that the attendant's prospective state employer had discriminated against her based upon her weight, a protected disability, and awarded the claimant $100,000 in compensatory damages.[82] Obviously, much confusion exists over how courts will treat weight discrimination claims in the future. That legal confusion (or uncertainty over future court decisions) can impact firms' expansion and hiring decisions.

Of course, a critical issue going forward from the particulars of this case is whether or not, or to what extent, similar court decisions would cause private firms and public agencies to hire obese people with the result being that other people's lives would be put in peril. We have to wonder who is in a better position to decide such issues, the courts and juries or firms and state agencies, especially when the latter can be open to legal damages for hiring workers who, because of their physical limitations, cause injuries and deaths to coworkers, customers, and suppliers.

Okay, I understand that many supporters of weight antidiscrimination laws fervently maintain that heavy people can't help their weight. Many people are genetically bound to be fat. Maybe so for a number of severely overweight people, but you have to realize that evaluating the ability of people as a whole to impose their will on their weight gain decisions requires that we also consider all people who are not excessively overweight. As one prominent economist once quipped, "If all you do is interview people who returned from World War II, you might get the impression that no one died in the war." There are simply hordes of reasonably trim (and far-from-heavy) people who may be just as genetically predisposed to weight gain as many currently heavy people are, but the trim people have worked very hard—incurred lots of costs – to keep the weight off. You can see many of these hardworking trim people in the gym and on bike paths all over the country.

So much for heavy people's weight being totally predetermined. It is best to say that people are more or less *predisposed* to gain weight, yet evidence from genetics has shown that people can purposefully and substantially modify their weight-gain predispositions through lifestyle changes.[83] Should people who control their weight be required to suffer penalties in the form of higher health insurance premiums, higher product and services prices, and possible job insecurities because other heavy people have not exercised whatever control they have over their eating and weight-gain propensities? The question is all the more poignant when you recognize that legal protection of heavy people from discrimination can magnify, through induced weight gain, the costs all others—heavy and trim alike, rich and poor alike—must incur from the excessive eating of many.

Remember that the most important goal of government should be to follow Google's widely touted mantra, "Do no evil." Beyond that, if one of government's goal is, or should be, to "internalize externalities" (as discussed earlier), then surely it should avoid, to the extent possible, encouraging the externalization of people's costs from their eating and exercise decisions. Fortunately, at least one appeals court found in 1998 that obesity per se is not a protected disability. The senior judge in a three-judge panel of the Sixth Circuit ruled, "We hold that to constitute an ADA impairment, a person's obesity, even morbid obesity, must be the result of a physiological condition."[84] However, you can imagine that advocates for the obese will be working hard to widen the range in which people's excess weight is the product of a "physiological condition," which, if successful, can give rise to more weight gain.

Concluding Comments

A word of caution as you conclude this chapter: If you are like many readers and me, you probably often imagine "overweight" or "obese" people in the worst of stereotypes, especially if you are trim or near-trim and/or find fat disquieting, if not disgusting. As you have read this book, you may have kept in the back of your mind an image of a fat person you have encountered, such as the big man who sat next to me on the airplane trip, related in the first chapter. Such images of the overweight and obese are often not pretty, and can be disturbing (as they can also be disturbing for obese people themselves).

When reading the obesity literature, it's easy to imagine all obese people as low-income, uneducated, and certainly unsophisticated. And why not? Those stereotypes certainly can validate researchers' claims that overweight adults they have studied are beset with extensive irrationalities, so much so that they, especially the obese, can't possibly be making responsible life choices, at least when it comes to food. The obese need the guidance of "choice architects" to improve their lives; they must be taxed into eating right and protected from themselves. They can't possibly be left "free to choose" their life courses without self-appointed or government-appointed coaches with offices in Washington or in remote state capitals.

But when two-thirds or more of American adults are said to be overweight or obese, such a statistic is reason enough to check stereotypes and reconsider just how hobbled, or not, this majority is in their decision making. Many of the obese people are like my very good friend, a world-class neuroscientist who swears his most productive years have been when he has weighed the most. Yes, he would love to lose some weight, but not at the expense of the full life he is living (and he won't have anything on his "bucket list" when he passes on, even at an early age). The obese and overweight category also includes the obese president of the University of California (if his pictures posted on the Internet are to be believed) and any number of his highly educated underlings, faculty included), and, at times, the extremely successful Oprah Winfrey, who, it appears, will live out her life at least among the overweight as she continues through her weight-loss/weight-gain cycles. Many heavy people are among those who are dear to us—our children, siblings, parents, grandparents, spouses, friends, and colleagues. Many are extremely well educated with lots of degrees at the end of their names—engineers, geneticists, and the proverbial "rocket scientists"—and even may be the Surgeon General of the United States, such as C. Everett Koop of decades ago and the current Surgeon General Regina Benjamin, appointed by Barack Obama. The overweight category includes me (marginally so) as I write this book (which I am working to correct as I write).

Granted, these people may be unhappy about their weights (and I am), but many are certainly not distressed and paralyzed. And many are deliberately and rationally making life choices that they (maybe not far-away life coaches) think are good ones for them. "I'll have a cheeseburger and add the fries."

A reality check is important because many proposals to control people's weights are based on the presumption that everyone, or a large majority, of heavy people are less than competent and consenting adults, in need of guidance and direction from self-appointed "choice architects." Granted, any number of people may fit the stereotype, but many are far more capable of making decisions for themselves— all very rationally—on what and how much they eat than all those high-powered people who presume that they can make better decisions for all others.

My parting caution: Be leery of messengers, especially those who are over-weight themselves, who engage in risky behaviors of their own, such as hang gliding, surfing, or drinking excessively at cocktail parties where they lament the obesity epidemic. Be leery of prophets of doom who believe they know what's best for others when they don't have a clue about the exact circumstances of many others' lives, much less the multitude of all those who live lifestyles they find offensive, repugnant, or maybe just disagreeable. And do keep in mind the quip of a heavy professor colleague and good friend, "I'm not overweight, I'm fat. Over-weight suggests I made a mistake in gaining all my weight. I didn't. I chose to get fat." That comment puts a serious wrinkle into the fat-tax and control debate that many, captured by all the "problems" of weight gain, may overlook.

Chapter 9
Dieting for Dollars

A headline in a newspaper caught my attention several years ago: "A Little Extra Cash Inspires Employees to Lose Weight, Study Shows." As an economist, my first reaction to the newspaper article was to scoff: So what else is new? "Incentives matter" is a fundamental axiom in economics on par with "there is no such thing as a free lunch." My second reaction was more reserved and concerned: Employers are rewarding the wrong workers, those who eat too much and run up their firms' health insurance costs. Firms should be rewarding workers who do not need incentives to lose weight. Otherwise, they run the risk of some workers gaining weight just to be paid to lose the added pounds. Employers who use weight-loss incentives also, inadvertently, encourage workers to gain weight before the first weigh-in! "Moral hazard," which has come up time and again in this book, is a real and abiding problem that can raise its ugly head in the strangest places (even workplaces).

One of my executive MBA students reported that his CEO offered to pay workers $3 for each pound they lost. What did the employees do? You may think the payment was too small to compensate many workers for the burden of actually losing weight, but it was sufficiently consequential to cause workers to fill up on water and heavy foods before the initial weigh-in. This means they could have been paid lunch money for phantom weight loss, both from the added water weight at the initial weigh-in and from the water weight lost as they dehydrated themselves just before the final weigh-in.

Moreover, payments for weight loss can backfire, in that the prospects of the payments themselves could cause workers to curb their own unpaid weight-loss efforts. Workers can reason that they can hold off their efforts until payment is tendered. Why give up the weight when there just might be a reward for weight loss in the future? The result can be an unforeseen outcome,

> Workplace payments for weight loss can reward phantom weight loss attributable to the incentive workers have to hydrate themselves before the initial weigh-in and to dehydrate themselves before the final weigh-in.

R.B. McKenzie, *HEAVY!*, DOI 10.1007/978-3-642-20135-6_9,
© Springer-Verlag Berlin Heidelberg 2012

when workers interpret payments differently than their employers. And incentives have had unforeseen and perverse effects in other settings. A widely cited study found that in Israel when a daycare center started fining parents for being late picking up their children, the parents responded by increasing their tardiness, figuring the fines were charges for additional babysitting time.[1]

A Diet Only an Economist Could Devise—And Not Understand!

My considered reaction occurred later in 2007, after thinking about the above weight-loss study's findings for a week. Why not do what George Mason University economist and *New York Times* business columnist Tyler Cowen has suggested and create my own weight-loss incentive, making it powerful, or as powerful as it needs to be for me? That is, I could create my own economist's designer diet, and lose weight to boot. After all, at the time I read the weight-loss news report, I had been trying to lose ten pounds for what seemed like a decade. And I figured at the time that I had lost a total of about 378 pounds during my yo-yo weight-loss struggle, only to remain nine pounds short of my target weight.

What's an economist to do? Four years ago I had given up on listening to advice from others on how to lose weight. "Eat vegetables." "Don't order cheese with your hamburgers; for that matter, eat your hamburger wrapped in lettuce, not a bun." "Go to the gym more often." "Eat off smaller plates." "Give up the wine." I really *knew* what to do, as do most (slightly or grossly) overweight people. Their problem and mine was, and remains, one of having the requisite incentive to do what we all know should be done. The weight-loss guiding rule is as simple as it is difficult to follow: consume fewer calories than are expended on a daily basis, and follow the rule consistently.

Whom could I call on to provide me with just the right incentive I needed to lose weight? Obviously, the only person I knew who was readily available at the time was . . . well, me! Hence, I cooked up my own "Economist Weight-Loss Incentive Plan," and I contracted with a friend to pay her $500 if I had not lost nine pounds at the end of ten weeks. I, my friend, and a witness (her husband) signed the pact. My friend similarly obligated herself to take the payment and to spend it on herself (and certainly not on me directly or indirectly, say, through a party to celebrate her reward to which I would be invited). She affirmed her solemn pledge with her signature, witnessed, again, by her husband, both of whom grinned broadly as they signed. I had her affirm her obligation with a signature because I wanted to make sure that, at the end of the contract term, she would not wimp out on me and refuse to take the payment out of guilt (she might have been

> Words on weight loss are cheap. Develop self-imposed incentives. Make a commitment to lose a doable amount of weight in a doable time period—and at some significant financial cost to yourself.

troubled by the thought, "I didn't do anything to earn the money"). I wanted to be bound for the full cost (and pain) of my commitment—$500—not some lower *expected* amount (and $500 payment would have a lower *expected* cost to me if there were some probability that my friend would not take and cash my check).

In other words, I wanted to maximize, within tolerable limits, my anticipated financial pain in order to maximize my incentive to lose the weight before the deadline. We tipped glasses of wine to seal the deal.

Had I really wanted to fully maximize my pain from not meeting my weight goal, I would have followed Cowen's advice more closely and have signed the pact with a stranger or committed to making the $500 payment to the campaign of my most disliked politician or, worse yet, to an organization I detest, for example, the American Neo-Nazi Party or the remnants of the Ku Klux Klan. I could have also made the goal weight the average of my weights over the course of, say, three days, to reduce the temptation to go without eating and drinking on one given target day. However, such thoughts have to be balanced by the fact that the greater my anticipated pain of not achieving the goal weight, the more inclined I might have been to set the goal weight higher or to set the payout lower, thereby resetting the anticipated pain downward.

Of course, I could have upped the payoff for "nonperformance" on my part to, say, $1,000 (which I considered), but let's face it, there is only so much I am willing to risk losing in weight and wealth, and the diet deal was something of a gamble on my part. Besides, once the contract was signed, my friend had an incentive both to withhold weight-loss advice and to fatten me up with free drinks, snacks, and carbohydrate-laden dinners, when given a chance. If I hiked the payoff to $1,000, I was afraid that her incentive to work against my goal of losing the nine pounds would be damn near irresistible. I wanted to keep her friendship, and incentives appropriately tempered.

A payoff of $500 seemed to be about right for me to optimize the probability of achieving my target weight—and, not incidentally, never having to make the payment.

Even though I am an economist and should have been able to fully anticipate the effect of my deal on me, I was amazed at how resistant I was to adopt my "Economic Weight-Loss Incentive Contract." I thought about it for weeks, given my poor weight-loss record of the past. After signing the contract, I was also equally amazed at how the looming $500 payment affected my behavior. While on my diet strategy, I judged practically everything I ate in terms of how much it would ultimately cost me in terms of making that $500 payment.

After gaining a pound the first day after signing the contract, I joined a gym, perfectly happy to pay the steep short-term rates. Why? Because the *full* price of the gym membership went down with my pact. The membership could, and did, help me reduce the probability that I would have to make the $500 payment. I also extended my exercise walks because, I figured, I was effectively paying myself to go the extra miles. I found myself sometimes spending three and four hours a day on exercise walks.

I even changed my morning breakfast of a bagel and a grande drip at Starbucks to a bowl of oatmeal at a local cafeteria—because the weight-loss pact translated into a threat of an added payment, which increased the *effective* price of the calorie-laden bagels and lowered the *effective* price of the calorie-light bowls of oatmeal. Similarly, the $500-payment threat increased the effective prices of fries, hamburgers, and chips and dip, while lowering the effective prices of raw oysters, fish, and snack packs of carrots. During the diet contract period, I ate more spinach salads than I ever ate on any other weight-loss program, which was to be expected from the first principle of economics, that the price and quantity consumed are inversely related (or when their effective price falls, the number of spinach salads consumed can be expected to rise). Early on, when the weight was not coming off at a promising rate, I even gave up wine at dinner.

I might have lost even more weight than I did had I not sometimes treated unexpected daily weight reductions (due, maybe, to water loss) as if I had been given a "real income" increase that, of course, I felt I had to "spend," say, by snacking and/or by putting wine back on the dinner menu.

When my weight-loss trend showed great promise *for me*, my friend with whom I contracted, and who is a gourmet cook and has her own catering business, extended an early invitation for me to be at her family's late Thanksgiving lunch, pointing out (with intended humor) in one email that "I cook out-of-this-world mashed potatoes with sour cream, cream cheese and butter—and with gravy! AND we always have mimosas and crab dip before lunch."

In a follow-up email, she added, "Forgot to tell you about the amazing dressing, ham, layered pea salad with sour cream and cheddar cheese topping, fresh cranberry/pear/peach compote, and of course pumpkin pie and lemon pound cake with chocolate icing. Oh yes, and yeast rolls with herbed butter. Everyone is allowed to nap after lunch! I then make fried potato cakes with the leftover mashed potatoes—cooked in butter." Of course, I had to decline her offer, but I couldn't resist asking my friend when she, her husband, and I met for drinks one day after work, "Would you pay $500 for the meal you propose I eat?" She was surprised by my question, with her answer obvious in her blank expression, which caused me to ask her, "Then, why expect me to do so, if you are not willing to pay the same price for your own cooking?"

A non-economist friend thought he was doing me a favor when he advised me four weeks into my diet period that if I got close to my goal, and needed some last-minute help in making my target weight, I could search out diuretics and laxatives at a drugstore days before the final weigh-in. He was surprised that I lamented his giving me that information. If taken seriously, his advice would have relieved the pressure I felt, and I wanted all the pressure I could get to lose the weight—no "safety hatches."

My total focus on my feared payment left me without a doubt toward the end that I would make or be below my goal weight on the official weigh-in day—and be there honestly. I in no way wanted to compromise my honor for the purpose of fooling others and avoiding the payment. Besides, with the pact in place, my honor was no longer an issue; the economics of it was all consuming. Indeed, I made my goal weight three weeks before the scheduled weigh-in. And, I am pleased to say, that I developed a comfortable three-pound weight-loss safety margin just before Thanksgiving to account for the fact that I might (just might!) "fall off the (weight-loss) wagon" because of excessive temptations that day on the dinner table. I should not have worried. The $500 penalty for yielding to temptation loomed very large and remained ever present, and I kept my safety margin with relative ease.

At the end of the ten weeks, I had lost fourteen pounds, five pounds more than the contract required!

Dieting for Even More Dollars

The questions I now ponder are "Why didn't I think of this strategy years ago?" and, "If other people are truly serious about shedding pounds, why don't they readily follow suit?" I have been amazed at people's resistance to adopt my diet strategy, even when they find the strategy novel and intriguing and profess that they sincerely *want* to lose weight.

After I explained to a waitress why I was ordering only vegetable soup and water for lunch, she said something to the effect, "Well, I guess you can make your deal if you have $500 to spare." I couldn't help telling her that she could set the contract payment and period at anything she wanted. "If $500 is too painful, then why not try $100?" She and others were unmoved, even after my explaining in some detail the effectiveness of the weight-loss strategy to that point.

Another friend, who lamented gaining eighteen pounds over the past six weeks, responded to my diet strategy in confidence, "Well, I **know** I can make my goal weight by the end of January. I don't need the added $500 incentive." Again, I had to make a point, "If you are so cocksure that you will make your weight, then why don't you agree to pay me $500 if you don't? It won't cost you a dime—if you are **certain** you don't need the extra incentive." He had

> If (or when) the first financial commitment to lose weight works, repeat as necessary.

no comeback, which suggests to me that many people who profess to be confident that they can hold to a weight-loss commitment aren't as confident as they profess. And I must confess that holding to my strategy was not easy. Clearly, given the expanding waistlines in the country, many Americans could use extra self-imposed incentives to hold to their weight-loss commitments.

I understand that my strategy may do nothing more than cause a continuation of my past yo-yo weight-loss/gain record, but I have an easy fix. I can renew my contract with my friend for six months and then repeat when that term is up. Indeed, after taking a break from the pressures of my diet incentive strategy, I re-upped the following winter with my friend for another ten pounds in weight loss for two months into the future, with, again, the $500 penalty for failure. After a second round of weight-loss success, I struggled for several months to get down to my high school graduation weight, which would require a loss of only five more pounds, but I found the struggle futile without the threat of a penalty. Hence, the following summer, I made another pact with someone I knew only in passing with a deal intended to reflect the greater difficulty of losing those last few pounds—five pounds lost in a month or a $500 penalty payment. Sure enough, it worked. I was elated at the end of the month when I was able to throw out all of my pants and replace them with new ones with waists the same as those I wore at my high school graduation (too many decades earlier to admit in print).

The Diet Non-Starter for Everyone Else

I remained amazed at how well my diet strategy worked, but I remained equally amazed at how readily others refuse to follow my lead. Not a single person I told in person adopted my strategy. I related my diet strategy in a column that appeared in the weekend edition of the *Wall Street Journal*, which was reprinted in a number of papers across the country and attracted a slew of emails from readers and any number of print, radio, and television interviews.[2]

Along the way, I learned that a couple of economists at Cornell University had, independently of Tyler Cowen, devised a similar diet strategy (although the particulars were different). They had gone so far as to establish a Web-based business in which they would allow people to make contracts with them to lose weight with a penalty payment.

Yet, to this day, I've been unable to make headway with reluctant others who have been unsuccessful in losing weight. I've repeatedly reacted, "Well, do I have a deal for you." I've told them, "Look,

- You can set the number of pounds you will lose—five, ten, or fifteen pounds.
- You can set the date; you can make the diet period as long or short as you like.
- And you can set the penalty payment, whatever suits you.
- Finally, you have a lot of control over your weight loss, especially if you are close to your goal weight on the target date (you cannot drink or eat on the target date and you can find ways to sweat like crazy, which can give you a safety margin of one to three pounds)."

But they won't bite. My initial thoughts were that these people really don't want to do what they say they want to do, lose weight. But I continued to puzzle over the near total absence of eager adopters of my "dieting for dollars." I couldn't get a question off the brain, "Why was it that I was willing to make the pact, but others have not been willing to follow suit?"

It took me more than a year of puzzling inside and outside my classroom over the matter before finding a solution that worked within my economic way of thinking. I might not have made the pact had I not been an economist who feels something of an obligation to make economics work in my daily life. I've always told my students, "Economics is not a discipline—it's a disease! If you catch it (that is, learn economics as a way of thinking applicable to virtually everything), the disease is terminal, because it will shape the rest of your life." Also, I have been able to use the diet experience for several years both in the classes I teach and in my writing.

I submit that I was willing to undertake the diet strategy because I am different from most others (and even most other economists). I received considerable pleasure from losing the weight, but, as I will explain, I don't think the weight loss alone would have been enough gain for me to walk all those extra miles and to give up all those hamburgers for all those (damn!) spinach salads. What may have driven me was the ancillary gains I got from being able to tell my students (and all others who would listen) about the strategy, and then to publish a piece in a highly visible newspaper. I got real pleasure making my economics work at a very practical level for me, and maybe others. And I received $700 from the *Wall Street Journal* for the column, more than I risked in the pact, I hasten to add (but a trivial consideration when compared to having the piece just appear in the *WSJ*).

Most others who want to shed a few pounds don't have these attendant benefits. They face the gains and pains from only the weight loss itself, with the balance not likely working in their favor. I say that because if a person assesses (in all honesty) the stream of gains into the future from weight loss to be greater than the stream of pains endured to get there, then that person need not make the pact. Why commit to a $500 (or any other amount) penalty? The person already has a favorable balance between the gains and pains. The person will lose the desired pounds in the desired time period.

If, on the other hand, the person assesses (in all honesty) that the pains of weight loss exceed the stream of gains into the future, the person is a candidate for making the weight-loss pact. That person needs some outside incentive, perhaps the concocted one, such as the $500 penalty for weight-loss failure in my pact. But, will the person make the pact? Not likely, because for the pact to have the intended effect, the person would have to figure that forking over the cash penalty on the specified weight-loss deadline would be more painful than all the pain from all the life-style changes necessary to lose weight before the deadline (minus the value of the weight loss). If the pain of the penalty payment were less than the net weight-loss pain, the pact would not induce the person to lose the weight. The person might as well fork over the payment at the time of the signing of the pact, which is something no sane person would do (if you are willing to do this, please contact me or a mental health professional ASAP).

The person could make the scheme workable, but only by increasing the penalty payment (say, from $500 to $1,000 to even $5,000) until it provides the proper positive incentive to lose weight. In other words, the person must add to the total net pain of not losing the weight. To start, the person assesses the gains of weight loss to be less than the pains. The pact must be one in which the pain of the penalty is greater than the net pain of the weight loss. Add the gains and pains with the pact, and the gap between the lower total gains and the greater total pains must expand with the pact, and adding to one's pains would appear to be a little irrational (a problem that is compounded when people are subject to "loss aversion," or subjectively weigh pains more heavily than gains).

Moreover, many people who have trouble losing weight also have trouble keeping the weight off when they lose it. They can reason that if they lose the weight because of the added dollar penalty, the threat of the penalty will no longer be there after the deadline, but all the temptations in the form of low-cost calories in widely available sugared and fatty foods (hamburgers and apple fritters) will be omnipresent all the time. They may figure that if they lost the weight, the weight-loss gains would be temporary, not worth very much. Why run the payout risks for gains that could be fleeting?

The "irrationality" of my dieting-for-dollars reminds me of a story my economist friend (and coauthor on other books) Dwight Lee told me. His story makes my point with greater clarity and with a bit of humor (albeit impolite humor). A man approached a "two'fer," a two-hole outhouse with two doors but no divider between the stalls. On opening the first door, he finds it is occupied. He goes in the second door and does his business. On getting up, he pulls up his pants, only to see a $20-bill flip out of his pant pocket and into the hole. He immediately pulls out his wallet and throws another $20 into the hole, causing the guy next to him to puzzle out loud, "Why the hell did you do that?" The first guy quickly responds, "You don't think I would go down in there for only $20, do you?" My weight-loss strategy requires, essentially, the same kind of perverse thinking.

In other words, my "dieting for dollars" strategy is irrational for people, aside for a few crazies like myself who have auxiliary reasons for adopting the strategy. But, then, my diet strategy based in economics is hardly the only one that economists and business executives have devised and adopted that won't work for everyone, at least not over the long haul.

Weight Loss Redux, Unfortunately!

But alas, I found out the hard way why my diet strategy might be a bad strategy even for me. As I was completing this book, I was asked to give a talk at a reception for newly admitted fully employed MBA students. The reception was held in May, with classes starting in late September. The reception organizers wanted me to give a short talk with light but substantive content. So, I decided to tell them about some themes from this book, as well as about my success with my diet strategy.

"Dieting for dollars," may be a potentially effective diet strategy for those willing to adopt it, but not many people can be expected to adopt it—for economic reasons.

Because I had regained a few of my previously lost pounds, I suddenly decided at the end of the talk to make the following commitment to the admitted students at the reception, "If I have not achieved my goal weight of 168 pounds by the first day of class [then four months off], I will cover the first $500 in a bar bill from a hospitality event I will hold after your first class." I think my error was to forget about the economics of procrastination discussed earlier in this book, given that my weigh-in date was then more than four months ahead. With that much time to go, I could reduce the discounted value of the weight-loss costs by postponing their incurrence a month or two or could ignore the commitment altogether—for a while. And not only did I procrastinate in getting to my weight loss path, I did something worse; I gained five pounds at the start. With three weeks to go before my first class, I still had those original extra nine pounds to lose.

> Even an economist (your author) can get caught by the hubris of his past dieting success and think his way into an impaired incentive to make his goal weight.

I then went on a crash diet because there was more than the $500 on the line; my professional credibility was also at stake. And I just might have to recast this chapter if I failed, which was the biggest of my worries. A week before the first class I was still five pounds over my weight goal. I doubled my exercise time. I drank cases of bottled water and downed bags of baby carrots to hold the hunger pains at bay.

I made my goal weight, I am pleased to report, but only barely, given that my weight two hours before my first class was 167.8 pounds. In the end, the day of my first class, I took a thirty-four-mile bike ride! This was not "cheating." In my mind, it was a playing of the strong incentive my "dieting for dollars" imposes. Whatever, I validated by weight to my first class with a picture I took of the scale with the weight and my feet clearly in the picture.

In addition to the procrastination error, I made two other mistakes that made for the close call that effectively lowered my real and imagined cost for not making my goal weight. First, I realized before the deadline that the commitment was a win-win for me. If I made the weight, I could imagine that my students would take my discussion of diet incentives with greater credibility. (I also would not have to alter the fundamental structure of the narrative of this chapter.) If I failed, the students would have a good laugh, and we would start the course with good cheer at a local tavern.

Second, I realized that the promised social could be construed as a school event, which my school sometimes holds to improve student attitudes toward the program. This meant that I might be able to use my school discretionary funds to cover the cost of the social. I never investigated whether I could seek reimbursement for the event, and don't know that I would have if I had not made my goal weight. Nevertheless, the mere prospect of my being able to sidestep the full cost reduced the incentive I had to make my goal weight. I believe that's why I came so close to failing. However, there was sufficient residual incentive—just enough—for me to cut my calorie intake and to increase my peddling on the bike path.

I know what you are thinking; I could have cheated in multiple ways. I could have taken laxatives and diuretics, or worse, just before the weigh-in. I could have been holding onto a bar out of sight of the camera, lowering the weight seen on the scale that was in the picture taken. I didn't do any of that, but the prospects of cheating will limit the market for, or just the workability of, my diet strategy.

But the people engaging me in such a contract might be unmoved because they have absolutely no "skin in the game." They have only the prospects of gain going into the deal, which helps to explain why I've never had anyone hesitate to make the contract with me, even with the prospects of cheating.

Why Fat Farms Work

"Fat farms," where heavy people make upfront payments to be forced onto a regimen of constricted calories and expanded exercise, obviously work for some people—but, I need to insert, for a relatively minor percentage of all heavy people. What makes fat farms viable for some at the same time my diet strategy is a nonstarter?

My explanation must be, admittedly, somewhat speculative, because research has not been done on the subject—to my knowledge. Fat farms could work because they simply increase the efficiency of weight loss with high-tech exercise equipment and special diets designed to ease the transition to low-calorie means, which is to say that they increase the gains from weight loss per dollar of expenditure or hour devoted to workouts, which is to say they offer the prospects of reduced pain from weight loss, all the while providing a vacation-like experience and increasing the opportunity for weight-loss rewards of approval coming from the staff and from mutually supportive other heavy people who all have much the same goal. Fat farms have to do *something*—provide value for dollars—if they hope to be profitable, and to survive. My diet strategy did none of that. I had the threat of making the $500 payment hanging over my head with no change in my weight-loss environment or in my support system, other than the changes I personally introduced all by my lonesome—at greater expense, of course.

The Lure of Employer Weight-Loss Payments

Economists love to repeat the refrain, "Incentives matter—a whole lot!" Clearly, pay matters, or else workers and their bosses wouldn't demand to be paid for their work and wouldn't be constantly scanning their employment horizons for better paying jobs. And a good rule is that the more boring the job, or less useful the work experience is to workers' personal lives, and the more difficult the workplace experience, the more pay matters. But do pay incentives matter a whole lot when it comes to matters of health, most notably weight? If they did, would we have so many overweight and obese people conceding to ever-present food temptations and incurring the wage penalties and social stigmas for their wanton ways?

Clearly, many (but not all) businesses have solid economic reasons to encourage their workers to live healthy lives. Healthy workers can be more productive and firms' can grow with output as workers become healthier. And, many people (co-workers, suppliers, and customers) view healthier workers as more attractive, a perception that can translate into greater firm sales and lower supply cost as more attractive workers may be able to negotiate better deals on materials and parts as well as larger and better deals on sales of firm products. And remember that research shows that more attractive workers receive a wage bonus for their good looks over their more homely counterparts, and weight can affect attractiveness.[3]

> Employers paying workers to lose weight can create counter-productive incentives and can reward the wrong (heavy) people.

Similarly, healthy workers are likely to be absent from work less frequently and to incur fewer medical costs than their unhealthy colleagues. The reductions in absenteeism and in health insurance premiums means lower overall production costs for their firms. As firms' costs decline, their profits, their stock prices, and mostly likely their compensation packages (salaries, bonuses, and value of stock options) will increase.

Indeed, executives who miss opportunities to increase their companies' profits through improving workers' health are putting their jobs and their firms at risk—unless, of course, unhealthy workers accept wages that are low enough to (more than) compensate for their reduced productivity and higher health insurance costs. Their investors can be expected to press top management to take every opportunity to maximize their firms' profit streams and, not incidentally, their firms' stock prices. Executives might also feel pressure from savvy entrepreneurs who may be ready and able to take over the misguided firms, and change the company wellness policies with the goal of increasing profitability. And the greater the effectiveness of wellness programs and incentives, the greater the market pressure will be to adopt them.

If healthier workers increase productivity and save health insurance and other costs, then firms can justify increasing these workers' wages, at least somewhat. Indeed, as we have seen, healthier workers are likely to improve their own employment-market positions, which can press their employers to raise their compensation in one form or another (higher wages or lower health-insurance premiums, for example). With higher compensation, both executives and workers can be happier, and their greater job satisfaction adds even more to firm output and profits.

But are employers' gains from having healthier workers worth what they would have to pay to get them? That is the crux of the economic incentives issue, and it could be that many incentive schemes are not worth their weight in . . . well, lost worker weight. There is always the ever-present prospect that having a fatter workforce is cheaper—more profitable—for many (not all) businesses than having a trimmer one. All depends on the exact responsiveness of workers to each dollar of incentive to lose weight and on the exact curb in business costs from the weight that is lost. It is easy to say incentives matter; it is quite another to find incentives that are worth businesses' trouble. Finding the *right* incentives is a far more complex business undertaking, with less assured success, than might be imagined, and devising the *optimum* health-related or weight-related incentive might be damn near impossible, but no less of a goal to seek.

Real-World Business Weight-Loss Incentive Strategies

One obvious route for firms to increase worker healthiness is to establish policies that will induce workers to reduce their excess weight, or at least get off their weight gain paths. And many firms have seen what they believe is the one and true economic light and have devised incentive schemes that they expect (or just hope) will induce significant (if not substantial) weight loss (or just a reduction in weight gain). Indeed, the Associated Press reported in 2010 that at least a third of major companies in the United States offer some form of incentive payments to workers to entice them to lose weight or to improve their health in other ways.[4]

To date, the adopted schemes have been varied with mixed and often disappointing results, as might be expected when firms are groping towards profitable reward systems with so little evidence about what works. After all, the real surge in people's weight began a half century ago and the rush of companies to find an incentive system to combat the weight-gain surge has a very short history, no more than a couple of decades. (Weight gains along with rapid increases in insurance premium have been relatively recent phenomena, and a half century ago, employers had to cope with nowhere near the same degree of urgency that they do today.)

Business experience with antismoking campaigns has offered some hope that similar incentive programs for weight loss would yield higher worker benefits and business profits. But although antismoking campaigns have had success, the results have not been dramatic.

One multinational company, based in the United States, offered only information on the benefits of quitting smoking to a group of 442 workers who smoked. It offered another group of 436 workers who smoked the same information but added financial rewards: $100 for completing the information program, $250 for having stopped smoking within six months after enrolling in the program, and $400 for not smoking six months after cessation of smoking. Not surprisingly (for economists), twelve months after enrollment the group that was offered financial incentives had a smoking cessation rate three times the rate for the group receiving only information on the benefits of not smoking, but the cessation rates were not astoundingly high, 14.7 percent for the incentivized group versus 5 percent for the nonincentivized group. The incentivized group had a cessation rate that was more than twice the cessation rate for the information-only group eighteen months after the program began, but still fairly low, 9.4 percent versus 3.6 percent.[5] Obviously, many new nonsmokers fell off the nonsmoking wagon, perhaps because, for some, they got on the wagon in the first place to collect the monetary payoff. Overall, should we expect monetary incentives of a few hundred dollars to quit smoking to have a major effect when all smokers are bound to know, by now, that long-term smoking can cause lung cancer and cut their lives short by eight to ten years? Failing to qualify for a monetary incentive of a few hundred dollars almost surely represents a trivial percentage increase in their lifetime costs.

The researchers did not report, I must note, whether the incentive program was more or less profitable than the nonincentive program. The company's productivity gains and the cost savings may not have been as great as the rewards paid out. No one knows. Yet this information is paramount to businesses, which are not charities or social welfare agencies, at least, not for the most part. If they set out to give money away in any substantial way with little to no positive effects, or with negative effects, on the companies' bottom lines, you can bet that the executives' job security would be in jeopardy.[6]

OhioHealth offered to pay the 9,000 workers at its five hospitals up to $500 for weight loss, with half of the company's workforce signing up for the incentive program (perhaps as much to curry favor with their bosses as to earn the rewards). The program obviously has had some effect. As of the middle of 2010, OhioHealth had paid out more than $377,000 in weight-loss bonuses, and workers reported that they had to buy new clothes.[7]

At Cornell University, in 2007, behavioral economists assigned fifty-seven healthy subjects between thirty and seventy years of age and with BMIs between 30 and 40 to three groups. [8] The first (control) group was required only to weigh in monthly—no external monetary incentives were provided. The second group would receive a monetary reward, determined by a lottery at the end of the program, if they achieved their goal weight. The third group had to deposit a sum of money that would not be refunded unless they achieved a weight loss goal of one pound per week for sixteen weeks; however, the subjects in this group would receive a reward twice their deposit if they achieved their goal weight loss.

After following the subjects for nearly a year, the researchers found the two latter incentivized groups lost on average nearly four pounds more than the control group. The lottery group lost an average of 13.1 pounds, whereas the deposit-contract group lost an average of fourteen pounds. The researchers expected the deposit-contract group to lose more than the other two groups on the theory that people are subject to "loss aversion," which is to say that people tend to dislike losing money more than gaining money of an equal amount. The effect of "loss aversion" in this study does seem to be modest, less than a pound (or less than a 7 percent) differential (but maybe the loss-aversion weight-loss premium was simply too small). Perhaps, also, the subjects in the third group were not responding to "loss aversion" at all; they might simply have faced a greater expected payoff than did the second group.

Another set of Cornell researchers studied the outcomes of more than 2,400 overweight workers (with a BMI at 25 or above) at seventeen workplaces who volunteered to participate on weight reduction programs with financial incentives.[9] One group of workers was paid nothing to participate in the weight-loss program but received bonuses each quarter based on the percentage of weight reduction. The bonuses were very modest—$25 to $50 for losing 20 to 30 percent of their baseline weights—and stopped altogether if workers' BMIs went below 25. The second group of workers followed the deposit-contract/bond scheme under which they deposited $9.95 per month into an account. Their deposit would be refunded at the end of the year, provided they had lost at least 5 percent of their starting weight. In addition, workers who lost 10 percent or more of their baseline weight received $100 bonuses and the "biggest loser" for the group received an additional $250 bonus. The researchers had a third control group who received neither penalties nor rewards.

The results were hardly a strong endorsement for the "incentives matter" refrain. Those who posted a "bond" (or made the monthly payments), perhaps succumbing to "loss aversion," lost the most, an average of 3.6 pounds. But those who received the quarterly reward lost slightly less, an average of 1.4 pounds, than the control group who received no incentives at all, which lost an average of 1.7 pounds. You have to wonder if the differences could have been, at least somewhat, a matter of self-selection, that is, those workers most determined to lose or those with the most to lose (in pounds, that is) going into the group requiring monthly payments. Moreover, the attrition rate during the twelve-month study was high for all groups, ranging from close to 50 percent for the group receiving monthly payments to over 76 percent for the group requiring the monthly "bond" payments. Hardly impressive results.

Cornell's researchers reviewed the findings of seven business programs that provided workers with cash rewards for losing weight. One of their more disappointing findings is that workers across all programs lost slightly more than a pound on average during the programs' time periods.[10] And we have to treat the findings in weight-loss incentives programs with caution; the researchers do not report how they prevented the incentivized and nonincentivized groups from tanking up on water and food before the initial weigh-in and from downing diuretics and laxatives before the final weigh-in. The economic way of thinking would suggest that the incentivized groups would have greater incentive not only to lose weight, but also to game the research study. The slight or modest difference in weight-loss outcomes could be partially explained by a difference in gamesmanship.

Weight-Loss Incentives and Recidivism

But should we expect these dieting-for-dollars programs to work very well? Perhaps not, considering the extent of people's weight problems. After all, overweight and obese workers already suffer financial losses in significant wage and fringe benefit penalties as well as poor self-images and a host of social stigmas, yet all have gained and maintained excess weight for years and many seem practically paralyzed to do anything about the problem.

For many of these people, the gap between what they perceive to be the gains of losing weight and the pain of doing so must be substantial. And the gain-pain gap is likely to expand with a proliferation of temptations to eat and a greater number of overweight people among the populace, which can reduce the personal costs of excess weight. In comparison to the gain-pain gap from weight loss, the rewards businesses have generally offered might seem paltry. The personal gain-pain gap for weight loss over time can easily exceed a maximum reward of $500 for losing some predetermined number of pounds or achieving some predetermined percentage reduction in people's baseline body weights. Remember, the reward is often a one-time deal or is a sequence of payments for a limited period of time.

Recidivism among weight-loss program participants is also unsurprising. The tendered rewards that filled the gain-pain gap will be gone at the end of the programs, but the gap can remain, as I noted was true in my own diet strategy. The pleasure (and necessity) of eating and the ever-present and spreading temptations to eat too much continuously press participants to return to old behaviors.

Of course, the rewards programs are often accompanied with wellness instruction aimed at helping people make permanent life-style changes. Such instruction will help to keep *some* participants on their weight-loss wagons (most of the time), but few heavy people on the planet do not already know most, if not all, of the nutritional advice offered under wellness programs. At its foundation, losing weight is not rocket science. You just have to eat fewer calories than your body expends in energy until you achieve your

> Many people who lose weight because of cash incentives from their employers can be expected to regain the weight when the incentives are withdrawn.

goal weight. There is probably not a minimally alert adult who lines up at Burger King for a triple-decker hamburger or downs deep-fried chocolate-covered strips of bacon at a county fair who does not know the likely weight-related consequences.

Of course, businesses could up the ante. But beyond some point, a progressively higher incentive for their workers' weight losses, extended ever longer into the future, can undercut the firms' profitability, which can undermine, albeit marginally, their competitive market position. It simply doesn't make business sense to pay more for weight loss than can be gained in cost savings and greater productivity. You also have to wonder if businesses are well positioned to become alternative "fat farms." You would think that most businesses' core competency is elsewhere, including repressing worker wages to reflect any lower net contributions to firm profits caused by their added pounds.

The Relevance of "Adverse Selection" and "Moral Hazard"

Dieting-for-dollar programs can also have perverse effects for businesses, especially in the long run, because of two problems—adverse selection and moral hazard. In brief, adverse selection occurs when people choose to do something because they know they will gain from participating, given their situation. Moral hazard amounts to the threat that a policy will actually change people's behavior for the worse.

Take the example of flood insurance. People who know they live in flood plains will buy flood insurance, while people on the surrounding hillsides will not. And the people in the flood plain will pay no more in premiums than their *expected* losses,

In developing weight-loss strategies, beware of two of the most important and weighty problems in economics and business: "adverse selection" and "moral hazard."

which means there is no way insurance companies can extract a profit (or charge policy holders premiums that exceed the expected flood-loss payouts). With this adverse selection at work, flood insurance is unprofitable for private insurance companies, unless the government subsidizes it. But with subsidies, a moral hazard can emerge with a vengeance. Knowing their flood damages can be recovered, more people will be willing to build in flood plains, and people living in flood plains can be expected to build bigger houses, stock them with higher quality and more expensive furniture, and do less to save their property when they know floods are coming.

Dieting-for-dollars programs can encounter many of these same problems. Overweight and obese workers—or just workers who feel threatened with future weight problems—can be expected to gravitate toward companies that have long records of rewarding those who lose weight (as well as imposing relatively lower wage penalties for excess pounds). With weight-loss incentives in place, the moral hazard problem can raise its ugly head with force, and with perverse consequences, with heavy workers who have obviously had poor records at weight control on their own signing up. Some workers can be expected to gain more weight than otherwise, or at the very least they may not worry as much about their weight moving them above some weight threshold (say, a BMI of 25) that qualifies them for the incentive program. In short, some workers may even gain weight so they can be paid to lose it.

A variety of ways to game the system are likely to emerge: As noted already, workers may deliberately gain pounds in the weeks and months before the program's initial weight-in or fill up on water just before stepping on the scales at weigh-in. They may resort to diuretics or laxatives or fast during the twenty-four hours prior to their final weigh-in. In short, incentive programs can cause firms to pay for (phantom) weight-loss pounds that may not have existed but for the incentive program.

Concluding Comments

The economic way of thinking as well as scientific evidence (subject to careful measurement) has a lot to say about the American and worldwide weight problem, but there is another potentially powerful yet unheralded force rarely mentioned in scholarly studies—the fading of meaningful personal responsibility felt in people's guts and hearts.

A hundred or more years ago, people assumed in large measure that they were the captains of their fates and responsible for what happened to them, in matters such as weight. To an important extent they were. We didn't then have the social safety nets that we now have, or the real incomes to recuse ourselves from our wayward ways.

Of course, way back then it was easy (or, rather, much easier) to control weight because eating opportunities were much more constricted than they are now. Over the intervening years, however, there has been a dramatic change in culture as scientists have found one reason or another to attribute weight gain, or whatever, to forces outside individual control. They attribute weight gain to lower prices, to real income increases, to the growing density of fast-food restaurants, and on and on. No doubt, these forces have been at work, but they contain a hidden message, "Your weight is not your fault. It's someone else's. It's due to some outside force. You are the *victim* of all these other outside forces." Such a take on life should be expected to bolster all the economic and social forces afoot pushing many people—self-perceived "victims"—toward greater weight gain, because these forces lower the costs many people must incur from gaining weight. "I didn't do it. Someone else (the devil) made me do it. I have no choice in the matter," which is tantamount to saying, "Why worry? Pass the hamburger, and don't hold the mayonnaise."[11]

In the "Perspective" at the end of this chapter, I have listed a few dieting rules, which emerge from the economic way of thinking used throughout this book, that you might want to consider. Otherwise, my best closing advice is simple and straightforward: If you believe your excess weight is a matter of genetics or someone else's fault, change your attitude. Make your weight your fault and your responsibility—really (not in a pretend manner). You will find that such a shift in attitude will immediately increase the cost of hamburgers and fries, as well as increase the future, ongoing personal pride (benefits) from weight loss. (No one would feel pride in weight loss if it were not his or her doing.) If you are overweight and you want to fortify your resolve to change your attitude toward your own weight, just look around at all the people who are close to being in your same circumstances—but who are trim. Are you somehow weaker than they? If so, give up. If not, then both of us can have hope for you (and me). But, then, if you are depressed, take care of those problems before venturing on a diet strategy of any kind. Most of all, try to find greater purpose in life. Don't underrate the economic value of hope for a better future. If you are hopeless, your circumstances are ideal. There literally is no reason to change. If you have hope for a better future, there is at least some room for improvement, some room for weight loss. Maybe a lot of room.

Perspective

Economic Rules for Successful Dieting? Maybe!

Economists are renowned (and are often chastised by non-economists) for assuming people are *rational*—more rational than everyone, including economists, know them to be.[12] But economics is a way of thinking about complex human behavior, and economists assume people act rationally to simplify the complexity of human behavior, thereby making analyses more manageable and revealing insights that might not otherwise be seen. True, rationality is a simplifying assumption. But behavioral economists also simplify things with their laboratory analyses, which are sterilized of much of the daily, real-world complexity of human experience.[13] But all attempts to explain and understand our terribly complex social and physical world require simplifying assumptions.[14]

Of course, people do not behave with complete rationality, and nowhere is this fact more apparent than in the realm of weight-loss. Fully rational people would recognize all the ill effects of excess weight and would know just what to do to achieve and maintain a healthy weight. No one need tell them or provide incentives for them to lose pounds. Fully rational people would know with precision the exact costs and benefits of everything they do, including eating, and would act accordingly. Weight-loss techniques would be meaningless because everyone would make rational—and healthy—decisions about his or her weight.

But, alas, such is not the world we live in. And because it is not, the economic way of thinking (both the conventional and behavioral variants) just might be able to offer some helpful insights for how people can achieve and maintain healthier weights. So here goes.

Any diet regimen aims to develop a negative energy balance—that is, eat fewer calories than your body burns, and you will lose weight. Knowing that, let's put cost/benefit analysis and the law of demand to work for you to achieve a negative energy balance. The general rule is this: Seek every way possible to raise the perceived *full* price of eating unhealthy, fattening, high-calorie foods and to lower the perceived *full* price of healthy, low-calorie foods. Likewise, seek all means to lower the perceived *full* price of exercise. Choose strategies that you can stick with over time—making permanent lifestyle changes. Here are some suggestions to start your thinking:

> A few principles of economic thinking can go a long way toward developing a successful diet strategy.

1. Recognize that with all the temptations to eat high-calorie foods, avoiding weight gain and losing weight requires hard work for most people, and more dedicated work now than in the past. Many—maybe most—trim people are as trim as they are because they have put in time to lose weight and to create barriers to succumbing to tasty temptations. Acknowledge that for many people, and this may include you, weight-loss is a full-time job.

2. Cutting back on food intake generally is a surer path to weight loss than increasing exercise, especially if you have a time constraint—and who doesn't. Remember, mindlessly eating a muffin or a bag of potato chips is far easier than working off those calories at the gym. Get a firm grip on the time cost of burning added calories—to burn off the calories in a single muffin, you will have to bike more than an hour or lift weights for nearly two hours. Consider what else you could accomplish in that amount of time, and throw that muffin in

the trash. (Forget, as best you can, about how much you paid for the muffin, if you already have it in hand, and be willing to throw half of it away. Next time, don't buy it in the first place.)

3. Surround yourself with thin people (or people thinner than you). We've stressed that excess weight can be contagious. When everyone in your social networks—friends, family members, coworkers—gains weight, the psychic and social costs of weight gain diminish. Everyone in the relevant group can experience the same cost reduction for eating and overeating. And studies do show that people who eat socially with heavy people tend to down more calories than people who eat with trim people.

   If you are packing excess pounds (no matter how many), try to do what does *not* come naturally: Pick friends (heavy or trim) who frown on excess weight. Your association with them will increase your personal cost of overeating. When you are intent on shedding pounds, the last thing you need are friends and family members who compliment you on your good looks—or excess pounds (or facilitate your gaining weight and break your resolve to lose weight).

4. Don't go it alone. Make your weight-loss strategy an affair to remember for family and friends. Enlist support, and join or form a weight-loss group. The cost of dieting for all can go down, heightening the probability of success.

5. Remember that our brains are our most scarce resource, with only so many neurons that can be devoted to a task, or multiple tasks. Because of our neuronal limitations, "distracted driving" (texting or applying makeup when on the road) has proven to be deadly. "Distracted eating" apparently can also be deadly—at least for weight-loss plans. When eating, research suggests, focus exclusively on eating. Avoid multitasking, that is, making calls, texting, watching television, working on computers, or just reading while eating. You can be distracted from just how many calories you are downing. In one experiment, twenty-two volunteers were given a meal to eat while playing solitaire on their computers. Twenty-two other volunteers were given the same meal and were left undistracted. Researchers found that the distracted eaters were worse at recalling how much they had eaten and felt less full than the undistracted eaters at the end of their meals, although the distracted eaters ate significantly more. At a taste test a half hour after their meals, the distracted eaters ate twice as many cookies as the undistracted eaters.[15] And it should be no surprise that people eat more when watching television.[16] The obvious lesson: Rather than eating driving you to distraction, distraction can drive you to eating more than you otherwise might.

6. Beware of diet schemes that cost more than they are worth in successful weight loss (for example, the so-called "caveman diet" that, if adopted, would require a substantial adjustment in the combinations of foods eaten).[17] The last diet you should want to adopt is one that packs on costs with few proven benefits. The cost of a diet will determine how long you stay with it. Just remember that compared with a high-cost/high-gain diet, a low-cost/low-gain diet can be more beneficial, over the long term, and can have a higher rate of return on your

investment in dollars and time because you are more likely to stick with it when budget limitations are pressing.

7. Jump at any chance to relocate to an area of the country where there are fewer overweight and obese people, for example, Colorado and Southern California—where, for cultural or other reasons, the personal cost of excess weight and/or weight gain can be higher than where you now live. Colorado residents have ready access to mountain biking and hiking trails, making the cost of exercise lower than in many other parts of the country. Southern California is blessed with good weather all year long, which means you can't spend much of the year hiding extra pounds with thick winter clothing or hiding out in air conditioned homes. Because other people have taken advantage of these and other local environments conducive to weight control, heavier people are more likely to stand out, and feel the attendant social pressure (cost) to control their weight. (If you have a choice where you live and work, avoid the "big-butt" states, most notably Mississippi and Missouri. Walking through the malls in those states can make you feel too comfortable, or even arrogant, about your own excess weight.)

8. If you are heavy, post a picture of yourself on your Facebook in an unflattering pose, which can increase the social costs you feel from your excess weight, which can increase your motivation to lose the weight. You can then post updated pictures as you lose weight, with the potential updates increasing your incentive to lose the extra pounds.

9. Seek to work for companies that impose a surcharge on their group health insurance policy for some level of obesity (or, better yet, excess weight). If such companies are hard to find, select companies that impose wage penalties for obesity. Again, the goal with such employment searches is to elevate the cost of overeating and to encourage controlled eating.

10. Many employers shun imposing health insurance surcharges for excess weight on the grounds that they might offend heavy workers. However, many firms are not so shy about providing health insurance discounts for workers who join wellness programs or who achieve specified health goals (for example, a reduction in weight, blood pressure, and BMI). And, as noted at the end of Chap. 6, the number of firms who provide health-related rewards will likely increase over coming years, given that the new national health-reform law specifically provides that employers can make health-related rewards (in the form of discounts) of up to 30 percent of their health insurance premiums. Seek out firms who institute such health-related reward programs for two reasons. The first reason is obvious: The rewards offer a payoff for healthy living. Second, the reward systems offer firms a not-so-obvious means of imposing costs on workers for their unhealthy living. The firms can simply raise their premiums for all workers, giving only healthy workers discounts, which is an indirect means of penalizing unhealthy workers (as if they had imposed a health insurance surcharge) and, again, of encouraging healthy living (which offer the prospects of reductions in health insurance premiums for all workers over time as more and more workers adopt healthier lifestyles).

11. Weigh yourself everyday on digital scales that show your weight to the first decimal place. You will see up close and in the very near term the cost of eating that apple fritter or skipping your workout. In general, find ways to feel the pain immediately from failing to keep your weight-loss commitment. Similarly, seek ways to get immediate gratification from the extra things you do daily to move your scale's dial downward by a pound, or even a tenth of a pound. Reward yourself as soon as possible, in nonfood ways (going to a movie, for example) when the dial changes.

12. If you can't rid your immediate environment of "goodies," put them at a distance—or in other ways increase the cost you must incur from dipping your hand into the cookie jar. For example, if you can't resist buying a large canister of chocolate-covered raisins at Costco for your workplace, at least place the canister in someone else's office down the hall (or, better, in the adjoining building). The walk down the hall (or across the ease way) will increase the cost of downing the extra calories, and reduce the expected calories consumed. Make sure the person in charge of the canister does not make the entire contents of the canister available for people to grab as many as they want. If a small amount of chocolate-covered raisins is available in the bowl, you and others will take fewer than when the filled canister is available.[18]

13. Replace your twelve-inch dinner plates with new ones that are no larger than ten inches in diameter—or better yet, use your old salad plates. Buy wine glasses suitable for elves and pick a tall and thin design. Research shows that diners ladle fewer calories on smaller plates than larger ones. Drinkers (and even bartenders) will pour fewer ounces, and calories, into small thin wine and champagne glasses than in large squatty ones (even when the different shaped glasses hold the same number of ounces).[19] If you have to refill your small plate and smaller glass, you will be more aware of how much you are eating, adding to the cost of consuming calories. Greater awareness and added costs will work to move back along your demand curve for additional food, increasing the probability that you will eat less.

14. Never pay for restaurant meals with credit cards that can obscure somewhat the immediate cost of meals, and dull your consciousness about the size of your meal and the number of cocktails you bought. Using credit cards may also increase the frequency of dining out. Instead, each month set aside a pre-determined wad of cash in an envelope dedicated for use on restaurant meals. Make sure that the cash store is significantly less than your average monthly expenditures at restaurants for the past half year. The constricted restaurant budget will force an increase in home-cooked meals, which will likely average fewer calories than you would have consumed in restaurant meals.

15. When you do go out for dinner, make it a real treat—choose an expensive restaurant. The meal is likely to be healthier and less fattening than at a more moderately priced establishment, and certainly a lot healthier and less fattening than at a fast-food restaurant. Then pick meals on the menu that are on the higher end of the restaurants' pricing scales. Such selections will encourage

you to order half portions and will further restrict the number of times you can, and will want to, eat out.

16. Better yet, go online to get restaurants menus to judge where to go, and when you get to the restaurant, ask for the list of menu items that gives the calorie count for the various menu items. You will be surprised at how many calories your favorite dishes carry, which represent a cost increase for dishes and an encouragement to order fewer of them.

17. Similarly, no matter how much you currently spend on a bottle of wine (or other alcoholic beverages) you buy, go upscale on future purchases. Higher priced wine will tend to reduce the number of bottles you buy and will likely cause you to drink the wine more slowly, reducing the number of calories downed in an evening. People who buy bottles of "Two-Buck Chuck" (Charles Shaw wine sold at Trader's Joe for $1.99 a bottle) for home consumption will not likely think very intensely about what they are giving up as they down one glass of wine after another. After all, the wine is a mere 50 cents a glass. Someone who buys bottles of Dom Pérignon Champaign at $120 each at Costco is going to think twice about gulping the wine, given that each glass will cost about $40 a glass (or at least $5 an ounce). More likely, buyers of such expensive wines will more likely sip—very slowly—and probably with friends and family who are following suit.

18. Join a gym that has a high upfront investment and low monthly payment, or low payment per visit. The low marginal cost that comes with the high upfront membership investment can encourage you to go more often. Indeed, behavioral economic research has shown that people who make sizable upfront investments for doing anything will undertake the activity more frequently, and will stay with the activity longer, than those who make little to no upfront investment. (I understand that this recommendation suffers from the same [rational] commitment problem my own dieting-for-dollar strategy has, discussed at the start of the chapter. I have no suggestion for remedying the commitment problem other than this one: As you are considering the upfront membership investment, have a few drinks to impair your inclination to think rationally, or to weigh carefully the current costs and the future benefits.)

19. If you don't like my drinking suggestion, find ways to add new and heightened value to losing weight or to add new and heightened cost to maintaining and gaining excess pounds. For example, do what celebrities have done and find ways to write and talk about your weight-loss experience. (Consider blogging about your struggle, if you can't sell your weight-loss story.) Try to determine as best you can the pay penalty you are suffering vis-à-vis your trimmer cohorts at work. Take to heart how much your added weight is costing you now in real dollars and how much more trying your retirement will be because of your extra pounds. Go out of your way to read news reports on the serious medical and social problems heavy people confront. Get a set of the DVDs of all seasons of "The Biggest Losers" television series, and watch and rewatch the episodes every chance you can. Feel their pain and hold on to the images of their "stomach aprons" hanging over their groins under their shorts. (Guys, hold

the images of the flopping breasts of the men contestants.) The more vivid you can make the images, the better, because their vividness can increase the psychic cost you can feel from overeating.

20. Learn to multitask while exercising to reduce the pain and increase the gain. My wife reads the newspaper while working out on the stationary bike at the gym. Buy an iPod (or other MP3 player) to make your workout go faster. I listen to audio books (mainly nonfiction books semirelated to my work) while road biking (on safe, little-traveled bike paths, I might add). I feel as though I am "working" while exercising, which means I increase the economic payoff from biking. Both my wife and I are convinced that our multitasking means that we *want* to exercise more often and we continue our exercise sessions for longer than we otherwise would.

21. If all else fails, try mental dieting—really! Imagine that you are eating your favorite snack, meal, or dessert. Imagine the smell, taste, texture, the chewing and swallowing of each morsel. Become enraptured by the experience that you string out as long as you can. This so-called "Imagine Diet" has been shown to work by researchers at Carnegie Mellon University. Normally, smells and tastes of foods can give rise to hunger, and overeating, but if you imagine eating the foods in detail and for an extended period, apparently you can trick your stomach and brain into believing that the eating experience is real, with an elevated probability that you will become habituated to the imagined foods. At any rate, the researchers found that those subjects in their experiments who imagined eating favorite foods were less likely to gorge themselves when presented with real food, when compared with subjects who did not adopt the Imagine Diet.[20]

Granted, these weight-loss strategies, grounded in economic thinking, won't work for everyone. But chances are they offer a greater chance of success than the usual run-of-meal (pun intended) diet recommendations that assume away, or just ignore, the powerful, ever-present economic forces that undermine people's best intentions. Diets that don't tip their hats to economic forces aren't likely to be worth a damn for very long. Extant economic forces, revealed in ever-present eating temptations, will be with us until our last breaths. Diet gurus won't be, can't be.

Chapter 10
Fat Freedom

W hat are we to make of America's "obesity epidemic" or the world's "obesity pandemic"? The problem cannot be denied: all we have to do is take a seat in any mall or stand on any street corner, and note the proportion of heavy people who pass by. But whose problem is it, and what—if anything—should be done? I propose a perspective on the problem and its solution that many weight researchers and policy advocates have tended to sidestep.

A sizable "obesity industrial complex" in the United States and most other advanced countries of the world seems determined to spotlight and then magnify where possible the scope of the weight problem. The transparent intent of the antifat warriors is to move what could remain a largely private problem with largely private consequences to a predominantly public one linked to a variety of public "fixes"—an array of intrusions into people's eating, exercise, and weight-gain decisions, which heretofore have been highly personal, subjective, and individualized. Many researchers, politicians, and just plain vanilla-liberal advocates of government intrusions have certainly honed their arguments, but their case raises a number of reservations. The more effective solution, I argue, is for the government and courts to reassert people's personal responsibility for their own weight-gain decisions, which is the only policy and legal route that will enable the country (and world) to ensure that heavy people do not impose the costs of their weight gain on others.

At the heart of the intensifying policy debate is a crucial concern for Americans: the extent to which individuals will remain free to eat what they want and to control their own girths based on their individual goals, or the extent to which those decisions will be manipulated, restricted, and directed by collective (democratic and bureaucratic) forces.

R.B. McKenzie, *HEAVY!*, DOI 10.1007/978-3-642-20135-6_10,
© Springer-Verlag Berlin Heidelberg 2012

The Case for Government Intrusion in Capsule

To summarize, advocates for government intrusions into people's eating and weight-gain decisions make the following major points:

- More than two-thirds of adult Americans are overweight or obese, and overweight and obese Americans continue to gain weight to boot, with ever more dire personal and social consequences. If current trends continue, perhaps half of the country's adult population will be obese by the end of this decade, with the percentage likely even higher by mid-century.
- Overweight is being passed on through generations as the population gives birth to heavier newborns who will, with a high frequency, morph into heavier children and teenagers, many of whom are bound to become obese adults with ever greater weight-related social, work, and medical problems. If the growth in the morbidly obese is not abated, Americans might experience within a decade or two a reversal in the country's average life expectancy (if the reversal hasn't already started).
- Excess weight causes a growing array of documented serious physical and mental impairments, emotional instabilities, and diseases, all of which result in hundreds of billions of dollars in added annual health-care costs, lost worker productivity, lower wages, and greater worker absenteeism, as well as the social ostracism that can contribute to a growing incidence of loneliness, depression, and suicide—which, in turn, can have feedback loops on heavy people's propensity to eat excessively and unhealthily and gain weight.
- Heavy people can't help themselves. Their weights are genetically determined, or they are just genetically predisposed, to eat more than they should because of evolutionary forces at work on the development of people's appetites long ago when food was scarce and uncertain. Alternately, obesity is a disease that has at least some markings of being socially contagious, which means that obesity can be self-accelerating in its spread through the population with mounting social and economic consequences for everyone.
- People of all stripes exude irrationalities, their decision-making errors abound, and they are especially prone to err when assessing the long-term consequences of eating fatty and sugared foods, a point of argument that seems amply validated in the number of excessively heavy people who fret about their weight but who seem powerless to restrain their eating. In its crudest form, this line of argument reduces to the proposition that many people (maybe including the vast majority of overweight folks) are either not responsible for their weight, and can't be, or are simply stupid and require intervention from others to make reasonable dietary decisions for them. (The researchers and antifat warriors basically argue that they know best for tens, if not hundreds, of millions of other people.)
- In a variety of ways (through, for example, higher food and drink taxes to cover their medical costs, lost workplace productivity, and higher prices at the pump), heavy people impose much (if not nearly all) of their excess-weight-related

costs on society at large, which is justification enough (if true, even for some hardcore free-market economists!) for government intrusions into people's heretofore private eating decisions.

> "Only governments have the authority to issue the policies and regulations needed to combat some of the forces contributing to the pandemic."

- Moreover, individual heavy people can't solve their own problems, or else they would have, and the country would not face the weight-related afflictions observed today. Government intrusions in the form of education, tax-and-subsidy incentives, and direct controls on what, where, and how much people eat and exercise are the only viable and effective paths to bariatric salvation. As one team of credible advocates of a broad array of government intrusions into people's individual eating decisions has argued,

> Governments – national, regional, and local – can play a uniquely powerful role in providing this support and encouragement and thereby catalyzing the creation of enough locally led social movements to change the pandemic's course. They are in a singular position to offer incentives to, and align the efforts of, all the organizations that have a stake in this issue. Only governments have the authority to issue the policies and regulations needed to combat some of the forces contributing to the pandemic. Governments have responsibility for the health and economic well-being of their populations, and they must shoulder many of the pandemic's costs.[1]

- If nothing else government can marshal a variety of choice "nudges" devised by "choice architects" to correct, at least partially, heavy Americans' wanton ways and to put everyone, heavy and trim people alike, on the path to gastronomical righteousness and economic prosperity.
- And finally, government's varied and deepening intrusions into people's smoking decisions, beginning in the early 1960s, worked with glorious results, dramatically reversing the growth in the percent of Americans who smoked, suffered debilitations, got sick, and died from the smoking-related medical afflictions. That considerable success of government policy can be duplicated with equal effectiveness to solve the country's overweight and obesity problem.

Case closed!

Problems with the Case for Government Intrusion

The antifat warriors fighting for government intrusion propose not only an expansion of nutrition education and labeling programs for people, with special attention to protecting children (an undisputed duty of government), but also an array of fat taxes and bans to make sure that consenting adults behave in ways that they—the politicians, researchers, and policy makers—deem necessary, if not just desirable. The smorgasbord of suggested reforms aimed at protecting both heavy and trim people alike from our wayward eating ways, and the associated social and private costs, expands with each report on just how serious the country's weight problems are and will become. But many advocates for government intrusions rarely admit certain inconvenient points of truth in the debate.

Most prominently, the basic BMI statistic on which the advocates claim an ample majority of the American population is overweight or obese is highly flawed (almost ludicrously so). I noted how my exceptionally healthy son, who has an extraordinarily low percentage of body fat because he lifts weights and exercises vigorously on a daily basis, is "obese" by the established BMI-based definition of obesity. I also pointed to a good friend and coauthor on several books whose BMI puts him in the normal-weight category but whose body fat (as measured by pinch tests) puts him into the obese category. When they were playing major league baseball, homerun sluggers Mark McGuire (six-foot-five and 250 pounds) and Barry Bond (six-foot-two and 228 pounds) had BMIs that made them borderline obese (or a fraction of a point below the obese lower limit). No doubt, any number of highly ranked professional athletes, especially in football, would break the obese bottom limit with ease. These are exceptional people, without doubt, but they certainly call into question the credibility of the BMI statistic for an unknown number of other people for whom BMI misrepresents their prospective health and longevity.

Never mind all the problems with the BMI statistics, researchers claim to *know* exactly how many Americans are excessively fat. The best of scientific statistical studies can produce a range of spurious results when starting with a demonstrably bad data series. You have to believe that so much of what is touted as serious scientific research on obesity is pure junk science, or just bunk, as one critic has documented at length.[2] Understandably, BMI is a poor predictor of people's health and longevity, not what researchers should want in their pursuit of the *science* of obesity.

And readers of the obesity literature should keep in mind that the BMI cutoffs for "overweight" (25) and "obese" (30) have not been set through some scientific process that establishes the numerical cutoffs as pivotal points at which medical problems suddenly begin to escalate. Rather they were set through political processes in which the vested interests in the obesity industrial complex, including antifat warriors such as research organizations and diet firms, press for low cutoffs to magnify the extent of the overweight epidemic. If the cutoff for the "overweight" category were returned to its level in the 1990s (then used by the National Institute of Health) of 27.5, tens of millions (maybe as many as forty million) Americans would no longer be counted as a part of the country's weight problem.[3] No doubt, some in the weight-control industry would likely oppose such a move because it would immediately and substantially reduce the perceived extent of the problem, limit funding for continued research, and diminish the political prospects that proposed reforms would be adopted.

Researchers also have clearly established many statistical *correlations* (or *associations*) between excess weight and three dozen or so serious diseases. But too often researchers and policy advocates allow the language in their reports to suggest that their *correlations* reflect *causation*. Maybe so in some cases, but maybe not in others. Third factors (genes or family circumstances) can be *causing* people's excess weight and their illness with no causative link between the two. That is, many heavy people might have developed diabetes or kidney failure anyway, even if they had controlled their weight. Certainly, it is a fairly safe bet that excess weight, at least beyond some level, can cause medical problems for some or many people, but we just can't now be as certain about the extent of the medical effects of excess weight as many researchers and advocates seem to believe (although it seems to be clear that medical problems mount when people become massively obese[4]). If their proposed policy intrusions are truly dependent on the actual *extent* of weight-related problems, then perhaps they should temper their enthusiasm for aggressive intrusions, at least somewhat.

Similarly, antifat warriors cite the hundreds of thousands of deaths each year that they say are *caused* by excess weight, or just fat. They have seized on the talking point that the rising count of deaths by fat in 2010 surpassed the falling count of deaths by smoking. Unfortunately, for all too many overweight and obese people who die each year there is no way to determine, directly or indirectly, when they die from their fat. When people are said to have died because of their weight, the declaration is often a subjective assessment based on appearance of the deceased, not autopsies. The widely reported count of deaths by fat is really an estimate based on statistical analysis of the difference in the count of deaths between heavy and trim people. Even when excessively fat people die of heart failure or kidney failure, it's all too often something of a leap of medical ideology to say that their fat was the true culprit. Again, maybe so in some cases; maybe not in many other cases. Again, a multitude of third factors may be driving both weight and the associated fatal diseases.

At any rate, when researchers at the Centers for Disease Control and Prevention took a critical and careful look at the causes of people's deaths, they found that the number of "deaths by fat" could be confidently validated at maybe 5 or 6 percent of the widely purveyed 400,000-plus deaths a year. [5]

As reports juxtapose magnified counts of overweight and obese Americans with recitations of all associated weight-related personal and social costs, many observers might get the impression that the overweight and obese are living wasted lives and are nothing but a drag on their families and the larger society. When put in such stark terms, the implied claims are patently false. If it were true for the two-thirds of the population that is overweight and obese, even with all the touted attendant problems, the American economy would surely have ground to a halt decades ago. Overweight and obese Americans are our neighbors and coworkers who contribute much to their family and friends, pay their taxes, and do creative things that benefit others. Many highly productive and creative heavy people can be lurking underneath findings so often reported as *average* outcomes for all people in the overweight and obese categories.

Moreover, as I have reported, some research shows that a few extra pounds can actually lower people's health-care costs and can actually lengthen many people's lives. Research has shown that the health-care costs of those officially classified as obese don't really begin to rise, *on average,* until BMI reaches into the high 30s.

And don't forget that underweight people (with BMIs less than 18.5) have been found to incur added medical-care costs, just as exceptionally heavy people do.[6] In fact, a graphing of the medical costs incurred on average by Americans at all BMIs, as assessed in one careful study, is U-shaped, with the bottom of the U more or less flat from BMIs in the low 20s to the high 30s.[7]

Heavy people are not likely the net burden on broader society that they are often made out to be. Research has shown that while weight matters at work and in determining health-care costs, heavy people can incur their extra medical costs themselves through lower wages and fringe benefits and fewer opportunities for workplace advancement. Indeed, one set of researchers has concluded that the wage penalty suffered by obese workers might more than compensate their employers for their added health-care costs.[8] In other words, obese people—not broader society— may be covering many, if not a large measure, of their weight-related costs that feed into group health-insurance premiums, albeit indirectly.

Some policy advocates include the additional outlays that overweight and obese people must make in food to maintain their body weight and in their larger size in clothing as societal costs of excess weight.[9] Well, excuse me; are these costs "society" must cover? No, not really. For the most part, those outlays are costs that obese people themselves cover, not taxpayers. And it's worth repeating time and again that many, if not the overwhelming majority of, overweight and obese people are responsible citizens—doctors, lawyers, automobile workers and coal miners, school teachers and professors, nurses and counselors—who are fully capable and prepared to cover their own costs.

Often researchers have shown that added weight increases the demand of the obese for resources, for example, fuel, as noted in Chap. 6. But the inference all too easily made is that if overweight and obese people were to control their appetites and weights, then there would be lower demands for and prices of many goods and resources. Maybe prices would fall for some goods and resources, but maybe not so much across a broad spectrum and by as much as might be expected. If overweight and obese people eat less, they will have more income to spend on other things, maybe including bigger and less fuel-efficient cars. But then they might forsake larger cars for more clothing, which requires resources, including energy, to produce. How prices will change throughout the economy is unclear because we can't be sure exactly how less eating and less weight will translate into shifts of demands and supplies across a multitude of products.

Many antifat warriors cite the risks that follow weight gain as justification for government intruding in people's decisions. But many heavy people offset the effects of their excess weight by healthy behaviors, such as undertaking exercise, sidestepping temptations to drink alcohol excessively, never picking up the smoking habit, controlling their stress, and taking prescription and nonprescription drugs (vitamins, aspirin, and Lipitor) daily. Surely, many ways abound for neutralizing at least some of the negative effects of excess weight that are rarely cited in anti-obesity crusades.

In addition, weight is hardly the only avenue by which people can incur risks. Indeed, a multitude of risky ventures are available, not the least of which are driving, hiking, skiing, parasailing, drinking alcohol, biking, surfing, working, fishing, playing, jaywalking—and on and on. Texting while driving has been proven deadly, but texting while not driving has also been associated with rising stress.[10] I dare say there are antifat warriors who engage in hang gliding or bungee jumping or excessive drinking. Should we control their behavior because they also drain resources and push up prices of those activities, and maybe impose costs on society at large?

And we should never forget that an untold number of heavy people are not distressed by their weights and attendant costs. Indeed, some prefer to incur the continuing costs of their added pounds than those costs, including stress, of weight loss to meet some standard set by people who have little to no knowledge of their exact life circumstances. I repeat the poignant point made by an obese college professor, "I'm not overweight, I'm fat. Overweight suggests I made a mistake in gaining all my weight. I didn't. I chose to get fat." We all need to remember the distinction the professor makes. Many people are "fat" by deliberate, calculated choices organized to maximize what *they* consider to be their life happiness.

And for many people, excessive weight is a transitory state. That is, they gain weight, only later to lose it (consider talk-show host Oprah Winfrey as the poster child for transitory excessive weight). The excessive weight statistics are snapshots of the population at given points in time. Many of the people caught in the snapshot will be overweight or obese only for some limited period of time, until they decide to change their lifestyles.

Moreover, targeting sugared and fatty foods themselves, not the people who eat them, can be a misguided policy, simply because people's decisions on portion sizes, not so much the identified fast foods or convenience foods, could be the greater culprit in weight gain. This point was made with force by a professor of nutrition at Kansas State University who decided to test the commonly acknowledged proposition in nutrition that it is the calories consumed and expended daily, not the exact foods consumed, that make all the difference in people's weights. He went on what he called a "convenience store diet" (what others have tagged as the "Twinkie diet") under which he limited his daily calorie intake to no more than 1,800 (when to maintain his body mass he required the consumption of 2,600 cal a day). For ten weeks in 2009, he downed daily a steady diet of Twinkies, powdered doughnuts, and nut-filled candy bars every three hours in lieu of the supposed more wholesome routine of three square meals.

Contrary to what you might think, he lost twenty-seven pounds, reducing his BMI in the process from 28.8 ("overweight") to 24.9 (borderline "normal weight"). He also experienced a 20 percent decline in his "bad" cholesterol (LDL), a 20 percent increase in his "good" cholesterol (DHL), and a 39 percent reduction in his triglycerides (a form of fat)—all of which is strong anecdotal evidence for guarding against blaming the foods and not the (over)eaters' extra calories.[11] While more carefully controlled scientific study is needed, the professor's experience suggests also that in combating weight, the target of food policy probably should be the (over)eaters and not the foods.

More Problems with Fat Intrusions

Before seeking to replicate the taxes and bans utilized against tobacco, policy makers and advocates concerned with Americans' growing waistlines need to keep in mind key differences between the past smoking war and the coming fat war.

First, in the smoking war the offending ingredient—tobacco—is used in a fairly narrow range of products, with cigarettes being the overwhelmingly dominant one, that are produced in a highly concentrated industry, which means few major firms need to be monitored and controlled. But the offending ingredients in the fat war, mainly sugar and fat (or just calories), are found in an ever-widening range of products developed and produced by hordes of firms in a highly diffuse food industry (or, rather, industr*ies*) that literally extends to the ends of the earth. Try to control people's intake of sugar or fat in one targeted product—sugared sodas or fast-food kid's meals—and they can stealthily move to another untargeted product for their sugar and fat fix. And entrepreneurs in hot pursuit of profits can get creative with all sorts of new products to escape and undermine fat taxes and bans.

Consumers who want sugar and fat and food producers who supply them have numerous ways to outmaneuver restrictions at every turn of the fat policy battles. Antismoking policies could stay focused on a few products, which made the policies narrowly intrusive and yet effective. On the other hand, to be equally effective, antifat policies must be expansively intrusive over a widening range of foods and drinks, ultimately impinging significantly on consumers' freedom of choice.

Second, and more important, in the antismoking campaign, the policies could narrowly target the offending parties—smokers—with taxes and bans on cigarettes. Nonsmokers did not have to pay the taxes or deal with the bans. Indeed, they could benefit from smoke-free environments the bans created. Antifat taxes and bans can't be so narrowly focused if they are to have a prayer of being effective (unless anyone dare suggest a fat test for purchases). Of course, they can be applied to some narrowly targeted product lines—again, sugared sodas and kids' meals—but note that the taxes and bans will penalize everyone, both trim and heavy people alike.

People who work at holding the line on their calorie intake and weight and exercise regularly will also have to pay the fat taxes and adjust their consumption decisions because of bans, and they (or their trim kids) also will be denied toys in their Happy Meals, just like heavy people (or their heavy kids) who make little to no effort to hold the line on their eating and do not move from their couches for reasons other than replenishing their stocks of snacks.

Do antifat warriors really want to penalize kids and adults who do what the warriors think is "right" simply to change the behavior of the kids and adults who do what they think is "wrong"?

Supporters of fat taxes and bans don't seem to appreciate that their favored policy proposals will also hit underweight kids and adults (some who have trouble packing on the pounds), poor and rich alike (although maybe disproportionately the poor), making it all the harder for them to get the calories they need at low prices to maintain a healthy weight. If the fat taxes and bans have the weight-loss effect proponents tout, then their policies can also increase the weight loss of the underweight kids and adults, or just thwart their weight gain struggles. And do remember that a significant percentage of many American households (15 percent in 2009) face "food insecurities" (or miss meals regularly for financial reasons).[12] A rather perverse policy outcome may result from food and drink taxes and bans: Not only will the underweight kids and adults suffer a reduction in their real incomes and welfare, but they also can be forced to confront increases in their medical-care expenditures. Is this right, fair, just? By what standard, for heaven's sake? Conveniently, the antifat warriors have sidestepped, ignored, or just buried such potential unforeseen and unintended consequences. Yet, using the economic theory undergirding their own policy proposals, we can certainly expect such consequences for underweight people.

Any number of weight experts and policy commentators argue that heavy people's excess weight is not their *fault*. They can't control themselves, so it is often argued. The cause of their excess weight is in their genes, in their childhood nurturing, or in their immediate environment. We shouldn't penalize heavy people for their wrongdoing, or just for their excess weight—which would mean imposing their weight-related costs on them. The experts and commentators don't seem to realize that many of the weight-related costs, medical and otherwise, are real; those costs don't go away by absolving heavy people of responsibility for their weight-related costs. If we absolve heavy people of their weight-related costs, then we impose those costs on others—who have no control (or surely less control) over what heavy people do. This means that for sake of consistency in argument, if nothing else, if we absolve heavy people of any responsibility for their weight-related costs because their weight is not their fault, then we surely can't hold all others responsible for the weight-related costs when they are not at fault.

Moreover, by shifting weight-related costs to nonheavy others, we encourage weight gain among a greater number of people. We magnify the problem. This is to say that by absolving heavy people of their weight, we hold others, who have incurred the costs of their weight control, at fault for a larger number of heavy people. If we can't fault heavy people for their weight problems, then surely we can't, and shouldn't, fault all others and hold them responsible for covering weight-related costs. Besides, I have noted in the book that much credible research indicates that almost all heavy people have at least some control over their eating habits (or some ability to override their genetic predispositions). In dealing with the country's weight problems, we need to enlist whatever residual control people have over what and how much they eat and weigh, and there is no more surefire method of doing this than making certain heavy people incur the full burden of their eating and weight. Remember the law of demand rules: The more you confront heavier people with a higher price (or greater costs) for their excess eating, the smaller the count of heavier people and the lower their weight. If some heavy people are relatively insensitive to price, because of, say, their genes, then that is all the more reason we need to make sure they suffer the full costs of their eating. We will need to achieve the maximum effect, with heavy people bearing the maximum cost. Partially subsidizing their costs can only limit their efforts to control their excess eating.

Free to Be Fat

What then is a reasonable strategy for solving the overweight and obesity problem *if* we are to continue to allow consenting adults the freedom to make whatever diet and weight gain decisions they want to make and at the same time curb societal costs from people's excess poundage? I understand, many advocates of government intrusions in all spheres of life don't care so much about individual freedom, except their own freedom to determine what so many others do (which makes their *freedom* a form of *power*, a force that has shaped much of human history, with hardly universally good effects). However, a whole lot of Americans care a great deal about their own freedom to do what they— *individually*—want. Indeed, many Americans are understandably outright hostile toward relinquishing their personal freedoms, especially on food fronts, to empower the "weight police" who literally have little knowledge of the detailed individual circumstances of those they would seek to control. And the weight police can never have enough information, regardless of how many research reports are issued.

Then, what can be done?

First, the government should adopt (to repeat) Google's mantra, "Do no evil" (or just no harm). As pressed at other points in this book, we can insist that government policies should not aggravate people's weight problems. If farmers, food processors, and restaurants are imposing their production costs on others through the rivers and airwaves, then by all means make them all incur their own costs. Otherwise, foods will be underpriced, encouraging excess eating and weight gain. Similarly, where the government is subsidizing the production of fatty foods, directly through payments to farmers (mainly grains) or indirectly through research to increase efficiency of production and distribution of fattening foods, the subsidies should be reduced, if not altogether withdrawn. Clearly, the government should not be in the business of padding the pockets of particular consumers or producers. Case in point: The U.S. Department of Agriculture, through an organization called Dairy Management, helped Domino's Pizza to revitalize its lagging sales in 2006 by developing a new line of pizzas with 40 percent more cheese and by devising and covering a $12-million marketing campaign for Domino's customers' and shareholders' benefit, according to one news report. Each slice of the new pizza carries two-thirds of the recommended daily intake of trans fat for an adult, and no doubt many Domino customers eat multiple slices at each sitting, which means the government has encouraged many pizza eaters to eat trans fats at several times the government's own recommended consumption level.[13]

Such governmental efforts to pad restaurateurs' and dairy farmers' pockets border on the absurd, and surely must be contrary to the nutrition and anti-obesity goals of the Department of Agriculture, which suggests such efforts should be abandoned. For similar reasons, governments at all levels should not be pressing farm policies that artificially raise the prices of fruits and vegetables, as agriculture researchers have found they do.[14] Also, the federal government should not be allowed to buy farm products, whether corn or peanuts or whatever, that go into sugared and fatty foods and then dump those food products on public schools, which can induce the public schools to fill school children's lunches with sugared and fatty foods. Kids and their parents need to pay the full cost of their sugared and fatty foods no matter where they eat them, in school or elsewhere. At the very least, trim and heavy taxpayers should not be called on to aid and abet food addictions, weight gains, and associated medical costs of heavy people.

Second, providing nutrition education for school children should be continued and possibly be expanded, mainly because such efforts allow people to make their own more informed food choices and because they can mute political drives to impose heavy-handed taxes and bans that constrict everyone's choices (other than maybe the "choice architects" who devise the taxes and bans).

Third, food suppliers should not be allowed to engage in consumer fraud by providing foods that are deceptive in terms of their nutritional value or their calories and fat grams. While many libertarians might object, food labeling laws, which require food suppliers to provide readily available information on the calories and fat grams of their menu items, can also be productive (if they are constrained in the details provided) in the sense that such requirements can make for more informed consumer decisions. Perhaps more importantly, such modest labeling requirements can thwart other political efforts to constrict consumer choices through taxes and bans. The Grocery Manufacturers Association, representing 300 large food and drink distributors, has already "voluntarily" agreed (at the behest of the Obama Administration) to place nutrition information on the fronts of packages and to make the contents easier to read.[15]

Personally, from a review of the limited research, I doubt that such information and labeling requirements will have much of an effect on people's weights. After all, nutrition information on labels of foods and drinks as well as food nutrition educational campaigns may have grown over the last fifty years more rapidly than people's weights. However, if such requirements are in place, we can be more confident that people's weight gains are the result of more informed decisions. This means that we can be more confident that people have decided that they prefer to have the food and weight gain and incur the attendant personal costs than to go without the excess calories. Again, labeling requirements may cause voters and their political representatives to be less inclined to impose more onerous taxes and food controls.

Fourth, children should be treated differentially from adults, as has long been the case. Legally, they are not deemed competent to make decisions that are in their own interests, because they don't always know their interests or the relevant short and long-term costs of achieving their interests. After all, their brains are not fully developed, or wired, until at least their mid-teens. We have to hold parents accountable for their children's weights. And it does appear that many parents are shirking their responsibility to control what and how much their children eat. Perhaps we should more aggressively prosecute (or threaten to prosecute) parents who allow their kids to become morbidly obese (or some such standard for child abuse and neglect). After all, the parents must be, for the most part, the enablers.

The last thing we should have is a range of government policies that enable irresponsible parents to enable their kids to become morbidly obese.

Fifth, we should recognize that junk-food advocates are right on one point: People will respond to food incentives and, therefore, to taxes and subsidies, which means prices can have some effect on our eating and drinking choices. The obesity research has confirmed time and again that the law of demand holds for food and drink, even for heavy people (and even for heavy people who have food addictions). We need to accept the law of demand as an article of faith in discussions of the country's weight problems, which means it can be a source of the solution to people's excess weight (as people themselves, not choice architects define "excess weight").

A core issue is this: As in the smoking war, should not government taxes and bans target the offending parties, the heavy people themselves and not food producers, distributors, and providers? In an effort to control people's weights, or the costs heavy people impose on others, why engage in carpet bombing when strategic bombing has far less potential for collateral damage?

Fat taxes applied only to the food and drink purchases of overweight and obese people could be a hard political sell, but at least should we not investigate how such can be done? Why should politicians and policy makers be more inclined to tax and control everyone's food intake than to tax and control only the offending parties? At any rate, if targeted taxes and bans are unacceptable, there is an indirect way of accomplishing much the same objective: *Hold heavy people fully and personally responsible for their weights by making sure that they incur, as much as possible, the full personal and societal costs of their excess pounds.* This means that airlines should remain free to ask heavy people to pay more for bigger seats (or two seats) when they fly, just as they have to pay more when they drive (through larger cars and more gasoline consumption). Ditto for when they go to ballgames and concerts.

The manager of Natural Nails may have the kind of "nudge" behavioralists (see Chap. 8) might welcome: Charge heavy people for the likely damage they do to pedicure lounge chairs. At least private firms should remain free to devise such surcharges. Requiring people to pay by the pound will be a cumbersome pricing rule for many firms, but it does convey a working principle, leading to any number of nudges that could fit the end-goals of self-appointed choice architects: We should make sure that firms at least retain the legal right to cover their added costs (and then some) that heavy people impose on firms and their other customers, with the profit included in prices to make sure firms have an interest in serving heavy people. While charging by the pound will unlikely be adopted by many firms, because such pricing strategies will be awkward on every public relations front, going forward into the future with growing weight problems, many firms might be able to devise pricing differentials for people in different weight categories, especially when weight does add significantly to cost. I am not at all suggesting that firms be *required to* impose surcharges on heavy people, but only that they retain the right to do so when their market circumstances permit (and there are groups who want to deny firms the right to price discriminate for weight on grounds of fairness and political ideology).

If rescue and hospital services for heavy people cost more than similar services for normal-weight people, the heavy people should be asked to pay a surcharge to cover the added expenses incurred. And we should make sure that heavy people have to anticipate the escalating costs of their currently added weight well into the future, just to get their attention and to have them adjust their current eating and drinking. I am fairly confident that firms that devise weight surcharges will likely phase them in, which will give people a chance to adjust their eating habits to avoid the future weight surcharges.

Many firms may be able to make many heavy people carry their full weight by adjusting group health insurance premiums for weight-related added risks, and we should make sure that employers continue to have full rights to discriminate against heavy people in hiring (or nonhiring) and in the wages and fringe benefits offered. If heavy people impose added work accommodation burdens on their employers, then employers must be able to recoup their added costs either by billing the employees directly or by lowering their wages and other benefits. The important point is that we should make sure that weight discrimination everywhere—in purchases and employment—is not made illegal. If it is made illegal, then we can expect people to gain even more weight because they can simply impose a portion of their weight-related costs on others, compounding the *social* problems of weight gain.

These proposals will appall some readers, but do note that heavy people already incur many of these personal and societal costs of their weight. Many (hardly all) of heavy people's lives are impaired. Still, if they are not paying their full way, then by all means let's adopt policies that ensure that they pay as much of their way as possible. Doing so will target heavy people themselves with the penalties of overeating, much as smoking bans and taxes targeted smokers, with the targeted penalties having a greater chance of actually changing behavior.

The cry might go up that heavy people won't respond to the greater burdens imposed on them. People are too irrational or face limited rational capacities, opponents may insist yet again. If that is the case, then all the proposed fat taxes and information/educational campaigns will not work either, and why should we tax everyone just to control the behavior of those people who, supposedly, can't control—or won't control—their eating and weight-gain proclivities?

Perhaps some people are truly afflicted with a disease, overeating. That's not an unsolvable problem, at least partially. We can make allowances and exceptions for that minority of the heavy population through medical examinations and certifications. The country already has a system in place for determining who is so disabled that they are allowed to park in parking spaces reserved for them. We can develop a similar system for excessively heavy people who have medically and genetically validated eating disorders (although, of course, the potential for abuse of such a system is huge).

Of course, the policy strategy to require the overweight to pay the full cost of their behavior is not likely to make the coming fat conflict any less intense. On the contrary, the conflict will really get divisive when people's weight problems start filling court dockets on two major grounds: fat discrimination and fat disabilities. Nevertheless, we should seek a balanced debate over the government's proper role in people's weight-control efforts. So far, much of the obesity-reform debate has been one-sided, favoring fat taxes, food controls, and weight antidiscrimination laws and court rulings. We need a debate that recognizes the importance of people, heavy and trim alike, retaining as much personal freedom as possible. The tried and true way of doing that is to make sure that personal responsibility and coverage of costs is central to the country's weight fix.

Concluding Comments

My criticisms of the BMI statistics and other flaws in weight research should not be interpreted to mean that I think the country does not have a weight problem. It obviously does, and it appears to be growing for any number of solid reasons, most notably economic reasons discussed in this book, many of which have been unheralded.

America and the world have become so productive, especially in calories, and so prosperous that temptations to eat, overeat, and gain weight abound. Today, people—even poor people—really must have more fortitude than they did a half century (or less) ago to resist the ever-present food temptations, and most people must work harder than they ever have to stay trim. Our prosperity as individuals and as a country has, indeed, been undercut by the effort we must now make and the costs we must incur to stay trim. In fact, we are now so prosperous that at least 40 percent of the food available in the country is never eaten. It is left in the fields, lost in distribution, but largely discarded as waste. Almost all participants in a survey reported having bought food that is never used, and food scraps from meals and snacks now make up nearly a fifth of landfills, eventually causing the release of more greenhouse gas, methane.[16] The uneaten and discarded food has an upside, less weight gain than there actually has been, although greenhouse gases might not be affected.

Without doubt, we as a country have a weight problem, period. The important issues, again, are twofold: Whose problem is it? And what is to be done about it?

Clearly, the bulk of people's weight problem is personal. Heavy people are the ones who must suffer a large measure of all the costs associated with excess pounds, as it should be and can't be otherwise—if we are to remain a largely free society, one in which individuals have the right to assess for themselves what to do with their lives. I might not like the sight of the excess pounds many people are carrying, but for the life of me, I can't see the justification for handing over to me the right to dictate to other consenting adults what they should eat and weigh, just as I can't see the justification for giving others the right to tell me what I should eat and how much I should weigh. I don't know other's value systems (which surely vary radically across people), and they don't know mine. Many overweight and obese people could be less unhappy than they would be if they constantly tried to stay as trim as I—or anyone else—might like.

The critical *economic* issue is whether or not people's individual excess pounds are materially undercutting the welfare of others, or whether there are spillover costs (an issue taken up at several points in this book). And there is a good economic reason for concern on that count. To the extent that people can impose the costs of their weight on others, they lower their own costs of eating, overeating, and gaining weight. Again, the law of demand rules, and the value of many of the pounds carried by heavy people can be lower than their full costs, clearly an outcome that undermines societal welfare across all people.

In this concluding chapter, I've argued for making heavy people fully and personally responsible for all costs of their weight gain because they—not all others—are the offending parties. Also, personal freedom and personal responsibility (for how freedom is used) are inextricably interlocked. Proposed food taxes and bans represent a real and abiding threat to individual freedom because food taxes can't be narrowly focused on a few firms or a few goods or ingredients in them. Narrowly defined taxes and bans will simply cause offending parties to get their food (or calorie) fixes elsewhere, which means that food taxes and bans, to be effective, have to be ever expanding, which means that governments' encroachments on all people's freedom of choice can be ever expanding. In short, my plea here for resurrecting the importance of personal responsibility in the debate over what to do about people's excess weight is a plea for the maintenance of personal freedom to the extent possible. Nutrition education and labels have one very important redeeming virtue; they can improve choices and, at the same time, can deflate political pressures for policies, like taxes and bans, that constrict choices.

Endnotes

Chapter 1

[1]As reported by Hard (2009).

[2]When it inaugurated its bag fee, it increased its baggage fee for three or more bags and for bags requiring special handling because of weight, size, or shape from $100 to $125 or $200 to $250, depending on item (CNN, June 13, 2009b, with the report accessed July 7, 2009b from http://www.cnn.com/2008/TRAVEL/06/13/airlines.bags/index.html.

[3]As reported by CNNMoney.com (February 9, 2011) at http://money.cnn.com/2011/02/09/news/companies/usair_bag_fees/index.htm.

[4]In mid-2009, United Airlines, the first major airline to institute a bag charge, followed the lead of US Airways and raised its bag charge by a third for the first bag, or from $15 to $20, and by a fifth for the second bag, or from $25 to $30. However, air travelers that paid the bag charges online could continue to pay the lower charge. Delta instituted the first charge for a second bag for international travelers (Pae 2009).

[5]The International Air Transport Association forecast in mid-2009 that its 232 member airlines, which provide 93 percent of all passenger miles, would incur a total of $9 billion in losses for 2009. Airlines in North America were projected to lose a total of $1 billion for the year, down from over the more than $5 billion lost in 2008 largely due to a dramatic spike in jet fuel prices (Wassener 2009).

[6]On this particular trip, the excess weight of the plane could have been due to several sources of added pounds, not the least of which are extra pounds of fuel and cargo. However, two airline pilots, one of whom tracks passenger weight for the airline industry, confirm that added passenger weight has been a growing source of departure delays.

R.B. McKenzie, *HEAVY!*, DOI 10.1007/978-3-642-20135-6,
© Springer-Verlag Berlin Heidelberg 2012

[7]Flights today also may *seem* fuller than they were three or more decades ago have increased the percentage of their seats filled, increased the number of rows of seats at the same time they have kept the distance between seatbacks more or less the same (by narrowing the backs of seats, and increased reliance on smaller regional planes that have lower ceilings (as reported by Yu [2009]).

[8]To make the very rough calculation of the gallons of jet fuel consumed for the added twenty-four pounds for each of the 216 passengers on the Continental flight, I used estimates of the added fuel consumption provided by Dannenberg, Burton, and Jackson in the *American Journal of Preventive Medicine* (2004). They estimated that a jet airplane consumed on average a gallon of jet fuel to transport 7.3 tons for one mile. They found that to carry the approximately ten pounds Americans gained on average during the 1990s, which required airlines to consume 350 million additional gallons jet fuel over what they would have consumed had Americans weighed in 2000 what they did in 1990. Since the added weight gain of Americans between 1960 and 2004 was twenty-four pounds, my estimate of the additional fuel consumption on all flights is, roughly, 840 million gallons. On my Orange County-Houston flight, the added weight gain over 1960 totaled 5,184 pounds, or 2.5 tons, which can be moved close to 2.8 miles on one gallon of jet fuel. Given the air distance between Orange County and Houston is 1,350 miles, the added passenger weight required the burning of 482 gallon of jet fuel that cost $1,205 at $2.50 a gallon. These are "rough" estimates because they are based the *average* fuel consumption per ton of weight. The *marginal* consumption of jet fuel per mile could be lower or higher than the *average* consumption.

[9]As reported by Reuters, April 22, 2010, accessed August 18, 2010 from http://www.reuters.com/article/idUSTRE63L1I020100422.

[10]Power and Schulkin (2009, p. 38).

[11]As reported by Injuryboard.com on May 13, 2003 at http://www.injuryboard.com/national- news/federal-aviation-administration.aspx?googleid = 27862.

[12]A substantial majority of scientists and the general public appear convinced that human activity has elevated the long-term global warming trend. This view on global warming is best represented by a report issued by the United Nations' Intergovernmental Panel on Climate Change (2007). The view has been popularized by Vice President Al Gore in his film and book, *An Inconvenient Truth* (2006). A minority of scientists concurs that global warming has been underway for centuries, but strongly disagrees with the view that human activity consequentially elevates global warming. These scientists also maintain that government-imposed curbs on human-generated greenhouse gases will not materially affect the global warming trend. For this minority perspective, see Singer and Avery (2007).

[13]As reported by the Mayo Clinic Staff (2010), citing Ainsworth et al. (2000). The link to the complete table is http://www.mayoclinic.com/health/exercise/SM00109.

[14]Johnsson 2009.

[15]Southwest.com 2009.

[16]As reported by "Today Show" contributor Marsh (2010).

[17]As reported by Lewis (2010).

[18]See the interview with Boston University professor Carolina Kobe on Fox Business News, April 20, 2009, as accessed on July 7, 2009 from http://www.foxbusiness.com/search-results/m/22123753/airlines-to-charge-obese-fliers-double.htm.

[19]See the letter posted by Adam Gilden Tsai on DenverPost.com on April 21, 2009, accessed on July 7, 2009 from http://blogs.denverpost.com/eletters/2009/04/21/airlines-should-reconsider-charging-for-obesity/.

[20]As reported by Starmer-Smith 2009.

[21]As reported by Johnsson 2009.

[22]As reported by the Associated Press and posted on May 17, 2007 on FreeRepublic.com, accessed on July 7, 2009, from http://www.freerepublic.com/tag/peopleofsize/index.

[23]As reported by Ben Mutzabaugh, USAToday.com, no date, as accessed July 7, 2009, from http://www.usatoday.com/travel/flights/item.aspx?ak=44010330.blog&type=blog.

[24]http://www.nber.org/papers/w15163.

[25]See reports on the support for the fat tax from the Center for Science in the Public Interest, January 28, 2004, accessed July 7, 2009 from http://www.consumerfreedom.com/news_detail.cfm/headline/2336. See also the report on a proposed fat tax in the United Kingdom from *Reuters*, July 12, 2007, accessed July 7, 2009 from http://www.reuters.com/article/healthNews/idUSL1254236520070712. See the Wikipedia entry for "fat tax" at http://en.wikipedia.org/wiki/Fat_tax.

[26]See the report on the proposed restaurant law, "Mississippi Law: 'No Fat People Allowed,'" *Itola.com*, February 6, 2008, accessed on July 7, 2009 from http://itola.com/business/new-mississippi-law-no-fat-people-allowed/.

[27]See a report on Maine's calorie-count law for restaurants at BangorDailyNews.com, June 18, 2009, accessed on July 7, 2009 from http://www.bangordailynews.com/detail/108646.html. At this writing several U.S Senators had struck a deal that would require restaurants chains with twenty or more outlets to provide patrons on request with information on fat, saturated fat, carbohydrates, sodium, sugars, dietary fiber and protein in their menu items (as reported by *LATimes.com*, June 10, 2009, as accessed on July 7, 2009 from http://latimesblogs.latimes.com/booster_shots/2009/06/deal-struck-to-post-calorie-counts-at-chain-restaurants-nationwide.html).

[28]The proponent of the formula for the fat tax is restaurant critic and London *Times* columnist Giles Coran (CalorieLab 2006). His formula is this:

$$F_{tax} = \left(\frac{\sqrt{BMI}}{100} \right) \times L_{tax}$$

where

BMI = the widely used Body Mass Index, which accounts for height in determining the extent to which people are obese, or just overweight,

F_{tax} = the fat tax, and

L_{tax} = the amount of a taxpayer's standard tax liability, which means that the fat tax will rise with income.

[29]For example, one study found that an extremely high (and unlikely) fat tax of 100 percent on unhealthy foods would reduce people's average body mass by a trivial amount, with the details of this and other studies considered later (Gelbach et al. 2007).

[30]See the scholarly work of Hamermesh and Biddle (1994) and Phann et al. (2000).

[31]Smith v. Hooters (2010) and as reported by Lewis (2010).

[32]Power and Schulkin (2009).

[33]For a discussion of some of the industry-based political forces that have sought to shape the measured and reported size and scope of America's weight problems, see Oliver (2006, Chaps. 1 and 2).

[34]French and Crabbe (2010).

[35]As reported by Schwartz (2011, March 3).

[36]As reported by Bounds (2011, February 22) for the *Wall Street Journal*.

Chapter 2

[1]See Speiser et al. (2005); and Power and Schulkin (2009).

[2]Karasu and Karasu (2010, p. 20), citing Price (2002) and Wadden and Phelan (2002).

[3]Karasu and Karasu (2010, p. 21), citing Maes (1997).

[4]Karasu and Karasu (2010, p. 21), citing Stunkard et al. (1986).

[5]Karasu and Karasu (2010, p. 20), citing Price (2002, p. 75).

[6]The scholarly literature on "self-control" or "self-regulation" is substantial. See, for example, Laran (2009) and Ferrari et al. (2010)

[7]Even if some extraordinarily virulent "fat gene" that gave afflicted people voracious appetites had appeared in the last century in response to say the spread of fast-food restaurants, evolutionary biologists would posit that, because of the so-called "evolutionary lag," it could take tens of thousands of years (maybe 50,000) for any adaptive genetic change to spread broadly in the human population, at least spread enough to prompt a genetic explanation of much of any observed rapid growth in people's weight, as recorded in the last half century (Levitan 2006).

[8]Li et al. (2010).

[9]The researchers found that for each DNA variant of the obesity genes a person has, he or she has a 16 percent greater risk of becoming obese. A person who exercises an hour daily has only a 10 percent greater risk. Also, each DNA variant that an inactive person, five-feet-six-inches tall, has is associated with a 1.3-pound increase in body weight. For the same person who exercises an hour a day, the body mass increase for each gene variant is 0.8 pounds, only half a pound but a 39 percent lower weight gain (Li et al. [2010]).

[10]"Conspicuous consumption" is a phrase coined by sociologist Thorstein Veblen in his *Theory of the Leisure Class* (1899) to denote expenditures on, say, cars and houses that people make to flaunt their high income and considerable wealth.

[11]Power and Schulkin (2009, p. 3).

[12]See Witcombe (2003).

[13]Power and Schulkin (2009, p. 3).

[14]Ibid., pp. 2–4.

[15]Malthus (1798).

[16]Power and Schulkin (2009, p. 1).

[17]Emmett (2006).

[18]According to economic historian Gregory Clark (2007, p. 2), "Jane Austen may have written about refined conversations over tea served in china cups. But for the majority of the English as late as 1813 conditions were no better than their naked ancestors of the African savannah. So, even according to the broadest measures of material life, average welfare, if anything, declined from the Stone Age to 1800. The poor of 1800, those who lived by their unskilled labor alone, would have been better off if transferred to a hunter-gatherer band."

[19]The increase in per capita income for the twentieth century is roughly estimated by the growth in real per capita Gross Domestic Product. For another graphical view of worker income growth during the nineteenth century, see Fig. 1.1 on per capita income in Clark (2007, p. 2).

[20] As reported by the U.S. "Population Clock," available on August 18, 2010 from http://www.census.gov/main/www/popclock.html.

[21] I discussed in the 1990s *The Paradox of Progress* (1997), which has been the continuing pervasive pessimism people harbor over their economic prospects for the immediate and long-term future in spite of the substantial progress that has been made in the immediate and distant pasts. Drawing on their own series of monographs done for the Federal Reserve Bank of Dallas, economist Michael Cox and journalist Richard Alms developed this theme independently in their *Myth of Rich and Poor* (2000). Science writer Matt Ridley most recently elaborated on the paradox of progress in *The Rational Optimist* (2010).

[22] Clark (2007, pp. 62–66).

[23] See the pictures of Adah Isaacs Menken, a variety stage star in 1860, at "the height of her voluptuous beauty," as well as ads of the early 1990s depicting much slimmer women (Stearns 1997, in the collection of photographs between pp. 136–137). See also the several pictures of Ms. Menkin and various other women of her era on Google images: http://images.google.com/images?hl=en&q=%22Adah+Isaacs+Menken%22&gbv=2&aq=f&oq=&aqi=.

[24] Stearns (1997).

[25] Ibid. (p. 133), citing Metropolitan Life Insurance Company 1966 and 1970, plus other sources.

[26] Stearns (1997, p. 133, citing Williamson 1953, Metropolitan Life Insurance Company 1966 and 1970, plus other sources).

[27] As reported with detailed tables by the National Center for Health Statistics (2009).

[28] National Center for Health Statistics (2009).

[29] Here is the official BMI formula:

$$\text{BMI} = \frac{(\text{Weight in pounds} \times 703)}{(\text{height in inches})^2}$$

[30] For the CDC's BMI calculator go to http://www.cdc.gov/healthyweight/assessing/bmi/adult_bmi/english_bmi_calculator/bmi_calculator.html. As opposed to typing in that long address, readers can simple search Google for "BMI calculator."

[31] Direct methods of measuring body fat include measuring the depth of folds of the skin at various set locations on the body, underwater weighing (to determine water displacement), and dual energy x-ray absorptiometry. For more on the BMI, see

http://www.cdc.gov/healthyweight/assessing/bmi/adult_bmi/index.html (as accessed July 7, 2009).

[32]See the World Health Organization discussion of the BMI, with the detailed breakdown of the BMI categories, at http://apps.who.int/bmi/index.jsp?introPage=intro_1.html (accessed August 7, 2009).

[33]Helmchen (2001).

[34]Ibid.

[35]Ibid. (p. 5), citing Flegal et al. (1998) and Fogel (1999) as the source of his data for obese white men for the 1988–1994 period.

[36]Helmchen (2001, p. 8).

[37]Helmchen and Henderson (2004, pp. 176–177).

[38]The data is drawn from the National Center for Health Statistics (2009).

[39]The average annual rate of increase in overweight Americans between the 1960–1962 and 2003–2006 surveys was slightly more than 1 percent a year. The annual rate of increase between the 1976–1980 and 2003–2006 surveys was 1.6 percent. The annual rate of increase between the 1988–1994 and 2003–2006 surveys was 1.4 percent. Between the 1999–2002 and 2003–2006 surveys, less than 0.7 percent.

[40]The estimated obesity rate for American men age twenty and older rose from 31.1 percent in 1999–2000 to 33.3 percent in 2005–2006. The estimated obesity rate for American women twenty and older rose from 33.2 percent in 1999–2000 to 35.3 percent in 2005–2006. However, the CDC judged the increases were not "statistically significant" changes, which means that they could be due to sampling errors (Centers for Disease Control and Prevention 2006).

[41]Between the 1960–1962 and 2003–2006 surveys, the obesity rate grew by an annual rate of 3.6 percent (less than the 4.5 percent annual growth for the Civil War veterans noted earlier). The annual obesity rate of increase between the 1976–1980 and 2003–2006 surveys was 4.8 percent. Between the 1988–1994 and 2003–2006 surveys, the annual rate of increase in the obesity rate was 4.8 percent. Between the 1999–2002 and 2003–2006 surveys, the annual growth rate was 1.2 percent.

[42]See Fig. 3, "Changes in the distribution of body mass index," in Centers for Disease Control and Prevention (2007). See also Helmchen and Henderson (2004, Fig. 1, p. 177). The data might suggest that only obese people were gaining weight. Not so. The overweight category (percentage of overweight people with BMIs 25–29.9) remained more stable than the obese category because the just-overweight category is constrained on both ends. To be just-overweight, the person's BMI is confined between 25 and 29.9, but there is no upper BMI constraint on the obese category. So, by 2006, many of those who were overweight in 1960 could have eaten their way out of the just-overweight category and into the obese category,

even as those who were already obese in 1960 continued to gain weight. Indeed, many normal weight people in 1960 very likely had eaten their way into the obese category by 2006.

[43]Readers can watch the spread of obesity from 1985 until 2008 in a PowerPoint slide show developed by the CDC at http://www.cdc.gov/obesity/data/trends. html#State. The slide show can also be downloaded.

[44]See the CDC's PowerPoint slides at http://www.cdc.gov/obesity/data/trends. html#State.

[45]Between 1960 and 2002, children ages six to eleven gained an average of nine pounds, or 14 percent. During those years, teenage boys between ages twelve and seventeen gained an average of fifteen pounds, or 12 percent. Girls of the same age gained an average of twelve pounds, or 10 percent. Boys and girls ages six to eleven averaged sixty-five pounds in 1960 and seventy-four pounds in 2002. Teenage boys ages twelve to seventeen averaged 125 pounds in 1960 and 134 pounds in 2002. Teenage girls twelve to seventeen averaged 118 pounds in 1960 and 130 pounds in 2002 (Odgen et al. 2004).

[46]Nationwide, in 2007, 17 percent of school-age children were obese and a third were overweight. The obesity rates for children ages ten to seventeen varied from just under 10 percent in Oregon to nearly 22 percent in Mississippi. In 2007, the five states with the lowest obesity rates for children ages ten to seventeen were Oregon (9.6 percent), Wyoming (10.2 percent), Minnesota (11.1 percent), Washington (11.1 percent), and Hawaii (11.2 percent). The five states with the highest obesity rates for children ages ten to seventeen were Illinois (20.7 percent), Louisiana (20.7 percent), Kentucky (21 percent), Georgia (21.3 percent), and Mississippi (21.9 percent). The obesity rates for children went down in ten states between 2003 and 2007 (Oregon, New Mexico, North Dakota, Iowa, Missouri, Wisconsin, Indiana, Michigan, West Virginia, and North Carolina) (National Survey of Children 2007).

[47]Centers for Disease Control and Prevention, May 28, 2009b, citing Ogden et al. (2002); Hedley et al. (2004); and Ogden et al. (2008), as accessed on August 9, 2009 from http://www.cdc.gov/obesity/childhood/prevalence.html.

[48]As reported by Healy (2010), citing Gordon-Larsen and Adair (2010, in press and unavailable at the time of this writing).

[49]As reported by the Centers for Disease Control and Prevention, Overweight and Obesity, citing various sources, May 28, 2009, as accessed on August 9, 2009 from http://www.cdc.gov/obesity/childhood/consequences.html.

[50]Centers for Disease Control and Prevention (2009), citing Ogden et al. (2002); Hedley et al. (2004); and Ogden et al. (2008), as accessed on August 9, 2009, from http://www.cdc.gov/obesity/childhood/prevalence.html.

[51]National Heart, Lung, and Blood Institute (1998).

[52]In a study of 88,000 women schoolteachers in California, researchers found that women who had added fat around their waists, causing them to have waistlines of 35.2 inches or greater, but who were not "overweight" (had BMIs of under 25) were one-third more likely to have asthma than other "normal weight" women. Obese women with large waistlines were even more likely to have asthma. However, it needs to be noted that only 7.5 percent of the surveyed women schoolteachers had asthma (Medline Plus, citing von Behren et al. 2009)

[53]Medline Plus, citing von Behren et al. (2009).

[54]Ibid.

[55]Ibid.

[56]Ibid.

[57]Kaplan (2010), citing Welsh et al. (2010).

[58]National Heart, Lung, and Blood Institute (1998).

[59]Kopelman 2000.

[60]Brownell (2005) and Puhl and Brownell (2001).

[61]As reported by Brody (2010), citing Adams et al. (2006).

[62]National Heart, Lung, and Blood Institute (1998).

[63]Flegal et al. (2005).

[64]National Heart, Lung, and Blood Institute (1998).

[65]As reported by Stein (2009), citing Berrington de Gonzales (2010).

[66]Cawley and Meyerhoefer (2010).

[67]The growth in health-care expenditures on obesity-related problems was attributable not so much to a growth in health-care expenditures per obese person, but rather due to the growth in the number of obese people. The count of obese Americans rose 37 percent between 1998 and 2006 (as reported by McKay 2009, citing Finkelstein et al. 2009).

[68]Flegal et al. (2005).

[69]Flicker et al. (2010).

[70]Cawley and Meyerhoefer (2010).

[71]Editors of the *Mayo Clinic Proceedings* (2010).

[72]As reported by Rosman (2010).

[73]Kuk et al. (2006).

[74]Ehrlich (1968).

[75]The quote is from William Dietz, director of obesity research at the Centers for Disease Control and Prevention, as quoted in the *Wall Street Journal* (Bialik 2009).

[76]Obesity researcher Isabelle Aeberli at Zurich's Swiss Federal Institute of Technology noted, "When the data of rather high obesity rates [for children] were first published in 2004, everyone was talking about it and we had calls . . . at the lab." There was little reaction when the obesity rate in children went down. She added, "It just seems to be *more* interesting to the general public to show something bad as compared to something good" (as quoted in Bialik [2009]).

[77]Rowland (2009).

[78]Karasu and Karasu (2010), citing Lichtman et al. (1992) and Tataranni and Ravussin (2004).

[79]Johns Hopkins Health Alert (2010).

[80]Flegal et al. (2005); Flicker et al. (2010); and Kuk et al. (2006).

[81]Gallagher (2004) and Araneta et al. (2002). One study has concluded that the BMI for overweight and obese Asians should be dropped to 23 and 25, respectively (Razak et al. [2007]).

[82]Oliver (2006, p. 3).

[83]Oliver (2006, pp. 3–4), citing Mokdad et al. (2004) and Flegal et al. (2005).

[84]Oliver (2006, p. 23).

[85]As obtained from the National Center for Health Statistics (2009), as accessed on October 4, 2010, from http://www.cdc.gov/nchs/.

[86]Gregg et al. (2005) and National Center for Health Statistics (2007).

[87]Flegal et al. (2005).

[88]As reported by Kolata (2006).

[89]Flegal et al. (2005).

[90]American males forty to fifty-nine years of age had an obesity rate of 40 percent; women, 41.1 percent. Males sixty and older, 32.2 percent; women, 30.5 percent. Males twenty to thirty-nine, 28.1 percent; women, 30.5 percent. (Centers for Disease Control and Prevention [2007]).

[91]Speiser et al. (2005); and Power and Schulkin (2009). But then other researchers have found a potential genetic source of obesity, given that among nearly 6,000 Utah subjects in the study, researchers found an increase in the frequency of the A allele with increasing BMIs. This is to say, the greater the subjects' BMIs, the more likely they would have the A allele, a possible genetic driver of weight gain with age (Hunt et al. [2008]).

[92]Silber (2008).

[93] As cited in Rossner (2002).

[94] Power and Schulkin (2009, pp. 132–134, citing an array of other studies).

[95] Paeratakul et al. (2002).

[96] Ibid.

[97] Thirty-nine percent of men see themselves as being overweight, whereas 54 percent of women perceive themselves as being overweight. The percent of whites, blacks, and Hispanics who perceive themselves to be overweight is 49, 47, and 41 percent, respectively. The percent of people in lower- and higher-income households who see themselves as overweight is 44 and 50 percent, respectively. Forty-four percent of people with less than a high-school diploma see themselves as overweight, whereas 47 percent of people with a high-school diploma or more education see themselves as overweight. However, only 20 percent of obese people in the survey saw themselves as having normal weight (Paeratakul et al. 2002).

[98] Of the surveyed American parents with children who are obese or extremely overweight at six to eleven years old, 43 percent assessed their children as having "about the right weight," with 37 percent assessing their children as "slightly overweight." Only 13 percent of the parents agreed that their children were "very overweight," but with the remaining 7 percent of parents (unbelievably) saying their children were "slightly underweight." Of parents with obese children ages twelve to seventeen, 56 percent said their children were "slightly overweight," but 31 percent did think their children were "very overweight." But still 11 percent of the parents said their children were carrying "about the right weight," with the remaining 2 percent of parents thinking their children were "slightly underweight" (as reported in Nation in Brief: Many don't see offspring's obesity. *Los Angeles Times,* December 25, 2007, A25).

[99] For example, Mayo researchers, led by cardiologist Francisco Lopez-Jimenez, found that women who have over 35 percent body fat, but with normal BMIs, are twice as likely as women who have lower body fat ratios to have heart problems and stroke (Winslow [2010]).

[100] Kemper et al. (1994); Stevens et al. (1994); and Powell and Kahn (1995).

[101] Abrams et al. (1993); Akan and Grilo (1995); Fitzgibbon et al. (2000); Kumanyika et al. (1993); Williamson et al. (2000).

[102] Flynn and Fitzgibbon (1998).

[103] In one study, 87 percent of men and women assessed their body weight to be in the socially acceptable weight range, with men more likely than women to believe that their body weights were okay (Rand and Resnick 2000). In a large-sample British study in which self-perception of body weight was assessed by the subjects' BMI classification, of men in the 18.5–24.9 BMI classification (which means they were of normal weight), 19 percent of men and 5 percent of women

thought they were too light, whereas 4.5 percent of men and 20 percent of women thought they were too heavy. In the BMI category of 25 or greater (which means the subjects were overweight or obese), 34 percent of men and 11 percent of women thought they had an appropriate weight. In this weight category, 73 percent of the women and 46 percent of the men reported that they were trying to lose weight (Kamel and McNeill 2000). See also Connor-Greene (1988).

[104] Williamson et al. (2000).

[105] The World Health Organization estimated in 2005 that, based on the BMI, the count of overweight and obese people in the world was 1.6 billion, 400 million of whom were classified as obese. The count of overweight and obese people was predicted to grow to 2.3 billion by 2015, with 700 million obese people included in that count (World Health Organization 2006). The count of overweight and obese people would be significantly greater if the BMI thresholds for overweight and obesity were lowered for Asians, since that ethnic group has more fat for any given BMI than other groups. The World Bank estimated the count of malnourished people in the world at 967 million in 2008 (Stewart 2008).

[106] See the figure in Cutler et al. (2003).

[107] European Association for the Study of Obesity (2005).

[108] Ibid.

[109] Ibid.

[110] In a study of 12,000 people who had been followed for thirty years, the chances of a person becoming obese increased 57 percent with obese friends, 40 percent with obese siblings, and 37 percent with an obese spouse (Christakis and Fowler 2007). In another study, 130 children ages nine to fifteen packed on 250 more calories in meals when they ate with their overweight friends than when they ate with overweight kids they did not know (Salvy et al. 2009).

[111] Indeed, on average the women ate 100 fewer calories for each man at the table, while the men's calorie intake was unaffected by the women at the table (as reported by Abedin 2009).

[112] In 2009, Americans consumed on average 787 pounds per capita of packaged foods (from sauces and dairy products to snacks and frozen pizzas). This per capita consumption level is:

• Between 4 and 6 percent more per capita than the closest "competitors," Spaniards and Frenchmen, respectively.
• A third more than Japanese.
• Nearly seven times more than the Chinese; and a whopping twenty times more than Indians.

On the other hand, in 2009, Americans consumed 602 pounds of fresh foods (vegetables, fruits, eggs, meat, and seafood) per person, which is comparable to the per capita consumption levels in Spain, France, Japan, Russia, but which is 40 percent less than in China. For more details on the consumption of various foods per capita across countries in 2009, see Fairfield (2010).

[113]Church et al. (2009).

[114]As reported by Severson (2010).

[115]Church et al. (2009).

[116]To date, researchers have been able to expose obese mice to cold treatments for just a few days and then burn off half of their white fat even while the mice ate 50 percent more than usual. The research could lead to curbs in childhood weight problems simply by turning down school thermostats to, say, 65, if not below. A hidden obstacle to this diet regiment of cold treatments is that people could compensate for the fat burned in body temperature control by simply eating more and maybe exercising less (as reported by Wang [2010], citing Arany et al. 2008).

[117]As reported by Wells (2010), citing the work of John P. Porcari, et al. in *Medicine & Science in Sports and Exercise* (2007).

[118]In the first edition of *The Joy of Cooking* that appeared in 1936, the average calories per serving for all of the menus was a modest 268. By the 2006 edition, the recommended portion sizes had increased and average calories per serving had increased by 43 percent, to 384, with the big jump in calories coming between the 1997 and 2006 editions (Stein [2009]).

[119]Wansink and Wansink (2010).

[120]Ibid.

[121]In the 1950s, the average dinner plate in the United States was nine inches in diameter. Today, it is thirteen inches, a doubling in the plate surface area in just a half century. But we still can't be certain whether the greater portion sizes are driving the growth in plates, or vice versa. I suspect that plate and portion sizes are, literally, "feeding" growth in the other, a finding that has led nutritionists to recommend a novel diet strategy: throw out your large plates and replace them with the average-size plates of the 1950s, the so-called "9-Inch Diet" (Bogusky and Porter [2008] and Wansink [2006]).

[122]As reported by Alderman (2011).

Chapter 3

[1]As reported by Stelter (2011).

[2]Andersen et al. (1998) and Grohol (2010).

[3]The calories, fat grams, prices for McDonald's menu items were found December 2, 2010 at http://nutrition.mcdonalds.com/nutritionexchange/nutritionfacts.pdf. The calories, fat grams, prices for Chili's menu items were found December 2, 2010 at http://www.calories-nutrition.buddyslim.com/chiles-southern-smoke-house-bacon-big-mouth-burger/.

[4]Islands is a sit-down restaurant chain that provides "casual dining" in Southern California and several southwestern states. The calorie data and prices for the fries and other menu items were obtained from the menu of a restaurant in Orange County, California, on January 1, 2010.

[5]Darwin (1859).

[6]Gregor Mendel, an obscure central European monk, was the first person to get the genetic transmission process correct—offspring did not blend the traits of their parents, but rather took on their parents' dominant traits – in an 1866 publication (seven years after the publication of the *Origins of the Species*). Then, Mendel's hypothesis faded from scholarly notice until the turn of the twentieth century. Darwin believed in "pangenesis," a wrongheaded view of the transmission process that was founded on the belief that "particles" in our bodies, which find their way into reproductive cells, are affected by what people do during their lifetimes. (See the report from the Institute for Science and Society, April 15, 2009, as accessed on December 3, 2010 from http://www.i-sis.org.uk/DarwinsPangenesis.php.)

[7]Darwin (1859, pp. 41–47, 59).

[8]Darwin (1859, Chap. 3). In Darwin's words,

> All that we can do, is to keep steadily in mind that each organism is striving to increase in a geometrical ratio; that each at some period of its life, during some season of the year, during each generation or at intervals, has to struggle for life and to suffer great destruction. When we reflect on this struggle, we may console ourselves with the full belief, that the war of nature is not incessant, that no fear is felt, that death is generally prompt, and the vigorous, the healthy, and the happy survive and multiply. (Darwin 1859, p. 87, end of Chap. 3)

[9]In the words of modern followers in evolutionary psychology, a species can have a "new design feature," such as a more sensitive retina:

> [T]he new design feature causes individuals who have it to produce more offspring, on average, than individuals who have alternative designs. If offspring can inherit the new design feature from their parents, then it will increase in frequency in the population. Individuals who have the new design feature will tend to have more offspring than those who lack it. . . Eventually, the more sensitive retina . . . will become universal in that species, typically found in every member of it. (Cosmides et al. 1992, p. 9)

[10]Over evolutionary time, there were, no doubt, some variations in finches along the development track with genetically grounded design features that were ill-adapted for survival and reproduction (for example, perhaps a second beak or just no beak). These varieties died out simply because of their inability to survive and procreate as well as their better (not perfectly) adapted finch "cousins."

[11]In his review of the manuscript for this book, Lorens Helmchen cautioned, "Given the very low levels of mortality from infancy all the way through the end of one's reproductive age, and the fact that sexual attractiveness no longer necessarily translates into reproduction, the speed of selection may be *slowing*. Put differently, in rich countries no one really dies nowadays before he or she has had a chance to reproduce and no one really reproduces even if (or especially if) he or she is considered good mating material. Thus, Darwin's 'evolutionary knife,' which only spared the fittest in the past, may be losing its edge," from personal correspondence with Helmchen, October 4, 2010.

[12]See Miller (2001).

[13]Of course, along the evolutionary path of peacock development, it is possible that some peacocks developed tails even more flamboyant than what we see today, but they could have quickly died out because their tails made them easier prey. In this way, evolution can optimize—has optimized, as suggested—peacock tail sizes, and every other characteristic in all other species as well, or so evolutionary biologists might theorize to good effect.

[14]Some evolutionary biologists worry that natural selection can't fully explain the size of the human brain today because there is no transparent reason for protohumans living hundreds of thousands of years ago, or their progenitors, to have needed a brain large enough to (eventually) develop calculus, conceive of black holes, not to mention the (much less demanding) task of writing a book on the economics of people's weight problems. Evolutionary biologists speculate that the large modern human brain can be chalked up to the fact that cleverness could have become a sexual attractor, enabling males to gain greater access to females (who find the wit and humor of males attractive, if not seductive, to this day, according to multicultural and multiethnic surveys). Maybe females' selection criterion was fairly straightforward: It's better to have a smarter mate than a dumber one, everything else (looks, speed, size, fertility, etc.) being equal. Or, perhaps the explanation is simpler: Both males and females were dumb enough to choose mates they thought were smarter (not realizing the added energy requirement of larger brains).

[15]Ruff et al. (1997).

[16]Cochran and Harpending (2009, p. 1).

[17]Ibid. (p. ix).

[18]In evolutionary theory, the human physique can be expected to adapt, eventually, to the environment and technology, as Cochran and Harpending (2009) have argued and documented, citing many other scholarly sources:

- When our ancestors of 100,000 years ago killed their prey in close combat with heavy spears, they needed stocky bodies (as Neanderthals had) and a lot of fuel to power them.

- When throwable spears and bows and arrows were developed, stocky bodies gave way to the thinner and taller bodies of Homo sapiens. With the development of fire for food preparation perhaps a half million years ago, the larger teeth of early humans, which were needed for grinding raw meats, gave way to smaller ones, perhaps because they required less energy. With the development of fire, early humans needed to use up less energy in breaking down foods in their digestion track, which freed up more energy for growing and maintaining a larger brain.
- The skeletal record reveals that human jaws have shrunk while our leg and arm bones have become longer and less dense and the protruding brow has almost vanished (aside for the aborigines of Australia).
- Dogs were domesticated from wolves about 15,000 years ago. The great variety of modern dogs suggest that, at least with human intervention, animal body size and styles and mental capacities can change dramatically in short order, especially when it is recognized that most dog breeds were no more than a thousand years in the making, and often in far less time. By breeding for tameness, a Russian scientist developed a domestic fox in just forty years! Border collies are clearly able to pick up commands far more quickly than, say, basset hounds.
- Teosite, a wild grass with seed, evolved with human encouragement, into corn in no more than 7,000 years.
- With food sources limited on isolated islands, elephants evolved from the largest animals on the plains of Africa to a little over three feet tall in just 5,000 years.
- Clearly, Scandinavians today would hardly be confused with members of African tribes, mainly because of their different skin coloring, with the lighter skin being an adaptation to the reduced direct sunlight in northern regions compared with equatorial Africa and the need to draw in vitamin D through the skin from sunlight.
- Modern humans, who arrived in northern Europe 40,000 to 50,000 years ago, replaced the Neanderthals, perhaps because of modern humans' superior hunting technology and skills and the inclination to trade at long distances. These advantages were amplified by modern humans' greater language skills, developed over the millennia through improvements in their larynx, perhaps attributable to selective (sexual) pressures for language, which had survival and procreation advantages.
- The development of agriculture 10,000 years ago resulted in a greater consumption of grains among humans and a reduced consumption of meats, which led to a protein deficiency in humans' diets. The protein-deficient diets led to an increase in tooth decay and anemia and a five-inch shrinkage in the average height of humans from about six feet when humans gave up hunting and gathering to about five feet 7,200 years ago. The average height for males has since recovered to about five feet ten today.
- Human tolerance for lactose (or milk) long ago shut down with the weaning of babies off breast milk. But with the development of agriculture and the vitamin deficiencies inherent in the shift from hunter-gatherer to agricultural diets,

humans developed, within the last 8,000 years, a more long-lasting lactose tolerance, which increased their intake of nutrients, especially of vitamin D.

- Human brain sizes for all populations could have decreased by 10 percent over the last 20,000 years (but only as evident in the decline in the size of the cranial volume, as revealed by the fossil record). The decrease could be attributed to the fact that farming was less mentally challenging than hunting and gathering (with all the attendant dangers of humans being prey as well as predators and not having steady and reliable sources of food) and because of people's submission to the growth in ruling authorities (which came with agriculture and the need to protect property rights to land and stored crops). For that matter, the cranial capacity, especially in the frontal lobe, among people who died from the Black Plague six to seven centuries ago, may have declined by 15 percent over the following two centuries (as evident in the comparative size of the cranial volume of the crew of a sunken ship in the mid-1500s).

- The scientific revolution that began in the 1600s could have changed the pressures from sexual selection, as brains replaced brawn in earning incomes, which could have speeded up the spread of "bright genes," which could have fed the development of new technologies and more varied employment of old technologies and which have had feedback effects on sexual selection.

[19]Stephen Jay Gould, as quoted by Cochran and Harpending (2009, p. 1). Cognitive scientist Steven Pinker, a prominent steady stater, elaborates on the constraints that human's evolutionary history has imposed on modern human's mental faculties:

> [Natural and sexual] selection operates over thousands of generations. For ninety-nine percent of human existence, people lived as foragers in small nomadic bands. Our brains are adapted to that long-vanished way of life, not to the brand-new agricultural and industrial civilizations. They are not wired to cope with anonymous crowds, schooling, written language, government, police, courts, armies, modern medicine, formal social institutions, high technology, and other newcomers to the human experience. . . Had the Pleistocene savanna contained trees bearing birth-control pills, we might have evolved to find them as terrifying as venomous spiders. (Pinker [1997, p. 42])

Evolutionary psychologists Leda Cosmides, John Tooby, and Jerome Barkow (as well as most other evolutionary psychologists and evolutionary biologists who accept the steady-state perspective) maintain that because of evolutionary forces, "there is a universal human nature, but that this nature exists primarily at the level of evolved psychological mechanisms, not of expressed cultural behaviors; . . . that these evolved psychological mechanisms are adaptations, constructed by natural selection over evolutionary [or over an extremely long period of] time; . . . that the evolved structure of the human mind is adapted to the way of life of Pleistocene hunter-gatherers, not necessarily to our modern circumstances" Cosmides et al. (1992, p. 5). The authors then add:

> [O]ur ancestors spent the last two million years as Pleistocene hunter-gatherers, and, of course, several hundred thousand years before that as one kind of forager or another. These relative spans are important because they establish which set of environments and conditions defined the adaptive problems the mind was shaped to cope with: Pleistocene

conditions, rather than modern conditions. . . Moreover, the available evidence strongly supports this view of a single, universal panhuman design, stemming from our long-enduring existence as hunter-gatherers (Cosmides et al. 1992, p. 5, who cite Tooby and Cosmides 1990a, b).

[20]Levitan (2006).

[21]Even had we been programmed mentally to deal with the growing array of complex particular conditions over eons, then surely the programs would have gone lame long ago as human's physical environments, not just humans themselves, continued to evolve. Any preprogrammed brain would likely have become obsolete, at least over evolutionary time, as did the DOS operating system for personal computers with ever-evolving technology. Ironically, had the human brain developed to use all its neuronal capacities to register only preprogrammed responses to varied conditions, we would *not* likely have the mental capacities we have today. A preprogrammed brain would not have allowed humans to be sufficiently adaptive to cope with myriad evolving physical and social conditions. Trapped by their preprogrammed responses to conditions, our human ancestors would have likely died out as sea levels ebbed and flowed and ice ages came and went. Being able to make real choices, and go with changing circumstances, has had (seemingly) survival value for humans and any number of other species, which is justification enough for economists' presumption that people make real choices. Having the adaptive capacity to make meaningful choices will be important later in the book when we begin to discuss solutions to modern people's weight problems.

[22]"Lucy" is the name the discovering paleoanthropologists Donald Johanson and Tom Gray gave to a fossilized partial skeleton of a species of early hominid, *Australopithecus afarensis*, which they dated as 3.2 million years old. Lucy, whose age at death has been estimated at twenty-five and who was three feet six inches tall, is considered to be an ancestor of modern *Homo sapiens*, in the main because she is believed to have walked upright. Lucy skeleton's was found in the Hadar region of Ethiopia in 1974. (To see the 40 percent of Lucy's skeleton that was found, go to http://www.talkorigins.org/faqs/homs/lucy.html.)

[23]Blaxter (1989) and Schmidt-Nielsen (1994).

[24]Kuzawa (1998).

[25]Flegal et al. (2005).

[26]Power (2004), Sterling and Eyer (1988), Rossner (2002), and Schulkin (2003).

[27]With brain sizes of various hominid species documented on http://www. talkorigins.org/faqs/homs/species.html, as accessed on March 25, 2010.

[28]For a review of the behavioral economic research on people's ability to discount the future appropriately, see Frederick et al. (2002).

[29]See Power and Schulkin (2009) who cite a host of other studies grounded in the argument being made here: Peters et al. (2002), Chakravarthy and Booth (2004), O'Keefe and Cordain (2004), Prentice et al. (2005).

[30]This may be true partially because their added pounds became markers for fertility, which evolutionary biologists believe was the case through the nineteenth century.

[31]Eaton and Eaton (2003).

[32]Clark (2007).

[33]With food coming in large "packages"—the size of a wildebeest, bison or giraffe—sharing was not necessarily a solely selfless enterprise. No one could eat a whole wildebeest, so sharing food with others had a zero cost. And, besides, *mutual* sharing could smooth out the differing food intakes and number of hunts among tribe members over time. No wonder people today have natural impulses to share and to follow the rule of tit-for-tat—such behavior enabled people to survive and procreate with greater frequency than those who followed other rules (a theme developed by Rubin [2002] with references to many scholarly sources).

[34]Power and Schulkin (2009, p. 38), citing a consensus statement on the causes of childhood obesity, reported in Speiser et al. (2005). "Power and Schulkin observe," "Most human obesity probably reflects complex interactions between genetic, environmental, and social factors often mediated through non-genetically derived changes in metabolism" (pp. 38–39).

[35]See, for example, Stunkard (1959) and Fairburn et al. (1998).

Chapter 4

[1]Marshall (1890, ¶ I.II.1).

[2]James Buchanan applied elemental economic principles to the political process, with an emphasis on how political institutions affect the economic (and other) policies politicians select. If economists assume that people are largely self-interested in markets and their private affairs, then there is no reason to believe that they are any less self-interested when they move into political circles. For example, with co-author Gordon Tullock, Buchanan argued that narrow special interest groups have undue political influence in electoral politics because they tend to be relatively small groups whose members have concentrated economic incentives to press for government expenditures from which they gain. The costs of these government expenditures, on the other hand, are imposed over a much more diffused public that has few personal incentives to even become informed on the policy agendas of

special interests, much less to contribute to political campaigns to defeat special-interest legislative drives. Thus, Buchanan and Tullock's lines of argument help to explain how fewer than three hundred South Carolina dairy farmers have pressed the state legislatures to impose restrictions on milk production that has caused the three million South Carolina consumers (whose incomes were often much lower than the incomes of the dairymen) to pay some of the higher milk prices in the country (Buchanan and Tullock [1962]). Buchanan had a healthy skepticism over the expressed noble intentions of politicians to "do good" for the rest of us. He and others carried with them a nagging question in the back (no, the front) of their minds: "What's in it for him?" Similarly, all the talk about an "obesity crisis" and "obesity epidemic" coming from obesity researchers and policy proponents (especially when they want to tax and control what people eat and drink) would cause him to worry that something else could be afoot. We might also worry today that the "antifat warriors" could be grossly exaggerating the country's weight problem with free use of hyperbolic labels, "crisis" and "epidemic" because they have a stake in the policy outcomes (Campos [2004] and Oliver [2006]). Such words could very well be strategically used to make a hidden policy agenda not necessarily motivated by concern for heavy people. Yes, economists can be a suspicious and cynical lot.

Gary Becker was more radical, applying economic principles not only to politics but also to a host of topics that may seem to have no economic foundation at all: discrimination, education, suicide, drug addiction, marriage and divorce, and crime ... and the list goes on (See Becker 1965, 1971a, 1971b, 1978, 1993, 1994, 1996, 1997). If people are inclined to maximize their well-being when they are buying cars and chewing gum, he reasoned, why would they be any less so inclined when it comes to committing robberies, buying street drugs, or preparing meals at home? In Becker's view, crime can be analyzed as an industry in which criminals seek to maximize their returns on their investments. They incur risks of being caught, prosecuted, and imprisoned, but all business entrepreneurs must suffer risks, albeit of a different sort. Why are people addicted to street drugs? Becker suggests that many are rationally addicted, but only in the sense that they weigh the costs and benefits (or gains and pains) of a lifetime of addiction *before* they take their first hit. He reasons that people who are depressed or who expect their lives to be cut short have stronger reasons to become drug addicted than others with more opportunistic life outlooks (see, for example, Becker [1978]).

[3]McKenzie and Tullock (1976, with five subsequent editions).

[4]See Levitt and Dubner (2005 and 2009).

[5]Levitt and Dubner (2009, p. 215), citing Lakshminarayanan et al. (2008).

[6]Gumert (2007).

[7]See two books in which my coauthors and I have developed at some length the economic way of thinking with many theoretical complexities: McKenzie and Lee (2010) and McKenzie and Tullock (2011).

[8]Okay, I grant you that many people may not seek their own self-improvement with the precision economists assume, and they may not stand ready to adjust readily to price changes, but so long as some people seek to do the best they can, the price change can have the directional effect economists expect. Also, I grant you that at the time the price of a good goes up or down, a lot of things can be changing (buyer preferences and weather, for example). But have no fear, the law of demand can still hold with only a minor modification. No matter what else changes, a reduction in the relative price of the good can still be expected to lead to more of the good being purchased *than would otherwise be the case without the price reduction.* When a local Ben & Jerry's lowers the price of its ice cream, the weather might turn cold, but we would still expect Ben & Jerry's to sell more ice cream under the cold conditions *than it would have sold if the store had not lowered its prices.*

[9]Lower food prices can, when demand is "elastic," result in lower total expenditures on food, which means more income consumers can use to buy other goods and services.

[10]Lakdawalla and Philipson (2002).

[11]Philipson and Posner (2003) also found that improvements in food-production technologies lowered the price of food and increased food consumption to boost the country's average weight and obesity rate.

[12]Goldman et al. (2010).

[13]HEALTHY Study Group and Foster (2010).

[14]The obesity rate for the group given instruction declined 18 percent (to 24.6 percent), and the control group's obesity rate declined 11–12 percent (to 26.6 percent), but, again, the researchers did not find the difference to be statistically significant, meaning that the difference in the drops could have occurred by chance (HEALTHY Study Group and Foster [2010]).

[15]As reported by Rabin (2010a).

[16]Fields (2004).

[17]Alson et al. (2007).

[18]As reported by the editors of the *Wall Street Journal* (January 22, 2011).

[19]As reported by Smith and Elliott (2008).

[20]Alson et al. (2007).

[21]As reported by MacFarquhar (February 4, 2011).

[22]Lakdawalla and Philipson (2002).

[23]Gelbach, Klick, and Stratmann (2007).

[24]Ibid.

[25]Powell et al. (2007).

[26]Americans average daily calorie intake was 2,157 in 2006, up from 1,826 in 1978 (as reported by Adamy [2010]).

[27]Helmchen and Henderson (2004).

[28]Costa and Steckel (1997), as cited by Cutler et al. (2003, Figure 1).

[29]Fogel (1994).

[30]As obtained from the U.S. Census Bureau, as reported in the online U.S. Statistical Abstract: 2010, accessed May 18, 2010, from http://www.cdc.gov/ nchs/data/nvsr/nvsr56/nvsr56_09.pdf and http://www.census.gov/compendia/ statab/cats/births_deaths_marriages_divorces/life_expectancy.html.

[31]Lakdawalla and Philipson have found that aging can add three to four points to people's average BMI and the percentage of cohorts who are obese can increase four or more times, but some of the weight gain with age can be attributed to people moving into less strenuous jobs (2002).

[32]As obtained from the U.S. Census Bureau, as reported in the online U.S. Statistical Abstract: 2010, accessed May 18, 2010, from http://www.cdc.gov/ nchs/data/nvsr/nvsr56/nvsr56_09.pdf and http://www.census.gov/compendia/ statab/cats/births_deaths_marriages_divorces/life_expectancy.html.

[33]Cutler et al. (2003), citing National Health and Nutrition Examinations Surveys I and III (1978 and 1996).

[34]As reported for *The New York Times* by Bakalar (2010).

[35]Ruhm (2009).

[36]As reported in "The recession's negative impact on health" by DietsinReview. com, accessed June 3, 2010, http://www.dietsinreview.com/diet_column/05/the-recessions-negative-impact-on-our-health/.

[37]As reported for *The New York Times* by Schultz (2010). According to the Zagat Survey, the Great Recession and sluggish recovery lead Americans to reduce the average number of meals eaten out of the home per week from 3.3 in 2007 to 3.1 in 2010. Also, in 2007, survey respondents reported that 47 percent of meals were eaten in restaurants in 2010, down from 53 percent in 2007. Nearly two-fifths of Americans surveyed also reported becoming more sensitive to the prices of restaurant meals. A third reported eating at cheaper places, and up to a fifth reported cutting back on appetizers and desserts. Zagat found that the increase in price of restaurant meals between 2007 and 2010 was three-quarters of the increase in the CPI (as reported by Zagat and Zagat, 2010).

[38]Dave and Kelly (2010).

[39]As reported for *The New York Times* by Foley (2010c).

[40]See the chart for the real price of gasoline for the 1918–2009 period at http://www.inflationdata.com/inflation/inflation_rate/Gasoline_Inflation.asp.

[41]Courtemanche (2010).

[42]Lakdawalla and Philipson (2002) found from analyzing self-reported individual data for the period 1981–1998 that women who work fourteen years at the least physically demanding jobs can expect to have BMIs 3.5 points higher BMIs than women in the most physically demanding jobs. And the added weight on women in sedentary jobs does not appear to be a consequence of heavy women choosing sedentary jobs. They seem to gain weight in their jobs because of the limited physical demands. See also Philipson (2001).

[43]Cutler et al. (2003).

[44]As reported by Adamy (2010).

[45]Putnam (1999) and Young and Nestle (2002).

[46]Courtemanche (2010).

[47]Flegal et al. (2010) as reported by Belluck (2010).

[48]With the added weight gain and upward pressure on gas prices, the pump price of gas could be rising or falling over time. The weight gain could keep the gas price from falling as much as it would have otherwise, or it could cause the gas price to rise by more than it otherwise would have.

[49]Jacobson and McLay (2006).

[50]In spite of Courtemanche's argument having intuitive appeal, we must remain somewhat cautious in accepting his analysis and conclusions as the last word on the tie between gas prices and weight gain, mainly because gas prices are only a small portion of *total travel costs* by car, and weight gain could be more affected by total travel costs than gas prices per se. This is the case because when Congress mandated for the first time in 1975 that automobile manufacturers meet corporate fuel economy standards, it *could* have affected the country's weight—but either up or down. In 1978, automobile companies' fleet of cars (with light pick-up trucks exempted) had to get a minimum average of 18 miles per gallon. By 2010, the minimum average had to be 27.5 miles per gallon. In 2007, the minimum corporate average fuel economy was set to rise to 30.2 miles per gallon in 2011 (with light trucks to be counted in the average for the first time), with the prospects of the standard rising to the mid-30s by 2020. While the implied reduction in the gas cost of traveling was lowered by the precipitous fall in the price of gas in the 1980s and 1990s (from a temporary peak in the early 1970s) and by the continuing hike in the fuel economy standard, the overall per-mile cost of traveling by car could have risen, because of the higher production cost of the cars themselves inspired by the progressively higher fuel economy standard. The gas cost of travel is only about 10 percent of the total cost of traveling a mile. This overall cost could have fallen, but

then again it could have increased, tempering people's inclination to drive places and to gain weight (if Courtemanche's econometrics are to be believed). Similarly, the increases in federal and state real gas taxes and tighter emission controls could also have, again, tempered somewhat people's weight gain. We can't be sure at this point. There is a good reason to fear that the cost per travel mile went up because of the fuel economy standards. If automobile manufacturers could have achieved the higher mileage standards at a lower car cost, which would have further lowered the cost of car travel per mile, then it seems that the fuel economy standards would not have been needed (other than for environmental reasons); the manufacturers would have achieved higher fuel economies without government direction.

[51]Bradford et al. (2005).

[52]See Bergsten (2005).

[53]As determined by data from the Bureau of Economic Analysis, U.S. Department of Commerce, at http://bea.gov/, as accessed on December 3, 2010.

[54]For a quick review of the spread of economic freedoms country by country over the last half of the twentieth century, see Sumner (2010). Sumner, among a growing number of "freedom researchers," also found a decisively positive relationship between the "index of economic freedom," devised by the Heritage Foundation, and real per capital income.

[55]As reported by Alesci (2010).

[56]Cutler et al. (2003).

[57]Powell et al. (2007).

[58]Rashad et al. (2005) and Raynor and Epstein (2001). On the increase in fat consumption in the United States, see Ippolito and Mathios (1995); and Frazao (1999).

[59]Nielsen and Popkin (2003).

[60]Raynor and Epstein (2001) have found that the growth in the variety of readily available foods over the last several decades has contributed to the growth in weight. Ewing et al. (2003) have found that the greater the conduciveness of urban areas to exercise, the lower the obesity rate. Other researchers have found that greater density of fast-food restaurants has led people to increase the consumption of more and fattier foods (French et al. 2000; Public Health Service 2001).

[61]These researchers estimate that with a 100 percent increase in the density of restaurants, the average BMI for adult Americans would rise by nearly 10 percent (assuming a starting average BMI of 25) (Rashad et al. [2005]).

[62]Chou et al. (2004).

[63]Three economists found that calories consumed at dinnertime actual decreased slightly between the mid-1970s and the mid-1990s, using U.S. Department of

Agriculture surveys of people who kept diaries and who self-reported the various foods they consumed (a data collection method that probably introduces the possibility of underreporting of food intake) (Cutler et al. [2003]).

[64]Ibid.

[65]The number of daily meals consumed averaged 3.86 during 1977–1978, as reported by the survey respondents. Daily meals averaged a reported 4.44 in 1994–1996. (ibid.).

[66]Ibid. Young and Nestle (2002) have argued that weight gain has been significantly affected by the growth in portion sizes.

[67]Block et al. (2004), citing Schlosser (2001).

[68]Block et al. (2004), citing Lin and Frazao (1999).

[69]Powell et al. (2007).

[70]In a study of the density of fast-food restaurants in New Orleans, predominantly white neighborhoods had 1.5 fast-food restaurants per square mile, whereas predominantly black neighborhoods had 2.4 fast-food restaurants per square mile (Block et al. [2004]).

[71]Maddock (2004) and Fuzhong et al. (2009).

[72]Cash et al. (2007).

[73]Cutler et al. (2003, Table 4).

[74]Guthrie et al. (2002). Similar results in the increased calories consumed by age groups were found by Nielsen et al. (2002).

[75]Cutler et al. (2003, Table 4).

[76]For reviews of the vast minimum-wage literature, see Brown (1988) and Brown et al. (1982).

[77]Editors, *The New York Times* (1987).

[78]Liu et al. (2007).

[79]Meltzer and Chen (2009).

[80]Meltzer and Chen (2009).

[81]The study deduced that the drop in the real minimum wage in the 1984–2006 period increased the BMI of those 10 percent of Americans with the highest BMIs by 0.13 (Meltzer and Chen [2009]).

[82]Salisbury et al. (2011).

[83]The history of the increases in the nominal federal minimum wage was available (in May 2010) on the Labor Law Center's Web page: http://www.laborlawcenter.com/t-federal-minimum-wage.aspx.

[84]Researchers have found that a 10 percent increase in the price of fast foods leads to a 0.4 percent decrease in the average BMI, a nearly 6 percent decrease in the probability of people being overweight, partially because the 10 percent increase in the prices of fast-food meals leads to a 3 percent increase in the frequency of consumption of fruits and vegetables (Powell et al. [2007])

[85]As accessed May 12, 2010, http://www.bls.gov/opub/ted/2000/feb/wk3/art03. htm.

[86]As reported by Gorski (2010) and Williams (2010).

[87]However, women working at least forty hours a week had median annual earnings that were 87 percent of men's median annual earnings. Cornell University economists have found that after adjusting for such labor-market factors as education, experience, occupation, the "gender pay [median earnings] gap" had narrowed to nine percentage points in 1998. The gender wage gap varies across fields from nearly 93 percent for computer programmers to under 61 percent for physicians (as reported in the *Wall Street Journal* by Bialik [2010]). See also Institute for Women's Policy Research (2010) for a different, more women-friendly view of the wage gap. For my own take on why women around the world, across all cultures and ethnic groups, tend to earn less than men (the pay gap today is partially explained by evolutionary forces long ago), see McKenzie (2008b, Chap. 12).

[88]Morrissey et al. (2011).

[89]Ibid. and Cutler et al. (2003).

[90]Ibid.

[91]Among African-American mothers, only 58 percent start out breastfeeding, with only 28 percent breastfeeding after six months and then with only 8 percent of babies exclusively breastfed after six months (as reported by the Office of the Surgeon General, January 20, 2011, as accessed January 28, 2011, http://www. surgeongeneral.gov/topics/breastfeeding/factsheet.html.

[92]Gillman et al. (2006); Grummer-Strawn and Mei (2004); Owen et al. (2005); and Toschke et al. (2007).

[93]Dewy (2006) and Nommsen-Rivers and Dewey (2009).

[94]Nommsen-Rivers and Dewey (2009).

[95]Kin and Peterson (2008); Benjamin et al. (2009); and Nommsen-Rivers and Dewey (2009). One caution to keep in mind is that day-care children could be a biased sample, given that they could be from homes dominated by unhealthy and fattening diets.

[96]Rowswell et al. (2008).

[97]Nommsen-Rivers and Dewey (2009) report that the median weight loss just after birth of breastfed babies is 6.6 percent compared with 3.5 percent of bottle-fed

babies. On average, breastfed babies regain their birth weight in 8.3 days compared with 6.5 days among bottle-fed babies, with some of the difference attributable to the lower weight loss among the bottle-fed infants.

[98]Nommsen-Rivers and Dewey (2009).

[99]Dewey (2006).

[100]Kin and Peterson (2008); Benjamin et al. (2009).

[101]Weimer (2001).

[102]Weimer (2001).

[103]Arizona Department of Health Services (2005) and as reported by the Office of the Surgeon General, January 20, 2011, as accessed January 28, 2011, http://www.surgeongeneral.gov/topics/breastfeeding/factsheet.html.

[104]Halfon and Lu (2010).

[105]Ludwig and Currie (2010).

[106]Ibid., online abstract.

[107]Ludwig and Currie (2010).

[108]Halfon and Lu (2010).

[109]Rosenow (2010).

[110]Cawley (1999); Naik and Moore (1996); and Schlosser (2001).

[111]Campaign for Tobacco-Free Kids (2010b).

[112]Rashad et al. (2005).

[113]Viscusi (1994).

[114]*Santa Monica Daily Press* (2010). The latest smoking ban takes effect, September 10, as accessed September 11, 2010, http://www.smdp.com/Articles-c-2010-09-08-70276.113116_Latest_smoking_ban_takes_effect_today.html.

[115]Becker and Murphy (1988) and Becker et al. (1994).

[116]Chou et al. (2004).

[117]Klick and Stratmann (2007).

[118]Peltzman (1975).

[119]Carpenter and Stehr (2009).

[120]Cutler et al. (2003).

[121]Ibid. (p. 13 in NBER version)

[122]Ibid. (p. 14 in NBER).

[123]Subar et al. (1998).

[124]As reported by Critser (2003) in reviewing a book by Pollan (2003).

[125]Cutler, Glaeser, and Shapiro found the correlation between the amount of commercial preparation of foods and their increased consumption to be 0.68 (Cutler et al. [2003, Figure 7]).

[126]Stewart (2006).

[127]Cutler, Glaeser, and Shapiro found that the correlation between the degree of branding of food products and calories consumed to 0.51. (Cutler et al. [2003, Figure 8]).

[128]The researchers found that a half hour saving in food preparation time is associated with a 0.5 point increase in people's BMI (Cutler et al. [2003, Figures 9 and 10]).

[129]Cutler et al. (2003, Table 7 and Figure 13).

[130]Researchers have found that one standard deviation in price controls is associated with close to a four percentage point decrease in the obesity rate (Cutler et al. [2003]).

[131]By "rational," economists generally mean three things: 1) people know, more or less, what they want; 2) they are able to order their wants from most preferred to least preferred, and 3) they are able to choose consistently among the goods in their ordering to maximize their well-being, and they individually determine their well-being.

[132]University of Chicago economist Richard Thaler and Harvard University law professor Cass Sunstein, who have been major players in the emergence of "behavioral economics," note in their widely read book *Nudge*, "If you look at economics textbooks, you will learn that homo economicus can think like Albert Einstein, store as much memory as IBM's Big Blue, and exercise the willpower of Mahatma Gandhi," which are hardly characteristics of real living human beings who can't do simple math problems (even with hand calculators), who have memory lapses (as well as false and distorted memories), get drunk, and become obese to their own regret (2008, pp. 6–7).

[133]Ariely (2008, p. xxi).

[134]See books by Wansink (2006), Thaler and Sunstein (2008), Ariely (2008), Marcus (2008), and Chabris and Simons (2010).

[135]I have countered the criticisms of economists' use of "rationality" in their economic models in a recent book. See McKenzie (2010a).

[136]See my *Predictably Rational?* (2010).

Chapter 5

[1] And there is a good economic reason why heavy people tend to dominate the clientele of all-you-can-eat restaurants rather than of restaurants that charge by the item. Heavy eaters tend to be attracted to the all-you-can-eat restaurants to eat all they can, with their excess eating driving up the heavy eaters' weights and the restaurants costs. The resulting higher prices for the all-you-can eat buffets drive out people who seek to control their weights by controlling their eating.

[2] Kemper et al. (1994); Stevens and Keil (1994); Powell and Kahn (1995); Abrams et al. (1993); Akan and Grilo (1995); Fitzgibbon et al. (2000); Kumanyika and Guilford-Davenport (1993); Williamson et al. (2000).

[3] Sharma et al. (2009).

[4] Centers for Disease Control and Prevention (2010b).

[5] Christakis and Fowler (2007) and Salvy et al. (2009). Some caution needs to be taken here in accepting these researchers' conclusion that obese friends and family members *cause* others around them to become heavier (as if fat is a communicable disease). These researchers may have only found an association. As health economist Lorens Helmchen, whom I've cited in earlier chapters, has reminded me in his review of the book manuscript, the found correlation could be the result of heavy people being exposed to the same obesogenic factors or are being attracted to other fat people to form clusters.

[6] Salvy et al. (2009).

[7] Puhl and Heuer (2009) and Brownell and Puhl (2001 and 2003).

[8] For a formal economic model of self-limiting weight gain, see Liu et al. (2007).

[9] Flegal et al. (2005).

[10] Becker et al. (1994).

[11] To make matters worse in obesity research, many 100–1000 of subjects per group are necessary to derive statistical power as to which gene variants are at work in effecting obesity. The best new way to study these complex behaviors is through "imaging genetics," which combines imaging, genetics, and physiological measures and where a much lower number of subjects is needed to derive scientific and clinical answers as to the exact causes of and treatments for obesity (Levin [2007]).

[12] As reported in the *Wall Street Journal* by Beck (2010a) on a study presented at the International Conference on Obesity held in Stockholm in mid-July 2010 with Susan Carnell the lead investigator on the study (the actual study was not available at this writing).

[13] As reported in the *Wall Street Journal* by Beck (2010b), citing an unidentified research study with Dana Small the lead investigator.

[14] De Araujo et. al (2008).

[15] As reported in the *Wall Street Journal* by Beck (2010a), citing a research study not found at this writing.

[16] As reported in Beck (2010), citing an unidentified research study.

[17] Knutson and Bossaerts (2007).

[18] Becker and Murphy (1988).

[19] Even if people are not as rational in discounting costs and benefits as the economic way of thinking might suggest, we can at least *think* about their being so, because intuition tells us that people often do at least roughly consider weighing costs against benefits, however imperfectly they might account for time and risk. As argued in Chap. 4, by using economic principles to *think* about addiction, we may deduce insights (and predictions) that could be otherwise missed and that are supported by empirical tests. I do not mean to suggest that the economic way of thinking will tell us all there is to know, or just want to know, about the problems of addiction and weight gain. I do cite the work of others throughout this book who assess addiction and weight gain from a number of perspectives, and we have seen how evolutionary biology and neurobiology offer ways of understanding people's decision making. Also, behavioral economists and psychologists are right that much understanding about human behavior can be gained through laboratory assessments of how people make their decisions. I take up these issues at considerable length and detail in another book (McKenzie [2010a]).

[20] Gelbach, Klick, and Stratmann (2007).

[21] See, for example, Twenge (2007).

[22] See the chart of the personal saving rate as a percentage of disposable income, which the Bureau of Economic Research in the U.S. Department of Commerce has computed from the 1930s to the present, accessed September 23, 2010, http://www.bea.gov/scb/pdf/2007/02%20February/0207_saving.pdf.

[23] See the chart of household liabilities-to-income ratio computed by the St. Louis Federal Reserve Bank, as accessed September 23, 2010, http://research.stlouisfed.org/fred2/series/CMDEBT.

[24] For example, people may not have felt a pressing need to set aside their disposable income into savings accounts to increase their wealth, and they may have felt that they could afford to take on more debt because they were gaining wealth (through their increasing equity in their stocks and houses). Note how the saving rate actually was negative for a quarter in 2005. The real (inflation-adjusted) interest rates on savings and debt were also on the decline during the period. Perhaps Americans also took on greater debt at the falling real interest rates because

the market for loanable funds became more global and more efficient, which means that Americans could tap more easily the proclivity of people in Asian countries (most notably, China) to save a relatively high percentage of their growing real incomes. If so, we have yet another economic cause for the fattening of Americans: the growing savings of other people in distant countries.

[25]The difficult problem for economists is explaining the growth in people's discount rate. The problem hangs not on a lack of potential explanations, but an abundance of them—and the absence of relevant studies, mainly because people's discount rates are mental, or subjective, constructs. Accordingly, I have to be speculative here. It could be that Americans yielded progressively to the growth in advertisements. Perhaps, as Americans consumed more of everything, they became progressively addicted to "keeping up with the Jones" in household luxuries—and eating out and moving up the quality and quantity food chains, a line of argument that Cornell economist Robert Frank has pressed in various books. (See, for example, Frank [2010].) The point is that there should be no surprise that the decline in the savings rate in the 1980s and 1990s went hand in hand with the rise in debt—and with the rise in people's weight, with both economic series driven partially by much the same force, Americans' rising discount rate. To be sure, in suggesting that people's discount rates may have risen during the last several decades of the twentieth century, I have strayed from the science of obesity into speculation, but sometimes speculations can drive future scientific inquiries. At the very least several data series marching in the same direction are certainly suggestive of a new research agenda for weight experts, determining the extent to which people's preferences—and their discount rates—have changed. Moreover, the falling saving rate and the rising debt rate could very well have been feeding (or funding) the flow of food from farms to grocery stores and fast-food restaurants and onto people butt-based "refrigerators." I grant perceptive potential critics that the fall in people's discount rates could also be due to a host of other factors, for example, relaxation of personal bankruptcy rules, credit underwriting and rating standards; demographic changes (more divorces, longer retirement); changes in medical technology; and health insurance coverage that exposes more to medical bankruptcies.

[26]Stigler and Becker (1977).

[27]The real interest rate, according to one literature review, fell from the 8–10 percent range in the early 1980s to the 2–5 percent range in the late 1990s and then dropped in the early 2000s (see Neely and Rapach [2008]).

[28]Becker and Murphy (1988).

[29]Akerlof (1991, p. 1).

[30]In 1978, 5 percent of Americans self-identified as "chronic procrastinators." In 2006, the rate was up to 28 percent (Steel [2007]).

[31]This is a theme developed by Abrahamson and Freedman (2007).

[32] Akerlof (1991).

[33] See Suanovic and Goldfarb (2007), citing Pasman, Saris, and Westerterp-Plantenga (2007), Hill (2004), and Field et al. (2003), on the tendency of people to gain weight as they go through weight–loss/weight–gain cycles.

[34] As reported by Greviskes (2010).

[35] As quoted in a press release from the Scripps Research Institute by McKeown (2010).

[36] As quoted in a press release from the Scripps Research Institute by McKeown (2010).

[37] Suranovic and Goldfarb (2007).

[38] Ibid.

[39] Gavin et al. (2010).

[40] Wenk (2010, Chapter 1).

[41] Grohol (2010).

[42] See, for example, Markowitz et al. (2008).

[43] As reported by Suicide.org, accessed July 4, 2010, http://suicide.org/suicide-statistics.html.

[44] As reported by the National Institute for Mental Health, citing Narrow et. al (1998), Blehar and Oren (1997), and Weissman et al. (1996), accessed July 4, 2010, http://www.nimh.nih.gov/health/publications/men-and-depression/depression.shtml.

[45] As reported by Fiore (2008).

[46] The genetics and environmental interactions here are currently the most active areas of research and may offer a deeper understanding of the etiologic causes of obesity.

[47] Lisi (2010).

[48] See Ariely (2008) and Thaler and Sunstein (2008).

[49] Bhattacharya and Sood (2007).

[50] To compute the externalized costs of weight, Keller et al. (1989) used a discount rate of 5 percent, coming up with a present discounted value of the lifetime externalized cost of $1,900 for 1989. I recomputed the real dollar value of that estimate using early 2010 dollars, which raised their estimate of the externalized costs to $3,346. However, some of the so-called external cost could be actually incurred by the heavy people themselves through lower wages, a subject to which we will return in the next chapter.

[51]Cannon and Balko (2004).

[52]Bhattacharya and Sood (2007).

[53]Levy (2002) and Bednarek et al. (2006) have shown that people in sufficiently high-income countries can be expected to carry body weights that exceed their physiologically optimum body weights, as well as to be happier in general than people in lower income countries.

[54]Epel et al. (2000), Peeke and Chrousos (1995), and Stöppler and Shiel (2007).

Chapter 6

[1]The names of people and places in this story have been changed because their exact identification is not important to the larger points that can be drawn from the story.

[2]As reported by Leibovich (1997).

[3]Ibid.

[4]Ibid.

[5]Ibid.

[6]Ibid.

[7]As reported by Goodyear (1997).

[8]As reported La Ganga (1998).

[9]See the critics' cases in Campos (2004) and Oliver (2006).

[10]As estimated by the Organization for Economic Cooperation and Development (2010).

[11]The makers of Twinkies, Hostess bakery, says on its Web site that it produces 500 million Twinkies a year (http://hostesscakes.com/twinkies.asp).

[12]Jacobson and McLay (2006).

[13]The two studies were done by Shelton Jacobson and his doctoral students (Jacobson and McLay [2006] and Jacobson and King [2009]). According to a *USA Today* report, Jacobson and McLay figured in their 2006 report that the added gasoline consumption would fuel two million cars. Jacobson and King (2009) report that gasoline consumption increased by 21 percent between 2006 and 2008, and I roughly estimate that the number of cars that could be fueled for the year is 2.2 million. Courtemanche (2010) came up with a similar estimate of the growth in gasoline consumption because of increased weight.

[14]The total annual consumption of gasoline for 2008 was reported by the U.S. Energy Information Administration, accessed July 9, 2010, http://www.eia.doe.gov/ask/gasoline_faqs.asp#gas_consume_year.

[15]Morris (2007) reports that the elasticity coefficient for the demand for gasoline between 1994 and 2006 was between −0.02 and −0.04.

[16]See Tillotson (2004) for a review of the historical tie between farm subsidies, especially in increasing farm efficiency, and American weight gain.

[17]Courtmanche (2007).

[18]To calculate the increased annual expenditures on gasoline, I have assumed that gasoline consumption remains at 137 billion gallons a year, the 2008 consumption level. Thus, when the price goes from $3.00 to $3.12 a gallon, total annual expenditures on gasoline increase from $411 billion to $427 billion.

[19]Dannenberg et al. (2004).

[20]Wassener (2009).

[21]Edwards and Roberts (2009).

[22]For arguments representing the scientific consensus on global warming (which has been popularized by Vice President Al Gore in his film and book [2006]), see a report issued by the United Nations' Intergovernmental Panel on Climate Change (2007). A minority of scientists concur that global warming has been underway for at least two centuries, but strongly disagrees with the view that human activity is consequentially elevating global warming. These scientists maintain that government imposed curbs on greenhouse gases will not materially affect the global warming trend. For this minority perspective, see Singer and Avery (2007).

[23]Razay et al. (2006).

[24]As reported by *Science Daily* (2009) on a study by Raji et al. (2010), accessed on July 23, 2010 from http://www.sciencedaily.com/releases/2009/08/090825090745.htm and from http://www3.interscience.wiley.com/journal/122539667/abstract?CRETRY=1&SRETRY=0.

[25]Raji et al. (2010).

[26]Cawley and Meyerhoefer (2010).

[27]Congressional Budget Office (2010).

[28]As reported by CBS News, "Forklift gets 900-pound man from bedroom," September 19, 2007, accessed July 26, 2010, http://www.cbsnews.com/stories/2007/09/19/national/main3276151.shtml.

[29]As reported by Zezima (2008).

[30]As reported by Hoholik (2010).

[31] Go to http://www.nytimes.com/2008/04/08/health/08ambu.html (Zezima [2008]).

[32] O'Connor (2009).

[33] As reported by Hoholik (2010).

[34] As reported by Waldrop (2010).

[35] As reported by Hollingsworth (2009).

[36] As reported on April 2, 2009 in "Obese gowns for hospital patients are wider than car," at *Telegraph.co.uk*, accessed July 26, 2010, http://www.telegraph.co.uk/health/healthnews/5095112/Obese-gowns-for-hospital-patients-are-wider-than-car.html.

[37] As reported by Mariano (2008).

[38] As reported by Pembrey (2010).

[39] Schlundt et al. (2007) and as reported by the Associated Press (2008).

[40] Sauer (2010).

[41] Ibid.

[42] As reported by Clifford (2010).

[43] Ibid.

[44] As reported by Loveys (2010).

[45] As reported by Watson (2010).

[46] As reported on GoTicket.com, accessed July 27, 2010, http://www.gotickets.com/venues/ny/new_yankee_stadium.php.

[47] One design firm has determined that the average seat width in 1,200 venues increased from twenty-one to twenty-two inches over the past two decades, as reported by FoxNews.com (2010).

[48] As reported by Yoshino (2007).

[49] As reported by Copeland (2011, March 21) for *USAToday*.

[50] As reported by Today Show contributor Lisa Marsh (Marsh [2010]).

[51] The survey literature is reviewed in Puhl and Brownell (2001), Brownell and Puhl (2003), and Puhl and Heuer (2009).

[52] Puhl and Heuer (2009), citing Roehling et al. (2007).

[53] The researchers found overweight survey participants were twelve times more likely to report workplace discrimination than normal weight participants. Obese participants were thirty-seven times more likely to report work-related

discrimination, whereas severely obese were 100 times more likely. Women were sixteen times more likely to report workplace discrimination because of their weight than men. Puhl and Heuer (2009), citing Roehling et al. (2007).

[54]Brownell and Puhl (2003), citing Puhl and Brownell (2001).

[55]These survey findings have been reported by Brownell and Puhl (2003), citing a number of other studies.

[56]Puhl and Heuer (2009), citing Foster et al. (2003).

[57]Puhl and Heuer (2009), citing Harvey and Hill (2001).

[58]Puhl and Heuer (2009), citing several nation-based studies of health care professionals on their attitudes toward overweight and obese patients.

[59]Puhl and Heuer (2009), citing Karnehed et al. (2006).

[60]Puhl and Heuer (2009), citing Wardle et al. (2002) and Crosnoe (2007).

[61]Puhl and Heuer (2009).

[62]Latner et al. (2005).

[63]Latner and Stunkard (2003).

[64]Puhl and Heuer (2009), citing Smith et al. (2007).

[65]Puhl and Heuer (2009), citing White et al. (1999) and Greenberg et al. (2003).

[66]Puhl and Heuer (2009), citing Blaine and McElroy (2002) and Geier et al. (2003).

[67]Puhl and Heuer (2009), citing Puhl and Brownell (2006).

[68]Puhl and Heuer (2009), citing Lauder et al. (2006).

[69]Brownell and Puhl (2003), citing Rand and Macgregor (1990).

[70]Bennett (2010).

[71]Of course, where heavy workers are unjustifiably paid less than their value to firms, we might expect some of the discrimination to go away with time as entrepreneurs realize they can gain a competitive advantage in their product markets by hiring heavy people who really are discriminated against, in the sense that they are really paid less than they are worth (after accounting for any productivity losses and/or added health-care costs, if there are any), a point to which we will return in this chapter.

[72]We should not forget that while heavy workers may be pleased that they have their own jobs, they can, and sometimes do, hold firmly to the weight-related stigmas, and many can be just as opposed to hiring other heavy workers for the same economic reasons that trimmers workers may hold dear.

[73]Hamermesh and Biddle (1994).

[74]Biddle and Hamermesh (1998).

[75]Persico et al. (2004).

[76]See Sorokowski (2010) and Stieger and Burger (2010).

[77]Persico et al. (2004).

[78]Ibid.

[79]Cawley and Meyerhoefer (2010).

[80]Mobius and Rosenblat (2006).

[81]In statistical assessment of 10,000 members of the Kaiser Permanente health care program between 1964 and 1973, when the members were forty-five years of age, research has shown that obesity does increase the chances of people having dementia later in life (Whitmer et al. [2005]). We've also noted that the elderly have progressively less brain tissue as they move from normal weight, to overweight, and then to obese (Raji et al. [2010]).

[82]Dor et al. (2010), citing seven studies (see Tables 2 and 3).

[83]Ibid., citing many studies.

[84]Wada and Tekin (2007).

[85]Cawley (2004).

[86]Dor et al. (2010), citing Averett and Korenman (1996); Baum and Ford (2004); Bhattacharya and Bundorf (2009); Cawley (2000, 2004); Han et al. (2009); Kim and Leigh (2010); Mitra (2001); Mocan and Tekin (2009); and Wada and Tekin (2007).

[87]Gregory and Ruhm (2009).

[88]Conley and Glauber (2005)

[89]This conclusion is also drawn by Averett and Korenman (1996).

[90]Mocan and Tekin (2009).

[91]Bhattacharya and Bundorf (2005). The authors actually found that the average hourly wage loss in 1998 was $3.41 an hour. I adjust that loss to 2010 prices.

[92]Bhattacharya and Bundorf (2005).

[93]Bureau of Labor Statistics (2010).

[94]According to Cawley and Meyerhoefer (2010) in their study involving 20,000 people, all obese nonelderly adults (twenty to sixty-four years of age) incurred in 2005 additional annual medical-care costs of $3,161 on average over and above what normal-weight adults incurred (with my adjusting the authors' estimates to late-2010 dollars). Obese men incurred additional annual medical-care

expenditures of $1,310 over normal-weight men. Obese women incurred additional annual medical-care expenditures of $4,133 over normal-weight women. Another duo of researchers found a lower average annual medical-care costs differential for obese and nonobese women and men of $1,457 and $405, respectively (adjusted to 2010 dollars). However, note that they, too, found the additional medical-care cost for obese women to be more than three times the additional annual medical-care costs of obese men (Bhattacharya and Bundorf [2005])

[95]Bhattacharya et al. (2010). The authors also found that making health-care insurance more generous for people who already have insurance has little to no effect on body weight.

[96]As reported by Lieber (2011) and Borrell (2011).

[97]As reported by Borrell (2011).

Chapter 7

[1]As reported by Borio (n.d.) and author's calculation on the number of cigarette packs per capita.

[2]For one video clip of Obama's apology covered by CBS News at http://www.cbsnews.com/video/watch/?id=5106630n (accessed August 23, 2010).

[3]Smith (1759 IV.I.10).

[4]Friedman (1973).

[5]Friedman (1962, p. 15).

[6]See Tullock (1967).

[7]Economists also argue that markets will fail to achieve maximum efficiency (or optimum allocation of resources) in the presence of "positive externalities," or when the actions of one or more people yield benefits to people who do not pay for the benefits. For example, a merchant who beautifies her storefront in a downtown shopping area may increase the traffic flow to other retailers in the shopping area, but because she is unlikely to be able to charge for the gains of others, she has an impaired incentive to beautify her storefront. Indeed, all stores can be in the same fix, with all missing out on additional sales that can come with all stores improving the looks of their storefronts. One recommended solution: a government requirement that all stores improve appearances. Another private solution is for an entrepreneur to buy up all the stores in the area, beautify all storefronts, and charge all merchants higher rents. I cover positive externalities in a footnote only because it has not been an issue, to date, in the smoking and fat wars.

[8]Of course, some firms may favor pollution abatement for their industry for ecological reasons, while others may favor pollution abatement for a good old-fashioned

economic reason: They may have a cost advantage in abating pollution over their industry rivals. The pollution controls can drive up everyone's costs—but differentially. Those with low pollution abatement costs will get a competitive cost and, therefore, a price advantage in their product market.

[9]Hayek (1944).

[10]Freedman (2010).

[11]Campos (2004) and Oliver (2006).

[12]Ariely (2008).

[13]See Thaler and Sunstein (2008) for a discussion of how appropriately constructed choices can be welfare enhancing and, at the same time, a form of "libertarian paternalism" that a majority of people would welcome.

[14]I have taken on the broad sweep of criticisms coming from behavioral economists in my own book (McKenzie [2010a]).

[15]See the transcript of the Hearing on the Regulation of Tobacco Products House Committee on Energy and Commerce Subcommittee on Health and the Environment, April 14, 1994, accessed August 9, 2010, http://senate.ucsf.edu/tobacco/executives1994congress.html.

[16]Levin (1950).

[17]Wynder and Graham (1950).

[18]Terry (1964).

[19]See the listing of twenty-nine reports on smoking issues by the Office of the Surgeon General, accessed August 3, 2010, http://www.surgeongeneral.gov/library/secondhandsmoke/factsheets/factsheet8.html.

[20]See, again, the transcript of the Hearing on the Regulation of Tobacco Products House Committee on Energy and Commerce Subcommittee on Health and the Environment, April 14, 1994, accessed August 9, 2010, http://senate.ucsf.edu/tobacco/executives1994congress.html.

[21]As reported in National Library of Medicine (n.d.), C. Everett Koop.

[22]Viscusi (1994).

[23]As related to me by a consultant to the American Tobacco Institute.

[24]Centers for Disease Control and Prevention (2010a).

[25]The American Heart Association reports that in the United States 23.1 percent of adult males smoke, while 18.3 percent of adult women smoke, accessed October 4, 2010, http://c2005.com/presenter.jhtml?identifier=4559.

[26]As reported in National Library of Medicine (n.d.) The report of the Surgeon General.

[27] As reported on a Web site maintained by the Campaign for Tobacco-Free Kids.

[28] As reported on the Centers for Disease Control and Prevention Web site, accessed August 3, 2010, http://www.cdc.gov/tobacco/data_statistics/fact_sheets/economics/econ_facts/index.htm, citing Centers for Disease Control and Prevention (2006). We need to be careful here in assuming from the $10.47 estimated medical costs per pack that smokers are covering only about half of the total costs of smoking through the price they pay for packs of cigarettes. After all, the CDC has made a strong case that smokers incur many medical costs during their shortened lives. They may not be paying all of those added medical costs, but they could be paying many of those costs through inflated health insurance premiums, direct medical bills not covered by insurance, and through lower wages. (Group health insurance policies do not always add a risk premium for smokers, which can cause employers to reduce their demand for workers who smoke, just as we have seen employers undercut the wages of overweight workers when health insurance premiums do not adjust for the medical-cost effects of added weight.)

[29] As reported by the Campaign for Tobacco-Free Kids on its Web site, accessed August 9, 2010, http://www.tobaccofreekids.org/reports/shs/.

[30] O'Neil (2006).

[31] As reported by the Campaign for Tobacco-Free Kids on its Web site, accessed August 9, 2010, http://www.tobaccofreekids.org/reports/shs/.

[32] As reported by Hernandez (February 3, 20011).

[33] For a timeline on key legislative and regulatory dates in the history of smoking, see the Web site provided by Forest – Voice and Friend of the Smoker, accessed August 7, 2010, http://www.forestonline.org/output/History-of-Smoking.aspx.

[34] All proposed labels for cigarette packs can be found at the FDA's Web site, accessed December 8, 2010, http://www.fda.gov/TobaccoProducts/Labeling/CigaretteProductWarningLabels/default.htm.

[35] See Bulow (2006).

[36] As reported on a Web site maintained by the Campaign for Tobacco-Free Kids.

Chapter 8

[1] Organization for Cooperation and Development (2010).

[2] See the Web site of Americans Against Food Taxes at http://www.nofoodtaxes.com/.

[3]For more details on the history of the smoking policy war, visit this Web site, accessed August 3, 2010, http://profiles.nlm.nih.gov/NN/Views/Exhibit/narrative/smoking.html.

[4]The actual total medical-care cost attributable to smoking in 2010 is $97 billion (Centers for Disease Control and Prevention [2010a]).

[5]Roan (2010), citing Biro et al. (2010).

[6]As reported by Bower (2010).

[7]Centers for Disease Control and Prevention (2010b).

[8]The CDC writes with urgency:

> Obesity is common, serious, and costly. In 2009, about 2.4 million more adults were obese than in 2007. This epidemic has affected every part of the United States. In every state, more than 15 percent of adults are obese, and in nine states, over 30 percent of adults are obese. The medical care costs of obesity in the United States are staggering. Recent estimates of the annual medical costs are as high as $147 billion (Centers for Disease Control and Prevention [2010b]).

[9]The CDC writes:

> Tobacco use is the single most preventable cause of disease, disability, and death in the United States. Each year, an estimated 443,000 people die prematurely from smoking or exposure to secondhand smoke, and another 8.6 million have a serious illness caused by smoking. Despite these risks, approximately 46 million U.S. adults smoke cigarettes. Smokeless tobacco, cigars, and pipes also have deadly consequences, including lung, larynx, esophageal, and oral cancers.

> The harmful effects of smoking do not end with the smoker. More than 126 million nonsmoking Americans, including children and adults, are regularly exposed to secondhand smoke. Even brief exposure can be dangerous because nonsmokers inhale many of the same carcinogens and toxins in cigarette smoke as smokers.

> Secondhand smoke exposure causes serious disease and death, including heart disease and lung cancer in nonsmoking adults and sudden infant death syndrome, acute respiratory infections, ear problems, and more frequent and severe asthma attacks in children. Each year, primarily because of exposure to secondhand smoke, an estimated 3,000 nonsmoking Americans die of lung cancer, more than 46,000 die of heart disease, and about 150,000–300,000 children younger than 18 months have lower respiratory tract infections.

> Coupled with this enormous health toll is the significant economic burden of tobacco use – more than $96 billion per year in medical expenditures and another $97 billion per year resulting from lost productivity (Centers for Disease Control and Prevention [2010a]).

[10]Surgeon General Satcher continues:

Many people believe that dealing with overweight and obesity is a personal responsibility. To some degree they are right, but it is also a community responsibility. When there are no safe, accessible places for children to play or adults to walk, jog, or ride a bike, that is a community responsibility. When school lunchrooms or office cafeterias do not provide healthy and appealing food choices, that is a community responsibility. When new or expectant mothers are not educated about the benefits of breast-feeding, that is a community responsibility. When we do not require daily physical education in our schools that is also a community responsibility. There is much that we can and should do together.

Taking action to address overweight and obesity will have profound effects on increasing the quality and years of healthy life and on eliminating health disparities in the United States. With this outcome in mind, I asked the Office of Disease Prevention and Health Promotion, along with other agencies in the Department of Health and Human Services, to assist me in developing this *Surgeon General's Call to Action to Prevent and Decrease Overweight and Obesity*. Our ultimate goal is to set priorities and establish strategies and actions to reduce overweight and obesity. This process begins with our attitudes about overweight and obesity. Recognition of the epidemic of overweight and obesity is relatively recent, and there remain enorous challenges and opportunities in finding solutions to this public health crisis. Overweight and obesity must be approached as preventable and treatable problems with realistic and exciting opportunities to improve health and save lives. The challenge is to create a multifaceted public health approach capable of delivering long-term reductions in the prevalence of overweight and obesity. This approach should focus on health rather than appearance and empower both individuals and communities to address barriers, reduce stigmatization, and move forward in addressing overweight and obesity in a positive and proactive fashion.

Several events have drawn attention to overweight and obesity as public health problems. In 1998, the National Heart, Lung, and Blood Institute in cooperation with the National Institute of Diabetes and Digestive and Kidney Diseases of the National Institutes of Health released the *Clinical Guidelines on the Identification, Evaluation, and Treatment of Obesity in Adults: Evidence Report*. This report was the result of a thorough scientific review of the evidence related to the risks and treatment of overweight and obesity, and it provided evidence-based treatment guidelines for health-care providers. In early 2000, the release of *Healthy People 2010* identified overweight and obesity as major public health problems and set national objectives for reduction in their prevalence. The National Nutrition Summit in May 2000 illuminated the impact of dietary and physical activity habits on achieving a healthy body weight and began a national dialogue on strategies for the prevention of over-weight and obesity. Finally, a Surgeon General's Listening Session, held in late 2000, and a related public comment period, generated many useful ideas for prevention and treatment strategies and helped forge and rein-force an important coalition of stakeholders. Participants in these events considered many prevention and treatment strategies, including such national priorities as ensuring daily physical education in schools, increas-ing research on the behavioral and environmental causes of obesity, and promoting breast-feeding.

These activities are just a beginning, however. Effective action requires the close cooperation and collaboration of a variety of organizations and individuals. This *Call To Action* seeks to recruit your talent and inspiration in developing national actions to promote healthy eating habits and adequate physical activity, beginning in childhood and continuing across the lifespan. I applaud your interest in this important public health challenge (Satcher [2007]).

[11] As reported by Harmon (2010). All calculations are based on demographic trends during the 1993–2008 period.

[12] Centers for Disease Control and Prevention (2010b). To see the map of spreading obesity rates, go to http://www.cdc.gov/vitalsigns/AdultObesity/StateInfo.html, accessed August 8, 2010.

[13] Christakis and Fowler (2007).

[14] Gershon et al. (2007).

[15] Friedman and Friedman (1980, p. 148).

[16] See the pictures of Koop at http://www.google.com/images?hl=en&source=imghp&biw=1197&bih=507&q=c.+everett+koop&gbv=2&aq=0&aqi=g1g-m1&aql=f&oq=C.+everett&gs_rfai.

[17] Posner (2009) and Andrews (2008).

[18] Leonhardt (2009b).

[19] Leonhardt pontificated in 2009b:

The solutions to these problems are beyond the control of any indi-vidual. They involve a different sort of responsibility: civic—even politi-cal—responsibility. They depend on the kind of collective action that helped cut smoking rates nearly in half. Anyone who smoked in an elementary-school hallway today would be thrown out of the building. But if you served an obesity-inducing, federally financed meal to a kin-dergartner, you would fit right in. Taxes on tobacco, meanwhile, have skyrocketed. A modest tax on sodas—one of the few proposals in the various health-reform bills aimed at health, rather than health care—has struggled to get through Congress. (Leonhardt [May 9, 2009])

[20]Smith (1776, V.3.76).

[21]As reported by the Campaign for Tobacco-Free Kids (November 9, 2009); accessed August 12, 2010, http://www.tobaccofreekids.org/reports/settlements/. See also Bulow (2006).

[22]Fast-food sales for 2010 were taken from Hoovers Web site, Industry overview: Fast food and quick service restaurants; accessed August 12, 2010, http://www.hoovers.com/fast-food-and-quickservice-restaurants/–ID__269–/free-ind-fr-pro-file-basic.xhtml. U.S. tobacco sales in 2005 totaled $2.6 billion, according to the latest Federal Trade Commission online report; accessed December 9, 2010, http://www.ftc.gov/os/2009/08/090812cigarettereport.pdf.

[23]Friedman and Friedman (1980, p. 227).

[24]Centers for Disease Control and Prevention (2010b).

[25]See the CDC's Web site that has the behavioral recommendations for individuals and all levels of government; accessed December 8, 2010, http://www.cdc.gov/Features/VitalSigns/AdultObesity/.

[26]Grimstvedt et al. (2010).

[27]For example, as early as 2003, Senate Majority Leader Bill Frist proposed providing federal grants to communities aimed at curbing the nation's obesity by encouraging people to exercise and eat well (rather than blaming the food industry for fat (accessed August 17, 2010, http://www.wate.com/Global/story.asp?S=1502798). In 2009, the Robert Wood Johnson Foundation solicited—grant proposals "to implement healthy eating and active living initiatives that can support healthier communities for children and families across the United States. The program places special emphasis on reaching children who are at highest risk for obesity on the basis of race/ethnicity, income and/or geographic location. This initiative will advance RWJF's efforts to reverse the childhood obesity epidemic by 2015" (accessed August 17, 2010, http://www.rwjf.org/applications/solicited/cfp.jsp?ID=20603). See also Richards et al. (2004) for an array of policies to change everything from schools and farm subsidies to architectural designs aimed at promoting healthier diets and greater exercise.

[28]As reported by Robertson (2010).

[29]Thaler and Sunstein (2008, p. 9).

[30]Ariely (2008, p. 242).

[31]Wansink et al. (2010).

[32]Thaler and Sunstein (2008, p. 11).

[33]McKenzie (2010a, especially Chap. 10).

[34]As reported by Robertson (2010), with a following report available from Food Safety News, December 3, 2010; accessed December 9, 2010, http://www.foodsafetynews.com/2010/12/child-nutrition-bill-ready-for-presidents-approval/.

[35]As reported by Pear (2010).

[36]See the discussion of the power of genetics in Karasu and Karasu (2010, especially Chap. 1).

[37]See photo of Brownell that accompanied a *Time* magazine column by Mike Huckabee in 2006 (http://www.time.com/time/magazine/article/0,9171,1187241,00.html).

[38]As reported by Baetlein (2009).

[39]Brownell and Frieden (2009).

[40]Smith et al. (2010).

[41]Brownell and Frieden (2009, p. 1806).

[42]Fletcher et al. (2010a, b).

[43]As reported by the American Council on Science and Health (January 24, 2011); accessed January 28, 2011, http://www.acsh.org/factsfears/newsID.2277/news_detail.asp.

[44]As reported by DeNoon (2005).

[45]As reported by Dahler (February 9, 2011).

[46]Fletcher et al. (2010a).

[47]As reported by Baetlein (2009).

[48]Ibid., citing Gelbach et al. (2007).

[49]Fletcher et al. (2010b).

[50]Epstein et al. (2010).

[51]As reported by Baetlein (2009).

[52]Epstein et al. (2010).

[53]Bulow (2006).

[54]Brownell and Frieden (2009, p. 1807).

[55]Hayek (1944).

[56]As reported by Bernstein (2010a).

[57]Ibid.

[58]As reported by Martel (2010).

[59] As reported by *The New York Times* Editorial Board (2010).

[60] As reported by Olson (2010).

[61] As quoted from an editorial, *The New York Times* Editorial Board (2010).

[62] As reported by Bernstein (2010a).

[63] As reported by Luna (2010).

[64] As reported by Huffstutter (2010b).

[65] As reported by *Science Daily* (February 15, 2011), citing Elbel et al. (2011).

[66] See the report on the Obama Administration's menu of anti-obesity efforts by Ambinder (2010).

[67] Backers of performance-based regulations for the food industry make no bones about their coercive intentions:

> This policy strategy rests on the moral argument that the food industry must take responsibility for child obesity consequences that flow from the consumption of the products from which they profit. It is a regulatory intervention that seeks to harness private initiative in pursuit of the public good. But it resists telling industry specifically what to do to address the problem. Instead, food companies are to be assigned outcome improvements in the form of reduced childhood obesity. Failure to achieve the regulatory target would result in substantial financial penalties (Sugarman and Sandman [2008]).

[68] As reported by Beato (2011).

[69] Cassandra Marie Smith v. Hooters of America. 2010. State of Michigan, Circuit Court for Macomb County, case no. 10-2213-CD, received May 24; accessed November 25, 2010, http://www.callsam.com/images/stories/news_docs_pics/Complaint_Smith-vs-Hooters.pdf.

[70] Smith v. Hooters (2010, p. 4).

[71] Ibid. (p. 6).

[72] Ibid. (pp. 7 and 8).

[73] This is a provision of the Michigan State statute titled Elliott-Larsen Civil Rights Act, Act 453 of 1976; accessed November 25, 2010, http://www.legislature.mi.gov/(S(ubnt3bm1wedhifncetm4uc45))/mileg.aspx?page=GetMCLDocument&objectname=mcl-Act-453-of-1976.

[74] Neavling (2010, June 7).

[75] As reported in Puhl and Heuer (2009).

[76] Puhl and Heuer (2009), citing Foster et al. (2003); Puhl and Heuer (2009), citing Harvey and Hill (2001); and Puhl and Heuer (2009), citing several nation-based

studies of health-care professionals on their attitudes toward overweight and obese patients.

[77]Wada and Tekin (2007); Mocan and Tekin (2009); Bhattacharya and Bundorf (2005); Dor et al. (2010), citing Averett and Korenman (1996); Baum and Ford (2004); Bhattacharya and Bundorf (2009); Cawley (2000b, 2004); Gregory and Ruhm (2009); Han et al. (2009); Kim and Leigh (2010); Mitra (2001).

[78]Cawley (2004); Dor et al. (2010), citing Averett and Korenman (1996); Baum and Ford (2004); Bhattacharya and Bundorf (2009); Cawley (2000b, 2004); Gregory and Ruhm (2009); Han et al. (2009); Kim and Leigh (2010); Mitra (2001); Mocan and Tekin (2009); and Wada and Tekin (2007).

[79]Bhattacharya et al. (2010).

[80]McKibben v. Hamilton County, Ohio. Accessed December 27, 2010, http://www. lexisone.com/lx1/caselaw/freecaselaw?action=OCLGetCaseDetail&format= FULL&sourceID=gdja&searchTerm=eaEN.jLda.aadi.YaXC&searchFlag=y& l1loc=FCLOW.

[81]Fredregill v. Nationwide Agribusiness Insurance. Accessed December 27, 2010, https://vpn.nacs.uci.edu/+CSCO+ch756767633A2F2F6A6A6A2E79726B7666617 26B76662E70627A++/hottopics/lnacademic/?

[82]The details of the case were accessed December 20, 2010 from http://openjurist. org/10/f3d/17/cook-v-state-of-rhode-island-department-of-mental-health-retardation- and-hospitals.

[83]Li et al. (2010).

[84]See the details of the case at http://caselaw.findlaw.com/us-6th-circuit/1143557. html, accessed December 20, 2010.

Chapter 9

[1]Gneezy and Rustichini (2000).

[2]Much of the commentary in the *Wall Street Journal* column forms the core of this chapter (McKenzie [2008]).

[3]See one of the articles on "beauty" and labor-market effects cited earlier (Hamermesh and Biddle [1994]).

[4]As reported by Stobbe (2010).

[5]Volpp et al. (2009).

[6]Whatever the findings on the efficacy of antismoking campaigns, quitting smoking is a category apart from losing weight. As noted earlier, smoking is not something

people need to do to sustain life, yet eating at some level is. And eating can compel people—especially those with food addictions and compulsions—to eat ever more, and to regain weight lost when employer-provided weight-loss incentives are no longer available.

[7] As reported by Stobbe (2010).

[8] Volpp et al. (2008).

[9] Cawley and Price (2010).

[10] As reported by Stobbe (2010).

[11] For a catalogue of all the arguments attributing people's weight gain to outside forces, see Karasu and Karasu (2010).

[12] I remind readers that behavioral economist Richard Thaler and behavioral legal scholar Cass Sunstein have mused, "If you look at economics textbooks, you will learn that *homo economicus* can think like Albert Einstein, store as much memory as IBM's Big Blue, and exercise the will power of Mahatma Gandhi." Thaler and Sunstein (2008, pp. 6–7).

[13] See my book *Predictably Rational?* (2010a) for a full discussion of why economists assume for their analyses that people are more rational than everyone knows people to be.

[14] See my book *Predictably Rational?* (2010a) for elaborations on this argument.

[15] Mitchell and Brunstrom (2005) and Oldham-Cooper et al. (2010), with the latter article summarized by Bakalar (2011).

[16] As reported by *NaturalNews* on January 7, 2009; accessed January 31, 2010, http://www.naturalnews.com/025252_television_water_watching_television.html (also at any number of other Web-based sites that can be found from a Google search).

[17] See Devany and Taleb (2010).

[18] Wansink (2006).

[19] Wansink (2006).

[20] As reported by Tierney (2010), citing Morewedge et al. (2010).

Chapter 10

[1] Algazy et al. (2010).

[2] Oliver (2006).

[3] As documented by Oliver (2006, p. 22).

[4]See Cawley and Meyerhoefer (2010).

[5]For the details of this line of argument, see Oliver (2006, pp. 3–4), citing Mokdad et al. (2004) and Flegal et al. (2005).

[6]See Cawley and Meyerhoefer (2010).

[7]Ibid. (see Fig. 2).

[8]Bhattacharya and Bundorf (2005).

[9]See Algazy et al. (2010).

[10]As reported by Rabin (2010b).

[11]As reported by Park (2010).

[12]As reported by Huffstutter (2010a), citing a U.S. Department of Agriculture survey of 46,000 households in 2009.

[13]As reported by Moss (2010).

[14]Alson et al. (2007):

[15]As reported by Neuman (2010).

[16]As reported by Parker-Pope (2010), citing Bloom (2010).

Bibliography

Abedin, S. (2009, September 3). The social side of obesity: You are who you eat with. *Time. com*. Accessed August 30, 2010, http://www.time.com/time/nation/article/0,8599,1919885,00. htm.

Abrahamson, E., & Freedman, D. H. (2007). A perfect mess: The hidden benefits of disorder – How crammed closets, cluttered offices, and on-the-fly planning make the world a better place. New York: Little, Brown, and Company.

Abrams, K. K., Allen L. R., & Gray J. J. (1993). Disordered eating attitudes and behaviors, psychological adjustment, and ethnic identity: A comparison of black and white female college students. *International Journal of Eating Disorders* 14(1, July):49–57.

Adams, K. F., Schatzkin, A., Harris, T. B., Kipnis, V., Mouw, T., Ballard-Barbash, R., Hollenbeck, A., & Leitzmann M. F. (2006). Overweight, obesity, and mortality in a large prospective cohort of persons 50 to 71 years old. *New England Journal of Medicine,* 355(August 24):763–778. Accessed Sept. 1, 2010, http://www.nejm.org/doi/full/10.1056/NEJMoa055643.

Adamy, J. (2010, May 12). White House obesity plan mixes carrots with sticks. *The Wall Street Journal*, p. A7.

Ainsworth, B. E., Haskell, W. L., Whitt, M. C., Irwin, M. L., Swartz, A. M., Strath, S. J., O'Brien W. L., Bassett D. R. Jr, Schmitz K. H., Emplaincourt P. O., Jacobs D. R. Jr, & Leon A. S. (2000). Compendium of physical activities: An update of activity codes and MET intensities. *Medicine & Science in Sports & Exercise*, 32(Suppl): S498–S516.

Akan, G. E., & Grilo C. M. (1995). Sociocultural influences on eating attitudes and behaviors, body image, and psychological functioning: A comparison of African-American, Asian-American, Asian-American, and Caucasian college women. *International Journal of Eating Disorders* 18(2):181–187.

Alesci, Christina (2010). Obesity in China doubled in 11 years with rising prosperity. *Bloomberg. com*. July 8, accessed November 26, 2010, http://www.bloomberg.com/apps/news? pid=newsarchive&sid=aD1hgKQESbCc.

Alson, J.M, Sumner, D.A., & Vosti, S.A. (2007, December). Farm subsidies and obesity in the United States. *Agricultural Resource Economics Update*. Davis, Calif.: Giannini Foundation for Agriculture Economics, University of California 11(2, November/December). Accessed January 10, 2011, http://agecon.ucdavis.edu/extension/update/articles/v11n2_1.pdf.

Akerlof, G. A. (1991). Procrastination and obedience. *American Economic Review,* 81(2):1–19.

Alderman, L. (2011, January 1). After surgery to slim down, the bills can pile up. *The New York Times*, B5.

Algazy, J., Gipstein, S., Riahi, F., & Tryon, K. (2010, October). Why governments must lead the fight against obesity. *McKinsey Quarterly*. Accessed November 2, 2010, http://www. mckinseyquarterly.com/Why_governments_must_lead_the_fight_against_obesity_2687.

R.B. McKenzie, *HEAVY!*, DOI 10.1007/978-3-642-20135-6,
© Springer-Verlag Berlin Heidelberg 2012

Ambinder, M. (2010, February 9). The Obama obesity proposals: The good, the bad, the missing. *The Atlantic*. Accessed August 17, 2010, http://www.theatlantic.com/politics/archive/2010/02/the-obama-obesity-proposals-the-good-the-bad-the-missing/35654/.

American Heart Association (2010). Cigarette smoking statistics. Accessed October 4, 2010, http://c2005.com/presenter.jhtml?identifier=4559.

Anderson, P., Butcher, K., & Levine, P. B. (2003). Maternal employment and overweight children. *Journal of Health Economics*, 22:477–504.

Andersen, R. E., Crespo, C. J., Bartlett, S. J., Cheskin, L. J., & Pratt, M. (1998). Relationship of physical activity and television watching with body weight and level of fatness among children: Results from the Third National Health and Nutrition Examination Survey. *Journal of the American Medical Association*, 279(12):938–942.

Andrews, E. L. (2008, October 23). Greenspan concedes error on regulation. *The New York Times*. Accessed August 16, 2010, http://www.nytimes.com/2008/10/24/business/economy/24panel.html.

Araneta, M. R., Wingard, D. L., & Barrett-Connor, E. (2002). Type 2 diabetes and metabolic syndrome in Filipina-American woman: A high risk nonobese population. *Diabetes Care*, 25:494–499.

Arany, Z., Foo, S., Ma, Y., Ruas, J. L., Bommi-Reddy, A., Girnun, G., Cooper, M., Laznik, D., Chinsomboon, J., Rangwala, S. M., Baek, K. H., Rosenzweig, A., & Spiegelman, B. M. (2008). HIF-independent regulation of VEGF and angiogenesis by the transcriptional coactivator PGC-1a. *Nature*, 451:1008–1012.

Ariely, D. (2008). Predictably irrational: The hidden forces that shape our decisions. New York: HarperCollins Publishers.

Arizona Department of Health Services (2005, April). Public input sessions: maternal child health block grant and needs assessment 2006. Accessed June 22, 2010, http://www.azdhs.gov/phs/owch/pdf/sum_perf_outcome_meas_2006.pdf.

Associated Press (2003, October 29). Frist proposal to reduce obesity goes to Senate floor. Accessed August 17, 2010, http://www.wate.com/Global/story.asp?S=1502798.

Associated Press (2007, May 17). Anti-discrimination law to protect short, fat people proposed in US state Massachusetts. Accessed July 7, 2009, from http://www.freerepublic.com/tag/peopleofsize/index.

Associated Press (2008, February 8). As waistlines expand, seat belt use shrinks. Accessed July 26, 2010, http://www.msnbc.msn.com/id/23070762/.

Averett, S., & Korenman, S. (1996). The economic reality of the beauty myth. *Journal of Human Resources*, 31(2):304–30. Accessed July 22, 2010, http://papers.ssrn.com/sol3/papers.cfm?abstract_id=3241.

Baetlein, L. (2009, September 1). Battle lines drawn over soda, junk food taxes. *Reuters*. Accessed August 17, 2010, http://www.reuters.com/article/idUSTRE5806E520090901.

Bakalar, N. (2010, December 27). Aging: Paying the physical price for longer life. *The New York Times*. Accessed December 29, 2010, http://www.nytimes.com/2010/12/28/health/research/28longevity.html.

Bakalar, N. (2011, January 4). Vital signs: Distracted eating adds more to the waistlines. *The New York Times*, D6.

Baum, C. L., & Ford, W. F. (2004). The wage effects of obesity: A longitudinal study. *Health Economics*, 13(9):885–99. Accessed July 22, 2010, http://www3.interscience.wiley.com/journal/107628895/abstract.

Beato, G. (2011, January). Watching what you eat: Why has the USDA been plumping up the food stamps program like a factory chicken? *Reason*. Accessed January 4, 2011, http://reason.com/archives/2010/12/10/watching-what-you-eat.

Beck, M. (2010a, July 13). Eating to live or living to eat? *The Wall Street Journal*, p. D1. Accessed July 13, 2010, http://online.wsj.com/article/SB10001424052748704288204575363072381955744.html.

Beck, M. (2010b, September 14). Freeze! Zap! Bye-bye fat! *The Wall Street Journal*. Accessed September 20, 2010, http://online.wsj.com/article/SB100014240527487034667045754896 80982668018.html.

Becker, G. S. (1965). A theory of the allocation of time. *Economic Journal,* 75(299):493–517.

Becker, G. S. (1971a). Economic theory. New York: Alfred A. Knopf.

Becker, G. S. (1971b). The economics of discrimination. Chicago: University of Chicago Press. (Originally published in 1957)

Becker, G. S. (1976). The economic approach to human behavior. Chicago: University of Chicago Press.

Becker, G. S. (1978). The economics of human behavior. Chicago: University of Chicago Press.

Becker, G. S. (1993). A treatise on the family (expanded edn.). Cambridge, MA: Harvard University Press.

Becker, G. S. (1994). Human capital: A theoretical and empirical approach. Chicago: University of Chicago Press.

Becker, G. S. (1996). Accounting for tastes. Cambridge, MA: Harvard University Press.

Becker, G. S. (1997). The economics of life. Chicago: University of Chicago Press.

Becker, G. S., Grossman, M., & Murphy, K. M. (1994). An empirical analysis of cigarette addiction. *American Economic Review*, 84(3, June):396–418.

Becker, G. S., & Murphy, K. M. (1988). A theory of rational addiction. *Journal of Political Economy*, 96(4):675–700.

Bednarek, H., Jeitschko, T., & Pecchenino, R. (2006). Gluttony and sloth: Symptoms of trouble or signs of bliss? A theory of choice in the presence of behavioral adjustment costs. *Contributions to Economic Analysis and Policy*, 5(1):1–46.

Belluck, P. (2010, January 13). Obesity rate hits a plateau in U.S., data suggests. *The New York Times*. Accessed May 12, 2010, http://www.nytimes.com/2010/01/14/health/14obese.html.

Benjamin, S. E., Rifas-Shiman, S. L., Taveras, E. M., Haines, J., Finkelstein, J., Kleinman, K., Gillman, M. W. (2009). Early child care and adiposity at ages 1 and 3 years. *Pediatrics,* 124 (2, August):555–562. Accessed June 18, 2010, http://pediatrics.aappublications.org/cgi/content/abstract/124/2/555.

Bennett, J. (2010, July 19). Poll: How much is beauty worth in the workplace. *Newsweek*. Accessed July 19, 2010, http://www.newsweek.com/2010/07/19/poll-how-much-is-beauty-worth-at-work.html?GT1=43002.

Bergsten, C. F. (2005). The United States and the world economy. Washington, DC: Peterson Institute.

Bernstein, S. (2010a, November 3). Happy Meals banned in San Francisco. *Los Angeles Times*, p. B2.

Bernstein, S. (2010b, November 12). Fast food battle comes to L.A. *Los Angeles Times*, p. B1.

Berrington de Gonzalez, A., Hartge, P., Cerhan, J. R., Flint, A. J., Hannan, L., MacInnis, R. J., Moore, SC., Tobias, G. S., Anton-Culver, H., Freeman, L. B., Beeson, W. L., Clipp, S .L., English, D. R., Folsom, A. R., Freedman, D. M., Giles, G., Hakansson, N., Henderson, K. D., Hoffman-Bolton, J., Hoppin, J. A., Koenig, K. L., Lee, I. M., Linet, M .S., Park, Y., Pocobelli, G., Schatzkin, A., Sesso, H. D., Weiderpass, E., Willcox, B. J., Wolk A., Zeleniuch-Jacquotte, A., Willett, W. C., Thun, M. J. (2010). Body-mass index and mortality among 1.46 million white adults. *New England Journal of Medicine*, 363(December 2):2211–2219. Accessed December 5, 2010, http://www.nejm.org/doi/full/10.1056/NEJMoa1000367.

Bhattacharya, J., & Bundorf, M. K. (2005, April). The incidence of the healthcare costs of obesity (Working Paper No. 11303). Cambridge, MA: National Bureau of Economic Research.

Bhattacharya, J., & Bundorf, M. K. (2009). The incidence of the healthcare costs of obesity. *Journal of Health Economics,* 28(3):649–658. DOI: 10.1016/j.jealeco.2009.02.009

Bhattacharya, J., Bundorf, M. K., Pace, N., & Sood, N. (2010, April). Does health insurance make you fat (Working Paper 15163). Cambridge, MA: National Bureau of Economic Research, Accessed December 7, 2010, http://www.nber.org/papers/w15163.

Bhattacharya, J., & Sood, N. (2007). Health insurance and the obesity externality. In: K. Bolin & J. Cawley (eds.), The economics of obesity (pp. 279–318). Bingley, UK: Emerald Group Publishing, Ltd.

Bialik, C. (2009, July 22). The slimming figures of childhood obesity. *Wall Street Journal.* Accessed December 10, 2010, http://online.wsj.com/article/SB124821547930269995.html.

Biddle, J. E., & Hamermesh, D. S. (1998). Beauty, productivity, and discrimination: Lawyers' looks and lucre. *Journal of Labor Economics,* 16(1):172–201.

Biro, F. M., McMahon, R. P., Striegel-Moore, R., Crawford, P. B., Obarzanek, E., Morrison, J. A., Barton, B.A., Falkner, F. (2010). Impact of timing of pubertal maturation on growth in black and white female adolescents: The National Heart, Lung, and Blood Institute Growth and Health Study. *Journal of Pediatrics* 138(6):636–643. Accessed August 9, 2010, http://www.jpeds.com/article/S0022-3476(01)04867-3/abstract.

Blaine, B., & McElroy, J. (2002). Selling stereotypes: Weight loss infomercials, sexism, and weightism. *Sex Roles,* 46:351–357.

Blaxter, K. (1989). Energy metabolism in animals and man. Cambridge, UK: Cambridge University Press.

Blehar, M. D., & Oren, D. A. (1997). Gender differences in depression. *Medscape Women's Health,* 2(2):3.

Block, J. H., Scribner, R. A., & DeSalvo, K. B. (2004). Fast food, race/ethnicity, and income. *American Journal of Preventive Medicine,* 27(3):211–217.

Bloom, J. (2010). American wasteland: How America throws away nearly half of its food (and what we can do about it). Cambridge, MA: Da Capo Lifelong Books.

Bogusky, A., & Porter, C. (2008). The 9-inch 'diet': Exposing the big conspiracy in America. New York: PowerHouse Books.

Borio, G. (n.d.). Tobacco timeline: The twentieth century 1950–1999 – The battle is joined. *Tobacco.org.* Accessed August 10, 2010, http://www.tobacco.org/resources/history/Tobacco_History20-2.html.

Borrell, B. (2011, January 3). Is it your boss' business? Two views on whether employers should offer discounts on good health. *Los Angeles Times,* E1.

Boulding, K. E. (1970). Economics as a science. New York: McGraw-Hill.

Bounds, G. (2010, 22 Feb.). When Man's Best Friend Is Obese. *Wall Street Journal.* Accessed http://online.wsj.com/article/SB10001424052748704476604576158372088195308.html.

Bower, B. (2010, March 5). Alcohol distills aggression in large men: Study supports notion that bigger men are meaner drunks. *Science News.* Accessed August 14, 2010, http://www.sciencenews.org/view/generic/id/56955/title/Alcohol_distills_aggression_in_large_men.

Bradford, S.C, Grieco, P.L.E., and Hufbauer, G.C. (2005). The payoff from global integration. Washington, D.C.: Institute for International Economics, May. Accessed February 6, 2011, http://www.piie.com/publications/papers/2iie3802.pdf.

Brody, J. E. (2010, August 30). Weight index doesn't tell the whole truth. *The New York Times.* Accessed September 1, 2010, http://www.nytimes.com/2010/08/31/health/31brod.html?_r=1.

Brown, C. (1988). Minimum wage laws: Are they overrated? *Journal of Economic Perspectives* 2 (Summer):133–145.

Brown, C., Gilroy, C., & Kohen, A. (1982). The effect of the minimum wage on employment and unemployment. *Journal of Economic Literature,* 20(June):487–528.

Brownell, K. D. (2005). The chronicling of obesity: Growing awareness of its social, economic, and political contexts. *Journal of Health Politics, Policy and Law,* 30(5):955–964.

Brownell, K. D., & Frieden, T. R. (2009, April 30). Ounces of prevention – The public policy case for taxes on sugared beverages. *New England Journal of Medicine,* 360(18):1805–1808.

Brownell, K. D., & Puhl, R. (2001). Bias, discrimination, and obesity. *Obesity Research.* 9 (12, December):788–805.

Brownell, K. D., & Puhl, R. (2003). Stigma and discrimination in weight management and obesity. *Permanente Journal,* 7(3). Accessed July 10, 2010, http://xnet.kp.org/permanentejournal/sum03/stigma.html.

Buchanan, J. M., & Tullock, G. (1962). The calculus of consent: The logical foundations of constitutional democracy. Ann Arbor, MI: University of Michigan Press.

Bulow, J. (2006, October 18). The tobacco settlement. *The Milken Institute Review*, pp. 41–54.

Bureau of Labor Statistics, U.S. Department of Labor (2010, June). Highlights of women's earnings in 2009. Accessed October 27, 2010, http://www.bls.gov/cps/cpswom2009.pdf.

CalorieLab (2006, June 6). Restaurant critic proposes fat tax formula. Accessed June 27, 2010, http://calorielab.com/news/2006/06/06/restaurant-critic-proposes-fat-tax-formula/.

Campaign for Tobacco-Free Kids (2009). A broken promise to our children: The 1998 tobacco settlement 11 years later. Accessed August 12, 2010, http://www.tobaccofreekids.org/reports/settlements/.

Campaign for Tobacco-Free Kids (2010). Accessed on August 3, 2010, http://www.tobaccofreekids.org/index.php.

Campaign for Tobacco-Free Kids (2010). Smoke-free laws: Protecting our right to breathe clean air. Accessed August 9, 2010, http://www.tobaccofreekids.org/reports/shs/.

Campaign for Tobacco-Free Kids (2010, April 29). Cigarette taxes reduce smoking, save lives, save money. Accessed May 12, 2010, http://www.tobaccofreekids.org/reports/prices/.

Campos, P. (2004). The obesity myth: Why America's obsession with weight is hazardous to your health. New York: Gotham Books.

Cannon, M., & Balko, R. (2004, October 21). Trimming fat two ways. *Washington Times*. Accessed June 4, 2010, http://www.washingtontimes.com/news/2004/oct/20/20041020-092925-6680r/.

Carpenter, C.S., & Stehr, M. (2009). Intended and unintended effects of youth bicycle laws. Accessed January 28, 2011, http://www.gse.uci.edu/docs/Carpenter_Stehr%20Bicycle_Manuscript_50409.pdf.

Cash, S., Goddard, E., & Lacanilao, R. (2007, June). Fast food outlet density and the incidence of overweight and obesity across Canadian metropolitan areas. *Social Science Research Network*. Accessed July 1, 2010, http://papers.ssrn.com/sol3/papers.cfm?abstract_id=992962.

Cawley, J. (1999). Addiction, calories, and body weight. Unpublished doctoral dissertation, University of Chicago.

Cawley, J. (2000). An instrumental variables approach to measuring the effect of body weight on employment disability. *Health Services Research,* 35(5, Pt. 2):1159–1179.

Cawley, J. (2004). The impact of obesity on wages. *Journal of Human Resources*, 39(2):451–474. Accessed July 22, 2010, http://jhr.uwpress.org/cgi/content/abstract/XXXIX/2/451?maxtoshow=&hits=10&RESULTFORMAT=&fulltext=The+impact+of+obesity+on+wages&searchid=1&FIRSTINDEX=0&sortspec=relevance&resourcetype=HWCIT.

Cawley, J., & Meyerhoefer, C. (2010, October). The medical care costs of obesity: An instrumental variable approach (Working Paper No. 16467). Cambridge, MA: National Bureau of Economic Research. Accessed October 22, 2010, http://www.nber.org/tmp/48003-w16467.pdf.

Cawley, J., & Price, J. A. (2010). Outcomes in a program that offers financial rewards for weight loss (Working Paper No. 14987). Cambridge, MA: National Bureau for Economic Research. Accessed July 29, 2010, http://www.nber.org/papers/w14987.

CBS News (2007, September 19). Forklift gets 900-pound man from bedroom. Accessed July 26, 2010, http://www.cbsnews.com/stories/2007/09/19/national/main3276151.shtml.

CBS News (2009, June 23). Obama's smoking struggle. Accessed August 23, 2010, http://www.cbsnews.com/video/watch/?id=5106630n.

Centers for Disease Control and Prevention (CDC) (2006). Sustaining state programs for tobacco control: Data highlights 2006. Atlanta: CDC. Accessed February 26, 2010, http://www.cdc.gov/tobacco/data_statistics/state_data/data_highlights/2006/pdfs/dataHighlights06rev.pdf.

Centers for Disease Control and Prevention (2009). Obesity prevalence among low-income, preschool-aged children – United States, 1998–2008. *MMWR Weekly*, 58(28):769–773. Accessed July 17, 2009, http://www.cdc.gov/obesity/childhood/prevalence.html.

Centers for Disease Control and Prevention (2009). Childhood overweight and obesity, consequences. Accessed August 9, 2009, http://www.cdc.gov/obesity/childhood/consequences. html.

Centers for Disease Control and Prevention (2010). U.S. obesity trends; Trends by state, 1985–2009. Accessed September 29, 2010, http://www.cdc.gov/obesity/data/trends.html#State.

Centers for Disease Control and Prevention (2010a). Tobacco use: Targeting the nation's leading killer. At a glance, 2010. Accessed August 3, 2010, http://www.cdc.gov/chronicdisease/ resources/publications/aag/osh.htm.

Centers for Disease Control and Prevention. (2010b). More states reach 30 percent obesity rate. Accessed August 5, 2010, http://www.cdc.gov/Features/VitalSigns/AdultObesity/.

Centers for Disease Control and Prevention (2010c). Economic facts about U.S. tobacco production and use. Accessed August 3, 2010, http://www.cdc.gov/tobacco/data_statistics/ fact_sheets/economics/econ_facts/index.htm.

Chabris, C., & Simons, D. (2010). The invisible gorilla: And other ways our intuitions deceive us. New York: Crown.

Chakravarthy, M. V., & Booth, F. W. (2004). Eating, exercise, and "thrifty" genotypes: Connecting the dots toward an evolutionary understanding of modern chronic diseases. *Journal of Applied Physiology,* 96:3–10.

Chang, V. W., & Lauderdale, D. S. (2005). Income disparities in body mass index and obesity in the United States, 1971–2002. *Archives of Internal Medicine,* 165:2122–2128.

Chen, E. Y., & Brown, M. (2005). Obesity stigma in sexual relationships. *Obesity Research,* 13:1393–1397.

Chou, S., Grossman, M., & Saffer, H. (2004). An economic analysis of adult obesity: Results from the behavioral risk factor surveillance system. *Journal of Health Economics,* 23:565–587. Accessed May 12, 2010, http://www.ers.usda.gov/publications/efan04004/efan04004d.pdf.

Christakis, N. A., & Fowler, J. H. (2007). The spread of obesity in a large social network over 32 years. *New England Journal of Medicine,* 357(4):370–377.

Church, T. S., Martin, C. K., Thompson, A. M., Earnest, C. P., Mikus, C. R., & Blair, S. N. (2009, February 18). Changes in weight, waist circumference and compensatory responses with different doses of exercise among sedentary, overweight postmenopausal women. *PloS One.* Accessed April 8, 2010, http://www.plosone.org/article/info:doi%2F10.1371%2Fjournal. pone.0004515.

Citing CDC Vital Signs (2010, August). Accessed August 5, 2010, http://www.cdc.gov/VitalSigns/ pdf/2010-08-vitalsigns.pdf.

Clark, G. (2007). Farewell to alms: A brief history of the world. Princeton, NJ: Princeton University Press.

Clifford, S. (2010, June 18). Plus-size revolution: Bigger women have cash, too. *The New York Times.* Accessed July 26, 2010, http://www.nytimes.com/2010/06/19/business/19plus.html.

Cloud, J. (2009, August 17). Why exercise won't make you thin. *Time,* pp. 42–47.

CNN (2009, February 24). TV viewing at 'all-time high,' Nielsen says. Accessed January 26, 2010, http://www.cnn.com/2009/SHOWBIZ/TV/02/24/us.video.nielsen/.

CNN (2009b, June 13). United, US Airways join in bag fees. Accessed July 7, 2009b, http://www. cnn.com/2008/TRAVEL/06/13/airlines.bags/index.html.

Cochran, G., & Harpending, H. (2009). The 10,000 year explosion: How civilization accelerated human evolution. New York: Basic Books.

Conley, D., & Glauber, R. (2005). Gender, body mass and economic status (Working Paper No. W11343). Cambridge, MA: National Bureau of Economic Research. Accessed July 22, 2010, http://papers.ssrn.com/sol3/papers.cfm?abstract_id=727123.

Connor-Greene, P. A. (1988). Gender differences in body weight perception and weight-loss strategies of college men. *Women & Health,* 14:27–42.

Congressional Budget Office (2010, september 8) How does obesity in adults affect spending on health care? Economic and Budget Brief, accessed July 6, 2011 from http://www.cho.gov/ 118xx/doc 11810109-08-Obesity_brief.pdf

Copeland, L. (2011, March 21). Overweight Americans throwing off safety of city buses. *USA Today*. Retrieved March 21, 2011, http://www.usatoday.com/news/nation/2011-03-21-busweight21_ST_N.htm.

Corporate fuel economy standard (2010). In: Wikipedia, the free encyclopedia. Citing the National Highway Traffic Safety Administration, Automotive fuel economy program: Annual update calendar year 2003. Accessed May 16, 2010, http://en.wikipedia.org/wiki/Corporate_Average_Fuel_Economy#Historical_standards.

Cosmides, J.H., Tooby, L., & Barkow, J. (eds.) (1992). The adapted mind: Evolutionary psychology and the generation of culture. New York, NY: Oxford University Press.

Costa, D., & Steckel, R. (1997). Long-term trends in health, welfare, and economic growth in the United States. In: R. Floud and R. Steckel (eds.), Health and welfare during industrialization. Chicago: University of Chicago Press, for the National Bureau of Economic Research.

Courtemanche, C. (2010, March). A silver lining: The connection between gasoline prices and obesity. *Economic Inquiry*, published online. Accessed November 30, 2010, http://papers.ssrn.com/sol3/papers.cfm?abstract_id=982466.

Critser, G. (2002). Fat land: How Americans became the fattest people in the world. Boston: Houghton-Mifflin.

Crosnoe, R. (2007). Gender, obesity, and education. *Social Education,* 80:241–260.

Cutler, D. M., Glaeser, E. L., & Shapiro, J. M. (2003). Why have Americans become more obese? *Journal of Economic Perspective,* 17(3, Summer):93–118.

Dahler, D. (February 9, 2011). Diet soda linked to higher risk of stroke and heart attack. *CBS New York*. Accessed February 10, 2011, http://newyork.cbslocal.com/2011/02/09/diet-soda-linked-to-higher-risk-of-heart-attack-stroke/.

Daily Telegraph (2009, April 2). Obese gowns for hospital patients are wider than car. Accessed July 26, 2010, http://www.telegraph.co.uk/health/healthnews/5095112/Obese-gowns-for-hospital-patients-are-wider-than-car.html.

Dannenberg, A. L., Burton, D. C., & Jackson, R. J. (2004). Economic and environmental costs of obesity: The impact on airlines. *American Journal of Preventive Medicine,* 27(3):264.

Darwin, C. (1859). The origins of the species. New York: Gramercy (reprinted in 1995).

Dave, D.M., & Kelly, R.I. (2010, December). How does the business cycle affect eating habits? (NBER Working Paper 16638). Cambridge, Mass.: National Bureau of Economic Research. Accessed December 29, 2010, http://www.nber.org/tmp/49552-w16638.pdf.

de Araujo, I. E., Oliveira-Maia, A. J., Sotnikova, T. D., Gainetdinov, R. R., Caron, M. G., Nicolelis, M. A. L., Simon, S. A. (2008). Food reward in the absence of taste receptor signaling. *Neuron,* 57(6, March 27):930–941.

DellaVigna, S., & Malmendier, U. (2006). Paying not to go to the gym. *American Economic Review*, 96(3):694–719. Accessed September 24, 2010, http://www.aeaweb.org/articles.php?doi=10.1257/aer.96.3.694.

DeNoon, D. J. (2005, June 15). Drink more diet soda, gain more weight. *FoxNews.com.* Accessed August 12, 2010, http://www.foxnews.com/story/0,2933,159579,00.html.

Devany, A., & Taleb, N. N. (2010). The new evolution diet: What our paleolithic ancestors can teach us about weight loss, fitness, and aging. Emmaus, PA: Rodale Books.

Dewy, K. G. (2006). Infant feeding and growth. In G. Goldberg, A. Prentice, A. Prentice, S. Filteau, K. Simondon (eds.), Breast-feeding: Early influences on later health. New York, Berlin, Heidelberg: Springer.

Diamond, J. (1987). The worst mistake in the history of the human race. *Discover*, 8(5):64–66.

DietsinReview.com (2009, May 25). The recession's negative impact on our health. Accessed June 3, 2010, http://www.dietsinreview.com/diet_column/05/the-recessions-negative-impact-on-our-health/.

Dor, A., Ferguson, C., Langwith, C., & Tan, E. (2010, September 21). A heavy burden: The individual costs of being overweight and obese in the United States. (Research Report). Washington, D.C.: George Washington University, School of Public Health and Health

Services, Department of Health Policy. Accessed October 7, 2010, http://www.gwumc.edu/sphhs/departments/healthpolicy/dhp_publications/?pubsdisplay=RecentPubs.

Dunstan, D. W., Barr, E. L., Healy, G. N., Salmon, J., Shaw, J. E., Balkau, B., Magliano, D. J., Cameron, A. J., Zimmet, P. Z., & Owen, N. (2010). Television viewing time and mortality: The Australian diabetes, obesity and lifestyle study. *Circulation* 121:384–391. Accessed December 13, 2010, http://circ.ahajournals.org/cgi/content/short/121/3/384.

Eaton, S. B., & Eaton, S. B. (2003). An evolutionary perspective on human physical activity: Implications for health. *Comparative Biochemistry Physiology,* 136:153–159.

Edelson, E. (2010, August 26). Wider waist boosts asthma risk: Even if women were of normal weight, extra fat around abdomen raised the odds, study found. *HealthDay News, Inc.* Accessed December 8, 2010, http://abcnews.go.com/Health/Healthday/story?id=8404081&page=2.

Edwards, P., & Roberts, I. (2009, April 19). Population adiposity and climate change [Electronic version]. *International Journal of Epidemiology.*

Ehrlich, P. R. (1968). The population bomb. New York: Ballantine Books

Elbel, B., Gyamfi, J., & Kersh, R. (2011) Child and adolescent fast-food choice and the influence of calorie labeling: a natural experiment [Electronic version]. *International Journal of Obesity,* February 15.

Emmett, R. (2006). Malthus reconsidered: Population, natural resources, and markets. *PERC Policy Series.* Bozeman, MT: PERC.

Epel, E. S., McEwen, B., Seeman, T., Matthews, K., Castellazzo, G., Brownell, K. D., Bell, J., Ickovics, J. R. (2000). Stress and body shape: Stress-induced cortisol secretion is consistently greater among women with central fat. *Psychosomatic Medicine,* 62(5, September/October):623–632.

Epstein, L. H., Dearling, K. K., Roba, L. G., & Finkelstein, E. (2010, February 5). The influence of taxes and subsidies on energy purchased in an experimental purchasing study. *Psychological Science.* Published February 5, 2010, as DOI:10.1177/0956797610361446. Accessed November 17, 2010, http://www.atg.state.vt.us/assets/files/Epstein%20et%20al%20-%20Influence%20of%20Taxes%20and%20Subsidies%20on%20Energy%20Purchased%20in%20an%20Experimental%20Purchase%20Study%20-%20Assoc%20Pysch%20Science%202010.pdf.

European Association for the Study of Obesity (2005). Obesity in Europe – EU platform on diet, physical activity and health (International Obesity Task Force: EU Platform Briefing Paper, March 15). London: The International Association for the Study of Obesity. Accessed July 17, 2009, http://ec.europa.eu/health/ph_determinants/life_style/nutrition/documents/iotf_en.pdf.

Everson, K. (2010, September 24). Told to eat its vegetables, America orders fries. *The New York Times.* Accessed September 25, 2010, http://www.nytimes.com/2010/09/25/health/policy/25vegetables.html.

Ewing, R., Schmid, T., Killingsworth, R., Zlot, A., & Raudenbush, S. (2003). Relationship between urban sprawl and physical activity, obesity, and morbidity. *American Journal of Health Promotion,* 18:47–57.

Fairburn, C. G., Doll, H. A., Welch, S. L., Hay, P. J., Davies, B. A., & O'Connor, M.E. (1998). Risk factors for binge eating disorder: A community-based, case-control study. *Archives of General Psychiatry,* 55(5):425–432.

Fairfield, H. (2010, April 4). Factory food. *The New York Times,* BU5.

Fat tax. (2010, November 17). In Wikipedia, the free encyclopedia. Accessed November 30, 2010, http://en.wikipedia.org/wiki/Fat_tax.

Ferrari, J. R., Stevens, E. B., & Jason, L. A. (2010). An exploratory analysis of changes in self-regulation and social support among men and women in recovery. *Journal of Groups in Addiction & Recovery,* 5(2):145–154. Accessed October 11, 2010, http://www.informaworld.com/smpp/ftinterface~content=a922043638~fulltext=713240928~frm=content.

Field, A., Austin, S. B., Taylor, C. B., Malspeis, S., Rosner, B., Rockett, H. R., Gillman, M. W., Colditz, G.A. (2003). Relationship between dieting and weight change among preadolescents and adolescents. *Pediatrics,* 112(4):900–906.

Fields, S. (2004). The fat of the land: Do agriculture subsidies foster poor health? *Environmental Health Perspectives*, 112:A820–A823.

Finkelstein, E. A., Flebelkorn, I. C., & Wang, G. (2003). National medical spending attributable to overweight and obesity: How much, and who's paying? *Health Affairs*, W3:219–226.

Finkelstein, E. A., Trogdon, J. G., Cohen, J. W., & Dietz, W. (2009). Health affairs: Annual medical spending attributable to obesity – Payer- and service-specific estimates. Research Triangle Park, NC: RTI International. Accessed July 29, 2009, via an emailed copy of the report from RTI International.

Fiore, K. (2008, September 12). Depression stalks five percent of U.S. population. *MedPage Today*. Accessed June 16, 2010, http://www.medpagetoday.com/Psychiatry/Depression/10901.

Fitzgibbon, M. L., Blackman, L. R., & Avellone, M. E. (2000). The relationship between body image discrepancy and body mass index across ethnic groups. *Obesity Research*, 8:582–589.

Flegal, K. M. (2006). Commentary: The epidemic of obesity – What's in a name? *International Journal of Epidemiology*, 35:72–74.

Flegal, K. M., Carroll, M. D., Kuczmarski, R. J., & Johnson, C. L. (1998). Overweight and obesity in the United States: Prevalence and trends, 1960–1994. *International Journal of Obesity*, 22 (1):39–47.

Flegal, K. M., Carroll, M. D., Ogden, C. L., & Curtin, L. R. (2010). Prevalence and trends in obesity among U.S. adults, 1999–2008. *Journal of the American Medical Association*, 303 (3):235–241. Accessed May 12, 2010, http://jama.ama-assn.org/cgi/content/full/2009.2014.

Flegal, K. M., Graubard, B. I., Williamson, D. F., & Gail, M. H. (2005). Excess deaths associated with underweight, overweight, and obesity. *Journal of the American Medical Association*, 293 (15):1861–1867.

Flegal, K. M., & Troiano, R. P. (2000). Changes in the distribution of body mass index of adults and children in the U.S. population. *International Journal of Obesity*, 24(7):807–818.

Fletcher, J. M., Frisvold, D., & Tefft, N. (2010a). Can soft drink taxes reduce population weight? *Contemporary Economic Policy*. Washington, DC: U.S. Department of Agriculture. Accessed September 23, 2010, http://info.med.yale.edu/eph/faculty/labs/fletcher/fft.pdf.

Fletcher, J. M., Frisvold, D., & Tefft, N. (2010b). Taxing soft drinks and restricting access to vending machines to curb child obesity. *Health Affairs*, 29(5, May):1059–1066.

Flicker, L., McCaul, K. A., Hankey, G. J., Jamrozik, K., Brown, W. J., Byles, J. E., & Almeida, O. P. (2010). Body mass index and survival in men and women aged 70 to 75. *Journal of the American Geriatrics Society*, 58(January 27):234–241.

Flynn, K. J., & Fitzgibbon, M. (1998). Body images and obesity risk among black females: A review of the literature. *American Behavioral Medicine*, 20:13–24.

Fogel, R. W. (1994). Economic growth, population theory, and physiology: The bearing of long-term processes on the making of economic policy. *American Economic Review*, 84 (3):369–395.

Fogel, R. W. (1999). Public use tape on the aging of veterans of the Union Army: Surgeons' certificates, 1860–1940, Version S-1, Unstandardized. Chicago: University of Chicago.

Foley, J. (2010). Fossil hominids: Lucy (AL 288-1). The Talk Origins Archive. Accessed October 5, 2010, http://www.talkorigins.org/faqs/homs/lucy.html.

Foley, J. (2010a). Hominid species. The Talk Origins Archive. Accessed March 25, 2010, http://www.talkorigins.org/faqs/homs/species.html.

Foley, J. (2010c, December 29). Food prices face a perilous rise. *The New York Times*, B2.

Forest – Voice and Friend of the Smoker. (2008). History of smoking. Accessed August 7, 2010, http://www.forestonline.org/output/History-of-Smoking.aspx.

Foster, G. D., Wadden, T. A., Makris, A. P., Davidson, D., Sanderson, R. S., Allison, D. B., Kessler A. (2003). Primary care physicians' attitudes about obesity and its treatment. *Obesity Research*, 11:1168–1177.

Fox Business News (2009, April 20). Airlines to charge obese fliers double. Accessed July 7, 2009, http://www.foxbusiness.com/search-results/m/22123753/airlines-to-charge-obese-fliers-double. htm.

FoxNews.com (2010, August 3). Larger audience members demand bigger seats. Accessed August 4, 2010, http://liveshots.blogs.foxnews.com/2010/08/03/larger-audience-members-demand-bigger-seats/.

Frank, R. H. (2010). Luxury fever: Money and happiness in an era of excess. Princeton, NJ: Princeton University Press.

Frazao, E. (1999, May). America's eating habits: Changes and consequences (Agriculture Information Bulletin No. AIB750). Washington, DC: U.S. Department of Agricultural. Accessed May 11, 2010, http://www.ers.usda.gov/Publications/AIB750/.

Frederick, S., Lowenstein, G., & O'Donoghue, T. (2002). Time discounting and time preference: A critical review. *Journal of Economic* Literature, 40(2, June):351–401.

Freedman, D. H. (2010). Wrong: Why experts keep failing us – and how to know when not to trust them. New York: Little, Brown and Company.

French, P, Crabbe M (2010) Fat China: How expanding waistlines are changing a nation. London and New York: Anthem Press.

French, S. A., Harnack, L., & Jeffery, R. W. (2000). Fast food restaurant use among women in the Pound of Prevention Study: Dietary, behavioral, and demographic correlates. *International Journal of Obesity*, 24:1353–1359.

French, S. A., Jeffrey, R. W., Story, M., Breitlow, K. K., Baxter, J. S., Hannan P., & Snyder, M.P. (2001). Pricing and promotion effects on low-fat vending snack purchases: The CHIPS study. *American Journal of Public Health*, 91(1):112–117.

French, S. A., Story, M., Jeffrey, R. W., Snyder, P., Eisenberg, M., Sidebottom, A., & Murray, D. (1997). Pricing strategy to promote fruit and vegetable purchase in high school cafeterias. *Journal of American Diabetic Association*, 97:1008–1010.

French S. A., Story, M., & Perry, C. L. (1995). Self-esteem and obesity in children and adolescents: A literature review. *Obesity Research*, 3:479–490.

Friedman, M. (1962). Capitalism and freedom. Chicago: University of Chicago Press.

Friedman, Milton. (1973). A 1973 interview with Milton Friedman. *Playboy*, as accessed on December 8, 2010, http://jeepers1.wordpress.com/2010/02/21/a-1973-interview-with-milton-friedman-playboy-magazine/.

Friedman, M., & Friedman, R. D. (1980). Free to choose: A personal statement. New York: Harcourt Brace Jovanovich.

Fuzhong, L., Hammer, P., Cardinal, B. J., Bosworth, M., & Johnson-Shelton, D. (2009). Obesity and the built environment: Does the density of neighborhood fast-food outlets matter. *American Journal of Health Promotion*, 23(3, August 21):203–209.

Gavin, A. R., Rue, T., & Takeuchi, D. (2010). Racial/ethnic differences in the association between obesity and major depressive disorder: Findings from the Comprehensive Psychiatric Epidemiology Surveys. *Public Health Report*, 125(5, September-October):698–708.

Gallagher, D. (2004). Overweight and obesity BMI cutoffs and their relationship to metabolic disorders in Koreans/Asians. *Obesity Research*, 12(3):445–453.

Gallup, Inc. (2010). Evolution, creationism, and intelligent design. (Data collected May 8–11, 2008). Accessed February 26, 2010, http://www.gallup.com/poll/21814/Evolution-Creationism-Intelligent-Design.aspx.

Geier, A.B., Schwartz, M. B., & Brownell, K. D. (2003). Before and after diet advertisements escalate weight stigma. *Eating and Weight Disorders*, 8:282–288.

Gelbach, J. B., Klick, J., & Stratmann, T. (2007, March 21). Cheap donuts and expensive broccoli: The effect of relative prices on obesity (Research Law Paper No. 261). Tallahassee, FL: Florida State University, College of Law. Accessed August 27, 2009, the Social Science Research Network, http://papers.ssrn.com/sol3/papers.cfm?abstract_id=976484

Gershon, R. R. M., Qureshi, K. A., Rubin, M. S., & Raveis, V. H. (2007). Factors associated with high-rise evacuation: Qualitative results from the World Trade Center evacuation study.

Prehospital and Disaster Medicine, 22(3, May/June):165–173. Accessed August 16, 2010, http://pdm.medicine.wisc.edu/Volume_22/issue_3/gershon.pdf.

Gillman, M. W., Rifas-Shiman, S. L., Berkey, C. S., Frazier, A. L., Rockett, H. R., Camargo, C. A. Jr, Field, A. E., & Colditz, G. A. (2006). Breastfeeding and overweight in adolescence: Within-family analysis. *Epidemiology,* 17:112–114.

Gneezy, U., & Rustichini, A. (2000). A fine is a price. *Journal of Legal Studies,* 29(1, January). Accessed November 16, 2010, http://papers.ssrn.com/sol3/papers.cfm?abstract_id=180117.

Goldman, D., Lakdawalla, D., & Zheng, Y. (2010, March 16). Food prices and the dynamics of body weight, a paper presented at a Conference on the Economic Aspects of Obesity, Robert Wood Johnson Foundation, November 10–11, 2008. Accessed December 15, 2010, http://www.rwjf.org/pr/product.jsp?id=62468.

Goodyear, C. (1997, December 18). Bedsores covered 680-pound girl, experts says. *SFGate.com.* Accessed June 25, 2010, http://articles.sfgate.com/1997-12-18/news/17764491_1_marlene-corrigan-christina-corrigan-christina-s-death.

Gordon-Larsen, P., & Adair, L. S. (In press). Timing of obesity onset in adolescents followed into adulthood: The role of maternal obesity. *Obesity.* Accessed November 10, 2010, http://www.cpc.unc.edu/projects/addhealth/pubs/61503.

Gore, A. (2006). An inconvenient truth: The planetary emergency of global warming and what we can do about it. Emmaus, PA: Rodale Books.

Gorski, E. (2010). College 'gender gap' favoring women stops growing. Associated Press, as posted January 26, 2010, at http://www.boston.com/news/education/higher/articles/2010/01/26/college_gender_gap_favoring_women_stops_growing/.

GoTicket.com. New Yankee Stadium seating chart and tickets. Accessed July 27, 2010, http://www.gotickets.com/venues/ny/new_yankee_stadium.php.

Greenberg, B. S., Eastin, M., Hofshire, L., Lachlan, K., & Brownell, K. D. (2003). The portrayal of overweight and obese persons in commercial television. *American Journal of Public Health,* 93:1342–1348.

Gregg, E. W., Cheng, Y. J., Cadwell, B. L., Imperatore, G., Williamson, D. E., Flegal, K. M., Narayan, K. M., & Williamson, D. F. (2005). Secular trends in cardiovascular disease risk factors according to body mass index in U.S. adults. *Journal of American Medical Association,* 293(9):1321–1326.

Gregory, C., & Ruhm, C. J. (2009). Where does the wage penalty bite? (NBER Working Paper 14984). Cambridge, MA: National Bureau of Economic Research. Accessed December 15, 2010, http://www.nber.org/papers/w14984.pdf.

Greviskes, A. (2010, March 30). Fast food as addictive as heroin, study confirms. *That's Fit.* Accessed October 19, 2010, http://www.thatsfit.com/2010/03/30/fast-food-is-like-heroin-studies-find/.

Grimstvedt, M. E., Kerr, J., Oswal, S. B., Fogt, D. L., Vargas-Tonsing, T. M., & Yin, Z. (2010). Using signage to promote stair use on a university campus in hidden and visible stairwells. *Journal of Physical Activity and Health,* 7(2, March):232–238. Accessed August 16, 2010, http://journals.humankinetics.com/jpah-back-issues/JPAHVolume7Issue2March/UsingSignagetoPromoteStairUseonaUniversityCampusinHiddenandVisibleStairwells.

Grohol, J. (2010, June 11). Link between depression, obesity confirmed. *PsychCentral.* Accessed June 14, 2010, http://psychcentral.com/news/2010/06/11/14513/14513.html.

Grossman, M. (2000). The human capital model. In: A. J. Cutler & J. P. Newhouse (eds.), Handbook of health economics, 1A (pp. 347–408). New York: Elsevier.

Grummer-Strawn, L. M., & Mei, Z. (2004). Does breastfeeding protect against pediatric overweight? Analysis of longitudinal data from the Centers for Disease Control and Prevention Pediatric Nutrition Surveillance System. *Pediatrics,* 113:E81–E86.

Gumert, M. D. (2007). Payment for sex in a macaque mating market. *Animal Behaviour,* 74:1655–1667.

Guthrie, J. F., Lin, B. H., Frazao, E. (2002). Role of food prepared away from home in the American diet, 1977–78 versus 1994–96: Changes and consequences. *Journal of Nutrition Education and Behaviors,* 34(3 May-June):140–150.

Halfon, N., & Lu, M. C. (2010). Gestational weight gain and birthweight. *The Lancet,* 376(9745, September 18):937–938. Accessed September 8, 2010, http://www.thelancet.com/journals/lancet/article/PIIS0140-6736(10)61024-0/fulltext#.

Hamermesh, D. S., & Biddle, J. E. (1994). Beauty and the labor market. *American Economic Review,* 84(5, December):1174–1194.

Han, E., Norton, E. C., & Stearns, S. C. (2009). Weight and wages: Fat versus lean paychecks. *Health Economics,* 18(5):535–548.

Hannan, P., French, S. A., Story, M., & Fulkerson, J. A. (2002). A pricing strategy to promote lower fat foods in a high school cafeteria: Acceptability and sensitivity analysis. *American Journal of Health Promotion,* 17:1–6.

Hard, J. (2009, June 15). What you should know about mishandled checked luggage on airlines. *About.com.* Accessed July 7, 2009, http://eventplanning.about.com/od/transportation/a/airline-baggage-checked-baggage-lost-luggage.htm.

Harmon, K. (2010, January 5). Obesity is now just as much of a drag on health as smoking. *Scientific American.* Accessed August 9, 2010, http://www.scientificamerican.com/blog/post.cfm?id=obesity-is-now-just-as-much-of-a-dr-2010-01-05.

Hartocollis, A. (2010a, October 7). City seeking to wean poor from sodas. *The New York Times,* A1.

Hartocollis, A. (2010b, October 8). Plan to ban food stamps for sodas has hurdles. *The New York Times,* A19.

Hartocollis, A. (2010c, October 9). For soda-banning mayor, a different policy at his company. *The New York Times,* A13.

Harvey, E. L., & Hill, A. J. (2001). Health professionals' views of overweight people and smokers. *International Journal of Obesity,* 25, 1253–1261.

Hayek, F. A. (1944). The road to serfdom. Chicago: University of Chicago Press.

HEALTHY Study Group (Foster, G. D.). (2010). A school-based intervention for diabetes risk reduction. *New England Journal of Medicine,* 363:443–453. Accessed July 14, 2010, http://www.nejm.org/doi/full/10.1056/NEJMoa1001933.

Healy, M. (2009, June 10). Deal struck to post calorie counts at chain restaurants nationwide. *Los Angeles Times.* Accessed July 7, 2009, http://latimesblogs.latimes.com/booster_shots/2009/06/deal-struck-to-post-calorie-counts-at-chain-restaurants-nationwide.html

Healy, M. (2010, November 9). Obesity often follows young into adulthood. *Los Angeles Times.* Accessed November 10, 2010, http://www.latimes.com/health/la-he-obese-teens-20101109,0,3643373.story.

Hedley, A. A., Ogden, C. L., Johnson, C. L., Carroll, M. D., Curtin, L. R., & Flegal, K. M. (2004). Prevalence of overweight and obesity among US children, adolescents, and adults, 1999–2002. *Journal of the American Medical Association,* 291:2847–2850.

Helmchen, L. A. (2001). Can structural change explain the rise in obesity? A look at the past 100 years (Working Paper). Chicago: University of Chicago. Accessed August 6, 2009, http://www.src.uchicago.edu/prc/pdfs/helmch01.pdf.

Helmchen, L. A., & Henderson, R. M. (2004). Changes in the distribution of body mass index of white US men, 1890–2000. *Annals of Human Biology,* 31(2):174–181.

Hernandez, J.C. (February 3, 2011). Smoking ban for beaches and parks is approved. *The New York Times,* A22.

Hill, A. J. (2004). Does dieting make you fat? *British Journal of Nutrition,* 92(Suppl. 1):S15–S18.

Hoholik, S. (2010, July 19). Burden of cots for obese may fall on taxpayers. *Columbus* [Ohio] *Dispatch.* Accessed July 26, 2010, http://www.dispatch.com/live/content/local_news/stories/2010/07/19/burden-of-cots-for-obese-may-fall-on-taxpayers.html?sid=101.

Hollingsworth, H. (2009, October 23). Obese patients get higher ambulance rates. *Associated Press.* Accessed December 7, 2010, http://www.allbusiness.com/health-care/health-care-facilities-clinics/13368458-1.html.

Hoovers (2010). Industry overview: Fast food and quick service restaurants. Accessed August 12, 2010, http://www.hoovers.com/fast-food-and-quickservice-restaurants/–ID__269–/free-ind-fr-profile-basic.xhtml.

Household sector: liabilities, household credit market debt outstanding (CMDEBT) (2010). [Data file]. St. Louis: Federal Reserve Bank of St. Louis. Accessed September 23, 2010, http://research.stlouisfed.org/fred2/series/CMDEBT.

Huckabee, M. (2006, April 30). Kelly Brownell. *Time.* Accessed November 6, 2010, http://www.time.com/time/magazine/article/0,9171,1187241,00.html.

Huffstutter, P. J. (2010a, November 16). 15% of families went hungry in 2009. *Los Angeles Times*, B2.

Huffstutter, P. J. (2010b, December 30). USDA requires nutrition labels for 40 popular cuts of meat. *Los Angeles Times*, B2.

Hunt, S. C., Syone, S., Xin, Y., Scherer, C. A., Magness, C. L., Iadonato, S. P., Hopkins, P. N., & Adams, T. D. (2008). Association of the FTO gene with BMI. *Obesity,* 16(4, April):902–904.

Inflationdata.com (2010). Inflation adjusted gasoline prices, updated July 21, 2010. Accessed November 29, 2010, http://www.inflationdata.com/inflation/inflation_rate/Gasoline_Inflation.asp.

Injuryboard.com (2003, May 13). Federal Aviation Administration increases weight estimates for passengers and luggage. Accessed December 8, 2010, http://www.injuryboard.com/national-news/federal-aviation-administration.aspx?googleid=27862.

Institute for Women's Policy Research. (2010). The gender wage gap: 2009 (Fact Sheet No. IWPR C350). Accessed May 12, 2010, http://www.iwpr.org/pdf/C350.pdf.

International Panel on Climate Change, United Nations (2007). IPCC Fourth Assessment Report, Working Group III. Accessed January 9, 2011, http://www.citizensenergy.com/fckupload/File/Energy_Forum_Reports/Climate%20Change/ipcc-mitigationrept040507.pdf.

Ippolito, R. M., & Mathios, A. D. (1995). Information and advertising: The case of fat consumption in the United States. *American Economic Review,* 85(2):91–95.

Itola.com (2008, February 6). Mississippi law: No fat people allowed. Accessed July 7, 2009, http://itola.com/business/new-mississippi-law-no-fat-people-allowed/.

Jacobson, S. H., & King, D. M. (2009). Measuring the potential for automobile fuel savings in the US: The impact of obesity. *Transportation Research Part D: Transport and Environment*, 14 (1, January):6–13. Accessed July 9, 2010, http://www.sciencedirect.com/science?_ob=ArticleURL&_udi=B6VH8-4V053N5-1&_user=10&_coverDate=01%2F31%2F2009&_rdoc=1&_fmt=high&_orig=search&_origin=search&_sort=d&_docanchor=&view=c&_searchStrId=1560723086&_rerunOrigin=google&_acct=C000050221&_version=1&_urlVersion=0&_userid=10&md5=24c3e7bea3579611284bf8903df454c1&searchtype=a.

Jacobson, S. H., & McLay, L. (2006). The economic impact of obesity on automobile fuel consumption. *Engineering Economist*, 54(4):307–323.

Johns Hopkins Health Alert (2010, September 15). How many calories should you eat in a day? COPD News of the Day. Accessed September 19, 2010, http://copdnewsoftheday.com/?p=4111.

Johnsson, J. (2009, April 16). United Airlines to start charging obese for two seats, or bump them from packed flights. *Chicagotribune.com.* Accessed June 27, 2009, http://archives.chicagotribune.com/2009/apr/16/business/chi-biz-united-airlines-obese-two-seats-april15.

Kamel, E. G., & McNeill, G. (2000). Men are less aware of being overweight than women. *Obesity Research,* 8:604.

Kaplan, K. (2010, April 21). Sweet tooth? Watch your heart. *Los Angeles Times*, AA1.

Karasu, S. R., & Karasu, T. B. (2010). The gravity of weight: A clinical guide to weight loss and maintenance. Washington, DC: American Psychiatric Publishing, Inc.

Karnehed, N., Rasmussen, F., Hemmingsson, T., & Tynelius, P. (2006). Obesity and attained education: Cohort study of more than 700,000 Swedish men. *Obesity,* 14:1421–1428.

Keller E. B., Manning W., Newhouse J. P., Sloss, E. M., & Wasserman, J. (1989). The external costs of a sedentary lifestyle. *American Journal of Public Health,* 79:975–981.

Kemper, K. A., Sargent, R. C., Drane, J. W., Valois, F., & Hussey, J. R. (1994). Black and white female's perception of ideal body size and social norms. *Obesity Research, 2*(2, March): 117–126.

Kim, D., & Leigh, J. P. (2010). Estimating the effects of wages on obesity. *Journal of Occupational and Environmental Medicine, 52*(5):495–500. Retrieved from SCOPUS database: http://www.scopus.com

Kin, J., & Peterson, K. E. (2008). Association of infant child care with infant feeding practices and weight gain among US infants. *Archives of Pediatric and Adolescent Medicine, 162*(7):627–633. Accessed June 18, 2010, http://archpedi.highwire.org/cgi/content/abstract/162/7/627.

Klick, J., & Stratmann, T. (2007). Diabetes treatments and moral hazard. *Journal of Law and Economics, 50*:519–538.

Knutson, B., & Bossaerts, P. (2007). Neural antecedents of financial decisions. *The Journal of Neuroscience, 27*(31, August 1):8174–8177.

Kolata, G. (2006, October 29). For a world of woes, we blame cookie monsters. *The New York Times.* Accessed August 20, 2010, http://www.nytimes.com/2006/10/29/weekinreview/29kolata.html?fta=y.

Kopelman, P. G. (2000). Obesity as a medical problem. *Nature, 404*(6778):635–643.

Kuk, J. L., Katzmarzyk, P. T., Nichaman, M. Z., Church, T. S., Blair, S. N., & Ross, R. (2006). Visceral fat is an independent predictor of all-cause mortality in men. *Obesity, 14*:336–341.

Kumanyika, S., Wilson, J. F., & Guilford-Davenport, M. (1993). Weight-related attitudes and behaviors of black women. *Journal of American Diet Association, 93*:416–422.

Kuzawa, C. W. (1998). Adipose tissue in human infancy and childhood: An evolutionary perspective. *Yearbook of Physical Anthropology, 41*:177–209.

La Ganga, M. (1998, January 10). Obese girl's mother found guilty of misdemeanor child abuse. *Los Angeles Times.* Accessed June 25, 2010, http://articles.latimes.com/1998/jan/10/news/mn-6819.

Labor Law Center (2010). Federal minimal wage. Accessed December 8, 2010, http://www.laborlawcenter.com/t-federal-minimum-wage.aspx.

Lakdawalla, D., & Philipson, T. (2002). The growth of obesity and technological change: A theoretical and empirical examination (Working Paper No. 8946). Cambridge, MA: National Bureau of Economic Research.

Lakshminarayanan, V., Chen, M. K., & Santos, L. (2008). Endowment effect in capuchin monkeys. *Philosophical Transactions of the Royal Society, 363*(October):3837–3844.

Laran, J. (2009). Choosing your future: Temporal distance and the balance between self-control and indulgence. *Journal of Consumer Research, 36*(April):1002–1015. Accessed October 11, 2010, https://moya.bus.miami.edu/~jularan/Papers/ISR4_Laran_JCR.pdf.

Latner, J. D., & Stunkard, A. J. (2003). Getting worse: The stigmatization of obese children. *Obesity Research, 11*(3):452–456.

Latner, J. D., Stunkard, A. J., & Wilson, G. T. (2005). Stigmatized students: Age, sex, and ethnicity effects in the stigmatization of obesity. *Obesity Research, 13*(7, July):1226–1231.

Lauder, W., Mummery, K., Jones, M., & Caperchione, C. (2006). A comparison of health behaviors in lonely and non-lonely populations. *Psychological Health Medicine, 11*:233–245.

Lavie, C. J., Milani, R. V., Ventura, H. O., & Romero-Corral, A. (2010). Body composition and heart failure prevalence and prognosis: Getting to the fat of the matter in the "obesity paradox." *Mayo Clinic Proceedings, 85*(7, July). Accessed September 1, 2010, http://www.mayoclinic-proceedings.com/content/85/7/605.full.pdf+html.

Leibovich, L. (1997, September 22). Mothers who think: The death of a fat girl. *Salon.com.* Accessed June 25, 2010, http://www.salon.com/sept97/mothers/obese970922.html.

Leonhardt, D. (2009, May 19). Sodas a tempting tax target. *The New York Times.* Accessed September 23, 2010, http://www.nytimes.com/2009/05/20/business/economy/20leonhardt.html?_r=2.

Leonhardt, D. (2009b, August 12). Fat tax. *The New York Times*. Accessed August 11, 2010, http://www.nytimes.com/2009/08/16/magazine/16FOB-wwln-t.html.

Leventhal, A. M., Mickens, L., Dunton, G. F., Sussman, S., Riggs, N. R., & Pentz, M. A. (2010). Tobacco use moderates the association between major depression and obesity. *Health Psychology*, 29(5, September):521–528.

Levin, B. (2007). Why some of us get fat and what we can do about it. *Journal of Physiology*, 583 (June 21):425–430.

Levin, M. L. (1950). Tobacco smoking and cancer. *Journal of the American Medical Association*, 144(9, October 28):782.

Levitan, D. J. (2006). This is your brain on music. New York: Dutton Books.

Levitt, S. D., & Dubner, S. J. (2005). Freakonomics: A rogue economist explores the hidden side of everything. New York: William Morrow.

Levitt, S. D., & Dubner, S. J. (2009). Superfreakonomics: Global cooling, patriotic prostitutes and why suicide bombers should buy life insurance. New York: William Morrow.

Levy, A. (2002). Rational eating: Can it lead to overweightness or underweightness? *Journal of Health Economics*, 21:887–899.

Lewis, A. (2010, August 29). The skinny on Hooters. *The Wall Street Journal*. Accessed September 28, 2010, http://online.wsj.com/article/SB10001424052748703669004575458183015136828.html.

Li, S., Zhao, J. H., Luan, J., Ekelund, U., Luben, R. N., Khaw, K. T., Wareham, N. J., & Loos, R. J. (2010). Physical activity attenuates the genetic predisposition to obesity in 20,000 men and women from EPIC-Norfolk prospective population. *PLoS Medicine*, 7(8, August). Accessed September 30, 2010, http://www.plosmedicine.org.

Lichtman, S. W., Pisarska, K., Berman, E. R., Pestone, M., Dowling, H., Offenbacher, E., Weisel, H., Heshka, S., Matthews, D. E., & Heymsfield, S. B. (1992). Discrepancy between self-reported and actual calorie intake and exercise in obese subjects. *New England Journal of Medicine*, 327:1893–1898.

Lieber, R. (2011, January 1). Incentivize your way to good health in 2011. *The New York Times*, B1.

Lin, B., & Frazao, E. (1999). Away-from-home foods increasingly important to quality of American diet (Agriculture Information Bulletin No. 749). Washington, D.C.: U.S. Department of Agriculture.

Lisi, C. (2010, March 15). New Jersey woman wants to be world's fattest woman. *New York Post*. Accessed July 4, 2010, http://www.myfoxny.com/dpp/news/dpgonc-donna-simpson-attempting-to-become-worlds-fattest-woman-fc-20100315.

Liu, L., Rettenmaier, A. J., & Saving, T. R. (2007). Endogenous food quality and bodyweight trend. In: K. Bolin & J. Cawley (eds.), The economics of obesity (pp. 3–22). Bingley, UK: Emerald Group Publishing Ltd.

Los Angeles Times (2007, December 25). Nation in brief: Many don't see offspring's obesity, A25.

Loveys, K. (2010, February 20). The fast and the furious: Stylist at London Fashion Week resigns over designer Mark Fast's decision to use size 14 model. *MailOnline*. Accessed July 27, 2010, http://www.dailymail.co.uk/femail/article-1214799/London-Fashion-Week-stylist-resigns-designers-decision-use-size-14-models-show.html.

Ludwig, D. S., & Currie, J. (2010, August 5). The association between pregnancy weight gain and birthweight: A within-family comparison. *The Lancet* (Early Online Publication). Accessed September 8, 2010, http://www.thelancet.com/journals/lancet/article/PIIS0140-6736(10)60751-9/abstract.

Luna, N. (2010, December 29). Bulking up diners' info: Laws requiring calorie counts aim to combat obesity, but effectiveness is unclear. *Orange County Register*, L1.

MacFarquhar, N. (February 4, 2011). Food prices worldwide hit record levels, fueled by uncertainty, U.N. says. *The New York Times*, A4.

Maddock, J. (2004). The relationship between obesity and the prevalence of fast food restaurants: State-level analysis. *American Journal of Health Promotion,* 19(2, November-December):137–143.

Maes, H. H., Neale, M. C., & Eaves, L. J. (1997). Genetic and environmental factors in relative body weight and human adiposity. *Behavioral Genetics,* 27:325–351.

Malthus, T. R. (1798/1999). An essay on the theory of population. New York: Oxford University Press.

Marcus, G. (2008). Kluge: The haphazard evolution of the human mind. Boston: Mariner Books.

Mariano, W. (2008, January 25). Hefty corpses straining morgues. *Orlando* [Florida] *Sentinel.* Accessed on July 26, 2010, the *Columbus* [Ohio] *Dispatch,* http://www.dispatch.com/live/content/life/stories/2008/01/25/1A_CORPSES.ART_ART_01-25-08_D1_G194O2F.html?sid=101.

Markowitz, S., Friedman, M. A., & Arent, S. M. (2008). Understanding the relation between obesity and depression: Causal mechanisms and implications for treatment. *Clinical Psychology,* 15(1, February):1–20. Accessed June 16, 2010, http://www3.interscience.wiley.com/journal/119412258/abstract?CRETRY=1&SRETRY=0.

Marsh, L. (2010, August 24). Nail salon charges her $5 extra for being overweight. *MSNBC.com.* Accessed August 24, 2010, http://today.msnbc.msn.com/id/38829032/ns/today-today_fashion_and_beauty/?GT1=43001.

Marshall, A. (1890/1920). Principles of economics. London: Macmillan and Co., Ltd. Accessed January 24, 2008, from http://www.econlib.org/library/Marshall/marP1.html.

Martel, F. (2010, December 13). Mayor Gavin Newsom vetoes San Francisco ban on Happy Meal toys. *MedialTE.com.* Accessed December 21, 2010, http://www.mediaite.com/online/mayor-gavin-newsom-vetoes-san-francisco-ban-on-happy-meal-toys/.

Maxon, T. (2008, April 27). Southwest Airlines sees no benefit in bag fees. *DallasNews.com.* Accessed July 7, 2009, http://www.dallasnews.com/sharedcontent/dws/bus/stories/DN-airlinebags_27bus.ART.State.Edition1.3b4ec20.html.

Mayo Clinic Staff (2010, September 20). Exercise for weight loss: Calories burned in 1 hour. *MayoClinic.com.* Accessed September 20, 2010, http://www.mayoclinic.com/health/exercise/SM00109.

McKay, B. (2009, July 28). Cost of treating obesity soars. *The Wall Street Journal,* D3.

McKenzie, R. B. (2008a, January 4). Dieting for dollars. *The Wall Street Journal.* Accessed August 10, 2010, http://online.wsj.com/article/SB119940580637766327.html.

McKenzie, R. B. (2008b). Why popcorn costs so much at the movies, and other pricing puzzles. New York, Berlin, Heidelberg: Springer.

McKenzie, R. B. (2010a). Predictably rational? In search of defenses of rational behavior in economics. New York, Berlin, Heidelberg: Springer.

McKenzie, R. B. (2010b, January 4). Predictably irrational or predictably rational? *Library of Economics and Liberty.* Accessed June 7, 2010, http://www.econlib.org/library/Columns/y2010/McKenzierational.html.

McKenzie, R. B., & Lee, D. R. (2010). Microeconomics for MBAs: The economic way of thinking for managers. Cambridge, UK: Cambridge University Press.

McKenzie, R. B., & Tullock, G. (1976). The new world of economics. Homewood, IL: Richard D. Irwin.

McKenzie, R. B., & Tullock, G. (2011). The new world of economics (6th ed.). New York, Berlin, Heidelberg: Springer.

McKeown, K. (2010, March 23). Scripps research study shows compulsive eating shares same addictive biochemical mechanism with cocaine, heroin abuse. Accessed October 19, 2010, Scripps Research Institute Web site: http://www.scripps.edu/news/press/20100329.html.

McMichael, W. H. (2009, November 5). Most U.S. youths unfit to serve, data show. *ArmyTimes.* Accessed September 21, 2010, http://www.armytimes.com/news/2009/11/military_unfityouths_recruiting_110309w/.

Medline Plus (2009) Wider waist boosts asthma risk: Even if women were of normal weight, extra fat around abdomen raised the odds, study found. Accessed on September 9, 2009, http://www.nlm.nih.gov/medlineplus/news/fullstory_88514.html.

Meltzer, D. O., & Chen, Z. (2009, November). The impact of minimum wage rates on body weight in the United States (Working Paper 15485). Cambridge, MA: National Bureau of Economic Research.

Metropolitan Life Insurance Company (1966). Trends in average weights: Insured men and women. *Statistical Bulletin of Metropolitan Life Insurance Company*, pp. 1–3.

Metropolitan Life Insurance Company. (1970). Trends in average weights, heights of men: An insurance experiment. *Statistical Bulletin of Metropolitan Life Insurance Company*, pp. 6–7.

Miller, G. (2001). The mating mind: How sexual choice shaped the evolution of human nature. New York: Anchor.

Miller, K. (2009, June 17). Baldacci signs bills to curb obesity. *BangorDailyNews.com*. Accessed July 7, 2009, http://www.bangordailynews.com/detail/108646.html.

Mitchell, G.L., & Brunstrom, J.M. (2005). Everyday dietary behaviour and the relationship between attention and meal size. *American Journal of Clinical Nutrition, 45*(3, December):344–355. Accessed January 5, 2011, http://www.sciencedirect.com/science?_ob= ArticleURL&_udi=B6WB2-4GPW6D9-2&_user=10&_coverDate=12%2F31%2F2005 &_ rdoc=1&_fmt=high&_orig=search&_origin=search&_sort=d&_docanchor=&view=c&_ searchStrId=1597490859&_rerunOrigin=scholar.google&_acct=C000050221&_version=1 &_urlVersion=0&_userid=10&md5= e851ab799d217442d48a897b33853354&searchtype=a.

Mitra, A. (2001). Effects of physical attributes on the wages of males and females. *Applied Economics Letters, 8*(11):731–735. Accessed from SCOPUS Web site database: http://www.scopus.com

Mobius, M., & Rosenblat, T. (2006). Why beauty matters? *American Economic Review, 96*: 222–235

Mocan, N. H., & Tekin, E. (2009, June). Obesity, self-esteem and wages (Working Paper No. 15101). Cambridge, MA: National Bureau of Economic Research.

Mokdad, A.H., Marks, J.S., Stroup, D.F., & Gerberding, J.L. (2004). Actual causes of death in the United States, 2000. *Journal of the American Medical Association, 291*:1238–1245.

Morris, M. A. (2007, March). Short-run motor gasoline demand model. Slide presentation at Energy Information Administration Energy Outlook, Modeling and Data Conference, Washington, DC. Accessed July 9, 2010, http://www.eia.doe.gov/oiaf/aeo/conf/pdf/morris.pdf.

Morewedge, C.K., Huh, Y.E., Vosgerau, J. (2010, December). Thought for food: Imagined consumption reduces actual consumption. *Science* 10:1530–1533.

Morrissey, T.W., Dunifon, R.E., & Kalil, A. (2011). Maternal employment, work schedules, and children's body mass index, *Child Development* 82(1, January/February, online). Accessed February 6, 2011, http://onlinelibrary.wiley.com/doi/10.1111/j.1467-8624.2010.01541.x/abstract.

Moss, M. (2010, November 8). While warning about fat, U.S. pushes cheese sales. *The New York Times*. Accessed November 10, 2010, http://www.nytimes.com/2010/11/07/us/07fat.html?_r=1&scp=2&sq=domino%20%20pizza&st=cse.

Mutzabaugh, B. (2008, January). Today in the sky: Canada – Airlines may not charge clinically obese fliers extra. *USAToday.com*. Accessed July 7, 2009, http://www.usatoday.com/travel/flights/item.aspx?ak=44010330.blog&type=blog.

Narrow W.E, et. al (1998). Acomparison of federal identifications of severe mental illness. Psychiatric Serviced. 49(12):1601–1608

Naik, N. Y., & Moore, M. J. (1996). Habit formation and intertemporal substitution in individual food consumption. *Review of Economics and Statistics, 78*(2):321–328.

National Center for Health Statistics (1978). National health and nutrition examination survey I. [Data file]. Washington: U.S. Department of Health and Human Services. Distributed by Interuniversity Consortium for Political and Social Research, Ann Arbor, MI.

National Center for Health Statistics (1996). National health and nutrition examination survey III. [Data file]. Washington: U.S. Department of Health and Human Services. Distributed by Interuniversity Consortium for Political and Social Research, Ann Arbor, MI.

National Center for Health Statistics (2007). Health, United States, 2007, with chartbook on trends in the health of Americans. Washington, DC: U.S. Government Printing Office. Accessed July 22, 2009, http://cdc.gov/nchs/data/hus/hus07.pdf.

National Center for Health Statistics. (2009). Health, United States, 2008, with chartbook on trends in the health of Americans. Hyattsville, MD: U.S. Government Printing Office. Accessed August 6, 2009, http://www.cdc.gov/nchs/data/hus/hus08.pdf.

National Heart, Lung, and Blood Institute (NHLBI) (1998). Clinical guidelines on the identification, evaluation, and treatment of overweight and obesity in adults: The evidence report. Bethesda, MD: NHLBI

National Institute of Mental Health, Public Information and Communications Branch (2010). Men and depression. Washington, DC: U.S. Department of Health and Human Services, National Institutes of Health. Accessed July 4, 2010, http://www.nimh.nih.gov/health/publications/men-and-depression/depression.shtml.

National Library of Medicine (n.d.). The report of the Surgeon General: Brief history. *Profiles in Science.* Accessed August 7, 2010, http://profiles.nlm.nih.gov/NN/Views/Exhibit/narrative/system.html.

National Library of Medicine. (n.d.). The reports of the Surgeon General: The 1964 report on smoking and health. *Profiles in Science.* Accessed August 7, 2010, http://profiles.nlm.nih.gov/NN/Views/Exhibit/narrative/smoking.html.

National Library of Medicine. (n.d.). The C. Everett Koop papers: Tobacco, second-hand smoke, and the campaign for a smoke-free America. *Profiles in Science.* Accessed August 9, 2010, http://profiles.nlm.nih.gov/QQ/Views/Exhibit/narrative/tobacco.html.

National Survey of Children (2007). [Data file]. Washington, DC: U.S. Department of Health and Human Services. Accessed September 8, 2009, http://nschdata.org/Content/#.

Neavling, S. (2010, June 7). Hooters case sparks debate about weight discrimination. *Detroit Free Press.* Posted to http://www.9news.com/rss/article.aspx?storyid=140484.

Neely, C.J., & Rapach, D.E. (2008, November/December). Real interest rate persistence: Evidence and implications. *Review* (Federal Reserve Bank of St. Louis), 609–642. Accessed December 20, 2010, http://research.stlouisfed.org/publications/review/08/11/Neely.pdf.

Neuman, W. (2010, October 27). Food association plans a package-front label showing nutritional data. *The New York Times.* Accessed November 12, 2010, http://www.nytimes.com/2010/10/28/business/28label.html.

Nielsen, S. J., & Popkin, B. M. (2003). Patterns and trends in food portion sizes, 1977–1998. *Journal of the American Medical Association, 289*(4):450–453.

Nielsen, S. J., Siega-Riz, A. M., & Popkin, B. M. (2002). Trends in food locations and sources among young adolescents and young adults. *Preventive Medicine,* 35:107–113.

Nommsen-Rivers, L. A., & Dewey, K. G. (2009). Growth of breastfed infants. *Breastfeeding Medicine,* 4(S1, October):S45–S49. Accessed June 18, 2010, http://www.liebertonline.com/doi/abs/10.1089/bfm.2009.0048.

O'Connor, M. (2009, July 30). Crews strain to help obese patients. *Omaha World-Herald.* Accessed July 26, 2010, http://www.omaha.com/article/20090730/NEWS01/707309966.

Office of the Surgeon General. (2007). 29 Surgeon General's reports on smoking and health, 1964–2006. Washington, DC: U.S. Department of Health and Human Services. Accessed August 3, 2010, http://www.surgeongeneral.gov/library/secondhandsmoke/factsheets/factsheet8.html.

Ogden, C. L., & Carroll, M. (2010). Prevalence of obesity among children and adolescents: United States, trends 1963–1965 through 2007–2008 (NCHS Health E-Stat). Atlanta: Centers for Disease Control and Prevention. Accessed August 9, 2009, http://www.cdc.gov/obesity/childhood/trends.html.

Ogden, C. L., Carroll, M. D., & Flegal, K. M. (2008). High body mass index for age among US children and adolescents, 2003–2006. *Journal of the American Medical Association, 299* (20):2401–2405.

Ogden, C. L., Carroll, M. D., McDowell, M. A., Flegal, K. M. (2007). Obesity among adults in the United States – No change since 2003–2004 (NCHS Data Brief No 1). Hyattsville, MD: National Center for Health Statistics. Accessed July 17, 2009, http://www.cdc.gov/nchs/data/databriefs/db01.pdf.

Ogden C. L., Flegal, K. M., Carroll, M. D., & Johnson, C. L. (2002). Prevalence and trends in overweight among U.S. children and adolescents, 1999–2000. *Journal of the American Medical Association,* 288(14):1728–1732.

Odgen, C. L., Fryar, C. D., Carroll, M. D., & Flegal, K. M. (2004, October 27). Mean body weight, height, and body mass index, United States 1960–2002 (Advance Data. No. 347). Washington, DC: U.S. Department of Health and Human Services, Centers for Disease Control and Prevention.

O'Keefe, J. H., & Cordain, L. (2004). Cardiovascular disease resulting from a diet and lifestyle at odds with our Paleolithic genome: How to become a 21st century hunter-gatherer. *Mayo Clinic Proceedings,* 79:101–108.

Oldham-Cooper, R. E., Hardman, C. A., Nicoll, C. E., Rogers, P. J., & Brunstrom, J. M. (2010). Playing a computer game during lunch affects fullness, memory for lunch, and later snack intake. *American Journal of Clinical Nutrition* (December 8). Accessed 5 January 2011, http://www.ajcn.org/content/early/2010/12/08/ajcn.110.004580.abstract.

Oliver, J. E. (2006). Fat politics: The real story behind America's obesity epidemic. Oxford, UK: Oxford University Press.

Olson, Walter. (2010, December 15). McDonald's suit over Happy Meal toys by California mom Monet Parham new low in responsible parenting. *New York Daily News.* Accessed December 21, 2010, http://www.nydailynews.com/opinions/2010/12/15/2010-12-15_mcdonalds_suit_over_happy_meal_toys_by_california_mom_monet_parham_new_low_in_re.html.

O'Neil, J. (2006, June 27). Surgeon General warns of second-hand smoke. *The New York Times.* Accessed August 9, 2010, http://www.nytimes.com/2006/06/27/health/27cnd-smoke.html.

Organization for Economic Cooperation and Development (OECD) (2010). Obesity and the economics of prevention: Fit not fat. Paris: OECD Publishing. Available from www.oecd.org/health/fitnotfat.

Owen, C. G., Martin, R. M., Whincup, P. H., Smith, G. D., & Cook, D. G. (2005). Effect of infant feeding on the risk of obesity across the life course: A quantitative review of published evidence. *Pediatrics,* 115(5, May):1367–1377.

Pae, P. (2009, May 16). WiFi returning to airlines. *Los Angeles Times.* Accessed May 17, 2010, http://articles.latimes.com/p/2009/05/16/business/fi-briefcase16.

Paeratakul, S., White, M. A., Williamson, D. A., Ryan, D. H., & Bray, G. J. (2002). Sex, race/ethnicity, socioeconomic status, and BMI in relation to self-perception of overweight. *Obesity Research,* 10(5):345–350.

Park, M. (2010, November 8). Twinkie diet helps nutrition professor lose 27 pounds. *CNNHealth.* Accessed November 8, 2010, http://www.cnn.com/2010/HEALTH/11/08/twinkie.diet.professor/index.html.

Parker-Pope, T. (2010, November 29). Trouble with food waste, and how to prevent it. *New York Times News Service.* Accessed December 13, 2009, http://bendbulletin.com/apps/pbcs.dll/article?AID=/20101129/NEWS0107/11290302/1159&nav_category=.

Pasman, W., Saris, W., & Westerterp-Plantenga, M. (2007). A behavioral model of cyclical dieting. In: K. Bolin & J. Cawley (eds.), The economics of obesity (pp. 49–78). Bingley, UK: Emerald Group Publishing Ltd.

Pear, R. (2010, December 3). Congress sends child nutrition bill championed by Mrs. Obama to the President to sign. *The New York Times,* A15.

Peeke, P. M., & Chrousos, G. P. (1995). Hypercortisolism and obesity. *Annals of the New York Academy of Science,* 771(December):665–676.

Peltzman, S. (1975). The effects of automobile safety regulation. *Journal of Political Economy*, 83 (4):672–678.

Pembrey, G. (2010, June 18). Coffin makers profit from obesity. *WeightWorld-United Kingdom*. Accessed July 26, 2010, http://www.weightworld.co.uk/health-and-diet-news/coffin-makers-obesity-1672.html.

Persico, N., Potlewaite, A, & Silverman, D. (2004). The effect of adolescent experience on labor market outcomes: The case of height. *Journal of Political Economy*, 112(5): 1019–1053.

Peters, J. C., Wyatt, H. R., Donahoo, W. T., & Hill, J. O. (2002). From instinct to intellect: The challenge of maintaining healthy weight in the modern world. *Obesity Review*, 3:69–74.

Petroleum Navigator – Annual Gasoline Consumption (2010, July). [Data file]. Washington, DC: U.S. Energy Information Administration. Accessed July 9, 2010, http://www.eia.doe.gov/ask/gasoline_faqs.asp#gas_consume_year.

Phann, G. A., Biddle, J. E., Hamermesh, D. S., & Bosman, C. M. (2000). Business success and businesses' "beauty capital." *Economic Letters*, 67(May, 2):201–207.

Philipson, T. (2001). The world-wide growth in obesity: An economic research agenda. *Health Economics*, 10:1–7.

Philipson, T., & Posner, R. (2003). The long-run growth in obesity as a function of technological change. *Perspectives in Biology and Medicine*, 46(3S):S87–S107.

Pinker, S. (1997). How the mind works. New York: W.W. Norton.

Pollan, M. (2003, January 12). You want fries with that? [Review of the book, Fat land: How Americans became the fattest people in the world]. *The New York Times*. Accessed June 4, 2010, http://www.nytimes.com/2003/01/12/books/you-want-fries-with-that.html?pagewanted=1.

Posner, R. A. (2009). A failure of capitalism: The crisis of '08 and the descent into depression. Cambridge, MA: Harvard University Press.

Powell, L. M., Auld, M. C., Chaloupka, F. J., O'Malley, P. M., & Johnston, L. D. (2007). Access to fast food and food prices: Relationship with fruit and vegetable consumption and overweight among adolescents. In: K. Bolin & J. Cawley (eds.), The economics of obesity (pp. 23–48). Bingley, UK: Emerald Group Publishing, Ltd.

Powell, M. L., & Schulkin, J. (2009). The evolution of obesity. Baltimore, MD: Johns Hopkins University Press.

Power, A. D., & Kahn, A. S. (1995). Racial differences in women's desires to be thin. *International Journal of Eating Disorders*, 17:191–195.

Power, M. L. (2004). Viability as opposed to stability: An evolutionary perspective on physiological regulation. In J. Schulkin (ed.), Allostasis, homeostasis, and the cost of adaptation (pp. 343–364). Cambridge, UK: Cambridge University Press.

Power, M. L., & Schulkin, J. (2009). The evolution of obesity. Baltimore, MD: Johns Hopkins University Press.

Prentice, A., Rayco-Solon, P., & Moore, S. E. (2005). Insights from the developing world: Thrifty genotypes and thrifty phenotypes. *Proceedings of the Nutrition Society*, 64:153–161.

Price, R. A. (2002). Genetics and common obesity: Background, current status, strategies, and future prospects. In T. A. Wadden & A. J. Stunkard (eds.), Handbook of obesity treatment (pp. 73–94). New York: Guilford.

Public Health Service, U.S. Department of Health and Human Services (2001). The Surgeon General's call to action to prevent and decrease overweight and obesity. Washington, DC: U.S. Government Printing Office.

Puhl, R. M., & Heuer, C. A. (2009). The stigma of obesity: A review and update. Obesity, 22 (January):1–24. Accessed July 10, 2010, http://www.yaleruddcenter.org/resources/upload/docs/what/bias/WeightBiasStudy.pdf.

Puhl, R., & Brownell, K. D. (2001). Bias, discrimination, and obesity. *Obesity Research*, 9 (12):788–805.

Puhl, R. M., & Brownell, K. D. (2006). Confronting and coping with weight stigma: An investigation of overweight and obese adults. *Obesity,* 14:1802–1815.

Putnam, J. (1999). U.S. food supply providing more food and calories. *Food Review,* 22(September-October, 3):246–249.

Rabin, R. C. (2010a, July 13). Obesity in young subjects drops in study. *The New York Times,* D6.

Rabin, R. C. (2010b, November 16). Too much texting is tied to risky activity. *The New York Times,* D6.

Rahilly, C. R., & Farwell, W. R. (2007). Prevalence of smoking in the United States: A focus on age, sex, ethnicity, and geographic patterns. [Electronic version published November 10, 2007]. *Current Cardiovascular Risk Reports,* 1(5):379–385. Accessed May 12, 2010, http://www.springerlink.com/content/t459r15463704w37/.

Raji, C. A., Ho, A. J., Parikshak, N. N., Becker, J. T., Lopez, O. L., Kuller, L. H., Hua X., Leow A. D., Toga, A. W., & Thompson, P. M. (2010). Brain structure and obesity. [Electronic version published August 6, 2009]. *Human Brain Mapping,* 31(3, March):353–364. Accessed July 23, 2010, http://www3.interscience.wiley.com/journal/122539667/abstract?CRETRY=1&SRETRY=0.

Rand C. S. W., & Macgregor, A. M. (1990). Morbidly obese patients' perceptions of social discrimination before and after surgery for obesity. *Southern Medical Journal,* 83(12):1390–1395.

Rand, C. S. W., & Resnick, J. L. (2000). The "good enough" body size as judged by people of varying age and weight. *Obesity Research,* 8:309–316.

Rashad, I., Grossman, M., & Chou, S. (2005, August). The super size of America: An economic estimation of body mass index and obesity in adults (Working Paper No. 11584). Cambridge, MA: National Bureau of Economic Research.

Raynor, H. A., & Epstein, L.H. (2001). Dietary variety, energy regulation, and obesity. *Psychological Bulletin,* 127(3):325–341.

Razak, F., Anand, S. S., Shannon, H., Vuksan, V., Davis, B., Jacobs, R., Teo, K. K., McQueen, M., & Yusuf, S. (2007). Defining obesity cut points in a multiethnic population. *Circulation,* 115 (16):2111–2118.

Razay, G., Vreugdenhil, A., & Wilcock, G. (2006). Obesity, abdominal obesity, and Alzheimer disease. *Dementia and Geriatric Cognitive Disorder,* 22:173–176.

Regents of the University of California (2010). San Francisco Division of the Academic Senate, tobacco CEO's 1994 statement to Congress news clip "Nicotine is not addictive." Accessed August 9, 2010, http://senate.ucsf.edu/tobacco/executives1994congress.html.

Reinberg, S. (2010). TV watching may shorten your life: Too much sitting raises your risk of dying from heart disease, researchers say. *HealthFinder.gov.* Accessed January 26, 2010, http://www.healthfinder.gov/news/newsstory.aspx?docID=634816.

Reuters (2007, July 12). "Fat tax" could save 3,200 lives each year. Accessed July 7, 2009, http://www.reuters.com/article/healthNews/idUSL1254236520070712.

Reuters (2010, April 22). Continental Air posts larger-than-expected loss. Accessed August 18, 2010, http://www.reuters.com/article/idUSTRE63L1I020100422.

Roan, S. (2010, August 9). Puberty age for some girls may still be falling. *Los Angeles Times,* A10.

Robert Wood Johnson Foundation (RWJF) (2008). Healthy kids, healthy communities, call for proposals. Princeton, NJ: RWJF. Accessed August 17, 2010, http://www.rwjf.org/applications/solicited/cfp.jsp?ID=20603.

Roberts, R. E., Kaplan, G. A., Shema, S. J., & Strawbridge, W. J. (2000). Are the obese at greater risk of depression? *American Journal of Epidemiology,* 152(2):152–163. Accessed June 16, 2010, http://aje.oxfordjournals.org/cgi/reprint/152/2/163.pdf.

Robertson, C. (2010, September 8). First Lady asks Congress to join childhood obesity fight. *The New York Times,* A15.

Roehling, M. V., Roehling, P. V., and Pichler, S. (2007). The relationship between body weight and perceived weight-related employment discrimination: The role of sex and race. *Journal of Vocational Behavior,* 71:300–318.

Rosenow, E. C. (2010). Quit smoking, gain weight: Is it inevitable? *MayoClinic.com.* Accessed May 19, 2010, http://www.mayoclinic.com/health/quit-smoking/an01437.

Rosman, K. (2010, April 27). A case for those extra 10 pounds. *The Wall Street Journal*, D1.

Rossner, S. (2002). Obesity: The disease of the twenty-first century. *International Journal of Obesity,* 26(Suppl. 4):S2–S4.

Rowland, M. L. (2009). Self-reported weight and height. *American Journal of Clinical Nutrition,* 52:1125–1133. Accessed August 18, 2010, http://www.ajcn.org/cgi/content/abstract/52/6/1125.

Rowswell, S., Rich, J., & Syben, H. (2008, February). Licensed child care in Washington State: 2006. Washington State Department of Early Learning. Accessed July 6, 2010, http://www.del.wa.gov/publications/research/docs/LicensedChildCareInWashingtonState_2006.pdf.

Richards, E.P., et. al. (2004) Innovative legal tools to prevent obesity. Journal of Law, Medicine, and Ethics 32(4):59–61.

Rubin, P. H. (2002). Darwinian politics: The evolutionary origin of freedom. Piscataway, NJ: Rutgers University Press.

Ruff, C. B., Trinkaus, E., & Holliday, T. W. (1997). Body mass and encephalization in Pleistocene Homo. *Nature,* 387:173–176.

Ruhm, C. J. (2009). Economic conditions and health behaviors: Are recessions good for your health? *North Carolina Medical Journal,* 70(4, July/August):378. Accessed October 13, 2010, http://www.ncmedicaljournal.com/wp-content/uploads/NCMJ/Jul-Aug-09/Ruhm.pdf.

Salisbury, A. C., Chan, P. S., Gosch, K. L., Buchanan, D. M., & Spertus, J. A. (2011) Patterns and predictors of fast food consumption after acute myocardial infarction. American Journal of Cardiology 2011 Feb 7. [Epub ahead of print]

Salmon, J., Bauman, A., Crawford, D., Timperio, A., & Owen, N. (2000). The association between television viewing and overweight among Australian adults participating in varying levels of leisure-time physical activity. *International Journal of Obesity,* 24(May, 5):600–606. Accessed January 26, 2010, http://www.nature.com/ijo/journal/v24/n5/full/0801203a.html.

Salvy, S., Howard, M., Read, M., & Mele, E. (2009). The presence of friends increases food intake in youth. *The American Journal of Clinical Nutrition,* 90(August):282–287.

Santa Monica [Calif.] Daily Press (2010, September 10). The latest smoking ban. Accessed September 11, 2010, http://www.smdp.com/Articles-c-2010-09-08-70276.113116_Latest_smoking_ban_takes_effect_today.html.

Satcher, D. (2007). Foreword from the Surgeon General, U.S. Department of Health and Human Services. In: The surgeon's call to action to prevent and decrease overweight and obesity: 2001. Rockville, MD: Office of the Surgeon General, U.S. Department of Health and Human Services. Accessed August 5, 2010, http://www.surgeongeneral.gov/topics/obesity/calltoaction/foreward.htm.

Sauer, A. (2010, September 7). Are pants lying to you? An investigation. *Esquire.* Accessed September 13, 2010, http://www.esquire.com/blogs/mens-fashion/pants-size-chart-090710.

Schlosser, E. (2001). Fast food nation: The dark side of the all-American meal. Boston: Houghton Mifflin Company.

Schlundt, D. G., Briggs, N. C., Miller, S. T., Arthur, C. M., & Goldzweig, I. A. (2007). BMI and seatbelt use. *Obesity,* 15:2541–2545. Accessed July 26, 2010, http://www.nature.com/oby/journal/v15/n11/abs/oby2007303a.html.

Schmidt-Nielsen, K. (1994). Animal physiology: Adaptation and environment. Cambridge, UK: Cambridge University Press.

Schulkin, J. (2003). Rethinking homeostasis: Allostatic regulation in physiology and pathophysiology. Cambridge, MA: MIT Press.

Schwartz, A. (2011, March 3). Obesity Shocker; Pace maker Zaps Stomach Internally to Aevent Overindulging. Fast Company occessed March 4, 2011 from http://www.fastcompany.com/1134252.

Schultz, J. S. (2010, May 29). The benefits of frugality. *The New York Times,* B4.

Science Daily (2009, August 25). More obesity blues: Obese people are at greater risk for developing Alzheimer's, study finds. Accessed July 23, 2010, http://www.sciencedaily.com/releases/2009/08/090825090745.htm.

Science Daily (2011, February 15). Calorie labeling has no effect on teenagers' or parents' food purchases, study finds. Accessed February 18, 2011, http://www.sciencedaily.com/releases/2011/02/110215102839.htm.

Severson, K. (2010, September 24) Told to eat vegetables, America orders fries. *The New York Times,* Accessed on December 13, 2010, http://www.nytimes.com/2010/09/25/health/policy/25vegetables.html

Sharma, A. J., Grummer-Strawn, L. M., Dalenius, K., Galuska, D., Anandappa, M., Borlund, Mackintosh, H., Smith, R. (2009). Obesity prevalence among low-income, preschool-aged children – United States, 1998–2008. *Morbidity and Mortality Weekly Report,* 58(28, July 24). Accessed June 1, 2010, http://www.cdc.gov/mmwr/preview/mmwrhtml/mm5828a1.htm

Silber, D. (2008). Want to lose weight, stress less! *Enzine Articles.* Accessed April 8, 2010, http://ezinearticles.com/?Want-to-Lose-Weight,-Stress-Less!&id=927347.

Singer, S.F., & Avery, D.T. (2007). Unstoppable global warming: Every 15,000 Years. New York: Rowman & Littlefield Publishers, Inc.

Sitton, S., & Blanchard, S. (1995). Men's preferences in romantic partners: Obesity vs. addiction. *Psychological Reports,* 77(3, 2):1185–1186.

Smith, A. (1759/1790). The theory of moral sentiments. London: A. Millar. Accessed September 17, 2007, from Library of Economics and Liberty, http://www.econlib.org/library/Smith/smMS1.html.

Smith v. Hooters of Roseville Inc. et. al, Circuit Count for Macomb County, Michigau, No. 10-2213-CD.

Smith, A. (1776/1904). An inquiry into the nature and causes of the wealth of nations (E. Cannan, ed.). London: Methuen and Co., Ltd. Accessed September 17, 2007, from Library of Economics and Liberty, http://www.econlib.org/library/Smith/smWN1.html .

Smith, C. A., Schmoll, K., Konik, J., & Oberlander, S. (2007). Carrying weight for the world: influence of weight descriptors on judgments of large-sized women. *Journal of Applied Social Psychology,* 37:989–1006.

Smith, Cassandra Marie v. Hooters of America (2010, May 24). State of Michigan, Circuit Court for Macomb County, case no. 10-2213-CD. Accessed November 25, 2010, http://www.callsam.com/images/stories/news_docs_pics/Complaint_Smith-vs-Hooters.pdf.

Smith, L., & Elliott, F. (2008, March 7). Rush for biofuels threatens starvation on a global scale. *The Times* [of London]. Accessed September 22, 2010, http://www.timesonline.co.uk/tol/news/environment/article3500954.ece.

Smith, T. A., Lin, B., & Lee, J. (2010, July). Taxing caloric sweetened beverages: Potential effects on beverage consumption, calorie intake, and obesity (Economic Research Report No. 100). Washington, DC: U.S. Department of Agriculture, Economic Research Service. Accessed September 23, 2010, http://www.ers.usda.gov/Publications/ERR100/ERR100.pdf.

Sorokowski, P. (2010). Politicians' estimated height as an indicator of their popularity. *European Journal of Social Psychology,* 40(7, December):1302–1309.

Southwest.com (2009). Southwest policies: Customer of size Q & A. Accessed June 17, 2009, http://www.southwest.com/travel_center/cos_qa.html.

Speiser, P. W., Rudolf, M. C. J., Anhalt, H., Camacho-Hubner, C., Chiarelli, F., Eliakim, A., Freemark, M., Gruters, A., Hershkovitz, E., Iughetti, L., Krude, H., Latzer, Y., Lustig, R. H., Pescovitz, O. H., Pinhas-Hamiel, O., Rogol, A. D., Shalitin, S., Sultan, C., Stein, D., Vardi, P., Werther, G. A., Zadik, Z., Zuckerman-Levin, N., Hochberg, Z.; Obesity Consensus Working Group. (2005). Childhood obesity. *Journal of Clinical Endocrinology and Metabolism,* 90 (3):1871–1887.

Starmer-Smith, C. (2009, April 22). Ryanair considers 'fat tax' for obese air passengers. *The Telegraph.* Accessed June 27, 2009, http://www.telegraph.co.uk/travel/travelnews/5199997/Ryanair-considers-fat-tax-for-obese-air-passengers.html.

Stearns, P. (1997). Fat history: Bodies and beauty in the modern West. New York: New York University Press.

Steel, P. (2007). The nature of procrastination: A meta-analytic and theoretical review of quintessential self-regulatory failure. *Psychological Bulletin,* 133:65–94.

Stein, J. (2009, February 17). Has the "Joy of Cooking" now become the "joy of obesity"? *Los Angeles Times,* A12.

Stelter, B. (2011, January 2). Television viewing continues to edge up. *The New York Times.* Accessed January 3, 2011, http://www.nytimes.com/2011/01/03/business/media/03ratings.html?_r=1&src=busln.

Sterling, P., & Eyer, J. (1988). Allostasis: A new paradigm to explain arousal pathology. In: S. Fisher & J. Reston (eds.), Handbook of life stress, cognition, and health. New York: John Wiley & Sons.

Stevens, J., Kumanyika, S. K., & Keil, J. E. (1994). Attitudes toward body size and dieting: Differences between elderly black and white women. *American Journal of Public Health,* 84(8):1322–1325.

Stewart, H. (2006, September 1). How low has the farm share of retail food prices really fallen? (ERR-24). Economic Research Service, U.S. Department of Agriculture. Accessed May 20, 2010, http://www.ers.usda.gov/publications/err24/err24a.pdf.

Stewart, H. (2008, October 8). World Bank warns on "human crisis" of high food prices. *Guardian.co.uk.* Accessed July 29, 2009, http://www.guardian.co.uk/business/2008/oct/08/worldbank.food.

Stieger, S., & Burger, C. (2010). Body height and occupational success for actors and actresses. *Psychological Reports,* 107:25–38.

Stigler, G.S., & Becker, G.S. (1977). De gustibus non est disputandum. *American Economic Review* 67(2, March):76–90.

Stobbe, M. (2010, June 21). Dieting for dollars? More workers are trying it. *MSNBC.com.* Accessed July 29, 2010, http://www.msnbc.msn.com/id/37385706/ns/health-diet_and_nutrition.

Stöppler, M. C., & Shiel, W. C. (2007, February 27). Stress, hormones, and weight gain. *MedicineNet.com.* Accessed June 17, 2010, http://www.medicinenet.com/script/main/art.asp?articlekey=53304.

Stunkard, A. J. (1959). Eating patterns and obesity. *Psychiatry Quarterly,* 33:284–295.

Stunkard, A. J., Sorensen, T. I., Hanis, C., Teasdale, T. W., Chakraborty, R., Schull, W. J., & Schulsinger, F. (1986). An adoption study of human obesity. *New England Journal of Medicine,* 314:193–198.

Sturm, R., & Datar, A. (2005). Body mass index in elementary school children, metropolitan area food prices, and food outlet density. *Public Health,* 119(12):1059–1068.

Subar, A. F., Krebs-Smith, S. M., Cook, A., & Kahle, L. L. (1998). Dietary sources of nutrients among U.S. children, 1989–1991. *Pediatrics,* 101(4, Pt. 1):918–923.

Sugarman, S. D., & Sandman, N. (2008). Using performance-based regulation to reduce childhood obesity. *Australia and New Zealand Health Policy,* 5(November 18). Accessed August 17, 2010, http://www.anzhealthpolicy.com/content/5/1/26.

Suicide.org (2010). Suicide statistics. Accessed July 4, 2010, http://suicide.org/suicide-statistics.html.

Sumner, S. (2010, July 5). The unacknowledged success of neoliberalism. *The Library of Economics and Liberty.* Accessed July 6, 2010, http://www.econlib.org/library/Columns/y2010/Sumnerneoliberalism.html.

Suranovic, S. M., & Goldfarb, R. S. (2007). A behavioral model of cyclical dieting. In: K. Bolin & J. Cawley (eds.), The economics of obesity (pp. 49–78). Bingley, UK: Emerald Group Publishing, Ltd.

Survey of Current Business (2007, February). Alternative measures of personal saving. [Data file]. Washington, DC: U.S. Department of Commerce, Bureau of Economic Research. Accessed September 23, 2010, http://www.bea.gov/scb/pdf/2007/02%20February/0207_saving.pdf.

Sydney Morning Herald (2009, June 19). Study tips scales the other way, overweight people live longer. Accessed June 22, 2009, http://www.smh.com.au/lifestyle/wellbeing/study-tips-scales-the-other-way-overweight-people-live-longer-20090618-cm13.html.

Tataranni, P. A., & Ravussin, E. (2004). Energy metabolism and obesity. In T. A. Wadden & A. J. Stunkard (eds.), Handbook of obesity treatment (pp. 42–72). New York: Guilford.

Terry, L. L. (1964). Smoking and health: Report of the Advisory Committee to the Surgeon General of the Public Health Service (Public Health Service, No. PHS 64–1103). Washington, DC: U.S. Department of Health, Education, and Welfare.

The New York Times Editorial Board (1987, January 14). The right minimum wage: $0.00. *The New York Times,* Opinion section. Accessed December 5, 2010, http://www.nytimes.com/1987/01/14/opinion/the-right-minimum-wage-0.00.html.

The Center for Consumer Freedom (2004, January 28). WHO wants a fat tax? Accessed July 7, 2009, http://www.consumerfreedom.com/news_detail.cfm/headline/2336.

The New York Times Editorial Board (2010, December 19). Not so Happy meal. *The New York Times.* Accessed December 21, 2010, http://www.nytimes.com/2010/12/20/opinion/20mon4.html.

Thaler, R. H., & Sunstein, C. R. (2008). *Nudge: Improving decisions about health, wealth, and happiness.* New Haven, CT: Yale University Press.

Tierney, J. (2010, December 14). Real evidence for diets that are just imaginary. *The New York Times,* D1.

Tillotson, J. E. (2004) America's obesity: conflicting public policies, industrial economic development and unintended human consequences. *Annual Review of Nutrition,* 24:617–643

Time (2006, April 30). Photograph of Kelly Brownell. Accessed December 8, 2010, http://www.time.com/time/magazine/article/0,9171,1187241,00.html.

Tooby, J., & Cosmides, L. (1990a). On the universality of human nature and the uniqueness of the individual: The role of genetics and adaptation. *Journal of Personality,* 58:17–67.

Tooby, J., & Cosmides, L. (1990b). The past explains the present: Emotional adaptations and the structure of ancestral environments. *Ethology and Sociobiology,* 11:375–424.

Toschke A. M., Martin, R. M., von Kries, R., Wells, J., Smith, G. D., & Ness, A. R. (2007). Infant feeding method and obesity: Body mass index and dual-energy X-ray absorptiometry measurements at 9–10 years of age from the Avon Longitudinal Study of Parents and Children (ALSPAC). *American Journal Clinical Nutrition,* 85:1578–1585.

Trust for America's Health (2009, July 1). New report finds obesity epidemic increases, Mississippi weighs in as heaviest state. Accessed August 11, 2010, http://healthyamericans.org/newsroom/releases/?releaseid=182.

Tsai, A. G. (2009, April 21). Airlines should reconsider charging for obesity. Posted to *DenverPost.com.* Accessed July 7, 2009, http://blogs.denverpost.com/eletters/2009/04/21/airlines-should-reconsider-charging-for-obesity/.

Tullock, G. (1967). Toward a mathematics of politics. Ann Arbor, MI: University of Michigan Press.

Tullock, G. (1994). The economics of non-human societies. Tucson, AZ: Pallas Press.

Twenge, J.M. (2007). Generation me: Why today's young Americans are more confident, assertive, entitled–and more miserable than ever before. New York: Free Press.

Tyson, P. (2009). Inquiry: An occasional column – Are we still evolving? *NOVA Online.* Accessed March 26, 2010, http://www.pbs.org/wgbh/nova/beta/evolution/are-we-still-evolving.html.

U.S. Census Bureau. (n.d.). U.S. and world population clocks. Accessed August 18, 2010, http://www.census.gov/main/www/popclock.html.

U.S. Statistical Abstract – National Data Book (2010). Births, deaths, marriages, & divorces: Life expectancy [Data file]. Suitland, MD: U.S. Census Bureau. Accessed May 18, 2010, http://www.census.gov/compendia/statab/cats/births_deaths_marriages_divorces/life_expectancy.html.

Veblen, T. (1899) Theory of the leisure class: An economic study in the evolution of institutions. New York: Macmillan.

Viscusi, W. K. (1994, October). Cigarette taxation and the social consequences of smoking (Working Paper No. 4891). Cambridge, MA: National Bureau of Economic Research. Accessed December 5, 2010, http://www.nber.org/papers/w4891.

Volpp, K. G., John, L. K., Troxel, A. B., Norton, L., Fassbender, J., & Loewenstein, G. (2008). Financial incentive-based approaches for weight loss: A randomized trial. *Journal of the American Medical Association,* 300(22):2631–2637. Accessed July 29, 2010, http://jama.ama-assn.org/cgi/content/short/300/22/2631.

Volpp, K. G., Troxel, A. B., Pauly, M. V., Glick, H. A., Puig, A., Asch, D. A., Galvin, R, Zhu, J., Wan, F., DeGuzman, J., Corbett, E., Weiner, J., Audrain-McGovern, J. (2009). A randomized, controlled trial of financial incentives for smoking cessation. *New England Journal of Medicine,* 360(7, February 12):699–709. Accessed July 29, 2010, http://www.nejm.org/doi/pdf/10.1056/NEJMsa0806819.

Von Behren, J., Lipsett, M. P., Horn-Ross, L., Delfino, R. J., Gilliland, F., McConnell, R., Bernstein L, Clarke CA, & Reynolds P. (2009). Obesity, waist size, and risk of current asthma in the California Teachers Study cohort. *Thorax,* 64:889–893.

Wada, R., & Tekin, E. (2007). Body composition and wages (Working Paper No. 13595). Cambridge, MA: National Bureau of Economic Research. Accessed July 22, 2010, http://www.nber.org/papers/w13595.

Wadden, T.A., & Phelan, S. (2002). Behavioral assessment of the obese patient. In T. A. Wadden & A. J. Stunkard (eds.), Handbook of obesity treatment (pp. 186–226). New York: Guilford.

Waldrop, M. (2010, May 28). Obesity ambulance takes to the road – capable of carrying 70 stone patient. *Daily Telegraph.* Accessed July 26, 2010, http://www.telegraph.co.uk/health/healthnews/7772735/Obesity-ambulance-takes-to-the-road-capable-of-carrying-70-stone-patients.html.

Wall Street Journal Editorial Board. (January 22, 2011). Amber waves of ethanol. *Wall Street Journal.* Accessed January 28, 2011, http://online.wsj.com/article/SB10001424052748703396604576088010481315914.html.

Wang, S. S. (2010, April 13). A new way to lose weight? Scientists see potential in the calorie-burning power of "good" fat in adults. *The Wall Street Journal,* B9.

Wansink, B. (2006). Mindless eating: Why we eat more than we think. New York: Bantam.

Wansink, B., Just, D. R., & McKendry, J. (2010, October 22). Lunch line redesign. *The New York Times,* A25.

Wansink, B., & Wansink, C. S. (2010). The largest Last Supper: Depictions of portion size and plate size increased over the millennium. *International Journal of Obesity,* 34(May):943–944. Accessed April 18, 2010, http://www.nature.com/ijo/journal/vaop/ncurrent/full/ijo201037a.html.

Wardle, J., Volz, C., & Jarvis, M. J. (2002). Sex differences in the association of socioeconomic status with obesity. *American Journal of Public Health,* 92:1299–1304.

Wassener, B. (2009, June 8). Airlines predict $9 billion global loss. *The New York Times.* Accessed June 9, 2009, http://www.nytimes.com/2009/06/09/business/global/09air.html?_r=1&scp=1&sq=%249%20billion&st=cse.

Watson, B. (2010, March 14). The plus-size furniture market expands as Americans widens. *DailyFinance.* Accessed July 27, 2010, http://www.dailyfinance.com/story/plus-size-furniture-market-expands-as-americans-widen/19388544/

Weimer, J. (2001, March). The economic benefits of breastfeeding: Review and analysis. (Food Assistance and Nutrition Report No. FANRR13, p 20). Washington DC: U.S. Department of Agriculture, Economic Research Service.

Weissman M. M., Bland, R. C., Canino, G. J., Faravelli, C., Greenwald. S., Hwu, H., Joyce, P.R., Karam, E. G., Lee, C. K., Lellouch, J., Lépine, J. P., Newman, S. C., Rubio-Stipec, M., Wells, J. E., Wickramaratne, P. J., Wittchen, H., & Yeh, E. K. (1996). Cross national epidemiology of major depression and bipolar disorder. *Journal of the American Medical Association,* 276(4):293–299.

Wells, S. J. (2010). Does work make you fat? *HR Magazine,* October, 26–32.

Welsh, J. A., Sharma, A., Abramson, J. L., Vaccarino, V., Gillespie, C., & Vos, M. B. (2010). Caloric sweetener consumption and dyslipidemia among U.S. adults. *Journal of the American Medical Association,* 303(15):1490–1497.

Wenk, G. L. (2010). Your brain on food: How chemicals control your thoughts and feelings. Oxford, UK: Oxford University Press.

White, S. E., Brown, N. J., & Ginsburg, S. L. (1999). Diversity of body types in network television programming: A content analysis. *Communication Research Report,* 16:386–392.

White House Task Force on Childhood Obesity (2010). Solving the problem of childhood obesity within a generation. Available from http://www.letsmove.gov.

Whitmer, R. A., Gunderson, E. P., Barrett-Connor, E., Quesenberry, C. P., Jr., & Yaffe, K. (2005). Obesity in middle age and future risk of dementia: A 27-year longitudinal population based study. *BMJ,* 330:1360.

Williams, A. (2010, February 5). The new math on campus. *The New York Times.* Accessed October 13, 2010, http://www.nytimes.com/2010/02/07/fashion/07campus.html?_r=2.

Williamson, D. A., Womble, L. G., Zucker, N. L., Reas, D. L., White, M. A., & Blouin, D. C. (2000). Body image assessment for obesity (BIA-O): Development of a new procedure. *International Journal of Obesity and Related Metabolic Disorders,* 24:1326–1332.

Winslow, R. (2010, January 26). The scales can lie: Hidden fat. *The Wall Street Journal.* Accessed February 14, 2010, http://online.wsj.com/article/SB10001424052748704762904575025313433081780.html.

Witcombe, C. L. C. E. (2003). Women in history: Venus of Willendorf. Accessed August 4, 2009, http://witcombe.sbc.edu/willendorf/willendorfgoddess.html.

World Health Organization (2006, September). Overweight and obesity. Accessed July 29, 2009, http://www.who.int/mediacentre/factsheets/fs311/en/index.html.

Wrangham, R. (2001). Out of the pan, into the fire: From ape to human. Cambridge, MA: Harvard University Press.

Wynder, E. L., & Graham, E. A. (1950). Tobacco smoking as a possible etiologic factor in bronchiogenic carcinoma: A study of 684 proved cases. *Journal of the American Medical Association.* 143(4, May 27):329–338.

Yoshino, K. (2007, November 9). A sinking feeling on "Small World" ride. *Los Angeles Times.* Accessed July 27, 2010, http://articles.latimes.com/2007/nov/09/business/fi-disneyland9.

Young, L. R., & Nestle, M. (2002). The contribution of expanding portion sizes to the U.S. obesity epidemic. *American Journal of Public Health,* 92(2):246–249.

Yu, R. (2009, October 29). Smaller jets squeeze big and tall fliers. *USA Today.* Accessed September 9, 2010, http://www.usatoday.com/travel/flights/2009-10-26-big-tall-fliers_N.htm.

Zagat, T., & Zagat N. (2011, January 25). The burger and fries recovery. *Wall Street Journal,* A15.

Zang, Q., & Wang, Y. (2004). Trends in the association between obesity and socioeconomic status in U.S. adults, 1971–2000. *Obesity Research,* 12:1622–1632.

Zezima, K. (2008, April 8). Increasing obesity requires new ambulance equipment. *The New York Times.* Accessed July 23, 2010, http://www.nytimes.com/2008/04/08/health/08ambu.html

CPSIA information can be obtained at www.ICGtesting.com
Printed in the USA
LVOW010354131212

311438LV00005B/154/P